NATURE DISPLAYED

NATURE DISPLAYED

Gender, Science and Medicine
1760–1820

Essays by
LUDMILLA JORDANOVA

LONGMAN
London and New York

Addison Wesley Longman Limited
Edinburgh Gate,
Harlow, Essex CM20 2JE,
United Kingdom
and Associated Companies throughout the world

*Published in the United States of America
by Addison Wesley Longman Inc., New York*

First published 1999

ISBN 0 582 301890 PPR
ISBN 0 582 301904 CSD

Visit Addison Wesley Longman on the world wide web at
hhtp://www.awl-he.com

British Library Cataloguing in Publication Data

A catalogue record for this book is available from the British Library

Library of Congress Cataloging-in-Publication Data

A catalogue record for this book is available from the Library of Congress

Set by 35 in 11/12pt Garamond
Produced by Addison Wesley Longman Singapore (Pte) Ltd,
Printed in Singapore

Contents

Preface

Nine of the twelve chapters in this book were published previously between 1981 and 1994; full details are given in the consolidated bibliography. I have made some changes to them and standardised the style of the footnotes, which have been made as economical as possible. The supporting material has been updated. In some cases the illustrations differ from those in the original versions. I have eliminated acknowledgements from the published pieces, but wish to renew my thanks to all those who helped with their preparation. I am most appreciative of both the individuals and the institutions who contributed to the previously unpublished essays by commenting on them and by inviting me to speak. I have left the final chapter, the inaugural lecture I gave at the University of York in December 1994, virtually unchanged since this was written for a special occasion and I wanted to retain its original flavour. The index is as full as possible in order to help readers locate the first reference to an individual, institution or idea. I hope that the essays can be read either as self-contained elements or as a connected series since there are many recurrent motifs.

Permission to reprint has been sought for all the previously published essays. I am grateful to those who responded so promptly and gave their permission and apologise to anyone with an interest who was inadvertently omitted – they are invited to contact the publisher. I would like to take this opportunity of acknowledging the support of the Wellcome Trust for much of the research upon which the following chapters are based.

For their help and encouragement in preparing this book, I am particularly grateful to: Malcolm Baker, Cathy Crawford, Patricia Fara, Christopher Gärtner, Sue Grace, Kristine Haugen, Clare Haynes, Roger Lonsdale, Andy Nolan, Andy and Jila Peacock, Steve Petford, Roy Porter, Richard Serjeantson, Pamela Sharpe, the administrative and support staff of World Art Studies, University of East Anglia, the staff of the Wellcome Institute Library and of the Wellcome Photographic Department and the staff of the British Museum Print Room. Hilary Shaw of Longmans has been exemplary in her patience and support. I owe a great deal to the following much-loved friends: Joyce Appleby, Cathy Crawford, Ann Dally and Philip Egerton, Leonore Davidoff, Andy and Jila Peacock,

Marcia Pointon and Marilyn Strathern. I give special thanks to Christopher Gärtner, Clare Haynes, and Lynda and John Williams for the help and friendship they have offered during the final stages of preparing this text.

Norwich, April 1998

Acknowledgements

The publishers would like to thank the following for permission to reproduce the following textual and illustrative material:

Chapter 3: 'Nature's Powers: a Reading of the Distinction between Creation and Production' first published (as 'Nature Powers: A Reading of Lanarck's Distinction between Creation and Production') in *History, Humanity and Evolution*, edited by J.R. Moore, Cambridge University Press, 1990;

Chapter 4: 'Melancholy Reflection: Constructing an Identity for Unveilers of Nature' first published in *Frankenstein, Creation and Monstrosity*, edited by S. Bann, Reaktion Books, 1994;

Chapter 5: 'The Authoritarian Response', first published in *The Enlightenment and its Shadows*, edited by P. Hulme and L. Jordanova, Routledge, 1990;

Chapter 6: 'The Popularisation of Medicine: Tissot on Onanism', first published in Textual Practice, vol. 1, no. 1, Routledge, 1987;

Chapter 7: 'Medical Meditations: Mind, Body and the Guillotine', first published in *History Workshop* (28);

Chapter 8: 'Guarding the Body Politic: Volney's Law of Nature', first published (as 'Guarding the Body Politic: Volney's Catechism of 1973') in *Reading Writing Revolution*, edited by F. Barker *et al.*, University of Essex, 1982;

Chapter 9: 'Policing Public Health in France 1780–1815' first published in *Public Health*, edited by T. Ogawa, Saikon, 1981;

Chapter 10: 'Naturalising the Family: Literature and the Bio-Medical Sciences in the Late Eighteenth Century', first published in *Languages of Nature: Critical Essays on Science and Literature*, edited by L. Jordanova, Free Association Books and Rutgers University Press, 1986;

Chapter 11: 'Gender, Generation and Science: William Hunter's Obstetric Atlas' first published in *William Hunter and the Eighteenth-Century Medical World*, edited by W.F. Bynum and R. Porter, Cambridge University Press, 1985.

ACKNOWLEDGMENTS

The British Museum for Plates 3, 4, 5, 10, © The British Museum; Cincinnati Art Museum (bequest of Mrs Mary M. Emery) for Plate 24; Indianapolis Museum of Art (gift of Mrs Albert J. Beveridge, photo © Indianapolis Museum of Art) for Plate 29; Trustees of the Wallace Collection, London for Plates 18 and 23; Wellcome Institute Library, London for Plates 1, 2, 6, 7, 11, 12, 13, 14, 15, 16, 17, 18, 19, 20, 21, 22, 25, 26, 27, 28 and 30.

List of Plates

For Sonya Alix and Zara Rose,
beloved daughters

CHAPTER ONE

Cultural Effort:
An Introductory Essay

In his seminal book *Imagined Communities*, Benedict Anderson analysed the cultural preconditions for a modular notion of nationhood: a type of nationhood came into being, composed of certain elements, and the resulting ensemble was adapted to suit other historical and geographical settings. Central to the pattern he identified were ways of imagining not just the nation itself but the relations between its members. He set out the social, cultural and economic mechanisms underlying the main means by which citizens who generally lacked direct personal contact with one another could, nonetheless, imagine themselves as part of a shared enterprise. 'Nation' was an abstract term given life in the minds and behaviour of ordinary people. His account implies that much of the work of creating and sustaining a sense of nationhood goes on in the head, and he stressed that such mental effort takes place in specific historical contexts and that it has particular, material preconditions. In other words, *Imagined Communities* is a book about what I am calling cultural effort.[1]

Nature Displayed is concerned with imagined relationships and examines the creation and use of modular concepts. Unlike Anderson, however, my domain is nature. I am especially interested in how those committed to producing authoritative knowledge in the late eighteenth and early nineteenth centuries worked to imagine abstractions, such as 'nature' and 'family', which concerned relationships. Even in the routine empirical business of medicine and natural history, these larger conceptual issues were always present. Although describing and classifying objects were important tasks for natural historians and medical practitioners, they were equally mindful of the need to understand the palpable affinities between living beings, especially human beings, as well as between God and nature, nature and nature's laws. Representing and conceptualising such kinships in terms of visible similarities was a complex enterprise, one that touched not only a sense of cosmological order but also the most intimate identifies of all concerned. The abstractions I write about were also, like 'nation', modular. Indeed, there can be no more modular concept than 'the family',

---

1. Anderson, 1991; I have tried to set out the potential usefulness of Anderson's approach for the histories of science and of medicine in Jordanova, 1996, and see also Jordanova, 1998.

which has, since the eighteenth century, carried the assumption that forms of human organisation share fundamental elements in common, that where there are not families there ought to be, and that the family is rooted in nature. Thus natural relations were imagined, and actively created, through cultural processes, not 'discovered' in the physical world. Thereby nature was indeed displayed.

We can express the same point in a different vocabulary. For Raymond Williams, nation and family are 'keywords', terms that are historically dense, whose changing meanings and uses contain broad social and cultural shifts. Scholars from several disciplines have noted how a limited number of concepts do a disproportionate amount of work – both analytical and emotional – at any given moment. Nature is certainly one such term and it has been functioning in this manner for generations. Especially at a time when *longue durée* history is unfashionable, it is hard to do full justice to ideas such as nature, to capture both their locally-forged specificities and their enduring associations. Furthermore, such keywords also tend to be elusive. Their richness of meaning brings with it on the one hand a flexibility and ambiguity that makes precision difficult, and on the other relevance to so many aspects of human experience that it becomes overwhelming. Nonetheless the centrality of these terms has drawn many writers to them. In some ways Williams and Anderson responded quite differently to the challenge – Williams, a literary scholar and socialist writer, always sought to show how complex texts worked to mediate changing social relations, while Anderson, a historian of South-East Asia, focused on constellations of collective practices, such as reading newspapers and administrative procedures. Neither, it should be said, has shown particular concern for the nature of visual experience, although it is implicit in Williams's work, especially on *The Country and the City*, that writers' visual responses to their immediate surroundings act as important triggers, especially of fantasies of other, better times and places, generally located in the past. 'Country' and 'city' are categories that take significant emotional charge, after all, from sensory experience – a point that also applies to 'nation'.[2]

I have mentioned Anderson and Williams as two hugely influential figures, especially for my generation; they have both, if in somewhat different ways, privileged the social and cultural processes that go on in the head without divorcing those processes from larger historical shifts. While I have found them inspiring, the writings presented here are very different. The essays that follow may signal some bigger shifts and attempt to open up the interpretative difficulties raised by keywords and modular concepts, but they are strictly limited in their focus. Most of them are based on readings of a small number of texts and images, although they make no pretence to being complete or exhaustive interpretations. But they are textually based because that is where I believe important cultural work gets done. My primary interest here is not in

2. Williams, 1983, 1975; Illich, 1983, drawing on Williams, organised his book around keywords; on nature, see Lovejoy, 1948, esp. chs 5 and 8; Wiley, 1962; Charlton, 1984. For a more recent approach to the complexities of nature and especially of natural history, see Jardine, Secord and Spary, 1996.

the means by which groups affirm and reaffirm their values, which generally involve forms of collective practice, although making, disseminating and responding to words and images is just such a practice. So, while I certainly assume that making cultural products occurs through complex social practices to be analysed as such, there is also room for work that emphasises the internal complexities of those products in their own right. I am fascinated by the way in which issues that are inevitably difficult, confusing, troubling and dangerous may be creatively handled through the processes of writing and image-making. I see the evidence for this in the cultural products themselves, and in the light of what is known about their context, I try to interpret and explain them. However, this is more a textual than a contextual study. The term 'text' itself is in fact rather slippery. I have used it to mean a consciously wrought artefact, made up principally of words, rather than as a generic term for all cultural products.

We should avoid reinforcing the idea that there is a self-evident distinction between texts and contexts, between, on the one hand, representation and, on the other, behaviour, action and structural forces. Yet it is undeniable that in the practice of each historian the interpretative weight tends to fall more on one than on the other. It is possible to understand this in terms of a combination of methodological preferences and disciplinary background. Those who pay attention to critical methods, and who often have a training weighted towards literature, art history and philosophy, give far greater emphasis to texts than do scholars with an interest in social, economic and political phenomena, coming from history and the social sciences. Many of those who would call themselves cultural historians have been anxious to blend the two approaches, as have historians and philosophers of science, especially those interested in the social construction of natural knowledge. There are a number of strategies available for accomplishing this: for example, to show how the production and reception of texts are themselves practices deeply embedded in the social, economic and political orders, and hence that texts are not fixed and static artefacts that exist in a separate world. Another is to expand the range of what counts as a text. One I find particularly compelling is to show how ideas, and the means by which they are expressed, act as mediations of the social conditions in which they exist. 'Mediation' suggests that ideas never passively reflect or directly express a prior state of affairs that is somehow more real than they are. It is used to stress both the transformations that ideas constantly undergo and their interested, ideological nature. Many historians, however, find the language of mediations and ideology baffling or unsuitable for their particular subject matter and intellectual style. Furthermore, historians genuinely differ over where and how at any given moment the most important things are happening, and, on the whole, conventionally trained ones have not given priority to the inner workings of texts and images. Yet for those interested in the generation of knowledge about nature, the use of concepts, the development of mental models of physical processes, and the role of metaphor are central issues. All these concerns encourage an emphasis on texts, although the diverse ways in which texts are handled needs to be stressed. Perhaps the variety of responses is most striking in the varying degrees to which texts are taken to be multi-layered, the products of different levels of consciousness.[3]

Historians of science and medicine have usually given priority to ideas, especially innovative ones, and to the individuals who produce them. The dangers of this type of privilege are well known, and have been expressed in attacks on triumphalism, on easy assumptions about the progressive nature of scientific knowledge and on Whig history. Nonetheless we continue to give a disproportionate amount of attention to those deemed the most outstanding innovators and discoverers. Such figures often acquire a paradigmatic status. Sometimes they are used as case studies of the way in which scientific and medical innovations function. At other times they are simply exemplary of great intellectual achievements. Or they can be indicators of intellectual trends, individuals who stand as indices to significant shifts and patterns. A number of figures recur in the chapters that follow, and I would like to clarify the status I give them. None of these men would be placed in the first rank of scientific innovators, although their historical significance is undoubted. I am not condoning the ranking mentality, but seeking to situate historiographically the individuals that interest me. I am certainly not claiming that they are 'representative' of the scientific and/or medical communities of their time. By definition they are likely to be exceptional individuals, where 'exceptional' is not about some universal intellectual superiority or genius (indeed such figures may be unusually ambitious, hubristic or greedy rather than clever), hence they are not representative in the usual sense of the word. But their writings may nonetheless be indicative of broader trends, articulating ideas with particular clarity, energy and force, making them especially valuable to historians. On the whole I have found in such figures themes and preoccupations that their contemporaries shared but expressed with less immediacy or only in a piecemeal fashion. Frequently it was the desire to generalise, to generate big pictures and comprehensive accounts that marked such figures out. I have often turned, for example, to the French naturalist Jean-Baptiste Lamarck to illustrate points about the trends towards a more naturalistic style of thinking. Lamarck rejected any hint of metaphysical explanation in natural history, natural philosophy and psychology – nature should be understood in terms of natural forces only. The breadth of his scientific interests and the nature of his intellectual ambition make him a valuable case study, as do his earnest attempts to present a cosmology and general methodological precepts for the pursuit of natural knowledge. But Lamarck, like many other figures discussed in the book, holds another kind of interest for me.

In *Camera Lucida*, Roland Barthes suggested that a photograph possesses what he called a '*punctum*' – a point that captured his interest and excited his curiosity.[4] It was not necessarily connected with the overt subject matter of the

3. Olby *et al.*, 1990, esp. chs 1, 5, 6, 9, 51; Bynum and Porter, 1993a, esp. chs 3 and 65; Wilson, 1993; Jordanova, 1995b; the articles in the journal *History of Science* provide an excellent insight into historiographic issues in the field. See also the works cited in note 7.

4. Barthes, 1993, esp. pp. 25–7, 42–5, 47, 53, 55. 'A photograph's *punctum* is that accident which pricks me (but also bruises me, is poignant to me)' (p. 27); 'the *punctum* is what I add to the photograph and *what is nonetheless already there*' (p. 55), emphasis in original.

image, and could be an apparently irrelevant detail. His attempt to conceptualise what captures an individual's attention in an image interests me because I am curious about its academic equivalent and more specifically about the ways in which scholars revisit the same figures and issues in their writings. I am struck by the way in which the ideas of certain thinkers have acted as a kind of *punctum* for me. What I like about Barthes's notion is that it does not seek to endow some aspect of a photograph with an independent value in and of itself; rather it acknowledges that capturing the attention is an individual matter, involving an intricate dynamic between viewer and image. Once the capturing has taken place, re-reading a text or viewing an image again becomes a journey motivated by love and familiarity – it is no coincidence, I think, that Barthes's book concerns his beloved mother's image, making it simultaneously an act of mourning and an exploration of the allure of photography.[5] Historians, having been lured to a person, period, text, image, country or theme, then examine the materials to which they have been led as thoroughly as possible, but often cannot fully explain how and why they were drawn there in the first place. Lamarck has constituted a sort of *punctum* for me, and at each visit I find something new in the themes he tackled. I have no desire to claim some kind of greatness for Lamarck on this account. I am merely asserting that I have found prolonged engagement with his ideas generative, that I believe their significance can be justified on historical grounds, and that they appeal because the issues they speak to are wide-ranging and not easily exhausted.

Indeed, I would extend the argument to the periods and places historians work on and to the issues that grab them. For many years I have been drawn to the later eighteenth and early nineteenth centuries. Possibly this reflects the life span of the figures I have studied. This era cannot simply be called the Enlightenment, which is generally deemed to have started somewhere between the mid-seventeenth century and the early eighteenth century and to have ended either with the French Revolution or shortly thereafter. Nor is it really the *late* Enlightenment, because criticism of that movement of ideas was already well-developed by the first decade of the nineteenth century. It could be claimed that this period has no real unity at all, split as it is by having that great divider, the French Revolution, right in the middle of it. Nonetheless for me 1760 to 1820 is a 'natural' period, but it is precisely my interests that make it so – I cannot and would not claim objectivity for its boundaries, partly because historical periods, however delineated, have blurred edges. This is not to say that they are arbitrary or lack intellectual plausibility, only that different scholars in interaction with their materials will foreground distinct chronological patterns. I could equally well describe the period these essays cover in terms of cohorts. Most of the people I discuss were products of the Enlightenment, rather than members of the generations that shaped it. It was already under way when they were born and as they grew to adulthood they absorbed its commitments. By the time some of them, such as Mary Shelley, arrived, disenchantment with it was under way. These individuals were liberal rather than

5. Ibid., pp. 60, 63ff., esp. 69.

conservative, reformist rather than reactionary. The exceptions, men such as Paley, Chateaubriand and de Maistre, figure here as foils to more liberal belief systems, such as transformism and the Enlightenment. Those whose ideas are given prominence in *Nature Displayed* were also largely professionals and middle-class, and hence influenced by the political and social debates of the second half of the eighteenth century, which, in their printed forms especially, were largely conducted by and on behalf of that class. They were also worshippers and students of nature, a concept that enjoyed an extraordinary degree of prestige in this period, which is precisely why critics of change and reform so often accused their opponents of un-naturalness.

I could also describe the periods to which I have long been attracted in style terms: late Baroque, rococo, neo-classical, romantic. Admittedly, style is a tricky concept, but I use it because it suggests both a historical and an aesthetic analysis: historical because styles are understood to be specific to a given time, and aesthetic because styles are taken to be composed of formal elements that produce particular kinds of beauty. Styles elicit strong reactions; their appeal may, ultimately, be inexplicable, but the powerful responses they evoke facilitate their capacity to act as *puncta*. Although I have not generally used stylistic classifications, it is nonetheless helpful to remember that aesthetic responses to cultural products and the contexts that produce them are integral to historical work, which, in my experience, is strongly driven by visual and intellectual pleasure. Since style refers to the recognisably shared features of diverse entities, which express their time of creation, it effectively yokes together historical and aesthetic approaches. I wonder whether there was, for instance, a cognitive style shared by many of the writers I have designated 'naturalist', which I have found particularly compelling. I have also mentioned style because its extension to fashion, to interiors, to food and so on, indicates that the styles we are drawn to give immediate pleasure and form part of daily life. Historians' choice of geographical areas is a closely related issue; places can also act as *puncta*. This was certainly the case for me in the early work I did on French science – France was a country I knew from infancy, and it excited my curiosity. Several essays were shaped by that interest. However, preferences also change, and although I still work on French materials, eighteenth-century Britain came to seem alluring; it too appeared seductive for reasons I cannot adequately explain. However, from the earliest research I ever did, I was drawn to comparisons between France and Britain, which still seem to me to be productive, although I certainly do not pursue here a structured form of comparative history. In other words, in the imaginations of historians the attractions of people, themes, periods and countries blend together, and change over a life course.

Above all knots or kernels of intertwined concerns, nexuses of problems demand intellectual revisiting. Several chapters deal with models of kinship, especially with the ways in which parent–child relationships have been understood and represented. Although I have some ideas about what kinship means to me at an intimate level, I cannot explain fully why I have found this an absorbing subject, capable of diverse manifestations, and always promising further complexities. It has certainly been a live political issue all the time I have been working on it, and its emotional significance is never in doubt. I also find appealing topics where there is no obvious final resting place, where a degree of mystery resides. These tend to concern human relationships that engage people at many different levels, that invite scientific and medical attention for this reason, but that prove somewhat resistant to full naturalistic analysis. Concepts such as health, nature, death, will, soul, Woman, exemplify the point. It is no coincidence that many of these topics are related to gender.

Perhaps I can adapt a remark by Ivan Illich and suggest that gender is what happens, not between the legs, but between the ears.[6] This signals a concern similar to Anderson's, that social categories require mental work, and I interpret them both as meaning that phenomena, like gender and nation, are to be understood culturally. 'Culture' and its cognates are notoriously slippery, but in terms of historical approaches an emphasis on culture generally implies an interest in the processes whereby human beings create meaning, that is, it gives weight to cognitive patterns, and to the resulting representations. It is no coincidence that the growth of interest in gender has occurred simultaneously with that in cultural history.[7] 'Gender' signalled a refusal to take biological categories at face value, and a pledge to search for the ways in which masculinity and femininity were given diverse, even contradictory meanings through historical processes. Considerable rhetorical emphasis was placed on gender being about culture, where sex differences were about nature. While debates about gender during the 1980s and 1990s have opened up and placed the culture/nature polarity under critical scrutiny, it remains true that there is an affinity between cultural approaches and an emphasis on gender.[8] One reason for the affinity is that while it is possible to construe gender as a variable, to be understood empirically in a similar fashion to race, class, religion and so on, this is widely perceived as unsatisfactory. It fails to explain why gendered associations are everywhere, why gender is among the most powerful and persistent of metaphors. We have come to call the approach that tackles such issues 'cultural'.[9]

Over the last decade there has been a particularly dramatic increase in studies on gender, although this has been accompanied by a certain looseness of definition. Gender may be a seductive and important topic but it is also an extremely difficult concept to work with. While I would like to make it manageable, and to be open about how I am using 'gender', both tasks are virtually

6. Illich, 1983, p. 68, and also p. 4. This quirky and stimulating book puts a very particular spin on 'gender' by appropriating it for a critique of modern capitalist societies; for Illich culture and economics are inseparable. 'Gender is in every step, in every gesture, not just between the legs. . . . Gender is something other and much more than sex.' 'Gender bespeaks a complementarit that is enigmatic and asymmetrical. Only metaphor can reach for it.'

7. Williams, 1981; Chartier, 1988; Hunt, 1989; cf. Illich, 1983, esp. ch. 4, pp. 130–1 and ch. 6. On definitions of culture, see Kroeber and Kluckhohn, 1952.

8. MacCormack and Strathern, 1980; see also the journal *Gender and History*. Other 'cultural' approaches to gender include Schiebinger, 1989, 1993; Crow, 1995; Benjamin, 1991; Davidoff and Hall, 1987; Maclean, 1980.

9. Marina Warner has paid particular attention to the cultural significance of gendered metaphors and images: 1976, 1983, 1985.

impossible. You have to watch it working in particular instances, and acknowledge its anarchic qualities, its refusal to lie down. In the chapters where ideas about family and reproduction are explored, gender is inevitably a central issue by virtue of the subject matter. When both male and female, masculine and feminine are involved, then we may legitimately use the term gender. Discussions of either sex and its dominant characteristics tend to imply the existence of the other, and hence of intricate relationships between two sets of sexualised attributes. Gender concerns not so much men and women as social constituencies, as the elaborate ideas and associations to which masculinity and femininity give rise. Gender tends, therefore, to be omnipresent and to be implicitly comparative, although it was rarely explicitly conceptualised by historical actors in this way. Scholars now use the term to refer to a wide range of areas where two sexualised elements, recognisably distinct and metaphorically rich, are compared and contrasted. It is precisely because we have a strong model of sexual *union* – in erotic love, in marriage and in reproduction – that the drive to conceptualise gender *distinctions* is so strong.

Inevitably, then, 'gender' raises the question of dualistic ways of thinking. In exploring these, I give weight to the manner in which they were presented in the original sources. While I want to note the persistence of some gendered dualisms over long periods of time, I emphatically do not think of them as universals. We can observe how often complexities, particularly moral ones, are resolved into two poles, without attributing to the human mind any innate predisposition to dualistic thinking. Dualisms that are persistent are also likely to be labile. These polarities are fascinating historical phenomena – capable of taking many different forms, yet with evident metaphorical linkages between them that follow certain patterns. At the same time, binaries do not map neatly and consistently onto each other – the role of gender in them is quite varied. Every major polarity, it seems, has the potential to be gendered, but this has occurred in different ways at different times. Most of the ones I discuss in the book are, simultaneously, moral and naturalised oppositions – a situation which makes the imaginative space between the two sides particularly fraught. This space may be thought of as a contested zone where boundaries are erected in order to bring clarity. Clarity and stability were important because, on the one hand, gendered distinctions appeared fragile, constantly under threat, and on the other, because nature, while a hugely authoritative concept, was hard to get a grasp on. Gender has long been a figure for perceived social change. The insult of calling something or someone 'effeminate', and the changing targets to which it is applied, illustrates the point.

Beneath this way of presenting dualisms, gender, science and medicine as forms of culture, lie a set of assumptions about how societies work, or rather models of social formations that I have found particularly congenial. The interest in boundaries, in the use of nature as an authoritative norm, and in the role of category distinctions in generating social order, derives from early exposure to the writings of Mary Douglas, who exercised great influence on historians and philosophers of science in the 1970s. There have been heated theoretical debates about the value and significance of her work, especially among philosophers of science. For historians the question has been whether her ideas help us to do historical business. Some have applied her ideas quite rigorously, I have not. Her writings are accessible, containing frameworks that she invited readers to apply to other contexts.[10] Mental frameworks – for that is what has interested Douglas – became important for at least some groups of historians as a result of a number of intellectual trends, such as the impact of the *Annales* school, general anthropological interest in belief systems, the dissemination of psychological and psychoanalytic ideas, the growth of cultural studies and media studies and the interest in critical methods beyond the confines of literary criticism, art history and philosophy. These are the very trends that have made cultural history important.[11]

The interest in mental frameworks has helped to expand the range of sources and topics available to scholars in the humanities. After all, traces of culture are present in everything. It is particularly striking that images have ceased to be the province of art historians, becoming much more integrated into a wide variety of historical practices. The point also applies to photography and film. While such integration is desirable, precisely because it serves to widen the scope of history writing, there are problems associated with it.[12] There is an unfortunate tendency to treat images as transparent, as windows onto other worlds, which, in effect, minimises or denies the cultural effort that goes into the creation of any artefact. Equally problematic, although more philosophically taxing, is the question of how applicable methods developed for the analysis of words are to visual materials. Many scholars have assumed that they are, with the result that whatever may be distinctive about visual experience is neglected and the issue of precisely what differentiates words and images is ignored. Since I place considerable weight in some of the essays on visual evidence, it is vital to assess how apt the approaches I have discussed so far are in relation to images, which have until recently been dealt with by distinct intellectual traditions, above all, by art history.

'Art', like 'science', carries an aura, confers status, and is implicitly normative. For most of those who have a scholarly investment in art, anything cannot count as art. For this reason, the term 'visual culture' is often preferred now, since it implies fewer value judgements, gives prominence to the varied nature of visual experience at any given historical moment, and expresses a preference for placing images in context rather than in pedigrees. It affirms that ways of seeing are historically specific, that there exists, to use Baxandall's term, a 'period eye'.[13] 'Visual culture' signals, in fact, an integration of history and art history.[14] As it happens, only a tiny proportion of the pictures I discuss are 'high' art, but no matter what aesthetic quality an image is deemed to possess,

10. Douglas, 1966; Douglas, 1973; Douglas, ed., 1973; Bloor, 1979; Olby *et al.*, 1990, chs 5 and 7; Rudwick, 1985; Jordanova, 1992.
11. Chartier, 1988; Hunt, 1989; Burke, 1990; Burke, 1991; Gay, 1985.
12. Works that successfully integrate art-historical and historical perspectives include: Brewer, 1997; Crow, 1995; Pointon, 1993 and 1997; Silverman, 1989.
13. Baxandall, 1988, part 3; see also Baxandall, 1985, esp. ch. 3.
14. On the integration of history and art history, see Rotberg and Rabb, 1988, and the works cited in note 12.

I seek to analyse it as a historically specific artefact, just like a text in some ways, in being both dense with meaning and capable of acting as a mediator. Thus, the approach I have sketched in is indeed appropriate to visual evidence in that it stresses responding to a whole cultural product rather than formal analysis. While we obviously need to know what specific visual symbols conventionally mean, iconography by itself is not enough. Partly it is insufficient because images, like texts, are so obviously parts of conversations in which many constituencies take part. Biographical information and detailed accounts of how an image is produced may be tremendously informative, but I emphasise its cultural life – the way in which it taps into trends, amplifies or contests them. This is why conversation seems an apt model; the interacting participants are of many different kinds, while each medium or genre will have special contributions to make. Several chapters offer such an argument; they present at least two very different perspectives on the same theme, which are dynamically shaped by the existence of the other side: man-midwifery/anti man-midwifery, transformism/natural theology, the Enlightenment/the authoritarian response. The conversational form applies to pictures as well as to words, which are so often responding to, engaging with each other.

There is no denying, however, the existence of significant differences between words and images. Yet, for my purposes here those differences are less important than their shared themes and preoccupations. Nonetheless, the fact that a picture can be viewed at a glance, that it can play in that moment with bizarre quirky ideas without discursive excess is significant. There is, so far as I know, no written equivalent to the extraordinary late eighteenth-century print *Nature Display'd* from which this volume takes its title (see plate 1, p. 11). A visual image may also possess its own distinctive way of expressing a complex idea – a straight line dividing human figures and faces, for example (see plates 2, 3, 6, 7, pp. 24, 26, 30, 31). A significant proportion of the images I use are prints: book illustrations, free-standing prints or based on a painting or drawing. This is not at all surprising given the changes in the nature and volume of publications in the period.[15] Many were designed to reach a wider audience, made up partly of professional people, often the peers of the authors and image makers, but also of literate and potentially more Enlightened classes, whose behaviour was capable of being moulded. Only a small proportion of medical and scientific books was illustrated, of course, and those with the most elaborate illustrations were within reach of limited numbers only. Nonetheless, the images that made documentary claims, even if they circulated in a limited fashion, were significant because they promised a fresh, authoritative view of nature, as, of course, did verbal descriptions of physical phenomena.[16] Satirical prints, which were probably more widely seen, indicate some of the more sceptical reactions to medical, scientific and gender issues.[17] Some of the

15. Porter, 1992, ch. 3 (by Fissell); Chartier, 1994; Burke, 1991, ch. 7 (by Darnton); Anderson, 1991, especially his discussion of newspapers; Jardine, Secord and Spary, 1996, ch. 7 (by Johns).
16. Bynum and Porter, 1993b, ch. 6 (by Kemp); Chapter 11, of this volume; Shapin and Schaffer, 1985, esp. 60–5, explore the making of authoritative views of nature through the concept of 'virtual witnessing'.
17. Donald, 1996; Haslam, 1996.

PLATE 1. *Anon., [James Gillray]*, Nature display'd, shewing the Effect of the Change of the Seasons on the Ladies Garden, *1797, engraving, Wellcome Institute Library, London.*

images mentioned started life as portraits and only became generalised through the titles they acquired in print form. From them we can gather something about how idealisations functioned, since in turning named persons into, for example, 'Nature', an elevation was involved from ordinary existence to an abstract idea with normative connotations.[18]

Whether in the form of pictures or words, there are a lot of abstract ideas in this book: nature, health, life, death, creation, identity and so on. Such ideas do not belong to any one domain or discipline, either now or then. They had a general cultural currency even if they were also claimed as part of the expertise of specific occupational groupings. Yet different types of knowledge and of

18. Emma Hamilton, a portrait of whom was issued as a print entitled 'Nature', provides an excellent example of the point, since we can understand the print as an idealisation of her. I discuss these issues in Chapter 2: Pointon, 1997, ch. 5; Jenkins and Sloan, 1996, pp. 266–75, esp. 269–70 on the 'Nature' print.

subject matter had been distinguished for centuries, and in some cases these distinctions found institutional expression. Similarly, occupations were minutely differentiated and classified and the existence of specialised knowledge, of expertise was recognised, even if the idioms through which recognition was expressed were rather different from our own. Hence, the organisation of knowledge during this period has to be taken into account. 'Organisation' is perhaps too grand a word for what was a piecemeal and geographically diverse situation. Few standard definitions of intellectual fields were available in the eighteenth century. In relation to medicine, which was comparatively structured, commentators differed in how they divided it up. There was no standard terminology even in universities, which mostly did not teach science in anything like the modern sense, and indeed disciplinary nomenclature was changing fast. In the period covered by the book the term 'biology' was coined and a number of specialist societies emerged to serve specific scientific disciplines (geology, mineralogy) rather than natural knowledge in general, which is what the Royal Society of London had done since the middle of the seventeenth century. In France there was more structure because the various Academies, which enjoyed state support, were organised by subject sections, and hence such divisions became more integrated into scientific and medical ways of life. Yet self-consciously modern, reformist institutions, such as the Royal Institution, London, founded in 1799, continued to offer lectures on 'natural philosophy' well into the nineteenth century.[19]

Of particular relevance to models of knowledge were periodicals and encyclopedias, which possessed two significant features. First, they gave expression to the widespread conviction that knowledge was growing and improving at an unprecedented rate and hence needed to be organised into manageable bits, and second, they responded to the desire of the literate classes to know as much as possible about the world in general. The first suggests a trend towards specialisation, the second the persistence of a common culture for those who could read and write. It seems that there was a fairly widespread sense that the nature and organisation of knowledge was in transition. It is significant that the period witnessed a number of attempts to develop systems for classifying knowledge, and to use visual models, such as the tree of knowledge in the *Encyclopédie*, to express the changing relationships between fields. This indicates both a utopian drive to make information widely accessible and a dawning awareness that there was already more than any person could grasp, hence the need to present an overall picture of knowledge, indeed to find ways of managing, if not reconciling, these two trends.[20]

That the organisation of natural knowledge was clearly in flux perhaps accounts for the importance of certain other aspects of scientific and medical culture of the period. Although some people placed an emphasis on where

19. Rousseau and Porter, 1980; Hahn, 1971; Berman, 1978; Morrell and Thackray, 1981; Corsi, 1988; Olby *et al.*, 1990, chs 63 and 64; Gillispie, 1980; Jardine, Secord and Spary, 1996, ch. 8 (by Roche); Whitley, 1984.

20. Shortland and Yeo, 1996, ch. 5 (by Yeo); Yeo, 1991; Darnton, 1984, ch. 5; Lefanu, 1984; Bynum, Lock and Porter, 1992; Kronick, 1991; Gascoigne, 1985.

knowledge had been generated, they were far more interested in how it was generated and by whom. It is a commonplace of historical writings on eighteenth-century science and medicine that there was an exceptional preoccupation with epistemology, that is, with theories of knowledge. The philosophical debates were complex, and when contradictory observations were made or divergent results were obtained from experiments, intricate arguments ensued, but by and large those who saw themselves as knowledge-creators consistently stressed careful empirical work and the meticulous application of reasoned arguments. While inevitably differences of detailed interpretation constantly arose, the broad contours of how reliable knowledge was to be produced were generally agreed upon. One result was that many people, not just metropolitan elites, but all those able to make fresh first-hand observations, claimed to be producing such knowledge. The reliability and trustworthiness of these individuals – travellers, naturalists and provincial practitioners – were accordingly extremely important, and this is why portraiture and biography arose as important genres within natural knowledge and medicine in this period; they provided evidence of an individual's character, behaviour and reputation. Hence, identity – an awareness of possessing and being shaped by recognised social values and roles – was an important issue. Identity-formation was as crucial for individuals as it was for groups, and in both cases identities were forged in dynamic interaction with others. Doctors, for instance, saw themselves as *not* quacks and *not* midwives, and defined themselves in more subtle ways in relation to their patients depending on the latter's wealth, status and gender.[21] A range of social constituencies was involved in the identity construction of writers examined in the book, for example, the state, the populace and active citizens in the case of reformers, hubristic over-reachers for writers such as Mary Shelley, the anarchic mob for commentators such as Chateaubriand, members of families for medical reformers and so on. I am assuming here, first, that those who produced knowledge paid particular attention to questions of identity, and second, that not only recognised professionals made claims to knowledge. It was not just those we retrospectively designate 'scientists' whose findings aspired to and enjoyed authority. When anyone asserted that nature was on their side, that palpable consequences followed from their specific views of nature's powers and authority, 'knowledge' was being claimed. In the process, students and teachers of nature constructed their identities. Image-makers fully participated in these processes of individual and group self-definition; they too had a stake in the nature and sources of legitimate knowledge.

In *Nature Displayed* I assume the importance of what can be called 'cultural effort' – the work that is done in the mind, the processes that go on between the ears. Such work is commonly prompted by cultural stimuli that are troubling, unfamiliar, or potentially subversive. The points I have just made about identity construction exemplify the approach. In *Frankenstein* Mary Shelley tapped

---

21. On identity in relation to scientific and medical biography, see Shortland and Yeo, 1996; on portraiture and biography see Jordanova, 1997 and 1998. On midwifery and quackery see Wilson, 1995 and Porter, 1989.

into and explored a widespread anxiety of her time, namely that those who sought knowledge of nature were prone to be melancholic, obsessive and introverted. The perceived crises of scientific and medical identity were not dealt with by the forms of action that are now conventional, such as lobbying, caucusing and so on, although these were just beginning to occur, but by distinctively cultural responses – writing and image-making. This is just as true of those who were critical of scientific and medical activities as of those who undertook them. The furious laymen who attacked man-midwifery did not raise funds for law suits against them, start schools for female midwives, or offer grants for births attended by women; they wrote and made prints, and thereby expressed, shaped and cultivated emotional reactions. From the nature and intensity of their responses we can infer the kinds of cultural management and psychic energy involved, and place them in the context of other related activities. Thus, for example, critical responses to the theories of William and John Hunter on the structure and function of the placenta reveal a great deal about the nature of their authority and the manner in which their intellectual claims were resisted.

It is obvious, at one level, that satire is precisely such historically-revealing cultural effort. But all too often it is read by historians as a transparent criticism of what was actually done rather than as a complex representation in its own right. The many satires on medical practitioners of the later eighteenth century tell us not what such practitioners really did but how they were perceived and where they touched collective sores. Their function was to transform and re-present their makers' responses and to do so in a form that would be instantly comprehensible to contemporaries. These processes require cultural effort, which takes many forms. Authors frequently internalised potential criticisms and then wrote in such a way as to pre-empt or to delegitimate them, as Tissot did at the beginning of his famous treatise on masturbation – this too is an example of cultural effort. I find the phrase helpful for two further reasons. First, it helps to maintain a focus on the place where cultural effort is most manifest – the texts and images themselves. Thomas Crow's recent book *Emulation*, an examination of the work of Jacques-Louis David and his pupils, is to my mind an exceptionally interesting example of just this approach. In a study that is particularly pertinent not just to the period but to loose homosocial groupings – the setting in which most natural knowledge and medicine as well as art was produced – Crow suggests that crises of authority, fatherhood and masculinity were worked through in the works of art themselves.[22] Second, the phrase 'cultural effort' serves as a reminder that, if much complex work is going on in the head, it is as likely to be shaped by emotion as by reason, by unconscious as by conscious processes. Indeed it suggests there are no easy separations to be made between form and content, between argument and affect, between explicit and implicit claims. In other words, 'cultural effort' stands for an approach well suited to the elusive but powerful intertwinings of science, medicine and gender, intertwinings that are above all in the domain of culture.

22. Crow, 1995.

The essays that follow were written between 1980 and 1997, and in that time the fields with which I have been most closely concerned have changed dramatically, as has the nature of my involvement with them. For most of that time I was working in departments of history, and teaching interdisciplinary courses, usually in collaboration with colleagues from sociology, philosophy, literature and art history. Now I work with anthropologists, archaeologists and art historians teaching courses around visual and material culture. My parent discipline, history and philosophy of science, has also changed markedly over the last two decades – cultural phenomena now play a considerably greater role, for example, and there have been real attempts to write at a level accessible to undergraduates and a general public, and hence to present a bigger picture of the history of science especially.[23] Historians of science, too, are becoming increasingly conscious of their relationships with the discipline of history, although the real bridge building is only beginning. This has occurred faster in the case of the history of medicine, partly because it has proved much easier to integrate medical history into the historical curriculum, where there is considerable student demand for the subject, and partly because in Britain the Wellcome Trust has funded a significant number of posts for historians of medicine, many of which are in history departments. The materials I use can be presented under a number of disciplinary labels; they also shed light on a number of different intellectual issues and approaches.

The history of science and the history of medicine possess different learned societies, journals and funding arrangements. Furthermore, they may be distinguished on intellectual grounds – science and medicine are distinct enterprises and each has its own history. Precision in such matters, as in the names we use to divide up fields of knowledge in a period without modern disciplinary categories, is vital. At the same time, there were considerable overlaps between the two in the period 1760 to 1820. We can illustrate the point by noting the intellectual affinities between Lamarck and Cabanis – the former was a naturalist, the latter medically qualified, although by no means a full-time or totally dedicated practitioner. Yet they had considerable interests in common, a pattern we find everywhere at the time. Two related features serve to distinguish science and medicine at that particular historical moment. First, medicine was primarily a form of practice, involving complex social negotiations between many different kinds of practitioners and equally diverse types of patients. Quite rightly, social historians wish to emphasise the importance, intricacy and historical specificity of these relationships.[24] I have not focused on medical practice here and mention it in order to place in context a particular way of thinking about health and about collectivities. Second, even if there was considerable geographical variation in their nature, medicine had its own institutions, from hospitals and medical schools to medical societies and dispensaries.

23. Bowler, 1992; Smith, 1997; *British Journal for the History of Science*, vol. 26, part 4, 1993, special issue on 'The Big Picture'. Biography is now playing an important role in bringing the history of science to a wider public: see Shortland and Yeo, 1996, esp. ch. 10 (by Moore).

24. The journal *Social History of Medicine* is an influential forum for this approach; see also, in addition to other works by him, Porter, 1987b, and Wear, 1992.

There were numerous niches available to the medically trained, not only in these institutions (and in 'private' practice), but also in prisons, philanthropic organisations, poor law institutions, local government, military, naval and colonial structures and so on. Relatively few such opportunities were available to 'scientists', and those that existed were in 'applied' science. These are important differences, but my concern has been with medical mentalities, and specifically with models of bodily phenomena, as well as with ideas about health. From that perspective, the picture looks rather different, with the affinities between 'science' and medicine predominating.

For a number of historians, medicine constituted a kind of common culture in the eighteenth century, with medical matters being widely debated and not only in medical circles, while literate laymen expected to, and did, converse with practitioners, sometimes on equal terms and sometimes as one educated person to another with special expertise but lacking absolute authority.[25] Physical well-being, illness and healing touched everyone. Furthermore, health was at the same time a central metaphor for social reform, and, as a matter of immediate importance to all, a significant element in debates that went far beyond the medical strictly speaking. Thus health, an ideal, was also a particular kind of icon in the period. By that token, it was a cultural commodity, traded far beyond the confines of medicine. Its aura derived from its strong associations with nature – health was the natural, that is the normal and desirable state of affairs, and was to be achieved through an understanding of nature and an ability to follow her precepts. Hygeia and Nature walked hand in hand.[26]

The materials available for examining the construction and representation of relationships in nature, for trying to understand thinking about gender and authority in the later eighteenth and early nineteenth centuries are extraordinarily rich. This richness is only just beginning to be appreciated – it demands a historiography which foregrounds cultural complexities. Yet there are many different ways of doing this, just as the materials themselves can be used in a variety of ways. Indeed, the following chapters were written within a number of different frameworks and I make no attempt to conceal that fact. For example, two chapters derive from an interest in science and literature, a fast-growing field, now quite substantial in size, especially in the United States, although this was not yet the case in the mid-1980s. At that time 'science and literature' was a novel and permissive framework that encouraged scholars, especially in the history of science, to open up questions about the nature of writing, the role of metaphor, the cultural reach of ideas in science. In fact, of course, it was not particularly new – we only have to think of the work of Marjorie Hope Nicolson to see that – but it felt like a fresh invitation.[27] 'Science and literature' offered something rather different to literary critics, for whom it was a permit to examine writings not previously within a conventional

25. Porter, 1985; cf. Jordanova, 1993b.
26. There is surprisingly little work on the cultural history of health as ideal, affect and image. But see: Rousseau and Porter, 1980, ch. 5 (by Bynum); Smith, 1985; Bynum and Porter, 1993a, ch. 12; Temkin, 1973; Coleman, 1974 and 1977a, b.
27. Nicolson, 1946 and 1976.

literary canon and to take their methods to new subject areas. One of these chapters also examines the theme of popularisation, a topic not much written about by historians of science and medicine at the time.[28] Priority had been given to texts that were authoritative, innovative in terms of content, and intellectually muscular, and quite specific assumptions had been made about the relationships between so-called elite and popular science, which it was important to challenge.

I have mentioned that the essays in *Nature Displayed* originated in a number of different debates, and that this diversity partly reflects broader changes in academic styles and preoccupations. It is inevitable that such changes take place. However, it is all too easy to see new approaches as already obsolete and dull even while they are in the process of becoming accepted. I fully grant the excitement that novelty brings, but, for a number of reasons, I do not want to see older frameworks simply marginalised. Keeping them alive is a way of remembering the history of our disciplines and of relations between them, and that is, in its most positive sense, a valuable heritage. Such a historical perspective also yields insights into how analytical vocabularies shift and the distinct insights they permit. For example, 'Policing Public Health' was written under the influence of the revitalised social history of the 1970s. This renaissance has been of lasting importance, so it is worth keeping in mind what it has offered to historical practice over the last two decades and its intellectual ancestry.[29] I have not sought to conceal or suppress changing approaches and attitudes in my essays. Neither, however, have I sought to emphasise change – the essays are arranged thematically rather than in their order of composition, which makes sense in the light of my earlier comments about the propensity towards revisiting themes, figures, sources.

Finally, I turn to the themes of interdisciplinarity and eclecticism. The chapters that follow are interdisciplinary in two specific senses. First, they use materials conventionally associated with a number of different disciplines. Second, they draw upon insights, approaches and frameworks derived from distinct academic fields. We could put the point differently by saying the essays are eclectic, which suggests almost a randomness, and a lack of guiding vision, whereas to call them inter-disciplinary suggests a breaking-down of arbitrary boundaries. Neither formulation works for me. There is a certain accidental quality to any scholarship; serendipity is a powerful force, especially when one engages open-endedly with materials that are relatively little known. Let us not endow interdisciplinary work with a false heroism, it is simply how some people's minds function, and it is supported, in this case at least, by the sources themselves. I prefer to call what I do cultural history, with an emphasis on ideas. The shape of *Nature Displayed* has been determined far more by the appeal of particular themes, historical moments, and delicious conjunctions than by any self-conscious anti-disciplinary project. Given a commitment to

28. Porter, 1992; Shortland and Yeo, 1996, chs 6 and 7 (by Cantor and Vicinus); Shinn and Whitley, 1985.
29. The journals *Social History* and *History Workshop Journal* not only reveal directly changes in social history, but also contain many reflexive pieces; Wilson, 1993.

gender, to cultural history, to a given period, and to scientific and medical ideas, then a particular kind of writing is likely to result. Necessarily this book has its idiosyncrasies, but I hope it explores some significant issues, both methodological and substantive, concerning nature, knowledge and gender between roughly 1760 and 1820.

PART I

NATURAL POLARITIES

Nature is a forceful, ever-present figure in Part 1. Since it is not possible to tie down what is meant by 'nature', its possible meanings and associations must be allowed to emerge from a variety of texts and images. However, a common thread in all these possibilities is that nature generates norms and thereby participates in moral polarities. Hence moral firmness was combined with semantic instability. What is good and natural was contrasted with what is bad and un-natural, and almost anything could go on either side of the equation. The pervasiveness of nature and its capacity to express moral oppositions accounts in part for its kinship with gender, a term which implies a special kind of duality. All dualisms are concerned with the simultaneous affinities and distinctions between their constituent terms and, as a result, they mediate ambivalence. Masculine and feminine are powerful, complex ideas, which do important cultural work, as indeed do nature, creation, production, authority and the other concepts discussed in Part 1.

If the essays that concern 'Natural Polarities' share major themes, it is important to recognise that they were written originally within quite distinct problematics. 'Feminine Figures' started with a set of questions about how nature was personified as female during the Enlightenment and it seeks to recognise that such questions are necessarily elusive, while also showing their relevance to social practices, such as the management of childbirth. 'Nature's Powers' was shaped by a desire to recast the history of evolutionary ideas into a more cultural-historical mode. It was therefore initially designed to address issues in the history of science, since evolution has been such a pivotal topic for the field, one furthermore in which the historiographical debates have been particularly intense. 'Melancholy Reflection' focuses on a single text, *Frankenstein*, which has become central for the recently constituted field of gender and science. The novel is often misinterpreted as a result of the still widespread wish to find unequivocal evidence of brute scientific power, and to demonstrate its gendered qualities. Hence *Frankenstein* has been read as an overt attack on masculinist science rather than as a general meditation upon the thirst for knowledge, the responsibilities of being a progenitor, and the kind of identity that is most appropriate for those with exceptional intellectual powers. 'The

Authoritarian Response' began life as a lecture in an interdisciplinary course on the Enlightenment; it concerns some extremely explosive dualities, forged during the French Revolution, an event often taken to mark the end of the Enlightenment. These paired terms, which are related to the emotionally-charged contrast between order and chaos, further intensified the stakes in the big concepts of the day. Nature was certainly one such concept. The result was oppositions of extraordinary violence – cannibalism versus civilisation, for instance.

Taken together, then, these four essays explore a number of moralised dualisms in which some of the complexities of 'nature' have revealed themselves, often, but not always, through their engendering.

CHAPTER TWO

Feminine Figures: Nature Display'd

In 1797 a bizarre print was published by Hannah Humphrey, entitled *Nature Display'd, shewing the Effect of the Change of the Seasons on the Ladies Garden* (see plate 1, p. 11). There is no top and no bottom – the image can be viewed equally well from four different angles. The reference to the 'ladies garden' – 'garden' was humorous slang for women's sexual parts – was intended to be if not exactly obscene at least titillating and would have been familiar to contemporaries. Thus these weird, incomplete female figures were associated with sexual pleasure. The four torsos meet in a zone marked with the words 'thunder, lightning, wind, rain', a zone that is around the lower abdomen of all figures; this feature serves to mitigate the immediate sense that nature and women are simply being associated with pleasure, since the words suggest changeability, unpredictability, and potential explosiveness. The figures have no heads and no legs. Instead of heads, three have plants sprouting from their necks; instead of legs they all have climatic conditions. The three plant-women present images and ideas that obviously reinforce familiar associations between femininity, sexuality, procreation, nature, plants, flowers and fruit. Winter, however, has a chimney pot for a head and 'hot house' written across her breasts. Hot houses are where plants are grown out of season or in otherwise unsuitable environments. They are artificial contraptions for what is, at other times and places, done naturally. It is possible that in referring to hot houses the print-maker had in mind the themes of fashion, self-indulgence, luxury and vanity that were a staple of eighteenth-century satirical idioms, particularly in relation to women. No matter how the detail of the print is to be interpreted, both the strong affinity between ideas of femininity and ideas of nature, as well as the ambivalence of such affinities, are evident. These female figures are associated with sexuality and reproduction as natural functions, with plants and gardens as areas metaphorically yoked to them, and with the regular, repeated rhythms of nature, the seasons. Overall, the print suggests that women's bodies are simultaneously erotic and troubling, and resolutely in the domain of nature.[1]

1. Partridge, 1961, p. 316. *Nature Display'd* was produced by Hannah Humphrey, a well-known print-seller with close associations with James Gillray: indeed, there has been some suggestion that this print was by Gillray himself, see Gillray, 1968, where *Nature Display'd* is among the so-called 'suppressed plates'; and also

Nature Display'd contains two themes I explore in this chapter – the complex eighteenth-century engagement with nature and the intricate interplay between femininity and nature, which was possible because the use of the female body to express a wide range of abstract ideas had been thoroughly conventionalised. Nature was a moral category of considerable weight available for and well suited to the expression of tensions concerning gender. The claim that an individual woman was or women in general were *un*natural was particularly effective rhetorically and mobilised a powerful sense of opprobrium. Furthermore, because abstract ideas, such as virtues and vices, were often personified in female form, while actual women were frequently portrayed as someone or something else (Hebe, a Vestal Virgin, Nature, Justice), numerous opportunities existed for exploring the gendering of urgent contemporary moral matters. Female figures were fluid and adaptable. This was difficult territory, however, because of the gap between women and female bodies on the one hand and the abstractions with which they were associated on the other. What served as the bridge? At a formal level, myth, history, long-used symbols and rhetorical figures served this purpose, but a degree of instability was nonetheless unavoidable. Despite the existence of conventions, it remained underdetermined how interpretation was to be performed, and hence uncertainty existed. The more formulaic the ways of filling the gap, the less uncertainty and the more stability there was. However, such formulae can also appear stilted and mechanical. The meanings of femininity and its kindred abstractions, although also shaped by custom, were similarly underdetermined, partly because there were simply so many possibilities. For viewers or readers to find particular associations apt at any given historical moment, symbols and so on had to be adapted and changed – pure convention was not enough to keep them fresh. Part of the pressure for change came from shifting presuppositions about gender, which allegory and personification helped to manage and clarify. 'Nature' was also subject to change. Both nature and gender altered because the practices that enlivened them were in flux and because new practices came into being that placed strain on existing representations and emotional configurations. When named women were presented as something else the possible slippages, the potential for ambiguity, were enhanced. In linking nature with feminine figures, attention could also be drawn to the fragility of gender roles, to the troubling implications of moving between identifiable persons, Woman and women, and to the need for clear boundaries, which appeared so elusive.[2]

Hill, 1976; Donald, 1996, esp. pp. 3–4, 32–3, which includes plates of many of Humphrey's prints; Robinson, 1996. Samuel Fores, to be discussed shortly, was also prominent in the world of prints, as Donald and Robinson make clear. *Nature Display'd* is discussed in George, 1942, vol. 7, p. 395, where it is also attributed to Gillray. It is possible to search the Wellcome Iconographic Collections by keywords, such as nature. I have examined a significant proportion of their relevant eighteenth- and early nineteenth-century holdings. Many secondary works on nature and gender are cited elsewhere in the book. See also the references in Illich, 1983, and the bibliographies in Jordanova, 1986b and Jordanova and Porter, 1997.

2. Warner, 1985; Abrams, 1993, entries for Allegory, Figurative Language and Symbol. He draws attention to criticisms of allegory in the late eighteenth and early nineteenth centuries as rigid, arbitrary and limited, pp. 207–8; Chapin, 1955. See also Agulhon, 1981; Pointon, 1997, ch. 5; Perry and Rossington, 1994, pp. 18–40; Woodall, 1997, ch. 2 (by Nicholson); Davis and Farge, 1993, esp. ch. 7; MacQueen, 1970.

Nowhere were these features more evident than in the passionate debates about man-midwifery during the eighteenth century.[3] The passion was generated by the increase in the numbers of men attending and seeking to attend normal birth and by the advent of the forceps – these were linked shifts that were perceived by some to threaten the modesty of mothers and the livelihoods of female midwives alike. The angry arguments that ensued have often been misunderstood because the attacks upon female and male midwives have been taken at face value, that is, they have been deemed to possess descriptive qualities, rather than being responses with their own emotional and political logic for which the conduct of childbirth was the trigger and conduit. Thus, although the attack on man-midwifery was a distinctive, even unique cultural episode, it can shed considerable light on more general patterns pertaining to the representation of female figures – the wife, the mother, the midwife and Nature herself. I am not claiming that diatribes against the presence of men in the birthing room bear no relation to changes in midwifery over the eighteenth century, but I am suggesting that a search for their truthfulness is misguided. I wish to place them in a different context – a broad cultural arena in which nature and feminine figures were playing off each other, where the moral and political stakes were felt to be phenomenally high.

The eighteenth-century midwifery debates in Britain produced one extremely striking image, often reproduced but rarely analysed, which gave dramatic expression to the need for clear, 'natural' gender boundaries (see plate 2, p. 24). This image was used as both advertisement and frontispiece for S.W. Fores's *Man-Midwifery Dissected; or, The Obstetric Family Instructor. For the Use of Both Sexes. Containing a Display of the Management of every Class of labour by Men and Boy Mid-Wives; also of their cunning, indecent and cruel practices. Instructions to Husbands how to counteract them. A Plan for the Complete Instruction of Women who possess promising talents, in order to supercede Male-practice. Various Arguments and Quotations, proving, that Man-midwifery is a personal, domestic and a national Evil.* Fores was a well-known print maker and he published this work under the name John Blunt. Given that it appeared in 1793, it is reasonable to assume that its heightened rhetoric gained force from contemporary political events in France – man-midwifery was strongly identified with everything French by its critics – and from a growing conservatism in Britain over the 1790s. Yet the basic themes and the intensity of affect had been present in writings on this subject for most of the second half of the century. In this light, the image becomes even more interesting since its venom is not carried in the figure or directly in visual detail, as it is in the Rowlandson cartoon of 1811, which depicts a huge, coarse, old woman carrying a bottle.[4] Her body is intended to repulse, whereas the figure in this frontispiece is undistorted. Rowlandson's image contains, I believe, the implication that feminine figures are ideally attractive – ones that are repulsive

3. Wilson, 1995; Bynum and Porter, 1985, part 3; Donnison, 1977; Roberts, 1993; Marland, 1993; Porter, 1987a; Gelis, 1984 and 1988.

4. This image is in the Wellcome collections, used on the back cover of Donnison's 1977 book, but not usually reproduced in books on Rowlandson. On Rowlandson, see Paulson, 1972 and Donald, 1996, esp. ch. 4.

PLATE 2. *John Blunt [Samuel Fores]*, A Man-Mid-Wife, *from his* Man-Midwifery
Dissected, *frontispiece, 1793, hand-coloured etching, Wellcome Institute Library, London. The
caption reads: 'A man-mid-wife or a newly discover'd animal, not Known in Buffon's time; for a
more full description of this* Monster, *see, an ingenious book, lately published price 3/6 entitled,
Man-Midwifery dissected, containing a Variety of well authenticated cases elucidating this animals
Propensities to crudity & indecency sold by the publisher of this Print who has presented the
Author with the Above for a Frontispiece to his Book'.*

constitute a kind of moral and aesthetic offence. Fores's image, by contrast, expresses its outrage in three other ways: the words, the abstract idea of the straight line cutting through, that is, dissecting a body, and by assuming and deploying general knowledge of contemporary cultures of midwifery. On one side of the sharp divide is the male practitioner, and his dubious activities are revealed in the forceps, instruments and potions that suggest violent, interventionist practice and questionable morals, since the medicines, on a shelf marked 'for my own use', were associated with the treatment of venereal disease. One bottle is marked 'love water', implying that the man-midwife sought 'to stimulate sexual desire in his patients'.[5] On the other side of the vertical line is the female figure, with few accoutrements at all, and the setting with its fireplace is clearly homely, in contrast to the male side, which suggests a shop or workroom. Physically speaking the figures are perfectly matched – the same face, the same height and build. There is absolutely no trace of distortion in the face or body, the line down the middle carries all the visual weight of the image. It is evident that Fores wants to play upon the 'mid' in midwife, since the word is positioned directly below the line, and from this basis he elaborates the idea that a man-midwife is and ought to be a contradiction in terms, an inappropriate, unnatural mixture of incompatible elements.

The script reads, 'A man-mid-wife or a newly discover'd animal, not Known in Buffon's time; for a more full description of this *Monster*, see, an ingenious book, lately published price 3/6 entitled, Man-Midwifery dissected, containing a Variety of well authenticated cases elucidating this animals Propensities to crudity and indecency sold by the publisher of the Print who has presented the Author with the Above for a Frontispiece to his Book'. So, the writing contains an open intensity and hatred that can inferred from the image but is not immediately apparent in it. A number of words are used that were frequent triggers for intense rage at that time – monster, animal, crudity, indecency.

The apparently cool abstraction of the straight line, especially when coupled with such intense emotions, is intriguing.[6] A number of prints from about 1760 onwards used the device of a vertical line to express a moral polarity. What they share is giving visual form to a dualism. Fores was after all a print maker and publisher, and I surmise that the image most akin to his frontispiece was known to him. *Cheek by Joul or the Mask* (see plate 3, p. 26) is an anonymous print of 1784 showing a face, divided by a straight line into male and female halves and accompanied by a verse. The print refers to the political campaigning in that year by Georgiana, Duchess of Devonshire on behalf of Charles James Fox. There are some striking similarities between the two prints in that they share a basic idea: mixing the sexes, who ought to be kept distinct, is unacceptable. The dividing line down the middle stands for gender distinctions. But in this case the faces do not match up perfectly, and that is precisely the

5. Donnison, 1977, caption to plate 3.
6. Cazort, Cornell and Robertson, 1996, pp. 25 and 27; *The Quick and the Dead* (1997). 'Half and half' waxes also existed.

Dfs. Devonshire   C. J. Fox.

Two faces here in one you see defign'd, | One rough & virulent, th' other fair & free,
Each ftrongly mark'd declares the inward mind, | with looks that promife fenfibility.
One feems ambitious of a daring foul, | when fuch as thefe in harmony unite,
The other foft the pafsions to controul. | The contraft furely muft amize the fight.

Publifh'd by E Hedges N.º 92 Cornhill May 8ᵗ 1784

PLATE 3. *Anon.*, Cheek by Joul or the Mask, *1784, engraving,* © *The British Museum, London. This is just one example of the many prints which attacked the involvement of Georgiana, Duchess of Devonshire with the political campaigning of Charles James Fox.*

point. Her elegant visage and elaborate hair do not fit with his larger, cruder face, fat chin, and darker simpler hair. As the verse put it:

> Two faces here in one you see design'd,
> Each strongly mark'd declares the inward mind,
> One seems ambitious of a daring soul,
> The other soft the passions to controul.
> One rough & virulent, th'other fair and free,
> With looks that promise sensibility.
> When such as these in harmony unite,
> The contrast surely must amaze the sight.[7]

The verse is considerably less forceful than the words on Fores's print, but the overall pattern is similar. The body remains undistorted, the visual effect is achieved by the straight line and the words supply the moral lesson. *Cheek by Joul* focuses on the face, and the verse uses appropriate ideas, such as the face being the index of the mind, whereas Fores has used the whole figure, suggesting perhaps that he is criticising social roles in their entirety. The most important feature shared by the two images is their appeal to the naturalness of gender differences. According to Colley, 'it was the unnaturalness of female participation in the public sphere that the cartoonists returned to again and again'. For her the print shows 'that their alliance was irregular, even monstrous', 'the split . . . was simply too great for fusion between them to be possible'.[8] Both images, then, reveal the force behind accusations of unnatural gender behaviour, and, in both cases, accusations of sexual impropriety were made. However, there is a subtle but significant difference in the way in which they present gender roles. In Fores's image, the two halves are identical except for the fact that one is in male, the other in female clothing. The implication is that viewers, like those who patronise men-midwives, could easily be deceived. Thus the 'truth' about gender distinctions and their consequences can be concealed, and requires writers like Fores to expose them. There is no confusion between the woman and the man in *Cheek by Joul*, the print appeals to the viewer to notice the obvious differences between men and women and respond accordingly.

The idea of the bisected figure had political currency in the 1790s, as we can see from its use in relation to Edmund Burke as a means of mocking his political inconsistencies. Satirists found a number of ways of expressing Burke's fickleness in visual form, and on the first day of 1793 an image appeared that bears striking similarities to *Man-Midwifery Dissected*. Two aspects of Burke, clothed entirely differently and divided by a straight line, display *The Shifting Orator*, who makes two different speeches and has two subtitles to illustrate his polarised positions.[9] The figure is crudely drawn and there are no contrasting settings as in Fores's print, but this image of Burke suggests that other moral polarities were handled in a similar way to those surrounding midwifery, and it conveys

7. Colley, 1992, p. 247, plate 55.
8. Ibid., pp. 245, 246.
9. Robinson, 1996, pp. 164–5.

PLATE 4. *Anon., [Thomas Rowlandson]*, The Contrast 1792 Which is Best, *1792, hand-coloured etching, after Lord George Murray,* © *The British Museum, London.*

particularly effectively the fear of slippage, of instability between positions about which people needed to feel secure and clear. There is even a sense of there being rights to clear demarcations.

In fact there were a number of ways in which the idea of sharp moral and political contrasts could be expressed visually. In the 1790s, for example, we find *The Contrast 1792*, which sets good British liberty next to bad French liberty (see plate 4, above), and *The Blessings of Peace, The Curses of War*, 1795 (see plate 5, p. 29), which contrasts an image of domestic contentment ('Such Britain was!') with a scene of devastation ('Such Flanders, Spain, Holland, now is!').[10] Both prints contain contrasting scenes inside juxtaposed roundels, and bold lettering to achieve a heightened emotional effect. *The Contrast* personifies types of liberty in female forms: British liberty is a seated Britannia, calm, attractive, holding the scales of justice and watching a ship; French liberty is a hysterical hag, holding a head on a trident, and presiding over a scene of devastation. Below each roundel is a set of keywords, including 'morality', 'personal protection' and 'happiness' for Britain, and 'anarchy', 'murder', and 'cruelty' for France. It was precisely these contrasts, these excessive vocabularies that writers against man-midwifery drew upon, hoping for ready emotional

10. Donald, 1996, pp. 152–7. On Rowlandson, see note 4; on Gillray, note 1.

PLATE 5. *Anon., [James Gillray]*, The Blessings of Peace, The Curses of War, *1795, hand-coloured etching and aquatint,* © *The British Museum, London.*

transfers between politics and medicine. Furthermore, it is striking that the prints not only deploy contrasting images of womanhood, but also dramatise the threat that political events pose for the family. *The Blessings of Peace The Curses of War* compares domestic happiness and intimacy with the death of the father, which leads to 'desolation'. In effect, the importance of the family, and hence of women's conduct, is elevated, endowed with national and international significance, and viewers thereby become accustomed to moving between different registers and levels of generality. It is as if female figures are particularly effective in facilitating such moves, which depend on a kind of emotional blur, on gushes of sentiment that promiscuously blend diverse loves, identifications and relationships.

It is not at all surprising that feminine figures were used in complex ways in writings about midwifery, given that the site of battle was both the mother's body and the role of female midwives. But outside the medical context, moral polarities also appeared particularly sharp in relation to women. Take, for example, *Life and Death contrasted – or, An Essay on Woman* (see plate 6, p. 30), which also uses the harshness of a rigid line dividing a figure, but here the axis is time rather than gender. There is even a pendant, *Death and Life contrasted – or, An Essay on Man* (see plate 7, p. 31), which carries some of the

PLATE 6. *Anon.*, Life and Death Contrasted – or, An Essay on Woman, *not dated*, c.*1760, hand-coloured etching, Wellcome Institute Library, London.*

PLATE 7. *Anon.*, Death and Life Contrasted – or, An Essay on Man, *not dated,* c.1760, etching, Wellcome Institute Library, London. *There are many versions of these two images. This pair is the version printed and sold by Bowles and Carver.*

same messages about vanity and the need to prepare for death.[11] Yet the male version, set in a rural churchyard with a temple in the background, lacks the bite of the female one, which is stuffed with admonitory quotations. And we know that vanity was a theme customarily associated with the female figure, that women bore the brunt of satires on fashion, that they were excoriated for their preoccupation with worldly pleasures. The objects in the foreground of *An Essay on Woman*, cards, romances, and a book about gaming, suggest precisely the widespread anxieties about women, frivolities and luxury that were present in Fores's diatribe. Although it was widely assumed by moralists that everyone should attend to their spiritual well-being, there was a special frisson attached to the idea of Woman – imagined as young and beautiful – reduced first to a skeleton and then to dust. Possibly the print trades on ideas of unveiling women, which carried a charge I have attempted to analyse elsewhere, on the pleasures and perils of masks, and on the notion of naked truth, a harsh reality, generally personified as female.[12]

The position taken up by Fores towards feminine figures was a complex one. He wanted to promote women as midwives, since this would protect the modesty of those giving birth, and in this he echoed female practitioners who defended their profession in the period.[13] But his attitude to parturient women themselves is considerably more ambivalent. In tracing the historical development of man-midwifery, he naturally noted its French antecedents and blamed French women for being loose in allowing themselves to be delivered by men, and their husbands for not controlling them. He was also hostile to the practice of women getting together during a labour. Although he was advocating greater use of female midwives, he referred to their inexcusable ignorance, which was to be tackled by proper training. The implication is that women are impatient for quick labours, that men-midwives play on this, and then make the mothers feel something amazing has been achieved. It follows from all these points that women need others to manage their modesty, that distinctively feminine virtue, on their behalf, and that all women, mothers and midwives, need to be better informed. It is noteworthy that he did not deny the need for male intervention in a minute number of difficult cases. Although the husband is the key figure in the book, the person whose interests should be defended and who should rescue his wife from the danger of accoucheurs, Fores also felt ambivalent about men: 'those pusillanimous husbands who feel themselves overborne by custom, and cannot muster up resolution enough to protect their wives' persons from injury and insult, may be compared to a captain who quits the ship

11. Donald, 1996, p. 78: '*An Essay on Woman* of 1769, probably designed by Valentine Green, bears inscriptions emphasising that responsibility for temptation and corruption is peculiarly female', a 'message that recurs endlessly in the social satire of eighteenth-century England'. See also pp. 217–18, note 25. Ribeiro makes similar points, 1986, esp. ch. 6, and chs 3 and 5, and she reproduces a similar pair of prints on p. 112. See also Brewer, 1997, figures 34 and 35. Cf. Nussbaum, 1984. Many historians of women and the family at this time have noted the intense moral investment in feminine (and ideally domestic) roles: for example, Davidoff and Hall, 1987 and Rendall, 1985.

12. Jordanova, 1989a, ch. 5; Warner, 1985, ch. 13.

13. On prominent female midwives see Marland, 1993, ch. 6 (by King) and 7 (by Gelbart); Porter, 1995, ch. 4. A number appear in Todd, 1984.

(whereof he is the sole owner) out of compliment to his pilot'. Husbands who permit the use of men-midwives, who are 'injurious to society', 'should have ass's ears'.[14] The implication, once again, that women cannot be trusted to manage their modesty alone is inescapable, as are the related implications that while mastery and ownership of women by men are desirable, indeed necessary, they are also fragile. Men have allowed themselves to be manipulated both by their wives and by other men, who have excluded them from the birthing room and thereby concealed the improprieties that occur there. Secrecy was a central issue – men-midwives were deemed to act in secret on women's private parts – it was in effect a code-word for sexual violation.[15]

Fores writes, as it were, in the name of the husband, but the figure with real power in the book is nature, personified as female and the ultimate arbiter. Fores does not present her as perfect, since 'nature does not *always* pursue her usual process', hence the need for special responses to 'preternatural cases'.[16] Nonetheless the power and autonomy of nature are constantly invoked. Nature works in her own time, which means that this work cannot and should not be hurried, that human beings have to learn to wait upon and respond to that pace: 'if *we wait with PATIENCE Nature of herself will do the work*', 'a female operator is obliged to wait NATURE'S *time*', which is a good thing since instruments, used to hurry things along, are his principal target.[17] Thus Fores urges respect for 'the powers of nature' rather than a slavish devotion to fashion. It might appear then that he has convention on his side, but the whole tone, particularly of the beginning of the book, suggests that this was not so. He felt the need to defend his work against the criticism that it was too explicit and unsuitable for women. He was not alone in this anxiety, and medical men writing popular books on family or sexual matters also had to deal with the charge. Fores was not a medical practitioner, and in defending himself he made common cause with William Buchan, the Scottish doctor whose *Domestic Medicine*, first issued in 1769, was one of the most widely read books of its kind ever published.[18] The defence of publishing details of the organs of generation and the process of birth was that everyone ought to know as much as possible about child bearing, precisely because it was of individual, familial and national importance. Fores quoted Buchan approvingly to the effect that women can easily be cheated out of their lives by their own ignorance. Both authors wanted the grand importance of their subject to act as a stabiliser, in case their discussions of reproduction themselves appeared indecent. They cast themselves as beneficent reformers, and drew upon an authoritative nature for rhetorical ballast.

But stability was not easily achieved. I suggest we can identify two points of special tension. The first concerns the nature of the power that men and women respectively have. Both sexes, for Fores, fail to inhabit their designated

---

14. Fores, 1793, pp. xv, 50.

15. Porter, 1987a; cf. Fores, 1793, pp. xii, xvi; pp. 309–29.

16. Fores, 1793, p. xxiii, his emphasis.

17. Ibid., pp. 37, 41, his emphases. Fores invokes Nihell in support of his position, p. 38.

18. Ibid., pp. xviii–xxiii. On Buchan see Lawrence, 1975, Rosenburg 1983, and Porter, 1992. Tissot, the subject of Chapter 6, felt vulnerable on just the same point.

roles and for both the consequences are grave. Yet the issue concerns women more immediately than men – it is they who might lose their lives – and, while he wants to empower women with information, he seems doubtful at the same time whether they can steer their own ship. Like other writers in this vein he dramatises the vulnerability of women to 'new fangled obstetric butchery lately invented at Paris', and further heightens the drama when he goes on about 'boys' as if the youth of male practitioners made the violation all the greater.[19] Women are intensely vulnerable, yet vital to the nation, they fail to exhibit proper modesty, yet can be empowered by advice and knowledge: they are blameless and culpable simultaneously. Men are equally culpable, but perhaps have greater potential as saviours.

The second point of tension concerns 'nature', that most elusive of concepts. It is now well-known that it was the centrepiece around which midwifery debates were organised in the eighteenth century. Fores's frontispiece (see plate 2, p. 24) made it abundantly clear that man-midwifery is unnatural, and the point is made in three ways. First, the man-midwife is an animal not a human. The boundary between human and animal was particularly crucial at this particular moment, when wild children, new races and societies, the capacities of monkeys, especially in relation to speech, were all being scrutinised with precisely the aim of working out where the dividing line was to be. Hostile comments on French revolutionary popular politics made liberal use of the idea of human beings descending to the level of the beasts.[20] Second, the man-midwife is a monster. Monsters are what should not happen, a mistake on nature's part, an interruption of business as usual in the natural economy. Although an interest in monstrous births was not new, it was intense, and more analytical in the eighteenth century, and there was speculation that man-midwifery increased the number of deformed children.[21] Third, the man-midwife is prone to be crude and indecent. The implied contrast here is with modesty, which for many eighteenth-century thinkers was a natural property of women. To violate feminine modesty was to be simultaneously immoral and unnatural, indeed these ideas were mutually defining.[22] For Fores, birth was a natural process: 'regular midwifery is only the superintendence of a process in nature, and the use of instruments (being the business of surgeons) is totally unconnected to it'.[23] But, as we know, 'nature' is not a stable concept. It could be invoked as a moral and ethical norm, yet the need to do so stemmed exactly from

19. Fores, 1793, p. xiii; there is a reference to 'boys' in the title, see also, for example, p. 57.
20. The man/animal distinction was fundamental to the human sciences of the period: Fox *et al.*, 1995; Smith, 1997. The connotations given to 'animal' behaviour by critics of the French Revolution are part of the general distaste for barbarism and anarchy: see Church, 1964; Chapter 5 of this volume; Paulson, 1983. The use of the tiger as a metaphor for revolution is an excellent example, discussed by Paulson, pp. 67, 72, 73, 97–102, 108–9.
21. The study of monstrosity was undertaken by medics and natural historians in this period, and it fed into the science of man. In addition to the works cited in note 20, see Huet, 1993, esp. ch. 5; Wilson, 1993, esp. ch. 5; Todd, 1995. Of course, *Frankenstein* is the obvious example of sustained thinking about monstrosity: see Chapters 3 and 4; Mellor 1988. Many critics of the French Revolution also spoke of monstrosity – see note 20.
22. Robinson, 1982.
23. Fores, 1793, p. 65.

the frequency with which what was perceived as *un*natural occurred. Women and the feminine seem to have been peculiarly implicated by the instability of nature as a term in this period. This is because their identification with nature was intense, fresh, multifaceted, while any deviations from a true path were passionately condemned, presented as errors to which women were particularly prone, such as vanity, immodesty and seduction by fashion. Women both partook of the prestige of one of the period's most authoritative concepts, and failed to manifest with sufficient consistency its defining traits.

Female figures, far more than male ones, have been used to carry ideals and abstract ideas over many centuries. We are used therefore to the doubleness of vision that ensues – a female form can be at once a body, even a body of a named person, and a virtue, vice, idea, nation, or whatever. We are equally used to accepting that the link between these two levels of meaning is not direct or literal but metaphorical, and metaphorical, furthermore, in some profound sense that appears strangely resistant to explanation. Why should time and death generally be male when nature and charity are conventionally female? (see plates 8, 9 and 29, pp. 36, 37, 221)[24] How do we associate a feminine form with areas from which women have been excluded?[25] Justice was commonly personified as a woman, although women were largely absent from the administration of the law. However, the gap between the two registers, and the fact that linking them requires mental effort, is precisely what makes allegory and personification possible. If this is the case, then processes that remove or close the gap are likely to lead to ambiguity and instability. The energetic reinvigoration of ideas of nature in the eighteenth century, its multiple and highly emotive links with the feminine, together with a widespread sense of upheaval in the most crucial areas of social practice where they came together – family life and procreation – indeed served to close the gap. Or rather, there was a perceived threat to close it, to blur the distinctions between women, Woman, and the feminine on the one hand, and between nature as a set of laws governing physical existence, nature as morality and nature as the source of life and fertility on the other. Femaleness and naturalness were hard to keep apart. Inside this conceptually unstable yet socially central zone, and in the throes of perceived dramatic change, sat birth and midwifery. Another diatribe against man-midwifery, this time by Philip Thicknesse, illustrates these points.

Man-Midwifery Analysed and the Tendency of that Practice Detected and Exposed was first published in 1764 by a man who became notorious for his ill humour (see cover illustration). Thicknesse tried many careers, including that of apothecary, was much married, thirdly to the feisty musician Ann Ford, herself the niece of a man-midwife, and published voluminously.[26] There were three eighteenth-century editions of his book on midwifery, the last of which in 1790 was published by Fores himself.[27] Many of the arguments in this ever-expanding book have

24. Eighteenth-century versions of Ripa's famous *Iconologia* illustrate the point: Ripa, 1971 and Richardson, 1979.

25. Warner, 1985, p. xx.

26. Thicknesse and Ford are discussed in Chapter 12.

27. Thicknesse, 1764, 1765 and 1790.

PLATE 8. *George Richardson*, Iconology, *London, 1779, volume I, plate XLI: 157, Investigation, 158, Conscience, 159, Discretion, 160, Ingenuity.*

PLATE 9. *George Richardson*, Iconology, *London, 1779, volume I, plate XLVIII: 185, Solitude, 186, Meditation, 187, Experience, 188, Exercise.*

already been noted in Fores, but some of its other features will serve to sharpen our understanding of the relations between femininity and nature in the eighteenth century.

There are three types of feminine figure in Thicknesse's text. First, he mentions a number of female midwives by name. He does so in order to bestow status on them, to suggest that they are a real option for women, who, by declining to use them, have sacrificed their modesty to fashion. Furthermore, since Royalty use these women, so should others. Thicknesse needs them to be real. The female figure of the midwife is thus rooted in particular, named women; she is not just a general type. In his text midwives were an occupational grouping made up of actual women.[28] Second, Thicknesse invokes a type of woman, one who is frequently a shadowy presence in diatribes against man-midwifery – the prostitute. Even where it was not openly stated it was generally implied that by allowing a man other than her husband to touch her private parts, the woman reduced herself to the status of a whore. Women who wish for a male attendant, having heard the arguments against them, are 'fashionable prostitutes', and may be called so by their husbands, according to Thicknesse. The language of prostitution not only reminds readers that money changes hands in midwifery and that a female body can be a commodity, but it evokes the sense that women are unreliable morally. Thicknesse associated the need to stamp out man-midwifery with 'the preservation of the Empire: for the FIRST MARK of the downfall of all great Empires has been the PROFLIGACY of the WOMEN'.[29] Third, Thicknesse personifies nature as a woman: 'Goody Nature . . . that excellent and never failing female midwife . . . This old lady, who had practiced the art of midwifery in every corner of the globe, for many generations, with amazing success, was, about fifty years ago, stifled in France between two featherbeds, by Messrs Doctors LaMotte and Mauriceau; and no sooner was the good old lady interred, than these, and many other male imposters in that fanatical country, endeavoured to intrude themselves on the public as her legitimate sons.'[30] Even though no woman is mentioned by name, this passage is notable in the way it brings together actual people, a profession doubly associated with women and the sustained use of female personification.

In his texts, Thicknesse moved between different kinds of women – fashionable women, the woman-midwife, the prostitute – he is naming individuals, many of them women, and he is invoking nature as an abstract idea to be personified, not just as female, but as a female midwife. Such writing, I contend, puts excessive strain on where, psychically and imaginatively, women are

---

28. e.g. Thicknesse, 1765, pp. 32–3; 1790, pp. xvii–xviii. Anon., 1772, used similar arguments, and included a list of eminent female midwives and their addresses, starting with Elizabeth Nihell, p. 73. It also constantly evokes 'nature' in its arguments.

29. Thicknesse, 1790, pp. 82 and 73, 79, 113, his emphases. Cf. Anon., 1772, esp. pp. 25, 27. Prostitution was a widely debated issue in the period; particular anxiety was expressed about the fall of young, previously virtuous, women, precisely the story Hogarth tells in *A Harlot's Progress* (1732): Shesgreen, 1973, nos 18–23; Paulson, 1975, ch. 3 and 1979, esp. pp. 19–23, 33–4, 118–20. See also the remarkable poem by Thomas Holcroft, in Lonsdale, 1984, p. 683.

30. Thicknesse, 1764, p. 3; on French midwifery see Gelis, 1984 and 1988 and his edition of de la Motte's treatise, 1979.

and Woman is. Describing Thicknesse's work in this way is an attempt to present the rage that was clearly present in him – and not only in him – in another language, one that may reveal what was at stake in responses to man-midwifery, while also hinting at how it fits into broader cultural patterns. A number of features of eighteenth-century society had produced this strain: the cult of or infatuation with nature, which had an erotic dimension that accentuated the gendered complexities of nature; a form of medicine that was increasingly preoccupied with family life and reproduction, both in theory and in practice, while it was also developing highly self-conscious literary and artistic treatments of women and femininity; the controversial nature of midwifery, expressed in a discourse that moved between abstractions, social types and accounts of real and imagined occurences. To these we should also add that demography and philanthropy, as practices and discourses, heightened col-lective emotional investment in motherhood, the prevention of infant death, and a growing population.[31] Furthermore, when laymen such as Thicknesse and Fores became enraged by the activities of men-midwives, they really had no option of going to institutions, professional bodies or the law for redress – the medical infrastructure, such as it was, offered few such possibilities. They relied instead on stirring up public opinion. Hence, they had every incentive to increase their emotional pitch.

The cult of nature had an erotic dimension, and the intense emotions elic-ited by man-midwifery suggest how important sexual anxieties about inappro-priate touching were. Men-midwives were, after all, accused of entering other men's 'gardens' and despoiling them. Nature in general, and gardens in particu-lar, carried strong connotations of pleasure, and by that token they could be feminised zones. Women were often depicted in unspecific 'natural' settings, vaguely associated with plants, endowed with qualities deemed characteristic of nature, or even portrayed as nature.[32] This was the context within which the intense man-midwifery debates took place. There the stakes were high and the talk was of violating, even suffocating, nature and women.

Hence it was crucial that women-midwives got nature on their side, which is exactly what Elizabeth Nihell sought to do in her *Treatise on the Art of Mid-wifery* (1760). Describing herself as 'professed midwife' on the title page, she defended her occupation, her fellow midwives and the interests of women in

31. The literature on the family and related matters in the eighteenth century is now huge. *Continuity and Change* publishes a range of work in this area, although its emphasis is more social than cultural. On the family in visual culture, see Duncan, 1973 and 1981; Leppert, 1988; Hautecoeur, 1945. Influential, although controversial, treatments of the family in the relevant period include: Ariès, 1973; Coveney, 1967; Davidoff and Hall, 1987; Flandrin, 1979; Pollock, 1983; O'Day, 1994.

32. See note 1. An admittedly impressionistic comparison of images of women with those of men in the period suggests that natural settings are far more frequent in the former than the latter. Precisely because of the rise of pleasure gardens, erotic experience was linked with garden settings, and specifically with the pleasures women offered, since most relevant representations were produced by men: Bryson, 1981, ch. 3; Solkin, 1993, ch. 4. Furthermore, women were particularly associated with flowers, amateur botany and flower painting: Bennett, 1991; Pointon, 1997, pp. 146–71; Schiebinger, 1993, ch. 1; Abir-Am and Outram, 1987, ch. 2 (by Schteir). See also Pugh, 1988, esp. pp. 102–121 on gardens and pleasure. It seems reasonable to assume that, even where no reference is explicitly made to it, the Garden of Eden was never far from people's minds.

general, not only by referring to her extensive professional experience, but also by claiming authority as a woman and a mother herself. Nihell saw women in general and herself in particular to be naturally better suited to practise mid-wifery than men. As she put it in relation to manual examinations by men: 'a midwife, duly qualified by Nature and art, with a shrewdness and delicacy of the touch, is, when requisite, capable of giving, in virtue thereof, a just account of a woman's condition'.[33] While she made some of the ritualised apologies for authorship that she imagined were expected of her, she confidently asserted the importance of her message and of her calling 'for the good of society': 'the voice of Nature and Reason' powerfully recommends 'the preservation of so valuable a part of the human Species as pregnant women, as well as that of their dear and tender charge, their children'.[34] Her dual emphasis on nature and reason is interesting, for she insisted that everyone could understand enough to make sound judgements about childbirth – nature had made sure of that. Nihell denied that male practitioners were safer, that is, able to reduce maternal and infant mortality, thereby revealing the centrality of arguments about popu-lation for the midwifery debates. Men certainly sacrificed the decency and modesty of their patients. Men-midwives do not, in other words, 'assist her [i.e. Nature]', indeed they have committed offences against her. The opposite of nature was, in one sense, 'Art': 'the men midwives, in their sistem [sic] of exalting their powers of Art over ours of Nature, keep no measures with truth'. In other words, she prefered nature with a little but competent art, to art, barbarously abused, 'without any Nature at all'.[35] Nihell foregrounded her own femininity, associated her profession with a feminised nature, and then claimed the authority of nature for her causes: the defence of women-midwives and modest mothers and the enhanced well-being of society as a whole.

Many other occasions for linking female figures with nature were far more anodyne. Perhaps this was necessarily the case, for they suggested a safer, far less treacherous world in which both nature and femininity were simpler, in which the more troubling oscillations between women, femininity and nature did not take place. The gap between the literal and the metaphorical levels could be more conventional, and less complex. This is the case in the 1784 print, entitled simply *Nature* and based on a painting of Emma Hamilton by George Romney (see plate 10, p. 41). The image deploys a number of devices that would have prompted contemporary viewers to think 'nature' – the background, the dog, the pose, the facial expression, all of which suggest a particular kind of nature, the nature of innocence and spontaneity, the nature, in fact, not so much of women but of children. One of the most notable extensions of the lan-guage of nature in the eighteenth century was into the world of childhood; although often associated with Rousseau's *Émile* (1762), it was already in flower in the 1740s in England, and contained its own complexities and contradic-tions. By calling this print 'Nature', relatively uncomplicated emotions were

33. Nihell, 1760, p. 312. On Nihell, see Todd, 1984, pp. 233–4 and Klukoff, 1970, who discusses Smollett's attack on her publications.
34. Nihell, 1760, pp. xvi and i of the Preface.
35. Ibid., pp. v and vii of the Preface.

Painted by G. Romney

Engraved by J.R. Smith.
Mezzotinto Engraver to his Royal
Highness the Prince of Wales.

NATURE

Flushed by the spirit of the genial year
Her lips blush deeper sweet, they breathe of Youth,
The shining moisture swells into her eyes
In brighter glow, her wishing bosom heaves
With palpitations wild.

London Published May 29 1784 by J.R.Smith No.1 Oxford Street.

PLATE 10. *J.R. Smith,* Nature, *1784, mezzotint after George Romney's portrait of Emma Hamilton, c.1782,* © *The British Museum, London.*

Nature

PLATE 11. *Anon.*, Nature, *not dated, engraving after Sir Thomas Lawrence,* Emily and Laura Anne Calmady, *exhibited at the Royal Academy 1824.*

mobilised, both because what was meant by nature was rather vague, and because by making Emma Hamilton child-like, any seduction can be a mere playful hint and all threat has been removed – this is not a Nature to be reckoned and grappled with.[36] There is little conceptual density here. These

36. Cadogan, 1748, is an interesting and early example of the portrayal of children as natural. Rousseau, 1911, Book 1, contains his ideas about early infancy. On the print, see Jenkins and Sloan, 1996, pp. 269–70. The verse on the print reads: 'Flush'd by the spirit of the genial year / Her lips blush deeper sweets, they breathe of Youth;/ The shining moisture swells into her eyes/ In brighter glow; her wishing bosom heaves / With palpitations wild.' I am deeply grateful to Dr Sloan for supplying me with the verse.

points are even clearer in a later print, also entitled *Nature*, made from a portrait by Thomas Lawrence of Emily and Laura Calmady (see plate 11, p. 42). Probably executed in 1823, it was exhibited at the Royal Academy in the following year: it was warmly received and a number of prints were made from it and a related drawing. The two girls are shown entwined, with a vague landscape in the background. Their pose suggests childish spontaneity, that is, it does not seem contrived or consciously posed – as Michael Levey affirms, 'Lawrence aimed at a totally "natural" impression'.[37] Here is nature at its least threatening, simplest, and most idealised, in the figures of two innocent girls (cf. plate 18, p. 172). The image seeks and elicits uncomplicated emotion, in effect it infantilises nature. There certainly was a measure of ambiguity in these images, but it was not troubling; there was no rage and little complexity.

The baby face of nature did not exist before about the middle of the eighteenth century and its legacy is still with us. Perhaps the soft, women-and-children image of nature arose in tandem with the profoundly unsettling aspects, to act as a kind of collective solace, creating a zone that could be entered for comfort. The other type of nature was also about women and children, but their darker, wilder sides. These were particularly, but not exclusively, evident in the impassioned disputes about midwifery. I have argued that there was special intensity surrounding Woman, women, and femininity in eighteenth-century discourse, and that this intensity is dramatically evident in the controversial nature of man-midwifery. It is important for my argument that such intensity is not interpreted as a simple, direct expression of changes in practice, that it does not merely reflect the supposedly increasing use of the forceps or changes in the composition of the occupation. After all, the vast majority of births were still attended by women. Rather the intensity came from what was invested by contemporaries in women's bodies and in the process of birth, and from the explosive moral connotations of the relationship between reproductively active women and their helpers. These investments in turn were made possible by representations that had long linked together women, female bodies, nature and abstract ideas. There were fireworks about midwifery because associations between the feminine and nature in the second half of the eighteenth century became more varied, more blurred, more unstable, more integral to larger political, social, and cultural shifts.

Thus, as nature became arguably the major source of moral legitimacy, the need for stable gender demarcations grew; it was met by apparently firm polarities that touched on those most sensitive areas – sexuality, family, nationhood – where rage was most easily triggered. I am proposing that this nexus of issues raised threatening and difficult questions, that it aroused powerful reactions because a number of key boundaries in fact lost their clarity. The assertion of crisp moral positions and the worries about the collapse and confusion of gender roles were two facets of a single situation. The straight line of Fores's frontispiece expressed the desire to restore clarity, to keep ontologically

37. Levey, 1979, pp. 74–5; Garlick, 1954, p. 30 and plate 99; Garlick, 1989, p. 161, plate 89. The painting was exhibited at the Royal Academy in 1824 and several prints were made from it.

distinct categories visibly apart. I have found evidence for the blurring of boundaries in books on midwifery, which, in their overt anxieties, consist of texts where real people, general social categories (gender, classes), social-cum-moral types (the prostitute, the fashionable woman), personifications and abstract ideas jostle together in texts and images, leaving the reader, like the writer, psychically adrift, and fearful of cosmic decline. In the shadows of these writings lay an ideal, ordered, stable universe, which was, of course, a chimera. Although the specific characteristics of medicine and midwifery are an import-ant element, this situation needs to be seen in broader contexts. The growth of reformist sentiment around the family, the increase in popular medical writing concerning family and sexual matters, the polarisation of moral issues, especially in the 1790s, and practices of personification are of special signifi-cance. In all of these trends the associated idioms of femininity and nature were deployed. Concerns about fuzzy gender distinctions also depended on the existence of a sense of drama around femininity, which could all too easily turn bad, with widespread detrimental effects. The gender drama was capable of being further heightened by many different kinds of crisis – in national politics, in foreign affairs, in the family – which were linked through highly emotive verbal and visual vocabularies. At the same time, these vocabularies were riven with tensions. The result was layer upon impacted layer of investment in femi-nine figures and their natural status, a burden they could hardly bear.

CODA

Uncertainty and openness tend to be devalued in scholarship, and in many fields speculation is considered unsafe, even sloppy. Where it is permitted, it tends to be presented as play, almost as if nothing much hinges on how we interpret texts and images. Here, however, I do not wish to play but to open up the maddeningly elusive issues that underlie the arguments of this chapter.

Two claims are often made: first, that women's bodies have been persistently used to allude to or explore something else, and second, that this is a particu-larly notable feature of eighteenth-century images, for example in portraiture. The first claim draws attention to persistent motifs, repeated with variations, in both words and images, over centuries. There is no doubting the existence of such motifs – the difficulty is offering an interpretation of them that eschews both essentialism (such as, men always seek to control women biologically and culturally and this is one manifestation of it) and ahistoricity (such as, in many periods when images of vice are sought, they turn to women, especially hags). A measure of historical specificity is important, and so is the recognition that the insidious power of 'women as . . .' is based on long habit, custom, conven-tion.[38] The real poser is why women are more linked with some traits and ideas

---

38. Weinsheimer, 1987; Perry and Rossington, 1994, esp. pp. 18–40; Woodall, 1997, ch. 2 (by Nicholson); Pointon, 1997, ch. 5.

than others. And men's bodies can be linked with 'something else' too, as a cursory inspection of illustrated editions of Ripa's *Iconologia* reveals. There have been times too when named men have been depicted as someone else, or in another time than their own, although it is true that the virtues in particular have been persistently personified as female. So, what exactly is the difference between men and women here?

What makes all this yet more vexing is that it is hard to see exactly how the links between female figures and abstract ideas function – a question Marina Warner poses most elegantly in *Monuments and Maidens*. Of course allegory and personification work because we are aware of the effort of decoding – indeed, being able to make that leap contributes a large measure to the pleasure they give. At the same time the leap could not be made at all if the links were purely arbitrary. It is true that objects, such as the scales of justice, act as triggers, but something deeper also occurs, so that it feels right in some way that is hard to articulate for women to represent certain ideas and entities. Even if it continues to feel right in some circumstances now, the disparity between the grandeur of the ideas involved and the mundane complexities of most women's lives is immediately apparent. The use of female figures to represent hygiene, electricity or inoculation appears ridiculous, hence it is hard to enter into the mind set that produced them.

While it is possible for historians to watch moments of decision making when symbols are chosen and assumptions that generally remain tacit are brought fleetingly to the surface, many unanswered questions remain. This is partly because the meanings of feminine figures resist full explication, and they appeal precisely for this reason. It may be helpful to confess their elusive quality – such a confession serves to acknowledge the power of mysteries, the inability of scholarship to completely dismantle processes of mystification. This does not mean we should stop trying to show how such figures work in particular historical circumstances, but it does mean that some interpretative tools are likely to be more useful than others. I would guess that these figures work because both men and women can identify with and project onto them. Thus the claim in relation to the seven female virtues Reynolds designed for stained glass windows in New College Chapel, Oxford, that he was working 'in a period when female personifications were generally designed merely to please the eye', is unhelpful.[39] It trades on facile assumptions both about gendered viewing, and about the period in question. Indeed, such a claim forecloses issues of identification and projection altogether.

'A man', opined Andrew Wilton in *The Swagger Portrait*, 'in even the most imaginary of costumes . . . or the most idealising of poses . . . is always himself . . . a woman is often shown as Venus, Diana, Chastity, Patience, or Truth.' He continued:

39. Penny, 1986, p. 291. For a different approach to Reynolds, see Postle, 1995, esp. pp. 168–81 on the New College project. Reynolds's work contains many interesting female figures, as, for example, in his 'Theory' (*c*.1779) and his allegorical portrait of James Beattie (1773). On identification see Laplanche and Pontalis, 1988, pp. 205–8.

There tends to be a stronger element of sheer make-believe in female portraiture; costumes are less likely to be those of current fashion, more fanciful or theatrical. Whereas men carry with them their own moral purpose, their own innate capacity for greatness, women, to whom, it was felt, few or no such qualities naturally attach themselves, need to be cast in the role of a moral archetype which develops and generalises the feminine virtues they are held to embody. But the sentimental identification of feminine virtues with women is exactly parallel to the (ultimately equally sentimental) assumption of manly virtues in men. The difference is that men are not required to impersonate an abstraction: their value is self-evident. This distinction does not necessarily denigrate women, though it reflects their position in a society which expected them to represent private rather than public virtues.[40]

Here Wilton is struggling with precisely the problem I have identified, and he works hard to avoid the implication that either his account or eighteenth-century representational practices is simply sexist. One implication of his approach is that women, relative to men, are semantically empty; they require additional props to make them meaningful. Woman is, precisely, a vessel. Another implication concerns the value given to women. Wilton sees this as fragile, hence the requirement that they 'impersonate an abstraction', a phrase which carries slight connotations of deceit. And his later point suggests that there may indeed be denigration involved. Marina Warner too was concerned with how women are valued through personification, but she assumed that it is generally, if only potentially, an occasion for affirmation. I fear that the question of value may be a red herring, and suspect that our interest in it stems from the tendency to look for one dominant mode or emotion in representations of women, to identify any particular representation as being either pro or anti women in general. This is to simplify the emotions involved, and to treat representations of women as indices of something else: 'value', 'status', 'esteem'. Some representations are themselves overtly simplifying and polarising as I have shown, but many are not. The more complex the abstractions they stand for, the less readily a stable moral stance may be deduced. Perhaps the question of value intrigues because it offers a way of connecting up representations with other areas of experience, especially with areas, such as politics, civil rights, employment, and the law, where the status of women is an explicit issue. Quite understandably, feminist historians by virtue of their own experiences have been preoccupied with women's status. My point is that we cannot infer status from representations, and that to attempt to do so is to ignore the fact that they are quite different types of category between which no direct translations are possible. They are related, but in highly complex ways, best explored in the language of 'mediation'.

Wilton's reference to make-believe is revealing, for what we are indeed talking about is fantasy. Over long periods of time, Woman has been a concept that gave permission for certain kinds of fantasy to take place. It is possible to construe this as a sort of semantic emptiness, or as resulting from relegation

40. Wilton, 1992, pp. 38–9.

to a private, domestic, sexualised zone, but it can also be understood as a special kind of potentiality and receptiveness. In saying this I too run the risk of essentialism or ahistoricity. However, I am advocating a particular approach to cultural history that gives historical specificity its due while being open to broad patterns and persistent themes. There are two stances such an approach requires and to which I am drawing attention in these remarks. The first is an openness to a wide range of materials and to the concepts that seem appropriate to their explication. Hence I have used, without explicitly theorising, notions such as 'rage', 'identification' and so on.[41] I want to see what kind of business can be done using them, drawing on the ideas readers will already have of their rich meanings. The second is an interest in creating cultural maps that help us see where particular themes come up, both vertically and horizontally: vertically over substantial periods of time, horizontally across diverse zones at a specific moment. And in mapping cultural motifs, we begin to discern shapes and patterns and to offer tentative explanations for them. In taking up both these stances, I find myself aware of how tentative *any* historical account must be, wishing nonetheless to try and offer suggestions, keen that a wide range of historical material should be drawn attention to, and conscious that any account of my materials that does not speak to their powerful emotions would be woefully inadequate. Furthermore, I know that the cultural life of feminine figures has lost none of its relevance, that their recalcitrance to full explanations stems from two facts: they are still constantly being used, often for utterly manipulative purposes, and we, women and men alike, are still seduced by their power and intrigued by their complexities.

41. These terms as I use them here are incipiently rather than explicitly psychoanalytic: cf. Laplanche and Pontalis, 1988 and Gay, 1985.

CHAPTER THREE

Nature's Powers: A Reading of the Distinction between Creation and Production

Every world view involves an emotional, as well as an intellectual apprehension of nature.

John C. Greene[1]

The distinction between creation and production lies at the centre of many world-views, and above all of Christianity. In the Nicene Creed, which declares, 'I believe in one God, the Father, Maker of heaven and earth . . . And in the Lord Jesus Christ . . . Begotten not made . . .', there is evidently considerable slippage in the way the verb 'to make' is used, as it expresses both divine and non-divine actions.[2] For centuries Western intellectual traditions have meditated upon both the differences and similarities between the kinds of making undertaken by people, nature and God(s), respectively. Natural philosophical traditions were no exception. The eighteenth century has been seen as a decisive turning point in the novel, direct and sustained use of a language of creation in relation to human performance that it witnessed.[3] The century was also marked by fundamental new interpretations of the notion of production. In setting the naturalist Jean-Baptiste de Lamarck in the context of such questions, I intend to achieve two goals. The first is to offer a reading of certain key aspects of his natural philosophy in the light of contemporary texts of a rather different kind: natural theological writings on the one hand and Mary Shelley's novel *Frankenstein* (1818) on the other. The second is to reveal the ways in which the elements of world-views articulate with one another and the forms that 'an

1. Greene, 1981, p. 18.
2. On the Nicene and other creeds, see Burn, 1910. A related example is the second verse of the hymn 'O come, all ye faithful', which reads, 'God of God, / Light of Light, / Lo! He abhors not the Virgin's womb; / Very God, / Begotten, not created . . .' (in *The New English Hymnal*, 1986, p. 65). This hymn, originally in Latin, dates from the eighteenth century. It echoes the Nicene Creed, which in modern versions refers to 'very God of very God, begotten, not made'. This form of words raises just the issues addressed in this chapter. The complexity of the verb 'to beget' is also relevant, as it embraces both creating and producing, as the *Oxford English Dictionary* makes clear. For an unusual slant on the status of Christ as 'begotten, not created', see Steinberg, 1983. Ginsburg and Rapp, 1995, contains discussions of the complexities of reproduction.
3. Kristeller, 1983, p. 106.

emotional . . . apprehension of nature' takes on. Both goals entail showing the stakes invested in the distinction between creation and production and the historically specific resonances it generated.

Lamarck employed a distinction, which is the subject of this chapter, between the creativity of God and the productivity of nature.[4] The pair of terms, creation/production, took on a special significance in the late eighteenth and early nineteenth centuries. They evoked authority, order and hierarchy; they spoke about origins, sequences and the historical underpinning of rulership; they described actions and processes as apparently diverse as work, reproduction, authorship and divine intervention. They served at once to link and to discriminate between human, natural and divine operations. The significance of these terms can be better understood if we place Lamarck, a 'forerunner of Darwin', in a wider cultural setting.

Reading Lamarck's ideas about life and its history in the context of contemporary natural theology sharpens our sense of what he was trying to do. His natural philosophy and natural theology seem almost deliberate inversions of each other. An examination of *Frankenstein* also facilitates our understanding of Lamarck's project. The literary licence Shelley took, by contrast, for example, with Lamarck or Paley, is important because it enabled her to open up and make explicit issues that surely troubled them but were far harder for them to write about. Yet she offered no settled answers to the problems she raised. Her novel neatly reveals the facets of the creation/production distinction present in European culture. It does so, furthermore, in a highly condensed, potent form. Her work shows that the distinction was important, not just at an intellectual level, but because it touched the nature of personal identity and cosmic meaning.

Thus this chapter is not about influences, but about distinct contemporaneous styles of thinking, their wider implications and their associations with transformism, as Lamarck's evolutionary ideas are most accurately termed. It is of the utmost importance that we comprehend what Lamarck was arguing against, namely, natural theological traditions. Contrary to common opinion, these were well-established in eighteenth-century France. Abbé Pluche's *Le spectacle de la nature* (1732–50) was, we know, widely read. The naturalist Réaumur, whose work Lamarck knew, employed the argument from design, as did Bernardin de Saint-Pierre, briefly a colleague of Lamarck's and a best-selling author.[5] Above all, the notorious hostility between Cuvier – also a naturalist, and one who enjoyed considerable intellectual and political prestige – and Lamarck included profound disagreements about religious matters. Although careful not to proclaim himself a natural theologian, Cuvier's ideas were widely understood by his contemporaries to have precisely this cast. Indeed it has

---

4. On Lamarck in general see Burkhardt, 1977; Burlingame, 1973b; and *idem*, 1973a, vol. VII, pp. 584–94. The most important recent work on Lamarck is Pietro Corsi, 1988. For a brief introduction to Lamarck's ideas, see Jordanova, 1984a. Lamarck's principal exposition of the distinction between creation and production may be found in Lamarck, 1820.

5. Limoges, 1975, vol. XI, pp. 42–4; Appel, 1987, pp. 13 and 56; Bernardin de Saint-Pierre, 1966; *idem*, 1982, esp. p. 11. Bernardin de Saint-Pierre is discussed in Chapter 10.

recently been claimed that 'Cuvier's functionalism ... gave support to the traditional argument from design'. Cuvier's protests against reducing 'Nature to a sort of slavery into which ... her Author is far from having enchained her', on the grounds that 'the world itself would become an indecipherable enigma', articulate the central tenets of a natural theological world-view in direct opposition to Lamarck and his sympathisers.[6] We can, therefore, confidently assert the historical appropriateness of juxtaposing Lamarck and natural theological writers.

There are additional reasons for setting Lamarck in the context of Paley, who was, after all, totally explicit about his metaphysical commitments. Throughout his *Natural Theology*, which appeared in England in 1802 and in a French version published in Switzerland in 1804, Paley consistently argued against the power of habit – a lynchpin of Lamarck's transformism. Inadvertently, then, Paley took issue with Lamarck, just as Lamarck, deliberately, criticized natural theology when he redefined God and nature. Furthermore, we can usefully compare Lamarck with Chateaubriand, whose *Génie du Christianisme*, also published in 1802, created a sensation in France, and who discussed the proof of the existence of God from the wonders of nature.[7] There is no evidence that Lamarck read either Paley or Chateaubriand, although he could hardly have been unaware of the latter's existence and ideas. He rarely cited other authors, few of his papers are extant, and only the meagre evidence of which books he owned at his death remains.[8] We know little of Lamarck's personal beliefs, but it is fair to assume that he was not a devout Catholic. It is not necessary to demonstrate direct links between these authors for the following arguments to work. I will be considering the intellectual possibilities available in a given culture, not seeking to establish lineages of ideas.

Lamarck's science always had a strongly reflexive dimension to it, beginning with his early botanical work and continuing into his last publications. This aspect of his thought has received surprisingly little attention. His reputation among historians is built on his botany, his theories of organic change, and his researches on invertebrates; other aspects of his natural philosophy have been neglected.[9] The meteorology, geology and 'psychology' remain little studied, as does Lamarck's last book, the *Système analytique des connaissances positives de l'homme* (1820). This was not a new work in any significant sense. It contains long quotations from earlier publications, especially *Philosophie zoologique* (1809) and the introduction to *Histoire naturelle des animaux sans vertèbres* (1815–22). In the *Système* he defined terms such as *Espèce, Faculté, Habitude, Homme, Idée, Intelligence, Jugement* and *Nature*.[10]

Lamarck expended considerable effort on elucidating key words. The results are revealing because they allow us to reconstruct the larger system of his

6. Quoted in Appel, 1987, p. 151; see also pp. 158, 173, 191, 213.
7. Chateaubriand, 1966, vol. I, pp. 149–93. Chateaubriand is also discussed in Chapter 5.
8. *Catalogue des Livres de la Bibliothèque de Feu M. Le Chevalier J.-B. de Lamarck*, 1830.
9. See the works cited in note 4. Cf. Jordanova, 1976.
10. Full details of these and Lamarck's other writings may be found in the bibliographies of the following works: Landrieu, 1909, pp. 448–70; Packard, 1901, pp. 425–45; and Burkhardt, 1977, pp. 261–8.

natural philosophy. While his definitions may appear rather simplistic in retro-
spect, they fulfilled a significant function in clearing the ground, so to speak,
in order that transformism could be planted in the right soil. Being sympathetic
to the *idéologues*, Lamarck was aware that sciences were well-made languages,
and he endeavoured to put this precept into practice.

Lamarck's ideas are generally structured by contrasting pairs of concepts,
giving his thought a strongly dichotomous character. The universe was divided
into matter and nature; and matter into living and inert; living things were of
two kinds – animals and plants. The organisation of the *Système analytique* to
some extent reproduces such a structure. It centres on man and is divided into
two principal parts devoted to phenomena inside and outside man respectively.
The latter were then divided into phenomena created and produced. There
were two sets of created phenomena, matter and nature, and likewise two
categories under production, consisting of inorganic and organic objects, and
so on. Lamarck employed other important dichotomies, such as his distinctions
between properties and faculties (the former are found in inert, the latter only
in organic bodies), active and passive (only nature is active, matter remains
passive), invention and imagination (the first is a useful skill for finding new
relations between objects, in contrast to the second, which results merely in the
formation of images), and fiction and reality (ideas not rigorously grounded in
observation as opposed to ideas rooted in nature).

Because Lamarck attempted to produce a consistent natural philosophy, it
was necessary for him to deal with God, nature and man. In order to show
what kind of a natural philosophy this was, and what its implications are for
our understanding of his transformism, a theory of natural production, I shall
examine Lamarck's definition of 'nature', first published in a natural history
dictionary in 1818 and reprinted in the *Système analytique* in 1820. Lamarck
began by establishing that nature was an 'order of things', a 'constantly active
power' of which man was a part and which should therefore be of primary
importance to him.[11] Like matter, nature was a created object, which it was
possible to know through observation. But Lamarck stressed the activity of
nature, by which he meant that natural laws regulated all phenomena. Nature
was, however, limited and – as he often put it – blind.

Other writers, according to Lamarck, used the word nature too literally and
vaguely – hence his attempts to clarify it. He had to purge the concept of
unwelcome associations. It was not, he emphasised, an intelligence or an individual being – terms which personified nature in unacceptable ways – but
something that acts out of necessity. Nature was 'a blind power, lacking intention or goal'.[12] It followed, for Lamarck, that God did not create natural objects
directly, but through the initial creation of nature and matter. Nature, a system
of dynamic laws, then produced all observable objects by acting upon passive
matter.

11. Lamarck, 1820, p. 20.
12. Ibid., p. 22.

In theory God could have created everything directly – that is his prerogative – but evidence in nature indicated that direct creations have not occurred. The evidence that Lamarck had in mind was indications of change over time. While physical objects appeared permanent, signs of change were present if one knew how to look for them. If natural objects were as old as nature itself, then it might be reasonable to assume them to have been created directly by God; whereas if they are of different ages and subject to continual change, they must be understood as products of nature. Furthermore, if natural bodies were created directly, Lamarck pointed out, nature itself would have no real existence or significance. In fact, science must concern itself with 'the power of nature'. To argue this point, Lamarck chose the example of the 'specious idea . . . concerning the original creation and immutability of species'.[13] People espouse it because they cannot directly perceive organic change, given the short life span of human beings. But close study of the 'monuments' on the earth's surface helps to dispel such a view. From these we learn of the continual activity of nature, evoked for the reader by geological and geographical examples.

For Lamarck, this ceaseless change was far from random. It could be resolved into two components: the destruction of bodies and their re-elaboration. This topic lay at the heart of his matter theory and had been explored at length in his earlier works, *Recherches sur les causes des principaux faits physiques* (1794) and *Mémoires de physique et d'histoire naturelle* (1797). Such change was invoked in the service of Lamarck's assertion that there was a 'general power' – nature itself – constantly acting.[14] But while Lamarck stressed the perpetual destruction and renewal of nature, he was equally concerned to show that this 'great power' was limited and lawlike. He argued that characterising nature in these terms is important, both for its own sake and so that we can determine how to study it. Lamarck was quick to point out that his own work had benefited from such a broad understanding of nature. It had, for example, enabled him to discover and use a 'general plan' of nature to establish a natural order among invertebrates.

Lamarck's next move was to clarify the relationships between nature and matter. Nature can neither create nor destroy matter, only modify it continually. Again, the possibility that nature might be construed as a reasoning being was set aside by considering the factor of time. Nature, Lamarck said, does nothing except through time, which is unlimited and universal. These characteristics are in explicit contrast to acts of creation, which are without duration. He was particularly concerned about the dangers of projecting human fantasies on to nature:

It is to this blind power [i.e. nature], everywhere limited and subordinated, which, however great it may be, can do nothing but what it actually does; which exists, in short, only by the will of the supreme author of everything; it is to this power, I say, that we attribute intention, design, resolution in its acts.[15]

13. Ibid., p. 27.
14. Ibid., p. 32.
15. Ibid., p. 35.

Such attributions were, for Lamarck, illegitimate.

So far we might summarise Lamarck's philosophy by saying that he argued against a natural theological perspective by carefully separating God from nature, creation from production. While natural theologians accepted these distinctions, they, unlike Lamarck, reconnected the dichotomies because they saw in nature the signs of God's creative power. Furthermore, Lamarck rigorously denied that nature can be seen in personal terms, although it was possible for him on occasion to refer to nature as 'this communal mother'. This was, I believe, a mere figure of speech, but it could well have been a rhetorical device knowingly used, a 'slip', or even a sign of the recalcitrance of language in being inevitably anthropomorphic.[16] Lamarck's argument for the existence of limited 'orders of things' could be applied to specific natural phenomena such as 'life'. Like nature, life was not purposive or an intelligent being, just a set of laws giving rise to organic phenomena. Yet expounding his views on life was not Lamarck's purpose in defining 'nature': it was to differentiate nature from God on the one hand and from the physical universe on the other. Those who confuse God and nature confuse the clockmaker with the clock, he asserted. To move from clock to clockmaker involved a deliberate and dramatic shift of conceptual level from natural effect to supernatural cause or agent. Lamarck objected to such moves. Natural theologians agreed that clock and clockmaker were distinct, but they wished to link them by treating nature as the signature of God. Thus when Lamarck separated clock and clockmaker, it was to banish the latter from the domain of science; when natural theologians did so, it was to distinguish between cause and effect, which, although separable, are also by definition linked. Therefore, Lamarck rejected any suggestion that natural knowledge should concern itself with the clockmaker. The very character of nature suggested to him that its workings were not the direct expression of divine will. Natural theologians agreed that maker and made were two different orders of being, but for them one was meaningless without the other. According to Lamarck, the difference in levels was crucial because one was accessible to human knowledge, whereas the other was not.[17] Lamarck thus implicitly rejected the idea that makers necessarily inscribe their marks on the end-product – the central tenet of natural theology.

Lamarck's distinction between nature and God was largely epistemological. But it signalled a larger style of thought. For him the different levels of creation and production were so profoundly distinguished – the one pure will acting out of time, the other visibly labouring – that to confuse them was to make a major category mistake. Nature does not contain evidence of another order of being; it merely reveals its own laws. For Lamarck this undercut the ideas of God as author and of nature as a book. His use of phrases like 'supreme author' was, I would suggest, mere convention.

16. Ibid., p. 36. On the recalcitrance of language, see Beer, 1983 and 1986.
17. Lamarck was particularly attentive to distinctions between conceptual levels. See Jordanova, 1981a, which discusses his 'psychology'.

Like other natural philosophers, Lamarck had to account for the origin and nature of activity. Matter was purely passive, all activity comes from nature. Yet in truth he did not account for the origin of activity beyond invoking a divine creative act in the beginning that made nature this way. For Lamarck, activity in nature derived from motion on the one hand, and laws governing motion on the other. Nature acts through space and time – significantly, Lamarck calls these the 'metaphysical entities which together constitute nature' – and they could be understood by the human mind in a way that God could not be.[18]

Lamarck then shifted key to take up one of his favourite themes, the *moral* importance of the study of nature, including man. He did not use the term 'moral' here; instead he claimed that knowledge of nature would help man know about his physical being, his preservation, his behaviour, and his relations with his fellow men.[19] Whereas Lamarck kept God and nature neatly distinct, man and nature are completely intertwined. Man is part of nature because he is subject to its laws, yet he is the only part of nature capable of understanding it. He ought to study nature for his own well-being, yet he perpetually misunderstands and projects his feelings onto nature. Lamarck used the example of monstrosities to illustrate this last point:

Certain irregularities in nature's acts, certain monstrosities which appear contrary to the ordinary workings of nature, reversals in the ordering of physical objects . . . are nonetheless the proper product of nature's laws and of the prevailing circumstances. . . . The word *chance* expresses only our ignorance of causes.[20]

Lamarck's repudiation of natural disorder does not, of course, mean that he saw everything as being under the governing hand of God. On the contrary it expresses his commitment to coherent explanation based on universal natural laws. Chance has no place in such laws. We attribute disorder to nature when something annoys or distresses us. What followed in Lamarck's discussion of 'nature' was an elaborate justification of the study of nature by that creature whose place within it, and, as natural historian and philosopher, outside it, is so complex. The programme set out here and in many other places in his writings linked natural history with natural philosophy. The empirical study of nature – Lamarck did much detailed natural historical work during his life – only made sense within a larger philosophical framework. This broad programme engaged with a wide range of issues and was a blend of epistemological, metaphysical and moral considerations. He found social questions in general and ethical ones in particular to be integral to his science.

Lamarck's 'psychology' was central to his philosophy of nature. It is best understood in terms of contemporary interest in the science of man. Indeed,

18. Lamarck, 1820, pp. 52–3.
19. Ibid., p. 55.
20. Ibid., p. 59, his emphasis.

he shared many of the central interests of that field, especially as articulated by his contemporaries, the *idéologues*, who placed themselves in the traditions of Locke and Condillac by insisting that all knowledge derives from the senses.[21] Lamarck's commitment to this position is clearly vital, as it spurred him to think through a naturalistic account of the nervous system and to reject any mental faculties, such as will and imagination, not strictly compatible with such an account. He downgraded those human activities that come under what he called 'the field of fictions'. By contrast, knowledge of nature acquired the status of the paradigm of all knowledge, and it was uniquely valuable to human beings. Lamarck took a dim view of those who strayed beyond 'the field of reality', declaring: 'it is forbidden for man to leave it'. He moved effortlessly from what it was possible for human beings to know, given their organisation and that of nature, to how they ought to conduct themselves generally. In so doing, his natural philosophy spoke to a wide range of social, moral and ethical questions. It has to be said that Lamarck was no moral philosopher; he displayed a simplistic view of what the study and knowledge of nature promised: 'man', he said, 'would conform more easily to natural laws, and escape from evil of all kinds'.[22]

Through his dialogue with other perspectives on God, man and nature, Lamarck attempted to elaborate a world-view in which his transformism played an integral part. Organic change was a paradigm case of nature's labours, of the successive production of bodies, to be explained naturalistically in terms of adaptation, habit, and so on. In this sense Lamarck gave nature a history even if his understanding of history lacked elements such as contingency. Lamarck both consciously constructed an alternative to a number of positions that he saw as determined by prior theological commitments, and offered an entire philosophical package, a blueprint for society as well as for science – in other words, a cosmology.[23]

In Lamarck's account, the history of nature has no real beginning. The history of life has, even if no date can be assigned to the appearance of the first organised being. He consistently emphasised the antiquity of the earth, but he had no means of conceptualising the initial act that brought the universe into being. We might say that this was because he was content to let the traditional biblical account stand, possibly to avoid giving unnecessary offence, or we might suggest that conceptualising a unique event within a naturalistic perspective designed to explain routine occurrences is extraordinarily difficult in itself. Either way, Lamarck did not offer a new view of the very beginning of existence. On the other hand, he did suggest that new beginnings were constantly occurring. His commitment to spontaneous generation – the ceaseless re-enactment of the history of life – to organic change and to the

21. Jordanova, 1981a, pp. 72–6; *idem*, 1976, pp. 20–3 and ch. 3. On the idéologues, see van Duzer, 1935; Moravia, 1974; Picavet, 1971; Boas, 1964, ch. 2; Gusdorf, 1978.

22. Lamarck, 1820, p. 79.

23. Desmond, 1987, examines one way in which Lamarck's ideas were deployed in the service of a politically inspired world-view. See also Desmond, 1989.

perpetual decay and reconstruction of physical bodies rendered the notion of a first, unique beginning less significant than it was in the Judeo-Christian tradition.

The little beginnings characteristic of Lamarck's natural philosophy had no special meaning for the human condition; they simply arose from the normal operations of nature's laws. Ultimately, Lamarck was able to derive a moral code from his philosophy of nature, but spontaneous generation contained no mythic implications in the way that, for example, the story of the garden of Eden does. He did not offer a strictly comparable account, although his writings could be seen as a loose alternative to traditional creation myths. But they offered a different kind of explanation, by emphasising workaday natural processes rather than cosmic meanings.

As part of his cosmology, Lamarck attempted to account comprehensively for a wide range of human phenomena, including suffering. I have already noted his fierce exclusion of chance and error from nature. From this it followed that, because man is a part of nature, things that go amiss for him cannot be explained in such terms. Nor, of course, can they be explained by some outside agency such as a devil; they have to be understood naturalistically. It must be admitted that Lamarck's attempts to produce a naturalistic account of social inequality, for example, were crude and simplistic. Yet this may be less important than the fact that he attempted to deal with such issues within his natural philosophical framework.

An interesting example is Lamarck's explanation of suicide, which he claimed must result from a disturbance of the nervous system. Yet because aversion to death was, for him, a basic propensity (following well-established traditions in political philosophy in which the preservation of life was an important instinct), he was reduced to saying that 'suicide is the result of an unhealthy state in which the ordinary laws of nature are inverted'.[24] In Lamarck's own terms this was hardly a satisfactory response, because he presented natural laws as fixed, universal and incapable of inversion.

Lamarck's attempts to account for inequality naturalistically were probably influenced by Jean-Jacques Rousseau. Like Rousseau, Lamarck criticised the social state for its inequality and artificiality, and for the tendencies of groups to exploit each other. Rousseau's *Discours sur l'origine de l'inégalité* (1754) not only offered a model of how gradual change can be explained naturalistically, but articulated powerful images of nature and society and the antagonism between them.[25] Lamarck and Rousseau also shared an interest in how man came to be as he is, and both were deeply ambivalent about the human race. Indeed,

24. Lamarck, 1820, p. 226.
25. For Lamarck's direct citations of Rousseau see Lamarck, 1820, p. 94 and Lamarck, 1815–22, vol. I, p. 330. See also Cantor, 1984, p. xvi; and Rousseau, 1973, pp. 27–113. On Rousseau's explanatory strategies in the Discourse, see Plattner, 1979. Plattner stresses Rousseau's indebtedness to contemporary science. To be sure, the Discourse considered only human development in naturalistic terms, but Plattner's book, especially ch. 3, shows how marked the similarities between Rousseau and Lamarck were. Another treatment of Rousseau in the context of contemporary science is Duchet, 1971, pp. 322–76. To a certain extent the whole of the *Système analytique* (Lamarck, 1820) is a study of man; part 2 is of particular relevance, however, to the Rousseau–Lamarck comparison.

Lamarck's transformism is notable for the ambivalent status it gave to man. In the order of production, man is very much a newcomer. Yet, at the same time, he occupies a special position as the only part of nature capable of understanding it. This privilege came 'naturally'; it is merely a by-product of organic superiority. However, man is also uniquely destructive. Only he causes the extinction of other species. Man represents the summit of nature's powers and the only element of disruption. Lamarck thought of the negative side of human beings as the product of society rather than of nature. And because nature is still in the process of unfolding, the human race cannot be the ultimate goal towards which nature/God works. Man's ascendancy would prove temporary if more complex beings emerged.

Although formally God takes priority in Lamarck's philosophy, He is absent from the history of nature and of life. Insofar as there is conflict in the world, it is within nature – among men and between human beings and the rest of nature. This conflict can be used pragmatically to help achieve a better understanding of where the human race went wrong, it has no cosmic meaning. Lamarck's refusal to give unquestioned centrality to human beings was consistent with his resistance to any suggestion that nature is a book to be decoded in the service of revealing its author. Nature embodies no personality – it remains blind, limited, law-like and labouring. There is no book of nature and hence neither authors nor readers – all ideas central to natural theology.

Many of the central arguments found in natural theological writings go back to the ancient world, yet it was not until the second half of the seventeenth century that the genre became well-established. At a popular level it persisted throughout the nineteenth century, with the Bridgewater Treatises, published in the 1830s, boasting among their authors some of the most distinguished names of the period. Paley's *Natural Theology* represents a cogent summary of the central tenets of a natural theological approach that flowered in the eighteenth century.[26] By the time of its publication in 1802, there were not only a number of well-established and distinct traditions of natural theology, but also a body of opinion strongly critical of it. A full history of natural theology in the eighteenth century remains to be written, and, until it is, placing Paley in a wide intellectual context remains difficult. However, his extensive influence together with the systematic way he approached his subject qualifies him as an exemplar of one style of thinking about God as the author of nature. Another style is represented by Lamarck's compatriot, Chateaubriand, and it is also appropriate to draw from his work in order to reveal the range of themes implicit in natural theology.

Natural theology took as its central image God the designer or contriver, and it was to this that Lamarck created an alternative. Natural theological language implied an analogy between God's creative acts and man's productive ones, or, strictly speaking, between the relationship God has with nature and

---

26. Paley, 1836–38; Gillespie, 1959; Russell, 1973; Goodman, 1973; Brooke, 1974, 1985 and 1991; Raven, 1953; Jordanova and Porter, 1979/1997, esp. chs 1–3; Yeo, 1979; Clarke, 1974; LeMahieu, 1976; 'William Paley', *Dictionary of National Biography*, vol. XV, pp. 101–7; Hume, 1948; Jordanova, 1992; Topham, 1992.

the ones human beings have with artefacts. Although it had powerful rhetorical potential, the analogy was by no means unproblematic, as can be seen, for example, in the Leibniz–Clarke controversy, where Leibniz objected to an argument that 'supposes God to perceive things . . . by a kind of perception, such as that by which men fancy our soul perceives what passes in the body'. At the end of the century, however, Thomas Reid revived the direct analogy between man and God, which had been subject to sustained attack, when he likened human intentional movements to the will of God.[27] In many other natural theological writings the analogy was used with little self-consciousness. By inviting their readers to imagine God as artisan and master craftsman, natural theologians blurred the very boundaries between creation and production that Lamarck was so concerned to strengthen. At the same time, they conveyed a sense of the profound gap between God and human beings. There were a number of different ways in which natural theologians achieved this double effect of similarity and difference, often generating considerable conceptual tensions in the process.

René de Chateaubriand, a romantic, reactionary, aristocratic writer and diplomat, who was deeply committed to Catholicism, came to natural theology with a set of assumptions quite distinct from those of the middle-class, Protestant, rationalist divine and moral philosopher William Paley. Chateaubriand relied heavily on visual reactions to nature as the trigger of sublime thoughts of an emotional and spiritual kind. The wonders of nature draw human beings, nature and God together in a transcendent movement. Nature is dense with visual indicators of the divine presence. It is also conceptualised as a language: 'Among men, tombs are the pages of their history; nature, by contrast, only prints on living things; she/it needs neither granite nor marble to make eternal that which she/it writes.'[28] Behind the inscribing hand of nature lay the ultimate author, God. Here Chateaubriand could unite God, man and nature by showing how they all write, yet he could also show that they do so in different ways. God, like man, makes things, but unlike man, His productions are not limited.

Chateaubriand used natural signs to link human life to its providential Creator by showing, for example, how the seasons have their markers that were recognised by people long before formal calendars existed. He characterised such knowledge as a form of divination. Chateaubriand's natural world is the occasion for human sensual pleasure, a temple for spiritual contemplation and a source of knowledge of basic rhythms and processes. It carries meaning in a number of different ways; it signifies at many different levels. Chateaubriand also used the familiar arguments about adaptation, design and purpose, yet he deployed none of the artisanal or technological vocabulary that was so central to Paley's writings. Hence his description of fish as 'real hydrostatic machine[s]' stands out as exceptional.[29]

27. Brooke, 1974, pp. 26, 48.
28. Chateaubriand, 1966, vol. I, p. 164. I have put she/it because it is hard to assess the degree to which French writers intended the personification implied by 'she'.
29. Ibid., p. 157.

In sum, Chateaubriand presented the similarities and differences between the human and the divine by using the powerful visual impact of nature to draw the mind from that which is clearly and intentionally made to the being capable of such creation. That for him God's role was associated with sensual and spiritual delight is revealed in his choice of the word *ordonnateur*, which includes, among other more sombre meanings, organiser of festivities and master of ceremonies. Yet Chateaubriand's was no domesticated God – He is in places of wild beauty and of solitude, a God of the desert not of the workshop. The contrast between Chateaubriand and Lamarck could not be more marked. Lamarck characterised nature as 'limited' because produced, as always subject to definable laws, whereas Chateaubriand refused any such constraint on the freedom of God's creativity, which he *saw* everywhere. In an apt image, Lamarck, whose descriptions lack visual richness, presented nature as blind. The blindness of nature suggests that it is self-contained; unable, as it were, to look outside itself. Nature is also without intention and and hence incapable of generating the providential signs that Chateaubriand discovered in abundance.

While Paley too conveyed wonder and pleasure in his arguments, his images differ from Chateaubriand's. He also stands in a somewhat different relationship to Lamarck, in that many of his arguments constitute a direct repudiation of the central tenets of transformism. I am not suggesting that this was intentional, although it is possible that he knew, and sought to refute, Erasmus Darwin's theories.[30] Paley, being steeped in eighteenth-century natural history traditions and in turn-of-the century English reactions to events in France, knew exactly where the threats to his belief system lay. Where Chateaubriand appealed to the reader's emotional response, inviting them to think not logically but in terms of emotionally-charged visual correspondences, Paley took a more rationalistic route.

Paley likened God's relationship to nature to that of human beings to their products, by presenting Him as a designer, contriver, carpenter, gardener, and so on. At the same time, he reinforced the differences between God and man by depicting 'art', in the eighteenth-century sense, as inferior to nature with respect to the skill it displays. Man and God are both makers, a point Paley stressed in order to show that the maker is always unlike that which he makes. In both cases, the signs of craftsmanship have a material existence and hence act as signifiers of the author. Yet any similarity between God and man ends when the level of skill is considered. The degree of fit between a humanly produced mechanism/machine and the purpose it is intended to fulfil hardly compares with God's – a discrepancy exemplified for Paley by the difficulty a workman would have designing a device to do all the things a spine can:

The chain of a watch, (I mean the chain which passes between the spring-barrel and fusee,) which aims at the same properties, is but a bungling piece of workmanship in comparison with that of which we speak [i.e. the structure of the spine].[31]

30. This is suggested by Clarke, 1974, pp. 96–7.
31. Paley, 1836–38, vol. I, p. 52. On earlier meanings of 'art', see Williams, 1983, pp. 40–3.

Or again:

In no apparatus put together by art, and for the purposes of art, do I know such multifarious uses so aptly combined, as in the natural organisation of the human mouth; or where the structure, compared with the uses is so simple. . . . The mouth . . . is one machine.[32]

This last sentence makes clear why Paley insisted on using man-made objects in his argument. We, as readers, can imagine the purposiveness of producing objects in which every detail serves some rational end. At the same time, we experience ourselves as separate from the tools we use, the process of manufacturing and the end-product. Paley's repeated stress on the mechanical character of organs reinforces the side of his argument that lures the reader into identifying human and divine capacities, while his stress on the fine, supremely beautiful fit between form and function affirms a sense of human inadequacy in the face of God's superior skill.[33] Both God and man, therefore, can be agents, causes, designers, authors and contrivers. Yet God alone has a single, total, overarching plan – a fact that Paley thought explained similarities between living things – and possesses the aesthetic capacities to generate true beauty.

Although Paley recognised that plants and animals were quite distinct, his emphasis on the gap between maker and made put them on a par with inanimate objects – both are 'passive, unconscious substances'.[34] Now the profound differences between Paley and Lamarck can be appreciated. For the former, a creative designer acts upon matter in a manner modelled on intention and will. By contrast, Lamarck moved the action away from a transcendental level and into nature, and more particularly into organic nature. Paley, it is clear, was perfectly aware of such arguments, for he explicitly countered them by ridiculing the idea that the parts themselves could contribute to their own form – a proposition that was absurd to him because he saw the plan and materials used to execute it as separate categories. Once activity was allowed to be present in natural things themselves, the uniqueness of God was subtly undermined. Paley's language of machines made the possibility that habit and the environment contributed to organic form, as Lamarck argued, seem preposterous.

Lamarck's task was to generate a fresh language appropriate to a naturalistic account of the historical changes organic forms had undergone. There were no suitable pre-existing models in natural philosophical discourse for him to draw upon, and there was certainly none that had the empirical richness or sensual immediacy of Paley's writings. Like Chateaubriand, Paley appeals to the eye. But he does so not in a spirit of pleasure, but of rational instruction:

32. Ibid., p. 67.
33. This argument was not only used by natural theologians; others also appreciated its general aesthetic importance. For example, see Hogarth, 1955. On the interpretation of Hogarth in the context of contemporary natural theology, see Jordanova, 1986a, pp. 48–51.
34. Paley, 1836–38, vol. I, p. 26.

A plain observer of the animal oeconomy may spare himself the disgust of being present at human dissections, and yet learn enough for his information and satisfaction, by even examining the bones of the animals which come upon his table.[35]

He put the same point more succinctly when he said, 'in every part of anatomy, description is a poor substitute for inspection'.[36] Like watches, plants and animals, pipes, automata, engines, flood gates, pumps and pistons were easy to visualise. But when Lamarck tried to describe the actions of the nervous system without lapsing into mechanistic explanations he had no such fund of images to draw upon. Paley, in other words, could employ a language of machines because he treated physical mechanisms as signs of God. Lamarck rejected the language of contrivance because it could not adequately express the dynamism within nature and especially in organic beings, which he did not perceive as machine-like. In repudiating assumptions and forms of argument based on a system of decoding nature to reveal God, Lamarck cut himself off from a long-established tradition. His careful definitions of words, such as creation and production, were attempts to recast the terms of reference of natural philosophy so that a naturalistic, transformist world-view could emerge. Comparing Lamarck with the natural theologians, we can see not only that they employed different images and metaphors, but that these were both rooted in and expressions of distinct modes of inference, methods and metaphysical systems.

The natural theologies of Paley and Chateaubriand, and the natural philosophy of Lamarck, expressed broad cultural concerns. The nature of God was clearly of prime interest to Paley, whose language was blatantly anthropomorphic. Lamarck, by contrast, considered the subject not amenable to rational discourse. The difference between them cannot be described solely in terms of content — what they believed — because it was a matter of how they conceived the human mind to arrive at its ideas. It is significant that Paley must be seen as both a rationalist and an empiricist: that is, he wanted all beliefs to be arrived at through the use of reason, and, just as fervently, he wanted the direct observation of nature to form the basis for religious experience.

Both Chateaubriand and Paley used the idea of the world of nature as a temple.[37] Temples were places where, for Chateaubriand, the individual soul communes with God; for Paley, where rational contemplation of the deity occurs. Because Paley held that God's existence and character must be totally demonstrable by a blend of reason and observation, he could plausibly stress the mechanical qualities of natural objects. God is a maker whose contrivances contain no mystery. Chateaubriand, however, held that there is mystery in profusion; the wonders of nature suggest the divine creator more by virtue of emotional than rational force. Whereas Paley's natural theology was closely tied to his moral and political philosophy, Chateaubriand's was linked with his fictional writings and his political commitment to the reinstatement of legitimate authority

35. Ibid., p. 51.
36. Ibid., p. 73.
37. LeMahieu, 1976, p. 90; Chateaubriand, 1966, vol. I, p. 171.

– both religious and secular – in France. A similar point can be made with respect to Lamarck, whose denial of the relevance of God to natural philosophy and assertion of a secular, naturalistic approach to society were expressions of well-established clusters of ideas with political dimensions.

In this period the ideological implications of a naturalistic approach to organic phenomena were widely debated. Transformism was particularly controversial politically. The special intensity of discussions in natural history, natural philosophy and medicine during the 1790s is now becoming clear. The most dramatic general features of the decade are well known, and their ideological impact has been widely discussed: the French Revolution, and particularly the execution of the king, and the reign of terror; the crisis surrounding the English Poor Laws; the impact of European war; artisanal radicalism; and the consolidation of American autonomy. Broadly, the decade saw, first, successful challenges to authority, especially of a patriarchal nature, and then a reaction against these challenges, culminating, in the first decade of the nineteenth century, in what I call elsewhere the authoritarian response. Hierarchical forms of power were reasserted, social stability sought, and the interests of the propertied elites defended. Integral to this process of reassertion were the imperialism of Napoleon, the revival of Catholic values in France, especially the Concordat with the Pope and the writings of Chateaubriand, the rediscovery of political-cum-social hierarchy and traditional values, and the flowering of 'Romanticism' in Britain and France, with its celebration of an inner life and of individual creative genius. The impact of such large-scale social and cultural movements on science and medicine is charted in work on early phrenology, the Lunar Society of Birmingham and networks of radical doctors and natural philosophers, the organisation of French science and the 'birth of the clinic'. Historians of philosophy have confirmed the special quality of the period during which the political stakes invested in the world of ideas were particularly visible.[38]

Ideas of authority and power at this time were closely bound up with prevailing notions of hierarchy: we can trace shared themes in natural knowledge, natural theology, philosophy, literature and political thought precisely because how and whether ideologies were to be naturalised was such a live issue. There were several, intertwining hierarchies in the thought of the period, through which the respective powers of God, nature and the human race were conceptualised: God, King, fathers, women, children and servants; the chain of being; God, Pope, clergy and laity; mind and body; complex animals . . . simple animals; First, Second and Third estates. To evoke one of these was to evoke others. The overlap between the hierarchies derives not just from the fact that they evinced a shared preoccupation with power, order and authority, but also from their expression in a common language. There was a limited set of

38. Important work on the politics of science and medicine includes: Cooter, 1984; McNeil, 1987; Weindling, 1980; Inkster, 1981; Outram, 1984; Schofield, 1963; Foucault, 1970; *idem*, 1973; Figlio, 1976; Pickstone, 1981; Schaffer, 1990b; Cunningham and Jardine, 1990. On philosophy see Boas, 1964, ch. 1 and Copleston, 1975. Also relevant are Colley, 1992 and Bergeron, 1981.

guiding metaphors that encouraged the transfer of meanings between the series – rulership, fatherhood, authorship, sovereignty, jurisdiction, ownership and degrees of spiritual or physical perfection. But to the sense of how deeply fraught overlapping vocabularies of power were in this period, we must add another dimension if we are to appreciate fully the significance of the creation/production distinction. It was a pivot around which stories were told, stories best understood as myths of creation.

Creation myths are stories about beginnings and about how things came to be.[39] They do not just account for the origin of the universe, but also for the place of human beings within it, their relations with their Gods and with worldly forms of authority. Thus, they must provide acceptable accounts of origins and speak to predominant human preoccupations, especially the nature of suffering. By providing frameworks of meaning, they address political, social, psychological, theological and aesthetic questions in such a way that these elements are closely bound together. There are a number of reasons for viewing Lamarck's transformism in this mythological context. He wrote at a time when myths of creation were being reconceptualised as primary vehicles for thinking about the nature of creation and for interpreting human existence. Indeed, it is possible to see evolutionary theories in general as offering versions of creation myths.[40] There were already many rich texts that sought to articulate these matters, but one that appeared in the same year as Lamarck published his definition of nature is particularly striking. There can be no doubt that Mary Shelley's *Frankenstein* raises questions about the distinction between creation and production.[41] It does so most obviously by showing the limitations of human capacities when applied to ends normally attainable only through the power of God. When a person strives to be a creator, the prerogative of God, he becomes in fact a mere producer.

It has been argued that *Frankenstein* must be seen in the context of the Romantic preoccupation with creation myths, and more particularly with attempts to rewrite, subvert and invent them.[42] In the novel, the 'modern Prometheus' clearly and knowingly transgresses the boundary between creation and production. He makes, or produces, a being that should either be generated biologically through reproduction or be created by God. The point is not just that Frankenstein assumes God-like creative powers, but that in the process he undertakes the wrong sort of production. It is necessary, therefore, to differentiate between the two sorts of production at issue in *Frankenstein* – the one biological, the other artificial – and this requires two major distinctions. First, human biological (re)production results from the union of male and female. Two different elements produce a third; Frankenstein, by contrast, undertakes his production alone. Secondly, a foetus grows as a unity; it is always an integral whole, whereas Frankenstein's creation is pieced together from different

39. Cantor, 1984; Shklar, 1972; Maclagen, 1977.

40. This theme is explored in Beer, 1983.

41. Poovey, 1980; Levine and and Knoepflmacher, 1983; Shelley, 1985. *Frankenstein* appeared in French in 1821. A stimulating recent interpretation is Musselwhite, 1987, ch. 3. See also Chapter 4 of this volume.

42. Cantor, 1984, esp. ch. 4.

bodies, stitched into a spurious integrity by its maker's hand. The monster was denied the experience of physical growth.[43] To these two kinds of production – biological and artificial – we can contrast a third, the one evoked by Lamarck, for whom nature's actions are a form of labour. Production is what nature does: it is a system of laws, acting uniformly in time and space. Production, like human labour, takes time, works sequentially and is a material process.

There are a number of ways in which the novel develops the production/ labour theme. It emphasises the arduous and unclear work Frankenstein undertakes, the difficulties he has in finding the right bits and piecing them together properly, and the poor results he achieves. The monster is not beautiful but repellent because he bears the marks of his method of assembly. Everyone who sees him treats him as abhorrent. His appearance is a cruel parody of the aesthetic qualities of nature. When the monster is heard telling his own story, it becomes perfectly clear that his appearance has caused him problems. His voice indicates a sympathetic person, aware, reflective and, initially, warm. The poignancy of his story rests precisely on the radical disjunction between his inner life and his external appearance; it is on the basis of the latter that people judge him.[44] His appearance indicates that he is neither a true creature of God, nor a natural child of a woman, but a mere product of a man.

Here the novel has special relevance for science and for natural theology. The assumption that human internal qualities could be inferred from external appearances remained widespread in the life sciences and medicine of the early nineteenth century, although it was not without its critics. Indeed, the physiognomic mode of inference had been a paradigmatic form of thinking for centuries.[45] The monster suffers and ultimately becomes evil because he is a victim of the unthinking application of this approach. There are two issues here, both of them germane to my theme. First, reactions to the monster cause us to question the propriety of a pattern of inference that moves from external traits to internal ones. Second, these reactions of revulsion are based on the accurate perception that there was indeed something amiss with the monster's appearance, which carried the signs of its improper construction. Mary Shelley thus called into question some settled assumptions by demonstrating the dramatic disparity between inner life and outward appearance. The relationship between inside and outside had traditionally been used to infer the presence of God in nature and the presence of the soul or emotions in human beings. Because the mental life of human beings was strongly identified with God, there was more than a formal analogy involved. At issue was a form of thinking that sanctioned inference from (physical) visual signifiers to a (spiritual) invisible signified.

43. Beer, 1983, p. 110.

44. Shelley, 1985; there are two crucial episodes in the novel where the plot turns on the revulsion inspired by the monster. The first is at the moment of his 'birth', when Frankenstein is repelled by the creature he had intended to be beautiful (described at the beginning of ch. 5); the second is when the monster reveals himself to the De Lacey family (end of ch. 15). In the latter context, it is only the *blind* old man who offers him any compassion.

45. Jordanova, 1986a and 1993a; Bryson, 1981, ch. 2; Tytler, 1982, Shookman, 1993.

The relationship between outside and inside, nature and God, seen and unseen, becomes all the more interesting in the light of a recent interpretation of Rousseau's *Discours sur l'origine de l'inégalité* as a major source of Romantic creation myths. From a non-physiognomical perspective, Rousseau suggested that a crucial moment in the development of the human race comes when people see themselves through the eyes of others, when there is a potential tension between self-perceptions and the judgements of others looking only at the outsides of their fellows:

The savage lives within himself; the sociable man, always outside of himself, knows how to live only in the opinions of others; and it is, so to speak, from their judgment alone that he draws the sentiment of his own existence.[46]

For Rousseau, this psychological turning point is indicative of the growing artificiality of society. More elaborate social arrangements encourage the development of 'masks', which promote self-interest and greed. In explaining the nature and genesis of human society, Rousseau made extensive use of a distinction between an inner and an outer man.

Rousseau's struggles to define 'nature' were deeply influential, specifically because he offered a naturalistic account of historical changes in human existence. These changes were not, of course, historical in the sense of chronicling events known to have taken place in particular societies, but by virtue of proposing a sequence of hypothetical processes, each emerging out of the previous one. This constituted a model for the transformist view of natural history, not unlike Lamarck's. Indeed, Lamarck seized the opportunity to include human interaction within his scheme, and he did so in terms recognisably derived from Rousseau. Rousseau's discourse spoke to the creation/production distinction by focusing on the production of human society, a process to be rationally reconstructed by examining its successive stages. It offered a fresh view of the present state of human existence in relation to a distant, almost mythical past – a state of nature. By tracing changes as much for their psychological as for their social and political implications, Rousseau was able to address many of the central issues embedded in creation myths.

Thus the significance of judging the monster from his appearance can now be specified more precisely. It is his ugliness, in fact, that first impels his creator to reject him. Later, the monster comes to recognise his gruesome body as the cause of his outcast status. In both natural theology and aesthetic theory it had become customary to compare the beauty of God's work in nature with the inferiority of human achievements. Mortal makers can never equal the Creator.[47] Frankenstein's monster is ugly because he was produced by man and constructed by illegitimate means. His ugliness denotes the violation of the distinction between creation and production that led to his existence. The beauty of nature, by contrast, is not just the sign of God's superior handiwork;

---

46. Quoted in Cantor, 1984, p. 126.
47. e.g. Hogarth, 1955, pp. 85–7; Paley, 1836–38, vol. I, p. 67.

it also serves as a constant reminder of the aptness of God's intelligence in fitting form so perfectly with function. Beauty and adaptation are two sides of the same coin – creation. The discrepancy between God's work and human productions is visually registered both in terms of aesthetic quality and in terms of functional fit. Those who refuse to accept the limited role human beings have been assigned are transgressors.

Anxieties about the distinction between creation and production were hardly confined to Lamarck's natural philosophy. Mary Shelley explicitly links both terms to science and to myth. Like other Romantics, she was deeply indebted to Rousseau, who was also a significant influence on Lamarck. The naturalistic method of Rousseau and Lamarck was historical and implicitly anti-physiognomic. It opened the way for a transformist mode of thinking that did not just assert organic change as a fact, but sought to reorientate the way people looked at nature and at society. In order to do this, the pre-existing alternative – natural theology – had to be disposed of. It was a difficult task, because this way of viewing nature and society had many ramifications across a wide spectrum of issues. My purpose has been to suggest that much of Lamarck's work was dedicated to this end, hence its preoccupations with definitions and method, with epistemology and classification, and its lack of visual engagement with nature.

Lamarck was the main thinker in the first decade of the nineteenth century who attempted to generate a language through which a new science of living things, sensitive to historical change, could be developed. Among the preconditions for this science were the ability to encompass all organic phenonmena, including human thought and behaviour, in a single naturalistic framework, purging references to agents external to nature from scientific thinking, the explanation of each level of organic complexity in terms of the preceding one, and demonstrating the basis of all faculties to be in organ systems. Lamarck's project therefore had to achieve two closely related goals: eliminating God, soul and vital principles from scientific discourse, and demonstrating the sufficiency of natural processes as their own explanation. To attain these, Lamarck had to undercut a physiognomic mode of thought, which drew people to search for natural signs, and then to decode them as evidence of a quite distinct and higher level of existence. For him it was necessary to stay with the phenomena.

I want to insist on the historical specificity of Lamarck's project. At just the moment when he was developing his full transformism, Paley published his *Natural Theology*. Although both writers emerged from eighteenth-century 'rationalist' traditions, yet, with Lamarck's theories, there came a radical split between a physiognomic and an anti-physiognomic mentality: Paley saw visual indicators of a divine author; Lamarck used abstract terms to reconstruct nature's processes. Natural theology was based on the idea that nature contained the palpable signs of God's creative hand. It was, in a sense, the equivalent of history painting, where great stories could be read in the canvas.[48] In order for

48. Bryson, 1981, ch. 2; Puttfarken, 1985.

natural theology to work effectively the evidence of design had to be utterly unambiguous, so that the story of the creation could readily be appreciated. This led Paley to stress repeatedly the mechanical nature of organic structures and processes. Just as human beings build their intentions into the objects they make, so does God.

Yet there was a danger here for natural theology. Paley's consistent use of a language of artisanship drew the reader inexorably to liken God to an artisan – an artisan whose work necessarily lacks mystery, because his design is totally transparent in what he makes. This language works against his own argument for God's transcendent existence and attributes, because it so readily identified God with man. Paley sought to reintroduce the mystery of God in two ways. First he argued that God has a total guiding plan, unlike human beings who plan only individual projects. There is magnitude and magnificence in God's plan that sets it apart from human designs, giving it an additional dimension. Secondly, Paley pointed to the beauty in God's work, which far surpasses anything people can achieve. In its scope and its aesthetic qualities, creation surpasses production. While it was also possible to evoke God's mystery, as Chateaubriand did, by stressing an emotional response to the providential aspects of nature, seen less as mechanisms than as marvels, for both writers, an intense visual engagement with nature was none the less fundamental to their project of finding God in nature.

Lamarck's transformism can now be placed in a larger context. It spoke to a very wide range of issues of the time, although these often remained implicit. By redefining terms such as creation, production, life and nature, Lamarck tried to generate a language purged of unwelcome theological associations, and to distance himself from natural philosophical traditions that rejected a science of life rooted in change over time, that is, in production. He wanted to set in place a vocabulary appropriate not just to his scientific concerns, but to his social and political interests, and for this the distinction between creation and production was essential. It embodied his metaphysics, his methodology and his social philosophy. It could work in many different ways and with considerable force because the two terms touched people so deeply. Creation and production not only stood at the very heart of the Christian tradition, which makes fundamental distinctions between begetting, that is, re-production, and creating, they also expressed concerns so basic to human existence that it is hard to articulate them without banality. What acts are people capable of? What kinds of things can they make? Is making babies, books, knowledge and machines the same kind of process? Can we imagine a non-human kind of making? What responsibilities does the maker owe to the made? The questions are as endless as the cultural possibilities they evoke. Lamarck's transformism, formulated in the absence of pre-existing models for the kind of scientific discourse he wished to generate, raised just such questions, answered them in an original manner, and did so in a context that gave debates about creation and production both a wide application and a sense of urgency.

Note: Throughout this chapter, I have, for the sake of simplicity, used 'man' as it was employed by eighteenth- and nineteenth-century writers. Such a convention implies no approval of the term itself.

The translations from the French of Lamarck and Chateaubriand are my own.

CHAPTER FOUR

Melancholy Reflection: Constructing an Identity for Unveilers of Nature

When Victor Frankenstein finally left his secluded home for the University of Ingolstadt following his mother's death, his feelings were ambivalent – loss combined with desire:

I . . . indulged in the most melancholy reflection . . . I was now alone. My life had hitherto been remarkably secluded and domestic . . . I believed myself totally unfitted for the company of strangers . . . as I proceeded, my spirits and hopes rose. I ardently desired the acquisition of knowledge . . . my desires were complied with . . .[1]

Shelley's choice of the term 'melancholy' was apt, since it encapsulated ambivalence. Although it suggested sad, gloomy and mournful feelings, it also evoked a sense of pleasure, of the delicious self-indulgence of such feelings. Melancholia was a disease, a neurosis, in the terminology of William Cullen, 'characterised by erroneous judgement'. One image of melancholy, a looser term, which in the early nineteenth century carried both medical and general emotional connotations, associated it with refined, learned and civilised men. While melancholy could be pathological, it also expressed the superior sensibilities of an intellectual elite.[2] Frankenstein's inability to keep his intimate, domestic self in a healthy balance with his thirst for knowledge, both of which had a melancholic aspect, constitutes the central monstrosity that the novel explores.

1. Mary Shelley, *Frankenstein*, 1985, p. 89. All subsequent references to Shelley's text are from this edition, edited by Maurice Hindle and hereafter cited as Shelley, 1985. Recently, scholars have been increasingly attentive to the differences between the 1818 and 1831 editions of the work. Hindle uses the 1831 edition. For a selection of recent work on the novel see Bann, 1994.

2. Morris, Kendrick *et al.*, 1807; the definition of 'melancholia' is in vol. II, not paginated. Definitions of melancholy and its cognates in the *Oxford English Dictionary* are also illuminating. On melancholy see Lepenies, 1992. Also relevant is Lawrence and Shapin, 1998, esp. ch. 2 by Iliffe. Some paintings by Joseph Wright of Derby could be said to touch on 'melancholy' in their exploration of the relationships between natural knowledge, the boundaries between life and death, contemplation, and introspection. Indeed Wright's *Hermit Studying Anatomy* of 1771–73 was used for the cover of the Penguin edition of *Frankenstein*. Equally interesting are *The Alchemist, in search of the Philosopher's Stone, Discovers Phosphorus* (exh. 1771; reworked and dated '1791'), *Miravan Opening the Tomb of his Ancestors* (1772), the portrait of *Brooke Boothby* (1781), and *The Indian Widow* (1785); see Nicolson, 1968, and Egerton, 1990. It is perhaps significant that Wright painted Erasmus Darwin, who is so often mentioned in connection with *Frankenstein*, five times.

Far from being a simple, moralistic tale of masculinist, scientific overreaching, drawing on simple definitions of 'science', 'medicine' or 'surgery', *Frankenstein* is a remarkably precise exploration of the internal conflicts felt by practitioners in a variety of fields, which we can conveniently yoke together as 'natural knowledge', and which are examined by Shelley with acuity. These conflicts are also historically specific, since they surfaced at a time when the expectations and claims of men of science and of medicine were disproportionate to their actual status and power. This mismatch was all the more frustrating because the idiom of scientific heroism, which became increasingly widely available in the first three decades of the nineteenth century, was enticing and seductive, yet insufficiently backed up by state support and cultural rewards.[3] Instability, uncertainty, ambiguity – these are key themes of Shelley's text, and they are explored with particular power through the account of his life that Frankenstein gives to Walton, the Arctic explorer. Walton's character, like Frankenstein's, is portrayed as an uneasy mix. On the one hand he is a daring explorer, a student of nature, possessed of an 'ardent curiosity' and of a desire to triumph over the elements, while on the other he is an isolated, lonely daydreamer, who is ultimately a failure. Walton and Frankenstein recognise their kinship, as the latter asks the former: 'Do you share my madness?'[4]

In order to pursue this argument I need to summarise *Frankenstein*'s structure and then to advance on two fronts, first by discussing the key chapters of Shelley's text, and second by analysing some of the issues portrayals of 'scientists' and 'doctors' raised in her time. In passing we must consider these occupational terms and note the anachronism if not of 'doctor' then certainly of 'scientist'. Although the term itself was not coined until the 1830s, there was nonetheless a sense well before then of men grouped together into some kind of collective, with shared concerns and values, and above all with a common epistemology.[5] This feeling of commonality, well before the word 'scientist' was current, among those who produced natural knowledge, is a significant phenomenon.

Shelley organised the work into three 'nested' first-hand accounts: Walton's letters to his sister, Frankenstein's account of his own life as told to Walton, and the monster's life story as told to Frankenstein. She thereby both shows a number of viewpoints and vividly evokes the suffering and trials of each narrator. In a state of extreme exhaustion, Frankenstein tells Walton of his happy childhood, the devastating death of his mother, his love for Elizabeth – who will be his bride – and his studies in Ingolstadt. It was in a spirit of benevolence, however deluded this proved to be, that he constructed a human being, having discovered the secret of life. When completed, however, the 'child' inspires horror, and its progenitor flees. The main portion of the book catalogues the subsequent meetings, disasters and misunderstandings that

3. Jacyna, 1983; Schaffer, 1990a; Knight, 1967; see also Desmond, 1989.
4. Shelley, 1985, p. 73.
5. It is sometimes said that Coleridge coined the term 'scientist' in 1833; for example in Levere, 1990, esp. 296, but see also Williams, 1983, pp. 276–80, esp. 279, where Williams attributes it to Whewell in 1840. Williams notes that the word 'scientist' was used very occasionally in the late eighteenth century.

occurred, culminating in the final climax on the Arctic wastes where Frankenstein dies and the creature goes off in sorrow to end his miserable existence.

In Mary Shelley's treatment, what is common to the different pursuits Frankenstein is enthused by is their capacity to open up nature's secrets, or at least they are designed to do so. They reveal or unveil something, personified as female, and presented as mysterious, enticing and potent. I wish to concentrate on the first four chapters, in which Frankenstein narrates his life until the time he is on the brink of completing his creation. From these chapters six themes, all important for my argument, emerge. First, seclusion and reclusiveness; these characterise his early family life long before he undertakes his solitary work on making the 'monster'. Second, passion; even as a child he is described as having a temper, being passionate, and throughout the account of his life his strong desires are foregrounded, above all his drive to learn the secrets of heaven and earth, to possess a kind of knowledge that is full of grandeur. These aspects of his personality were presented by Mary Shelley as overwhelming him, as forces he could neither resist nor control. Third, there was an absence of satisfaction. Frankenstein was often left unsatisfied by the activities he undertook, by the knowledge available to him, and accordingly he is set apart from others, suffering an inner emptiness. Fourth, he was drawn to particular kinds of natural knowledge. It is striking that he felt attracted to domains that were marginal, contentious or on the boundaries of what could be controlled, such as alchemy and electricity, and that he changed his mind so often about what interested him. This intellectual fickleness led him to discard areas in emotive terms: 'I at once gave up my former occupations, set down natural history and all its progeny as a deformed and abortive creation.'[6] Here fields of knowledge are treated in the way his monster was to be. Fifth, Frankenstein had powerful responses – both positive and negative – to those in positions of intellectual authority over him: his father, his father's friend who explained electricity to him, and his two very different teachers at Ingolstadt: Krempe, who repels him, and Waldman, to whom he feels drawn. It is important to note that in the last case this included a strong physical reaction to their persons and demeanour. Shelley's account gives credence to the idea that the character of men of science was to be 'read' in their appearance. It was also to be 'read' in their signatures, which were often reproduced beneath their printed portraits.[7]

Finally, the *history* of natural knowledge is a significant issue for Frankenstein. The contentious nature of some of the areas to which he is attracted derives from the fact that they are archaic: they belong to a past, not a present. Specific mention is made of Cornelius Agrippa, Paracelsus and Albertus Magnus. Humphry Davy's *Elements of Chemical Philosophy*, which Mary Shelley read in

6. Shelley, 1985, p. 86.

7. The most important source for scientific and medical portraits is Burgess, 1973; my impression is that signatures were particularly likely to be added to portraits when prints were published as frontispieces to the collected works of medical authors or as illustrations to obituaries. On medical portraits of the period see Jordanova, 1997. Lawrence and Shapin, 1998, use many scientific and medical portraits to explore the somatic identities of those who produce natural knowledge. Recent work on French eulogies is also relevant: Outram, 1978; Roche, 1980; Paul, 1980.

PLATE 12. *Robert Newton*, Sir Humphry Davy, *1830, engraving after Sir Thomas Lawrence, 1810/11, Wellcome Institute Library, London.*

1816, opened with a 'Historical View of the Progress of Chemistry' (see plate 12, above). His purpose was to place earlier chemical traditions, including alchemy, in a broad framework, which defined how proper chemical knowledge was to be acquired, specified its usefulness to humankind, and asserted its status as part of an 'intelligent design of the system of the earth'. For Davy, history helps to reveal the stable aspect of experiment, which 'is as it were the chain that binds down the Proteus of nature, and obliges it to confess its real form and divine origin'.[8] Furthermore, Frankenstein revealed his scepticism about the 'modern professors of natural science'.[9] It is true that this refers to his early years, but his evocation of a sense of there being a *history* to natural knowledge is nonetheless significant: 'I had retrod the steps of knowledge along the paths

8. Davy, 1821; p. 503; the 'Historical View of the Progress of Chemistry' is pp. 1–60. On Mary Shelley's reading see White, 1947, vol. II, pp. 539–45, and Feldman and Scott-Kilvert, 1987, vol. I, pp. 85–103. Hindle comments on her reading of Davy: Shelley, 1985, pp. 24–5.
9. Shelley, 1985, p. 91.

of time . . .'.[10] His sense of history was reinforced by Waldman, who 'began his lecture by a recapitulation of the history of chemistry', as did many lecturers in the eighteenth century. What really inspired Frankenstein was Waldman's way of presenting 'the ancient teachers of science' as mere speculators, and 'the modern masters' as the real miracle-workers.[11] The appeal of performing miracles and probing secrets is still there, but now, thanks to Waldman, it is associated with the moderns. Yet, Waldman's humanity allows the historical figures others dismissed to become those who laid 'the foundation' of modern knowledge. A historical perspective allowed Frankenstein to embrace the present, which he had previously rejected. Here, as elsewhere in the book, Shelley explored different modes of knowledge, not in order to rank and evaluate them, but rather to probe their moral and psychic qualities.

One reading of Shelley's depiction of Frankenstein's development and inner life is as an unambiguously critical portrayal of perverted science. And it has been claimed that the science she described bears little resemblance to the behaviour of medical practitioners and students of nature at the time she was writing. I want to suggest that, on the contrary, she was acutely sensitive to areas of uncertainty and ambiguity felt by those who studied medicine and/or the natural sciences and whose relations with the past of their 'disciplines' were being carefully negotiated at just this time. Many practitioners wrote histories precisely in order to work out the extent of their debt to the ancients and to their other forebears, to gain a perspective on 'modern' achievements, to place themselves in a lineage.[12] This was important precisely because they felt deeply implicated by the past, which was not yet separate enough to be put aside safely, but was still sufficiently close to require active management. Those who studied medicine at universities had to read some of the ancients very closely indeed; they would have been well aware of attempts to give a shape to the history of their field, which included compilations and codifications of medical writings.[13] It was because savants felt vulnerable to the suggestion that magic, and an improper concern with death and the supernatural, were still part of the scientific enterprise that they felt the need to repudiate them so firmly. Debates about mesmerism, and about physiognomy, with its troubled kinship with divination, as well as the violent contests over definitions of quackery, can all be characterised in these terms.[14]

In the early decades of the nineteenth century, many if not most of those who studied nature in practice worked largely alone, and in a domestic rather than an institutional setting. They more often worked with members of their own families and with servants than with their peers. At a time when students of nature were forging their masculine professional identities, they were most likely to be collaborating with female relatives, who were skilled at drawing, and

---

10. Ibid.

11. Ibid., p. 92.

12. Webster, 1983; Christie, 1990.

13. Rosner, 1991, conveys most effectively the ways in which medical students encountered the ancients and the more modern masters.

14. Jordanova, 1993a; Darnton, 1968; Porter, 1989.

at classifying and preserving specimens.[15] The more formal collective activities, such as those promoted by the British Association for the Advancement of Science, which started in the 1830s, and the specialist 'disciplinary' scientific societies, which began to be founded in the early nineteenth century, were important because they were new, or relatively so. Indeed it is arguable that provincial medical societies, starting in the 1770s, and medical periodicals, produced by groups of like-minded men from the mid-century onwards, played a central part in what is conventionally called 'professionalisation', and that they did so because they were strikingly innovative.[16] They worked against the grain of most medical practice, which was solitary, and carried out in domestic settings. The importance of hospitals derives in part from their capacity to bring together medical men, whose other forms of practice were more individual. These features made the personal qualities of practitioners yet more important.

Institutions can be understood as having symbolic functions: they presented the public face of science and/or medicine as a collective enterprise. It is not contradictory that the late eighteenth and early nineteenth centuries are characterised both by the making of individuals into scientific heroes and by institutionalisation; rather, these are complementary faces of the same coin. Heroes on their own could be construed as unstable, their idiosyncrasies untethered, while institutions without heroes were impersonal, lacked flair and could be felt to be dull. Even if it was to be decades before stable scientific and medical cultures were firmly established, the tacit goal of early nineteenth-century practitioners was to generate more security – psychic and social – for those who studied nature as a group. The persistence of the amateur is a notable feature of nineteenth-century British science, thus those who insisted that it should be a recognised occupation with collective rights were demanding something for which few indigenous models existed. Medicine, in a limited sense, did provide a model, since its practice could generate a regular source of income. Yet even doctors had little collective power in the early nineteenth century. Despite placing Frankenstein in a European setting, Shelley uses themes familiar from the British scene, especially insofar as her hero pursues an individual quest inspired by a thirst for natural knowledge and by a sense of the history of science.

It is true that Mary Shelley makes Frankenstein's reclusiveness and inability to communicate with those close to him into a morbid state, but in doing so she took up a theme that had been common in the medical literature of the eighteenth century. After all, the condition of being a man of thought or reflection was one that, like other social conditions, possessed its own distinctive pathology.[17] To have a well-developed intellect could be seen as a mark of status, a way of differentiating mental refinement from cruder skills based on manual capacities, but it was also a precondition of a particular kind of

15. Allen, 1981; Schiebinger, 1989, Davidoff and Hall, 1987, esp. pp. 289–93; Morrison-Low, 1991.
16. Lefanu, 1984; Inkster and Morrell, 1983; Emerson 1990; Morrell, 1990; Gelfand, 1993; Morrell and Thackray, 1981.
17. e.g. Tissot, 1758 and 1767; and *idem*, 1768 and 1771; see also Bynum and Porter, 1993, vol. I, pp. 584–600, esp. 589–92.

pathology – introspection, melancholy, obsession. There is also a sexual issue here: masturbation was called the solitary vice and associated with selfish self-absorption; Frankenstein's transgressions rendered him less capable of forming normal adult relationships, especially with the woman destined to be his bride. Perhaps it is also significant that she was chosen for him, above all by his mother, and that she died before their relationship could be consummated. Tissot's famous admonitions concerning male masturbation, first published in the mid-eighteenth century, stressed that its reclusive nature required hunting out and exterminating, and that it disabled the indulger from living a full and productive adult life.[18]

There were many reasons why those who were devotees of science and/or practitioners of medicine wanted to present themselves as men of reason, whose intellectual capabilities, combined with deep humanity, were their most striking feature, and as the modern equivalents of earlier philosophers. As vehicles for this presentation, they used styles and idioms that had authoritative connotations. This entailed a distancing from trade, from manual labour, from crude manners and from rudimentary educational attainments. At the same time, a thirst for knowledge, which produced an uncommon commitment to unveiling nature, was an important element of scientific/medical heroism. Natural knowledge was best produced by conspicuously disinterested behaviour, by a desire to generate knowledge for its own sake, for the sake of mankind and not for one's own personal advancement, for mere selfish gratification. Philanthropic activities were one vehicle through which these points could be made. The desire for knowledge came to occupy a different category from other kinds of desire, with which it might otherwise be confused. Two pairs of prints from the 1780s are relevant here; they both contrast the Benevolent Physician (see plate 13, p. 76), who is generous to his patients, with the Rapacious Quack (see plate 14, p. 77), who robs them. The dominant issue was clearly money, but the broader implications of setting benevolence, the desire to do good, against rapaciousness, and of presenting desire as greed for money, possessions and sexual domination, are unavoidable.[19] Just as there was a potentially pathological aspect to solitary, contemplative work, so there was to the desire to know nature, which could become a consuming passion, and, by that token, something abnormal. In all these cases – history, seclusion, thirst for knowledge – a careful balancing act was required in practice. Mary Shelley picked this up, and showed the absence of balance. She thereby pointed up the importance of equilibrium, not the unproblematically 'bad' qualities of scientists in general or of Frankenstein in particular.[20]

18. Tissot, 1766; Tissot is the subject of Chapter 6.

19. Details of these two pairs of prints may be found in the *Catalogue of Prints and Drawings in the British Museum* (1877 and 1935). The 'Benevolent Physician' prints are discussed in vol. V covering 1771–83 (nos 6347 and 6350, *c*.1783), the 'Rapacious Quack' ones in vol. III covering 1752–60 (nos. 3797 and 3798, *c*.1760). Since the 'Physician' and the 'Quack' were pendants, the implication is that the prints were issued twice, once *c*.1760 and again *c*.1783. Despite the titles, these two pairs are quite different in design.

20. On this point it is suggestive that, in the preface he wrote for the 1818 edition, Percy Shelley specifically insisted that no 'inference [was] justly to be drawn from the following pages as prejudicing any philosophical doctrine of whatever kind' (Shelley, 1985, p. 58).

Printed for & Sold by CARINGTON BOWLES, **The BENEVOLENT PHYSICIAN.** at Nº 69 in St Pauls Church Yard, LONDON.

The Benevolent Physician takes no Fee —
Of those that need him much in Poverty.

To Poor distress'd, and those of small estate
He Money gives, takes only of the great —

486

Published as the Act directs

PLATE 13. *Anon.,* The Benevolent Physician, *not dated, 1780s, mezzotint, Wellcome Institute Library, London. By refusing payment from a family, the benevolent physician becomes a special kind of philanthropist.*

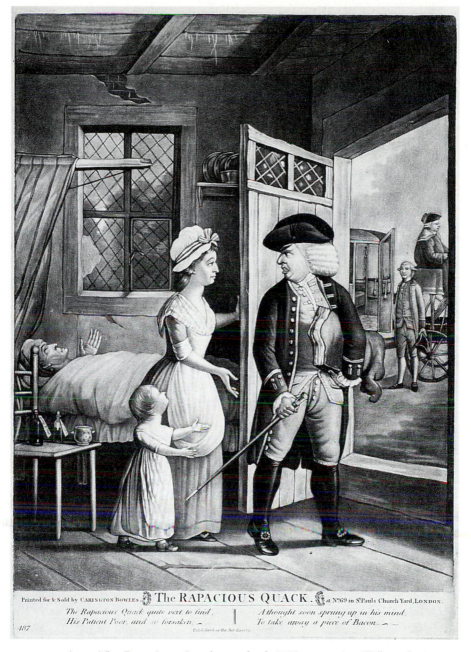

Printed for & Sold by CARINGTON BOWLES ▷ The RAPACIOUS QUACK. ◁ at N.º 69 in S.ᵗPauls Church Yard, LONDON.

The Rapacious Quack quite vext to find,   *A thought soon sprung up in his mind,*
His Patient Poor, and so forsaken,   *To take away a piece of Bacon.*

487   Published as the Act directs.

PLATE 14. *Anon.*, The Rapacious Quack, *not dated, 1780s, mezzotint, Wellcome Institute Library, London. The quack, who has by implication no medical training, is cast as a thief.*

One of the most striking features of Frankenstein's personality is that he feels driven to act on his new enthusiasm for natural knowledge, and that his efforts meet with success. He is portrayed as, in a specific sense, highly interventionist. Although no mention is made of it in the text, one recent edition of the book associates his activities with surgery: '[Mary Shelley] was of course writing in the early 1800s when liver transplants and open heart surgery were but considered fantasies in the minds of a few inventive surgeons.'[21] In the early nineteenth century, surgery consisted largely of bleeding, the removal of limbs, the treatment of wounds, and dealing with ailments such as bladder stone. Other operations were performed, but these mostly consisted of *removing* growths and related procedures. Thus surgery was active and manual, but not until the second half of the nineteenth century did it involve much entry into body cavities. Surgery was clearly *not* what Mary Shelley had in mind. Her emphasis was on anatomy and physiology, on understanding life through the processes of death. Opening organic beings for inspection, and then using them, or parts of them, again, were the ways in which Frankenstein's interventionism manifested itself.

The fluid boundary between death and life – a dominant theme in the biomedical sciences of this time – was of such importance that Frankenstein imagined that, in time, he might be able to 'renew life where death had apparently devoted the body to corruption'.[22] The belief that the boundary between life and death was reversible was widely held at the time: for most of the eighteenth century there had been sustained interest in suspended animation, techniques for reviving the drowned and the hanged, premature burial – indeed in any aspect of medicine that held out the hope that death could be delayed, avoided, held at bay.[23] Medical writers imagined doctors in a quasi-divine role, shedding new light on nature's processes. For example, according to David Ramsay, medical practitioner and early historian of the American Revolution, experiments on animals have 'tended to enlighten physicians in the god-like work of alleviating human misery'.[24] Ramsay was eloquent about the medical benefits of treating the drowned: 'How many must have been lost to their friends and the community, before mankind were acquainted with the god-like art of restoring suspended animation?'[25] Ramsay often used metaphors of light, referring, for example, to 'a blaze of medical knowledge'.[26] 'From the midst of this darkness a sudden light broke in upon me – a light so brilliant and wondrous, yet so simple, that . . . I became dizzy with the immensity of the prospect which it illustrated'; this is Frankenstein's description of his discovery of 'the cause of generation and life'.[27] Mary Shelley has grasped perfectly the

---

21. This was published in 1986, by New Orchard Editions, and is accompanied by wood engravings by Lynne Ward.
22. Shelley, 1985, p. 98.
23. McManners, 1981; Ariès, 1983; Maulitz, 1987; Richardson, 1988.
24. Ramsay, 1801, p. 15.
25. Ibid., p. 16.
26. Ibid., p. 34.
27. Shelley, 1985, p. 96.

PLATE 15. *Henry Meyer, Sir Astley Paston Cooper, 1819, engraving after F. Simoneau, Wellcome Institute Library, London. Cooper, whose education included stints in Edinburgh and Paris, and attendance at John Hunter's lectures, was a superstar surgeon who was given a baronetcy by George IV after performing a small operation.*

fantasies of at least some medical practitioners of the time, which involved imagining transcendent powers that were almost their own.

These fantasies comprised claims both to intellectual penetration and to active skills. They were nurtured by a new breed of metropolitan medical men, who were becoming successful in acquiring institutional power and social prestige and were rather assertive about their achievements as medics. Examples of the phenomenon include John Abernethy, Matthew Baillie, Sir Astley Paston Cooper (see plate 15, above) and Samuel Foart Simmons, all of whom were painted by Sir Thomas Lawrence, who also put the likenesses of other medical

PLATE 16. *H. Robinson*, Sir Anthony Carlisle, *1838–40, engraving after Sir Martin Shee, c.1795, Wellcome Institute Library, London. Carlisle was a prominent surgeon, who had been taught by, among others, John Hunter. He became Professor of Anatomy at the Royal Academy of Arts, London in 1808, a post he held for sixteen years.*

and scientific heroes on canvas – Sir Joseph Banks, Sir Humphry Davy (see plate 12, p. 72), Edward Jenner and Thomas Young.[28] Other members of this new breed were Sir Anthony Carlisle (see plate 16, above), professor of anatomy at the Royal Academy, and Sir Charles Bell, author of one of the Bridgewater Treatises of the 1830s, who shared an interest in the relationships between medicine and the fine arts.[29] Measuring power is impossible, but the power of these men was probably more symbolic than it was real; however, creating a *culture* of medical and scientific power was one way of securing the thing itself.

28. Garlick, 1989.

29. Biographies of all these medical men may be found in the *Dictionary of National Biography*, which in a significant sense constitutes a primary source, since the entries were written in the idiom of nineteenth-century heroism. Cf. the *Dictionary of Scientific Biography*, the first volume of which appeared in 1970, edited by Gillispie.

The portraits of such men are, in a significant sense, romantic; they make their subjects assertive and exciting but are not afraid to suggest the kinship between medicine and death. At first sight, the inclusion of skulls and bones in a number of these images is surprising, since they evoke a topic, death, which practitioners generally found difficult to cope with. After all, doctors were widely seen as the agents of death, and, in their anatomical role, as tormentors of the dead.

The most unpleasant sides of Frankenstein's activities involve an inappropriate contact with and disturbance of dead bodies. There is no evidence to indicate that the links between medicine and death became any less troublesome in the years leading up to 1831 – the year the second edition of *Frankenstein* appeared – and Ruth Richardson's work suggests that, with the Anatomy Act of 1832, they became far more so, especially at a popular level.[30] How, then, are we to account for the fact that such troubling associations surface in portraits of elite medical practitioners? (see plates 15, 16, 17, pp. 79, 80, 82).

Three possibilities present themselves, which are by no means mutually exclusive. The first is that these are the men who *legitimately* look death in the face, who know mortality in a way that *they* are claiming to be acceptable. They may be making such claims in the face of opposition, but they are making them nonetheless from a position where their rights and expertise were gradually being acknowledged by members of social groups whom they would accept as their peers, and by those who were still clearly their superiors. Second, being an old emblem, the skull could be used in this context to evoke long traditions of *memento mori* and of the contemplative life. Precisely because these were part of established traditions in high culture, they might be understood as alluding to the medical contact with death and with the human condition in its morbid states, in a manner that was softened, rendered elegant, by centuries of conventionalised use.[31] If skulls and bones had a certain formulaic quality, then the possibility that associations with death suggest a sharp, urgent critique of science and medicine would be lessened or undermined. The third possibility is that the presence of skulls may be understood in terms of a romantic portrayal of science and medicine at this time as domains of daring. Proximity to death had a certain sublime quality to it. There is absolutely no doubt that in building a set of self-images for those who unveiled nature, the vocabulary of romantic heroism and genius had huge importance.[32] Thus the frisson generated by the macabre side of medicine/death enhanced the image and self-image of those who studied such subjects.

The language of genius was also taken up by those in scientific circles more strictly defined, the pre-eminent example being Humphry Davy (see plate 12, p. 72).[33] Certain biographical traits were commonly picked up in accounts of students of nature. Individual struggle was a frequent prelude to discovery, suggesting a sustained commitment to an overarching ideal. Uncommon talent

30. Richardson, 1988.
31. Hall, revised edition, 1979, pp. 94 ('Death'), 130–1 ('Four Temperaments'), 285 ('Skull'). Hall stresses the direct links between melancholy, contemplation, books and a skull. (See also note 2, above.)
32. Cunningham and Jardine, 1990.
33. Ibid., esp. pp. 13–22 and 213–27.

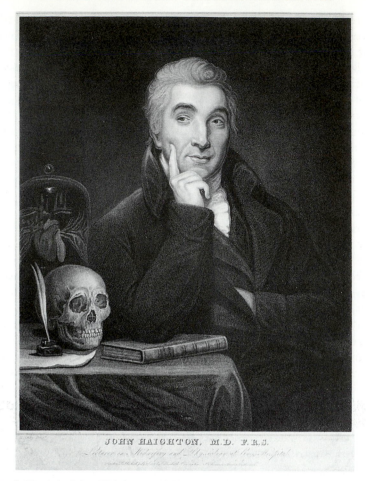

JOHN HAIGHTON, M.D. F.R.S.

PLATE 17. *I. Kennerly,* John Haighton, *1818, mezzotint after H. Ashby, Wellcome Institute Library, London. Haighton, a physician with strong anatomical skills, was interested in physiology and obstetrics, hence the book,* Haller's Physiology, *and the obstetrical case on the table, on which there is also a skull. He had a complex and somewhat rivalrous relationship with Sir Astley Paston Cooper.*

was made manifest at a young age. Such men showed a predilection for long hours of work, for solitary study, with the implication that they sacrificed their own health in the process. They also possessed the ability to stick with ideas, even in the face of opposition, displaying bravery, tenaciousness, even a zeal, a passionate commitment. These themes were developed in the growing number of published biographical accounts in the early nineteenth century.[34] It was not even necessary for individuals to be at the top of their field or in the eye of

34. Marten Hutt has recently completed a doctoral dissertation on medical biographies in the late eighteenth and early nineteenth centuries: Hutt, 1995. See e.g. Aikin, 1775 and 1780; Towers, 1766–80.

a wide public for a romantic idiom to be applicable.[35] The traits I have just noted were present in Frankenstein's life and labours, but developed to such a degree that they became pathological. This was *always* a possibility for scientists and medical practitioners, and the extreme importance attached to reputation at this period suggests how fragile – both psychically and economically – their careers were. Perhaps 'careers' is not the best term, because it suggests a far more structured course of life than was usually the case. Although by the 1830s many doctors had institutional affiliations, these rarely offered them any kind of security and most were 'honorary', while those about to be designated 'scientists' had far fewer such niches available to them. Often a scientific and/or medical life was pieced together, like Frankenstein's monster, made up of bits of lecturing, writing and practising medicine, with the possibility of patronage from friends, relations or sympathetic aristocrats.

In these circumstances, it was attractive to create a certain aura around scientific and medical activities, presenting them not just as worthwhile in terms of contributing to the progress of knowledge and to human well-being, but as thrilling. A good deal of mythologising was involved in terms already established as plausible at this particular historical moment. Nonetheless, this image/self-image was fragile, it was delicately poised between social benefits deriving from knowledge well used, and disaster derived from certain kinds of excess. Practitioners had recourse to a range of devices to cultivate the former and keep the latter at bay. Histories of their subjects did just this. These were quite explicitly about fatherhood in both its good and bad forms. Hippocrates was the father – the good progenitor – of medicine, Galen was the self-indulgent obscurantist – the bad father – just as Frankenstein was.[36] Portraits of practitioners, which would embody – literally – desired values, can be viewed in a similar way. Other devices included the elaboration of intraprofessional etiquette, cultivation of patronage relations, and assertions of moral and/or religious conformity.[37]

My argument has been that, in the early nineteenth century, the ambivalence surrounding a thirst for natural knowledge could not be laid to rest. Perhaps it never has been – the afterlife of *Frankenstein*, the history of science fiction as a genre, and the interest in films such as David Cronenberg's *Dead Ringers* (1988) suggests as much. The resulting tensions and ambivalences had to be actively negotiated. In the area of gender and sexuality there was a need to create a secure masculine identity for practitioners of science and medicine, which allowed that natural knowledge was exciting and to be sought in the fashion of a quest, but which resisted any suggestion that it was totally seductive. This would have led to a loss of self-control, or generated auto-eroticism. It was important that the power flowing from natural knowledge was purged of

35. e.g. Thomas Garnett and John Haighton in the *Dictionary of National Biography*, 1949–50, vols VII and VIII respectively.

36. A particularly clear example of such histories is Black, 1782.

37. Baker, 1993, esp. pp. 861–8. These themes emerged particularly clearly in the early nineteenth-century medical reform movement: Desmond, 1989; Loudon, 1992; French and Wear, 1991; Jordanova, 1997 and 1998.

its magical and hubristic elements. In other words, the cardinal tenet of the Enlightenment, that rational knowledge was a proper source of secular power, had to be further refined and clarified. The unveiling of nature, that profoundly unstable term, was a source of valued insights, but it could also unleash that which was dangerous. This tension is much more apparent in languages like English, where gendered personifications stand out. And, as I have pointed out elsewhere, it is evident in the very idea of a veil, which simultaneously conceals and reveals and is thereby erotically charged.[38]

I am not claiming for *Frankenstein* some kind of 'documentary' status it does not possess. Rather in its powerful evocation of the internal life of a student of nature, it tapped into a turbulent unconscious life that was experienced in a variety of ways by practitioners of the time. They tended to present this life in its most stable form, Shelley in its least stable one. One of the monstrosities of the book is, of course, Frankenstein's psyche. We cannot understand the scientific/medical enterprises of the time without paying due attention to their internal psychic dimensions. Admittedly such a claim is not unproblematic, since it raises questions about what constitutes evidence of the psyche and about the manner in which it is to be interpreted. There are sources, however, in which these dimensions are so dramatically expressed that it seems perverse not to respond accordingly. For example, the theme of monstrosity was taken up quite explicitly in one place within medicine – man-midwifery. This is an important area because of the ways in which it has been invoked in writings on *Frankenstein*, as if Mary Shelley were mounting an explicit critique of men as midwives.[39] This was not, I believe, her concern, but the attack on man-midwifery did deploy the language of monstrosity. *Man-Midwifery Dissected* (1793) contains a well-known frontispiece, that of a figure divided down the middle by a straight line; on one side is a male midwife with his drugs and obstetrical instruments, on the other is a female midwife, who requires few aids (see plate 2, p. 24).[40] The image is all of a piece with the text, by a man, which decries man-midwifery as a French perversion, a threat to the nation's morals. In the caption beneath the image, the man-midwife is referred to as a monster lately discovered but not known in Buffon's time. Buffon's natural history, with which Mary Shelley was familiar, was not only a huge compendium of the natural world written by a prominent and powerful French savant, but a work widely read and appreciated for its literary elegance.[41] The monstrosity alluded to is of many kinds, but it is especially sexual. It rests partly on the idea that to join two utterly unlike things together – a man and a woman – in the role of midwife, is going against nature, and by that token against morality. This example indicates the heightened language that already existed in the 1790s around the practice of medicine, and, by extension, science, a point that is

38. Jordanova, 1989a, ch. 5.

39. e.g. Roberts, 1993. For very different views of man-midwifery see Bynum and Porter, 1985, part IV; Wilson, 1995.

40. Fores, 1793. See also Chapter 2.

41. Feldman and Scott-Kilvert, 1987, vol. I, p. 100; Hampson, 1968. Buffon is still widely read as a stylist in France, and as a result remains available in cheap editions.

reinforced by the equally vitriolic disputes about quackery.[42] Practitioners knew this, feared charges of improper conduct, and hence were already anxious about their identities on these grounds before the end of the eighteenth century, and the more they strove for respectability, the worse their fears, the higher the stakes became.

It is clear from her journals that Mary Shelley both read widely in what I have called natural knowledge, and that she was acquainted with a number of medical practitioners.[43] Percy Shelley was often preoccupied with his own health, and construed the resulting experiences as integral to his imaginative life.[44] In this sense the Shelleys drew on a cultural context in which science and medicine were not set apart, but were openly available to educated persons as intellectual and emotional resources. They were vehicles for general thought. It is mistaken, on a number of grounds, to see *Frankenstein* as a direct critique of science. It is more helpful to interpret the novel as an exploration of intellectual energy, of practices that manipulated nature, and of the desire for mastery. Put this way it becomes clear that Mary Shelley was probably thinking about a number of different modes of knowledge – literary and philosophical as well as magical, scientific and medical, and possibly also about their diverse manifestations in different geographical and historical locations. Thus science was not unique, but like other activities in some respects, if not in others. Historians of science are likely to be intensely aware of its uniqueness – scholars often carry the baggage of the domain they study – and to wish to trace that uniqueness backwards. This accounts for the widespread tendency to see *Frankenstein* as a prophetic work, and to present twentieth-century science as the direct legacy that confirms its prophetic status.[45]

I have suggested another point of view, one in which Mary Shelley is a cultural commentator on a highly fluid situation, in which medical and scientific practitioners were striving to carve out niches for themselves, often against the grain of their actual situations. They wished for forms of social and cultural stability they could only fantasize about, while Mary Shelley imagined knowledge in its most unstable, transgressive form. This was possible, I have hinted, not so much because of the content of natural knowledge at the time, which is only lightly sketched in by her, as because she sensed something of the psychological complexities of a thirst for grand knowledge. Since the idioms she deployed were of her time, we can appreciate their immediacy in the context of late eighteenth- and early nineteenth-century anxieties about what unveilers of nature were like. Such people were potentially monstrous, in historically specific ways. At the same time, we, like Mary Shelley, can also appreciate that the dangers of desiring knowledge are not limited to a particular historical moment, hence fears of monstrous forms of knowing can never be assuaged.

42. Schaffer, 1990b; Porter, 1989.

43. Feldman and Scott-Kilvert, 1987, vol. I, e.g. pp. 26, 39, 47, 55, 65, 67, 124, 180.

44. Leask, 1992.

45. Easlea, 1983, pp. 28–39; Maurice Hindle makes a similar point in his introduction in Shelley, 1985, pp. 41–2.

CHAPTER FIVE

The Authoritarian Response: The French Revolution and the Enlightenment

The end of the Enlightenment is my concern here. I am interested in the uses made of representations of the Enlightenment in the 1790s and the early years of the nineteenth century by those who were critical of it. Such critics certainly welcomed the end of a movement of ideas they deemed pernicious, and the circumstances in which they found themselves encouraged their sense of its monstrosity. How, when and why the Enlightenment ended are formidably complex questions, but end it did. Its demise can be linked to a series of interrelated processes that marks a major point of transition in European and, possibly, in world history – the French Revolution. Even at the time, perhaps we should say especially at the time, the Revolution was yoked to the Enlightenment; thus disenchantment with the Revolution often went hand in hand with disenchantment with the Enlightenment. Some commentators went further and suggested that the Enlightenment caused the Revolution.[1] They were able to do so by associating the Terror, which was in reality only one phase of the long and intricate revolutionary process, with the values of the Enlightenment. By taking the Terror as emblematic of '1789', commentators were able to depict in fearsome terms the darkest, the most threatening shadows of the Enlightenment. I shall not comment on the explanations that have been offered of the end of the Enlightenment or of the causes of the Revolution, which continue to generate impassioned debate. My aim here is to re-view that phenomenon we call the Enlightenment through the menacing shadows it was claimed to have cast.

In the 1790s and early 1800s a particular, reified version of the Enlightenment was constructed. It is important not to confuse this with the historical phenomena we now study, although these too are, of course, constructs – ones for other times, other places. An understanding of the Enlightenment as perceived through the terrifying chaos of Revolution has much to teach us. Commentators concerned to re-impose authority saw, if largely in their mind's eye, the shadows of the Enlightenment only too clearly. Shadows cast gloom, they

---

1. Church, 1964. On the relationships between Enlightenment and Revolution see also Day, 1996; Outram, 1995, ch. 8; Hampson, 1968, ch. 8. On the French Revolution in world history see Roberts, 1995, esp. pp. 693–716 and 773 and Fehér, 1990, chs 1 and 6.

invite those who live under them to account for their darkness. A monstrous Enlightenment was fabricated in order to achieve precisely this. The exact form the monstrosity took tells us much about the worst fears of those who stood in shadow. The relationships between objects and their shadows are complex – the latter bear a resemblance to the former, but there is always an element of distortion. What I am calling 'the authoritarian response' reveals some of the Enlightenment's most menacing shadows, and by that token in fact permits a more rounded view of the complex movement of ideas that supposedly cast them.

Hence I shall not be concerned here with establishing either the causes or the origins of '1789', but with the links assumed to exist between the Enlightenment and the Revolution, links that encouraged the formulation in the early nineteenth century of an authoritarian response that sought to supersede both the Revolution and its associated world-view. Naturally, when such associations were made they served, rhetorically, clear political ends. The case of Edmund Burke is among the best-known examples of this phenomenon.[2] In fact, the Enlightenment was invoked both by those who deemed themselves 'revolutionary' and by those who presented themselves as 'counter-revolutionary'. Hence ideas and political events stood in manifestly close, if sometimes fraught, relation to one another.

The end of the Enlightenment was bound up with the rise to power of Napoleon Bonaparte. Obviously he did not single-handedly cause the end of an intellectual and cultural movement. Rather he embodied the gradual, and general, withdrawal of confidence in some of the most cherished ideas associated with the Enlightenment. His life exemplifies the shift all the more elegantly because he was educated in an Enlightenment manner, and initially presented himself to the French people as the saviour of the true Revolution. Indeed, many groups, especially outside France, continued for some time to idolise him as a liberator. But as he acquired more political power, disillusion about him spread, while he became ever more vigilant to control not only French society but the images of him that were present in it. He encouraged movements, institutions, and individuals with an altogether distinct, and more authoritarian, perspective and discouraged those with Enlightenment values. The mere fact of his existence as Emperor, his Concordat with the Pope, and his elaboration of a matching symbolic order indicated publicly a change of major proportions.[3]

This change, although it took place in France, and responded to a whole range of issues and problems that were distinctively French, was noted and had a profound impact far beyond the geographical boundaries of 'France'. There were three main reasons for this. First, French writings and ideas were widely disseminated in Europe and North America, and they were used in very different contexts to canvass the major philosophical, political, and cultural questions of the day.[4] It was inevitable, therefore, that events that openly bore on the fate and standing of such ideas were watched with interest elsewhere.

2. Cf. Reedy, 1981; Hulme and Jordanova, 1990, ch. 9 (by Musselwhite).
3. Lyons, 1994; Bergeron, 1981; Woolf, 1991; Kennedy, 1978, esp. ch. 3.
4. e.g. Commager, 1978; Porter and Teich, 1981.

Second, the French Revolution, following rather closely on the American Revolution, became an example, a paradigm of revolution. Its fate was thus of general interest; it allowed people to speculate about the nature of revolutions, about deep change, about new and old orders.[5] Third, the Revolution itself was not confined to France, but directly involved, once war was declared, the rest of Europe, including Russia.[6] Naturally, threats had been felt elsewhere long before that, but these were made tangible by the subsequent long military engagement and the appalling suffering that it brought to many areas.

Whilst we have a name for revolutionary turmoil, we do not have a term for the reaction against it. To call it counter-revolution would be seriously misleading, since this suggests political movements dedicated to counteracting the Revolution directly.[7] What I am describing was less focused politically yet more extensive culturally. I designate it 'the authoritarian response'. Clearly, a key issue here is the complexity of 'authority' as an idea. Deriving as it does from the cluster of concepts around 'author', 'authority', according to the dictionary, refers back to a source, an originator, instigator, actor, or begetter. In the late eighteenth and early nineteenth centuries, it generally implied a single source of legitimated power. Authoritative power can be both over the conduct and actions of others and over their beliefs and opinions. This power can be general, as in the case of government or Church, or more focused and knowledge-based, as it is when particular books or persons are endowed with the power to give authoritative testimony. The authority of natural knowledge, which we now conceptualise in terms of expertise, is especially significant, both because it was presented as new and distinctive and because it remained contentious. In the social sciences as they have developed since the nineteenth century, authority is primarily construed in political terms, and we now have a range of theoretical vantage points from which authority may be viewed – inspired by more recent political experiences – none of which was available to observers of the end of the Enlightenment.[8] In this context, the crucial points about authority are its metaphorical richness and the fact that debates about its foundations were exceptionally raw.

I use the notion of authority because it has been applied to a wide range of phenomena, thereby enabling us to draw out the shared qualities of apparently disparate aspects of a single society. In early nineteenth-century France, for example, it is possible to discern a shift towards an authoritarian mode in literature, art, religion, politics, philosophy, and science, to name only the more obvious areas. The changes these fields experienced, in the wake of distaste for Enlightenment assumptions and revolutionary excess, have much in common with one another. To see the authoritarian response in a fuller context, we need to return to the Enlightenment itself, indeed to its early stages. Before doing so, however, it is necessary to establish a general point about authority.

5. Palmer, 1959 and 1964. The period has, following Eric Hobsbawm's extremely successful book, become identified as 'the age of revolution', 1962.

6. Lyons, 1994, chs 14–16; Woolf, 1991.

7. Cf. Beik, 1970; Best, 1988, pp. 129–53; Roberts, 1990, esp. ch. 5.

8. Michels, 1948; Peabody, 1968; Ragan and Williams, 1992.

Authority is, as I have already indicated, a metaphor; it has a long history and a capacity to reach the enormously varied and quite palpable experiences of power that lie at the heart of most societies. At the centre of these experiences are the powers of gods and of rulers, both of which have been linked with other manifestations of authority, such as the privileges of the husband, father or head of household. Legal theory and practice, political thought, and the constant use of metaphor have served to effect such linkages. Apparently diverse forms of authority were both spoken about and experienced in related ways. There have been places and periods when these relationships are made perfectly explicit. The legal formulation in England that a wife killing her husband is petty treason, the patriarchalist apologia of Robert Filmer, the complex discourses and symbolism of absolutism, and in particular the endowment of Louis XIV with quasi-divine powers are all examples of the point.[9]

The intertwining in language, symbol, and experience of these forms of authority means that areas such as religion, politics, and philosophy were, at many different levels, bound together. More specifically, it alerts us to the fact that eighteenth-century societies were the inheritors of rich religious, political, and philosophical traditions for which authority was a central term – traditions that were deeply troubling to many eighteenth-century people. Locke's liberal refutation of Filmer's defence of patriarchal authority is a well-known example of this reaction against assertions of the traditional and unassailable nature of overarching authority.[10] There are innumerable other examples of a struggle to get away from the multiplicity of crushing authorities that 'absolutism' in all its forms represented. I mean to refer here both to the historically-specific political formulation generally called 'absolutism', and, by extension, to general assumptions that power of any kind could be 'absolute'. It is important to stress that absolutism embodies *models* of power – the extent to which it was successful in actually achieving its ends must remain a moot point.[11]

Let us take, for example, the authority of God. It is, I think, quite wrong to place strong emphasis on the rejection of God's authority during the Enlightenment, although there were, to be sure, a few people who took this route. Rather, there was a loosening of the bonds of that authority, through explorations of what more distant relationships between God and 'man' might look and feel like. Natural religion, a term that can be used to characterise the belief systems of many radical thinkers of the day, represents the desire for a certain space between the deity and the earthly world – one that leaves considerable room for manoeuvre.[12] God was no longer a force who swaddled humankind,

9. Wolf, 1968; Schochet, 1975; Butler, 1978; Marin, 1988; Burke, 1992; Lyons, 1994, p. 296. In using the term 'power' I do not wish to imply that power and authority are identical. Many types of power do not involve authority, whereas the possession of authority generally implies some kind of power.

10. Locke's *Two Treatises of Government* were published in 1690; he was reading Filmer in 1679 and 1680, according to Laslett, 1965, pp. 70–2. Filmer's ideas had been formulated some decades earlier. See also Filmer, 1991.

11. Cf. Bonney, 1987.

12. e.g. Mary Wollstonecraft's use of religious ideas in her *Vindication of the Rights of Woman*, first published in 1792. See also Kennedy, 1989, part 3, esp. ch. 3; Outram, 1995, ch. 3; Fox *et al.*, 1995, e.g. p. 33; Porter and Teich, 1981.

but the one who permitted loose dress, freedom of movement. The tightness that had been present in Filmer's patriarchalism or Louis XIV's absolutism was altogether too constricting. Binding together the ideas of God, monarch, sun and father, for example, led to a sense of suffocation; the weight of overlapping hierarchies was crushing.[13] Rigid ideas of hierarchy, in parenting as in politics and religion, came to seem outmoded, inappropriate, repugnant to a sense of natural justice. This change of mood can be linked with the development of 'individualism', which, although, like 'liberalism' a highly problematic term, refers to a very real sense that human beings were endowed with a shared human nature, with intrinsic worth and definable rights. Such assertions were about the value of individual persons, in and of themselves. There was no need to refer upwards, as it were, in search of transcendent properties, since the key qualities were inherent in human beings themselves. The tremendous interest in 'the science of man', which was central to Enlightenment intellectual endeavours, was an expression of the interest in a human nature that could be studied empirically and used as a basis for social reform.[14]

There was another central characteristic of the Enlightenment, which was integral to the reaction against absolutism, but which has been remarked upon less often. The absolutist model assumes the existence of defined foci of power. After all, the image of a sun king implies just such a centre point. The main foci, although of different types, were thought of as overlapping, even co-extensive. They were conceptualised in similar terms; the existence of emotive and flexible metaphors, such as those around paternity, was useful in this respect. The 'absolutist' framework had implications not only for the nature of rulers (seen as active), but especially for the ruled (seen as passive). Accordingly, the ruled seem relatively inert; they bask in the sun, they worship and adore, they bow down before it, they are awed by it. By the middle of the seventeenth century, the sun was the acknowledged centre of the universe. The sun is generative, a single dynamic source. In this mind set it is difficult to imagine order, coherence, and responsibility emanating from the people themselves, without imposition from above. These qualities come, in the absolutist framework, from a different order of being that is beyond and apart from society. Authority was thus associated with a qualitatively distinct level of existence, and with central sources of power. Dominant models of authority during the Enlightenment made quite different assumptions; above all, they were naturalistic.[15]

Much Enlightenment thinking, in a whole range of domains, was dedicated to challenging 'absolutist' models. Order could, it was argued, derive from people/believers/citizens themselves, or, in the case of the physical world,

13. The use of metaphors such as swaddling and suffocation is deliberate on my part – the well-known Enlightenment attacks on the swaddling of infants drew upon and helped to shape widespread assumptions about education and human nature. Although generally associated with Rousseau's *Émile*, 1762, they were articulated by earlier writers, e.g. Cadogan, 1748.

14. Kennedy, 1978; Fox *et al.*, 1995; Smith, 1997, part 3, esp. chs 8 and 9.

15. Chapter 8 examines just such a naturalistic model. The relationships between mind and body were a central issue through which conflicting models of authority were mediated – Rousseau, 1990. See also works cited on the science of man.

from nature's own laws, even if these were, ultimately, the product of God's will. God's will was distant, nature was immediate; it was there, to be seen, touched, used as a material and intellectual resource. Similarly, if people came together and made a contract, and then governed themselves in a consensual manner, the kinds of authority involved were immediate and man-made, quite different from the absolutist intention where a single, remote, divinely-sanctioned will was the sole legitimate source of authority. Far from emanating from a unitary, distant and higher level, authority could be conceptualised by participants in the Enlightenment as arising from below, that is, from the very same level in which it was exercised. I do not mean to imply that the political participation of the masses was taken as unproblematic, far from it, but it was at least conceivable that citizens – and much hung on how that term was defined – could govern themselves. For authority to come from among people rather than from beyond them came to seem perfectly plausible.

There is a further implication contained within the Enlightenment distrust of imposed, transcendent authority that bears on the themes of this chapter. If authority could be located within society, that is, within human beings rather than in gods or in quasi-divine monarchs, then people themselves as sources of power become enormously more interesting. One major way of pursuing such questions was through the detailed examination of mental faculties. Accordingly, the study of human nature was central to the Enlightenment project. With ideas such as free will, soul, and spirit under siege, fresh approaches to human nature took on a new importance. A naturalistic approach was developed to supersede an overtly theological one. And because terms like 'will' have such a wide range of referents, including to the faculties of the understanding, rethinking such categories became a matter of the widest interest. I have already noted how there were overlapping vocabularies for speaking about power in the period. Thus, if one of the cornerstones of a traditional approach to authority was challenged, we would expect a related adjustment in the whole range of discourses. If the will as an expression of political and divine action is invalidated, how could it be deployed to describe mental acts?

There were, therefore, quite particular reasons for changes in ways of thinking and talking about human beings, and especially their mental lives, during the Enlightenment. But the shift was more extensive than this. After all, one of the most powerful impulses that lay behind that phenomenon we call the Enlightenment was the drive to explain all aspects of the physical world, including living things, in naturalistic terms; to find scientific explanations for natural and social phenomena. This included human beings as a matter of course, hence the development of the new discipline known as 'the science of man'.[16] The science of man had many aspects in the eighteenth century – it was closely allied to medicine and natural history and to what is now termed anthropology. It also enjoyed a special relationship to widespread speculation about how the human mind worked and the ways in which it was linked to bodily phenomena. This last interest was nurtured by studies of the brain as the

16. See Moravia, 1980, in addition to the works cited in note 14 above.

presumed physical location of thought, experience and the soul, by the philo-sophical concern with building plausible models of mental action and more especially by sensualism – the assumption that all knowledge derives ultimately from the senses.

In fact, the philosophical issues here were exceedingly complex. Nonethe-less, the cultural reach of sensualism was extensive and a simplified version of the sensualist position was widely disseminated in the eighteenth century.[17] As a result, debate about how the senses worked, about how the mind functioned, about whether the soul existed, and, if it did, whether it could be located in a specific anatomical place, was enjoined by a great variety of people.[18] What role willing might play in human life was thus an obvious candidate for discussion, both because much hung on it and because of the general curiosity about human nature. The will was a major concept through which concerns about the uniqueness of humanity could be explored.

The Enlightenment began with a struggle with established authorities; it sought to create alternative sources of validation, above all from nature and from human nature, and it ended in the wake of a renewed political, theological, and philosophical authoritarianism, even a revival of absolutism. The conflicts between the Enlightenment and the authoritarian response of the early nine-teenth century found one of their most powerful expressions in 'psychology'. This word is, of course, somewhat anachronistic if used of periods before the mid-nineteenth century, but I deploy it here as a shorthand for the concern with the nature of mental life that attempted to explain the processes of think-ing naturalistically. Hence psychology was allied with philosophy, and especially with epistemology, on the one hand, and with the natural and medical sciences, particularly physiology, on the other. Psychology was at the centre of the sci-ence of man, a project of the Enlightenment, as it was also at the centre of the authoritarian response.

An exemplification of these points may be found in the fate of 'ideology', the science of ideas, a new area of study that emerged at the end of the eighteenth century.[19] Its students were followers of Condillac, and they grouped themselves around Destutt de Tracy, around the salon of Madame Helvétius at Auteuil, and from 1795 around the Second Class of the *Institut National* in Paris, which was devoted to the moral and political sciences. Although the intel-lectual interests of the *idéologues* were very broad, their shared commitments both to a science of human nature and to an understanding of the phenomena of consciousness were of paramount importance. They were indeed heirs of the Enlightenment, striving to produce ever more sophisticated accounts of human experience based on observation.

A medical approach was influential here since clinicians had a fund of ex-amples to draw upon that illustrated the enormous variety of human nature, both normal and pathological, and the complexity of mind–body interaction.

17. e.g. Baxandall, 1985, pp. 74–104; Stocking, 1982; Rousseau, 1990; Fox *et al.*, 1995, ch. 4 (by Smith); Smith, 1997, ch. 5.
18. Figlio, 1975; Smith, 1997, chs 4 and 7.
19. Picavet, 1971; Moravia, 1974; Gusdorf, 1978; Kennedy, 1978; Head, 1985.

This last point is important because eighteenth-century savants were generally reluctant to see mind and body as separate; they exhibited a preference for showing how the two were necessarily intertwined. Some savants were still dualists, but their understanding of mind–body interaction was exceedingly sophisticated, so that the difficulty *in practice* of separating these two elements was clear to them. Indeed, it was suggested that, as the prominent medical *idéologue* Cabanis put it, the physical and the moral were at their base the same, both facets of 'organisation'.[20] He meant by this that it was possible to understand all the functions of living things in terms of their structural complexity. The implications for a science of man were clear; even the most elaborate mental processes where to be explained biologically, by reference, for example, to the anatomy and physiology of the brain and nervous system.[21] Not only were 'mind' and 'body' two manifestations of a single set of natural phenomena, but strong claims about the existence of a soul or free will easily appeared implausible. It is worth being quite explicit about why this was the case.

I mentioned earlier the question of active and passive elements; under political absolutism the populace was relatively passive, the king, active. That, at least, was the theory. Similarly, it was possible to imagine the human body as relatively passive, the soul, mind, will, or spirit as more active. And so it was with nature too, which was often seen as the inert substratum upon which God acted via laws of nature. Although it would be a mistake to imply that there was a consensus on these matters, we can gather much about the common assumptions made about them from the violent reaction elicited in the eighteenth century by theories that attributed activity to mere matter. By the end of the century, however, natural philosophers had developed elaborate ways of understanding living things that followed a delicate middle ground. They rejected crude dualism partly because neither soul nor free will did the necessary explanatory work in producing a convincing and naturalistic account of organic action. Equally, they mostly had little time either for overt materialism or for theories of active matter, which were generally deemed subversive.[22]

The approach taken by Cabanis and by many of his contemporaries, which involved the study of 'organisation', stemmed from precisely this newly-found middle ground, one that was especially attractive to those who were self-consciously progressive, both socially and politically. We should note the affinity between the physiological and biological approaches just outlined, and political assumptions that people could make ordered societies themselves. Such societies were deemed capable of manifesting considerable organisational complexity, without the intervening hand of a separate and higher active power. Furthermore, the overlap, play and analogies between the human body and the body politic were, as commentators have noted, recognised at the time.[23] It was

20. Figlio, 1976; Moravia, 1980, p. 264; Elizabeth Williams has also discussed medicine and the science of man, but from a totally different vantage point: Ragan and Williams, 1992, ch. 4 and Williams, 1994. See also Fox *et al.*, 1995, ch. 3 (by Porter).

21. Staum, 1980 and Cabanis, 1956.

22. Schaffer in Rousseau, 1990 gives a particularly compelling analysis of these issues; cf. Fox *et al.*, 1995, ch. 7 (by Hatfield).

23. Pickstone, 1981; Outram, 1989.

equally evident that the problems of explaining action, whether this was divine, natural, or mental, were different facets of a single philosophical cluster. It should therefore come as no surprise to discover that the *idéologues* were deeply interested in the science of man, and especially 'psychology', in scientific method, and in the natural, the political and the moral sciences broadly defined.

All the issues mentioned so far could be explored at a variety of levels and through a wide range of specific instances. For example, at a more detailed level much of debate hinged on the faculties of the understanding, especially because there was no consensus as to what the basic faculties were. Some commentators simply eliminated will as a fundamental faculty or claimed that ideas of free will were no more than a theological trick. For others the will was not demoted completely – for de Tracy, a leading *idéologue*, the basic faculties were feeling, remembering, judging, and willing. Nonetheless, he did not see the will as detached from and superior to other bodily and mental processes. It was one faculty among others to be understood naturalistically. However, by the 1790s there was a growing awareness of the inadequacies of the basic sensualist model, of the complexity of mental life and hence of the need to alert and expand the terms within which psychology was discussed.[24] There is no better exemplification of this point than the changing ideas of Maine de Biran.[25]

Maine de Biran was an influential philosopher who was concerned above all with introspection, with explaining our inner mental lives. He is considered to be of 'pivotal importance in the history of French thought', a figure who 'helped create nineteenth-century French Spiritualism and twentieth-century French Existentialism'.[26] Initially, he was enthusiastic about *idéologie*; both de Tracy and Cabanis responded positively to his early work, and he in turn was indebted to them. Indeed, in many ways de Tracy's own dissatisfaction with Condillac's sensualism paved the way for Maine de Biran's more searching critique and for the alternative that he developed. But he became disaffected with the *idéologue* approach and sought his own path. He retained, however, a conviction that constructing a science of human nature was a task of paramount importance and himself attempted to produce a synthetic account of the field – a psychology or philosophical anthropology, to use his own terms. He held a deep conviction in the importance of human consciousness, i.e. inner experience, as a source of knowledge and thus introspection was a central method for him. More than this, the inside of human beings could not, for de Biran, be seen as passive. Rather he sought an active human centre in the will. This had two implications. First, de Biran was interested in the nature of willed effort by which the self knows or feels itself through the resistance it encounters. Second, he used this as a paradigm of causality. Indeed, the will is so central to his philosophy that it may be summed up in the phrase, 'I will, therefore I am'.[27]

24. Copleston, 1975, pp. 19–36; Fox *et al.*, 1995, ch. 7; Kennedy, 1978, chs 2 and 3; Head, 1985.
25. *Les Études philosophiques*, 1982; Huxley, 1950, pp. 1–152; Moore, 1970; Kennedy, 1978, ch. 3; Smith, 1997, ch. 10.
26. Hallie, 1959, p. viii.
27. Copleston, 1975, p. 30.

In the career of a single individual, nurtured in the major traditions of the Enlightenment, we can trace the progressive disenchantment with those traditions. Maine de Biran was an agnostic early in his life, he died a Catholic. He began with an interest in thinkers such as Locke, Bonnet, and Condillac, then he became involved with the *idéologues*, especially Destutt de Tracy and Cabanis, and finally he moved away from them towards more mystical approaches and philosophies where the existence of God and the spiritual dimensions of human life occupied a more central position. Along with his insistence on human activity, on 'man' as a free agent, and on the basic distinction between our experience of the external and internal worlds, went a deep conviction in dualism. It is everywhere in his later ideas. Indeed, dualism was at the heart of the authoritarian response.

For Maine de Biran the differences between mind and body, between the spiritual and the material realms, between active causes and passive effects, and between God and His created world were of paramount importance. These distinctions had a number of facets. They enabled him, for example, to stress the special nature of the human mind, which, for both theological and philosophical reasons, was a centrepiece of his thought. Free will was contrasted with matter, which was determined by laws of nature. Such distinctions also expressed a revulsion against 'levelling tendencies', against the crassness of lumping things together – a complaint often directed against the Enlightenment by its critics. An approach that rests heavily on the existence of distinct orders of being, and that then construes these as ranged along a hierarchy, be it of power, value, morality, or degree of spirituality, requires a philosophy of difference. And, at this historical juncture, dualism was the major and the most attractive candidate.

I am not suggesting that Maine de Biran was somehow inherently reactionary, although his politics can certainly be characterised as conservative. Like many of the *idéologues* he was a public figure for large parts of his adult life. For most of the period of Napoleon's rule he was an administrator and a representative in national assemblies, although he, again like them, came to oppose the Emperor. He was once more active under the restored monarchy. It is possible to argue that his philosophy was consonant with a more authoritarian approach in general and that his emphasis on the spiritual aspects of human existence supported more than an introspective approach: it actively encouraged ideas of distinct levels, some of which – God, the life of the spirit, the will – were 'higher' than others.

The authoritarian response manifested itself in a number of forms – some of which were closely linked with 'Romanticism'.[28] It is important to recognise that there were major differences of opinion among those we identify as the principal exponents of an authoritarian position.[29] There was, for example, no consensus on the merits of Napoleon's rule, on the role an aristocracy should assume, on the precise form monarchy should take. Nor was there agreement

28. Porter and Teich, 1988, esp. pp. 240–59; Day, 1996.
29. Beik, 1970.

on what the principal causes of Revolutionary turmoil were, although many commentators saw the Enlightenment as a major, if not its sole cause. That exponents of the authoritarian response possessed highly individual perspectives on philosophical, religious, and political matters in no way undermines my analysis of their shared position as influential propagators of the belief that clear, transcendent authority was indispensable to the well-being of human society. A revealing, if idiosyncratic, example of the cult of authority is Chateaubriand – noble, royalist, and Romantic writer. Chateaubriand's memoirs, published in 1849, provide eloquent testimony to his reactions to the Revolution, while his famous *Génie du Christianisme* (1802), which came at a strategic moment in France's relationship with the Papacy, was an enormously influential statement of the inspirational power of religious belief. As a writer of extraordinary emotional energy, he was able to present many different aspects of the need for authority – a prominent argument in *Génie* is that adoration of the deity brings aesthetic rewards.[30]

We can contrast the picture of the satisfaction afforded by Christianity, which Chateaubriand painted in *Génie*, with the painful one of the Revolution in his memoirs:

The Revolution would have carried me with it if only it had not begun with a series of crimes: I saw the first head carried on the end of a pike and I recoiled. In my eyes murder will never be an object of admiration or an argument for freedom; I know of nothing more servile, contemptible, cowardly, and stupid than a terrorist. . . . On 14 July came the fall of the Bastille. . . . In the midst of these murders, the mob indulged in wild orgies. . . . The 'victors of the Bastille', happy drunkards declared conquerors by their boon companions, were driven through the streets in hackney carriages; prostitutes and *sans-culottes*, who were at the beginning of their reign, acted as their escort. . . . I was standing at the window of my hotel with my sisters and some Breton acquaintances when we heard shouts of 'Bolt the doors, bolt the doors!' A troop of ragamuffins appeared at one end of the street. . . . As they came nearer, we made out two dishevelled and disfigured heads. . . . The murderers stopped in front of me and stretched the pikes up towards me, singing, dancing, jumping up in order to bring the pale effigies closer to my face. One eye in one of these heads had started out of its socket and was hanging down on the dead man's face; the pike was projecting through the open mouth, the teeth of which were biting on the iron. . . . If I had had a gun, I should have fired at those wretches as at a pack of wolves. They howled with fury . . . Those heads, and others which I saw soon afterwards, changed my political tendencies; I was horrified by these cannibal feasts. . . .[31]

I have quoted from Chateaubriand at length in order to convey the powerful manner in which he builds up an image of Revolution as terror to serve his larger purposes (cf. plates 4, 5, pp. 28, 29).[32] He deploys two main strategies:

30. Chapter 3 examines Chateaubriand in a rather different intellectual context – natural theology.
31. Baldick, 1965, pp. 121, 127, 128–9.
32. On images of revolution see Donald, 1996; Cuno, 1989; Bindman, 1989; Paulson, 1983.

the use of a specific vocabulary that generates an emotional response and the selection of episodes in the Revolution as emblematic of the process as a whole. He does indeed achieve his principal goal – to shock his readers into an instinctive revulsion – but the precise way in which this is accomplished is significant. Fragmentation of an entire society as well as of individual bodies is a major theme. The severed head does an enormous amount of work by allowing us to move from bodily mutilation to political chaos. The chaos, which is specifically associated with the mob, has a quite particular set of characteristics: it is criminal, bestial and sexual. Both literal and metaphorical promiscuity are at issue here. And, the ultimate accusation is that of cannibalism. The mob, according to Chateaubriand, is no longer human, it is less than human since it carries out the worst transgressions that we can imagine. The Revolutionary processes were filthy and chaotic, how then could France be cleansed and reordered?

There were a number of responses to this question, which was felt to be an extremely urgent one by many members of that society. There were political, religious and philosophical responses – what they had in common was an authoritarian cast of mind. Napoleon, to take the most obvious example, saw his destiny as providing a political solution to what he saw as 'the spirit of faction', 'the disorder' of the 1790s, since these were 'hurling the nation into an abyss from which the time has at last come to rescue it, once and for all'.[33] In concrete terms, this strategy took a number of forms: the gathering of military and political power to himself, eventually as a hereditary ruler, the elaboration of a highly structured administrative apparatus to serve his needs, the imposition of the famous Napoleonic codes, which, among other things, asserted the rights of the husband/father within the family, and the pursuit of an imperialist project.[34] Furthermore, Napoleon was far from being liberal when it came to intellectual matters. He discouraged dissent, and most famously in 1803 he abolished the Second Class of the *Institut National*, the home of the *idéologues*, many of whom had welcomed his political participation in the early days, but who became increasingly disenchanted as his tyrannical aspects and megalomaniac aspirations emerged.

An equally revealing parallel response was the development of 'traditionalist' philosophy.[35] Here was an attempt to generate a coherent philosophical reaction to both the Revolution and to the Enlightenment that had supposedly given birth to it. In place of faction, the traditionalists wanted organic unity, instead of a social contract, they asked for a divinely-sanctioned political order uniting God and monarch. Order was God-given, not made by human beings; accordingly, notions such as the sovereignty of the people and democracy represented monstrous detours from a true path. Religion and politics should be reunited, they felt. This project for a new coherent synthesis entailed, among other things, recouping the idea of revelation as able to do important philosophical

33. Thompson, 1934, p. 81.
34. Bergeron, 1981; Lyons, 1994, ch. 8.
35. Dunning, 1920, ch. 5; Copleston, 1975, pp. 1–18; Bergeron, 1981, ch. 8; Reedy, 1983.

work.[36] Not only was revelation the ultimate source of authority, but a dramatic claim was made about the acquisition of knowledge in general. The traditionalists attacked Bacon – an Enlightenment superhero – and the scientific traditions indebted to him, and they attacked sensualism for its denial of innate ideas. In place of a view of knowledge as acquired by human effort through processes that could be understood, they substituted the idea of knowledge as, ultimately, a gift from God. Accordingly order, of whatever kind, is given from on high, not acquired from below.

One of the most important exponents of this position was Joseph de Maistre, a conservative Catholic monarchist, who saw the Enlightenment as the direct begetter of Revolution.[37] For him the Revolution was 'satanic', it was a time of 'orgies', and the philosophers who unleashed it could be deemed the cause of murders, they were 'monsters' and 'scoundrels'.[38] The accusations of moral depravity are indeed striking, not least in the similarity they bear to Chateaubriand's. Of course, they partly served a rhetorical purpose, to heighten the split between the Revolution and what should succeed it – if the former could be made all bad, the goodness of the latter could emerge more vividly. But if a traditionalist response was to convince, it had to do more than denounce the Revolution and the philosophes – it had to generate a fresh and compelling account of political and social order. For de Maistre one of the main routes for doing so was rethinking the nature of sovereignty, a project he was already engaged in by the mid-1790s.

Joseph de Maistre clearly needed to undermine the radical implications that emanated from the sovereignty of the people, since these served to negate the overarching character of divine power. At the same time he recognised that God acts through people and not supernaturally when it comes to the social and political order. For him, God 'has *willed* society, he has *willed* also the sovereignty and laws without which there would be no society' and hence secular order derives ultimately from divine will.[39] It further followed that ideas such as the state of nature and the social contract are completely misleading. God made people sociable, and he made them into nations: 'the same power that has decreed social order and sovereignty has also decreed different modifications of sovereignty according to the different character of nations. . . . The Creator has traced on the globe the limits of nations . . .'.[40] Thus, nations have character traits similar to human beings, and enjoy a kind of organic unity. Each nation has its own appropriate form of government, which cannot be derived from abstract general principles – it is God-given and natural. We may notice at this point how de Maistre is bringing together diverse kinds of power and treating them all as properly deriving from God's will.

36. The force of such claims about 'revelation' are brought out particularly clearly when the contrast with natural theology – the discovery of God through the empirical study of his works – is considered.
37. Lively, 1965; Lebrun, 1969; Beik, 1970, pp. 62–72.
38. Church, 1964, pp. 15, 19, 20, cf. Paulson, 1983.
39. Lively, 1965, p. 94.
40. Ibid., p. 99.

The deployment of nature in the service of de Maistre's argument is instruct-ive. Indeed, in doing so, he was employing a standard device of Enlightenment writers for invoking authority, but to quite different ends: 'the aristocracy is a sovereign or ruling class by nature, and the principle of the French Revolution runs directly contrary to the eternal laws of nature'.[41] Such a claim is consist-ent with the accusations of evil, monstrosity, and depravity that he made against the philosophes, and with his distrust of reason. When people attempt to be architects of societies, they exhibit exactly that false pride, shallow self-confidence, and disrespect for the true laws of God and nature of which the Enlightenment was so often accused. In his own way de Maistre explored the problem we associate with Frankenstein and with Faust.

One of the main props of de Maistre's view of sovereignty is the importance of unity: 'however sovereignty is defined and vested, it is always one, unviolable and absolute'.[42] Interestingly enough, this is quite compatible with one of the cornerstones of Revolutionary thought – the unity of the nation – it would therefore be mistaken to assume that Revolution and tradition were always polar opposites. We can see the desire for a comforting wholeness in some of the 'sacred laws' that de Maistre enumerated. These included, '1. The king is sovereign; no one can share sovereignty with him, and all powers emanate from him', and '2. His person is inviolable; no one has the right to depose or judge him'.[43] The essence of such 'laws' is that they are not derived from human reason, but 'are written only in men's hearts, and more particularly in the *paternal* relationship between prince and subjects'.[44] In de Maistre's work we can see how the familiar battle lines are clearly drawn. On the side of the Revolu-tion and the Enlightenment we have reason, abstraction, hubris, faction, chaos, depravity and artificially constructed societies, while on the side of order and monarchy we find moral feelings, faith, unity and cohesion, clear and tran-scendent sources of power, the divine will and 'nature'. In the first the people themselves try, profanely, to construct an ordered society; while in the second, God, working with monarchs, the aristocracy and the Church, creates social and political order.

By examining the writings of a number of prominent thinkers we can see more readily the ways in which the Enlightenment was reified and then used in a specific historical setting as a vehicle for debating wide and deep questions about order and authority. These debates were symptomatic of a larger crisis. It was not only savants who perceived and tried to conceptualise an unstable situation, although their views are of additional interest because of both their active participation in a number of regimes and their attempts to produce coherent intellectual reactions to social and conceptual change. These conflicts were felt by the populace too. We know, for example, that the women of the people quickly turned against the anti-Catholic fervour of the Revolution; they tried to clean churches, to atone for profane acts, to continue traditional

41. Ibid., p. 105.
42. Ibid., p. 112.
43. Ibid., p. 117.
44. Ibid., my emphasis.

worship, and to support their priests.[45] When dealt with at an intellectual level, the Enlightenment, the Revolution, and the reactions against them all appeared more clear-cut than they were in reality. To an extent, this was inevitable. After all, a battle of words, images and symbols had been enjoined, and all protagonists wanted to effect a moral polarisation for their own rhetorical and political purposes.

In referring to rhetoric I do not mean to trivialise in any way the shadows constructed by writers who epitomise the authoritarian response. Such rhetoric was important in its own right as well as being the main vehicle for intense emotion. Furthermore, we know the Enlightenment through the successive versions of it constructed by many generations of commentators. The version produced at the end of the eighteenth century has special interest. The Enlightenment that was invented in the wake of the Revolution arose at a momentous turning point in European history. There was both a freshness and a rawness in responses to the Enlightenment at that time, because it was felt with such intensity that this movement had cast deeply threatening shadows. By examining those shadows we arrive at a better understanding of the Enlightenment itself, because these two elements, although their forms may change, remain inseparable.

45. Hufton, 1971.

PART II

BODY MANAGEMENT

Medicine is a dominant theme in Part 2, yet the term 'medicine' needs some unpacking. To interpret medicine in narrowly professional terms would be anachronistic for a time when there was so little uniformity of medical training and practice and so many interested parties. We can usefully distinguish four of its aspects. First, medicine possesses a distinctive subject matter – the human body in sickness and in health. While practitioners invariably presented their understanding of the body as authoritative and systematic, they have never been able to exercise exclusive rights over it. The body is at once so implicated in the quotidian existence of every human life and so supercharged with meaning that it can never be owned by a set of occupations. Second, medicine has generated a number of vocabularies for speaking of what goes on in relation to bodies, hence its idioms penetrate other domains. To be sure these are complex processes that are far from uniform, but the seepage of medical language is a significant historical phenomenon, to be distinguished from its subject matter. Languages may be distinguished too from medical world-views, the third aspect. These world-views are equally pervasive, but they possess a distinctive level of generality. By medical world-view I mean a general framework, such as environmental medicine or the germ theory of disease, that is capable of making sense of a wide range of phenomena and of shaping broad patterns of behaviour and thinking – anxieties about infection and specific measures to eliminate it, for instance. Finally, medicine is a set of practices; literary and visual as well as diagnostic and therapeutic. Clinical practice is where social negotiations necessarily take place; it is also where the messiness of bodily phenomena have to be made sense of if at all possible. Important implications follow from these distinctions for the theme of body management. In Part 2 I argue that a good deal of that management occurs textually. Yet we should not put undue emphasis on the power that medical writers could exercise when they had, if not exactly a free rein, at least a wider imaginative space in which to work. The body, especially in disease, was recalcitrant, and clinical practice provided one kind of brake on medical thinking. Prevailing assumptions concerning social, political and economic priorities acted in a similar fashion.

In 'The Popularisation of Medicine', I examine a text, first published in 1760 by a practitioner with a huge European reputation, who could draw on his extensive clinical experience in advocating a particular kind of body management. For Tissot each individual had to manage meticulously their own sexuality and should be taught to do so in childhood. In a significant sense the renowned Swiss physician was a reformer, who manipulated his readers' emotions in order to bring about changes that would start with individuals behaving differently, but would eventually yield a collective improvement. By contrast, the body management at issue in 'Medical Mediations' is at once more philosophically subtle and politically brutal. It is a familiar idea that the French Revolution acted as an intensifier of cultural trends, and that the body played a central role in its ideological conflicts. In responding to the guillotine, medical thinkers had to both think through its physiological effects and assess its moral impact. The issues raised by the guillotine were intricate, both philosophically and politically, hence the need to manage its perceived effects within medical discourse. 'Guarding the Body Politic' concerns medicine much more loosely. The author of the text with which it is concerned was not medically-trained, although he was interested in both natural philosophy and natural history. Volney's catechism resembles Tissot's *Essay on Onanism* in that, by seeking to inculcate good habits in individuals and thereby in society as a whole, it is openly reformist. Although both draw on long-established languages of sinfulness, their framework is naturalistic in being based on the existence of natural laws, which should be followed – the authority of nature rather than that of God is invoked. It was possible to do this because 'health' was a term with powerful affect, suggesting an absolute good, for both individuals and collectivities. Health was also a norm, an ideal, a state that was 'natural'. Such investment in health as a concept is the context for 'Policing Public Health', which examines some of the ways in which the well-being of groups was conceptualised and the practices designed to promote it.

Medicine was, these essays suggest, a complex cultural construction, with a potent reformist, even utopian dimension. In a sense it stood for the search for a better society to be achieved through individual body management. It was also a metaphorical domain within which general issues such as 'lifestyle' and mind–body relationships could be explored. Accordingly, it is inappropriate in this period to think of medicine as a profession or a discipline, rather it was a rich cultural terrain of which no single group had exclusive possession.

CHAPTER SIX

The Popularisation of Medicine: Tissot on Onanism

Popularisation has been surprisingly little studied by historians of science and medicine.[1] Although common-sense meanings of popularisation are obvious enough, for the purposes of historical analysis it is vital to consider how popularisation is best characterised and what approaches suit its investigation. The dramatic proliferation of works which can only be described as 'popular' on scientific and medical subjects during the Enlightenment is a significant historical and literary phenomenon. While it would be possible to present this trend as simply a spin-off of economic expansion and social mobility, such an approach lacks analytical bite. Important questions include: who wrote these works, for whom and why, what kind of process is 'popularisation'? In fact the very idea of 'popularisation' is problematic, since it apparently confirms an unfortunate dualism, with 'knowledge' and those who produce it on one side, and a diluted form of that knowledge and its consumers on the other. One way of overcoming the consequences of a way of thinking that reinforces a schism between science/medicine and society is to treat scientific and medical texts as literature, and not to worry about their epistemological status, about their originality or the quality of their knowledge. It is then possible to examine different genres, styles and textual strategies in a way that respects the dominant themes and openness of eighteenth-century culture, the enormous interplay between areas we have subsequently come to hold separate. Writings on matters of health participated fully in larger trends, and there is an aspect of eighteenth-century 'popularisation' that is particularly relevant here: the profound didacticism so many medical publications of the period shared with literary productions on other subjects.

Popular medical works in the eighteenth century did not consciously seek to expound the results of 'research'. Frequently targeted at specific social groups (women, mothers, families, people with a particular social status or occupation), they generally addressed, advised and exhorted the reader in some way. It does not follow from this that they were highly simplified. Indeed, there

---

1. See Ehrenreich and English, 1979; Lawrence, 1975; Rosenberg, 1983; Cooter, 1984; Porter, 1985; Secord, 1985; Shinn and Whitley, 1985; Porter, 1992.

were wide variations in the amount of technical or linguistic knowledge pre-supposed. There seems to have been a degree of unity in their approach in that the relation of 'lifestyle' to health was mostly the central issue. This in part reflects the widespread continuing commitment to notions of constitution and temperament, to the importance of habit and regimen, and to the impact of the environment on human beings.[2] Consequently self-help and the preven-tion of disease occupied a prominent place in writings that exhorted people to strive for the ultimate ideal, health, through a 'medicine of avoidance and prevention'.[3]

In addition to the explicit advice given, popular medical texts assumed that robust health was a general good and that illness had adverse economic and political consequences. The idea of 'lifestyle' as embodied in these texts is, in fact, rather complex and was developed in a number of different ways. Gen-erally these involved the whole person – mind and body – in their immediate context, especially the family. Lifestyle could be a way of speaking about class, gender or even whole nations, as in the growing concern in the second half of the century with generating an adequate population to underpin the strength of the state.[4] Since medical advice books were sold to individuals, they consid-ered the relationship between their readers and the larger social fabric as a matter of course, although they tended not to concern themselves with the health of collectivities. This is an important point because these volumes had to hold together a sense of individuals' responsibility for their own health and of the tangible effects of their condition on others. The presentation of health in terms of selfhood is particularly striking.[5] To be healthy was to have a competent, coherent identity; to be ill as a result of one's own behaviour was to have fallen into a state that was somehow less than fully human – much the same was said about the body politic.

Didactic literature proliferated in the eighteenth century. Several scholars who have studied general conduct books have noted their popularity, their tendency to re-use well-established and successful models, and the ways in which they were closely related to other forms of literature, often being formed by rear-ranging excerpts from publications of quite different kinds.[6] Medical advice books should thus be seen in the larger context of conduct books in general. It would be easy to suggest rather general explanations for the increased output of such literature: concern about social mobility, anxieties on the part of the mobile themselves, attempts to assert control by groups seeking to establish or maintain hegemony, the social ambitions of the writers who produced them, and so on. This chapter has an altogether more modest aim: to examine more closely the form and content of such publications through a case study.

2. Smith, 1985; Riley, 1987.

3. Riley, 1987, p. xv. Riley provides an excellent discussion of environmental medicine in order to understand how endemic and epidemic disease was tackled in the eighteenth century, hence his focus is on aggregate rather than individual health.

4. Glass, 1978; Buck, 1982; Taylor, 1979 and 1985; Riley, 1985, esp. chs 3 and 4.

5. I am well aware that the self is a tricky concept. Porter, 1997 outlines a range of historical approaches, see especially part II – Enlightenment.

6. Curtis, 1981; Hornbeak, 1938; Paulson, 1979, part 2, ch. 3; Armstrong and Tennenhouse, 1987.

Surveys of broad categories of popular literature run the risk of neglecting the actual strategies that writers employed and the nature of the reading experience they offered their audiences. Of course, it would be naive to suppose that we can ever reconstruct that experience. For one thing, we do not know how these works were used. Were they read from cover to cover, dipped into only when needed, or even bought to impress and never read at all? Furthermore, which family members read them? Were the numerous books addressed to mothers about female and childhood complaints read by the women themselves? The questions are endless – only the immense popularity of these texts is clear. Snippets of information about such matters can be gleaned from diaries and private papers, but these are, by their very nature, both fragmentary and unreliable.[7] Careful study of popular medical publications can, however, tell us quite a lot about the audiences constructed by the author, about languages of health and illness, and about the rhetorical strategies deemed most appropriate to the subject.

I propose to analyse one such text, in order to illustrate how it works at a number of levels, developing a complex, even contradictory role for the reader. This work can safely be designated as 'popular' in the most basic sense. It was evidently commercially successful, enjoying numerous eighteenth-century editions and being translated from the original Latin into French, English, Dutch, Italian and German.[8] I refer to Tissot's famous, or rather notorious, *Essay on Onanism* of 1760 – a work which has been credited with exercising enormous influence on attitudes towards sexuality over a considerable period of time. Be that as it may, it is, in my opinion, an extraordinary piece of *writing*. At this point it may be objected that such a work is not 'typical'. This may be true, but then searching for the 'typical' can be a misconceived and fruitless activity. It does, however, contain motifs found in other works of medical advice. Nonetheless, it may be helpful to point to two characteristics of the book which are indeed unusual. First, the presence of the author is exceptionally powerful. Often books of this kind were multi-authored, comprising extracts from existing works, or the identity of the writer was relatively inconspicuous. Second, and directly related to this, was Tissot's prominence in the medical and literary worlds of his day. He published on a wide range of controversial topics, including smallpox inoculation, plague, the people's health, fevers, epilepsy and nervous diseases. Many of the major figures of the Enlightenment, such as Voltaire and Rousseau, were among his friends.[9] By contrast, many eighteenth-century medical advice books were written by little-known practitioners, who lacked the public acclaim that Tissot enjoyed. The only comparable figure was the feisty Scot William Buchan, whose *Domestic Medicine* of 1769 was an extension of and an act of homage to Tissot's *Avis au Peuple sur sa Santé*, 1761.

7. Beier, 1985; Lane, 1985.

8. Although I know of no definitive bibliographical study of the numerous editions of Tissot's work, the catalogues of the British Library, the Wellcome Institute Library, the National Library of Medicine and the Library of Congress list many different editions. See also Emch-Deriaz, 1992 and note 10 below.

9. Eynard, 1839; Lejeune, 1974; Minder-Chappuis, n.d. [1973]; Tarczylo, 1980; Emch-Deriaz, 1992.

While it would be fallacious to suppose that any significant degree of consensus existed in medicine, the themes and strategies used by Tissot appeared
in other contemporary works, and many of his preoccupations were quite
simply commonplaces of medical writings. There are, in fact, many extraordinary pieces of medical writing, although, like unhappy families, each is extraordinary in its own way. I make no apology, then, for choosing a single work, which
is both noteworthy and indicative of broad historical trends.[10]

*An Essay on Onanism, or a Treatise upon the Disorders produced by Masturbation: or
the Dangerous Effects of Secret and Excessive Venery* is a work often referred to but
seldom read. It was written in an almost autobiographical mode, full of references to people Tissot knew or had corresponded with, anecdotes he had
heard about, and his own clinical experiences. Since the author's presence was
established so strongly, Tissot could address the reader directly, as in a conversation, yet with authority. Needless to say, however, in the course of cataloguing
self-inflicted woes, he appealed to other kinds of authorities. Many of these are
major medical sources from the seventeenth and earlier eighteenth centuries,
such as Boerhaave, Haller and Hoffmann; others are classical, ranging from the
expected use of Galen and Hippocrates to the more surprising invocation of
sources such as Plato, Horace and Plutarch, who are cited in Latin. Tissot in
fact quoted widely, from St Jerome and Montesquieu, Aristotle and Linnaeus,
often with minimal references, which implies that he expected a part of his
audience to be well-read. Yet he also made it clear that one could skip the Latin
bits without losing the gist of his arguments, which implies that he expected
some readers to be familiar only with a vernacular.[11] When coupled with the
direct style, this gives the 'information' conveyed, at least to our eyes, a variety
of epistemological statuses. These range from 'I have seen myself . . .' to 'Someone has written to tell me that he has heard/seen . . .', and include the standard
citations of prominent medical authors like Harvey, La Mettrie and Boissier de
Sauvages. Constant movement between these levels enabled Tissot to relate
endless individual case histories, sometimes about named or identifiable
people. This certainly served to heighten a sense of drama about health, which
Tissot appeared to cultivate knowingly, even claiming that he will 'terrify by
examples'.[12] Many of the cases he recounted end in gruesome death, and thus
embody all the features of moral fable. The overt messages were unambiguous,
simple and unoriginal. At heart there was only one lesson, 'moderation', a notion
that dominated not just medical but the vast majority of didactic writings in the

10. I have relied heavily on the edition printed in Dublin in 1772, translated from the French ('the last
Paris edition') by A. Hume, MD, about whom little is known, although it seems he was the author of a
medical advice book, *Every Woman her Own Physician; or, the Lady's Medical Assistant*, 1776. Other editions which
have been consulted, and other relevant works by Tissot, are listed in the bibliography. Emch-Deriaz, in
Porter, 1992, p. 154, n. 17, gives some bibliographical information. Tissot had published in Latin on masturbation in 1758. The first edition of the work I discuss here is normally given as Lausanne, 1760. See Blake,
1979, pp. 451–4.

11. Tissot, 1772, p. vi.

12. Ibid. Many of these examples are given in part 1 of the book, 'The Symptoms', and especially in
section 4, 'Observations of the Author'. The following three parts concern, 'The Causes', 'The Cure' and
'Analogous Disorders'. Section 10, 'The Practice of the Author', provides a detailed account of Tissot's
clinical practice, outlining the cures and remedies he used and assessing their efficacy.

eighteenth century. Moderation implied self-control, constant self-management, and the ability to monitor one's own behaviour in the light of a larger perspective, which included comparisons between the sexes, classes, ages and occupations. Where the 'self' is not up to these tasks, as with children, the control must be exercised by others. Accordingly, the moral tales in Tissot's *Essay* were addressed to a variety of audiences – the young, parents, guardians, other medical practitioners and also possibly the 'general reader'.

So far, the special nature of the subject matter has not been mentioned, yet this dominates the book as it has dominated its reception.[13] It discusses that which is not normally discussed; it penetrates the secret lives of those whose stories are told and, by implication, those who read it. In this way it resembles eighteenth-century writings on man-midwifery, which, in explaining childbirth and assessing how it should be managed in the name of decency, had to negotiate a delicate path – keeping to a moral high ground while avoiding transgression. Not only did Tissot's *Essay on Onanism* speak, at length, about things 'unmentionable', but it did so specifically in relation to a group of people for whom the implications are particularly shocking – children. Tissot's text assumed the existence of childhood sexuality, implied the need for its control, and argued that failure to curb and direct it had permanent consequences because of the peculiar damage that results from the loss of such an important entity as the seminal fluid before maturity is attained.[14]

We may reasonably suppose that children themselves did not read Tissot. Nonetheless, with an adult audience in mind, he acknowledged the difficulty of finding the right language:

I can venture to aver that I have not neglected any precaution that was necessary to give this work all the decency, in point of terms, that it was susceptible of. . . . Should such important subjects be passed over in silence? No, certainly. The sacred writers, the fathers of the church, who almost all wrote in living languages; the ecclesiastical writers, did not think it proper to be silent upon crimes of obscenity, because they could not be described without words. . . . I hope to deserve the acknowledgement and approbation of virtuous and enlightened men, who are acquainted with the proneness of men to evil.[15]

Tissot thereby simultaneously claimed the right to speak on 'indecent' matters, and modelled his discourse on that of the Church, invoking St Augustine specifically as support. While there are many differences between his approach and a theological one, his invocation of the example of the early Church fathers is nonetheless interesting. It allowed him to introduce quasi-religious notions of evil and sin, which were coupled with the naturalistic arguments against sexual excess. And it is worth noting that he chose a biblical reference for the

13. See Boucé, 1980 and 1982; Engelhardt, 1974; Hare, 1962; McLaren, 1973–74; Stanton, 1993; Bennett and Rosario, 1995.

14. On the history of childhood, see Ariès, 1973; Boas, 1966; Plumb, 1975; Sommerville, 1982; Pollock, 1983. Cf. Scarre, 1989.

15. Tissot, 1772, p. iv.

main title. Furthermore, these allusions fitted well with the confessional tone of much of the work. Case histories often took the following form: a patient has some symptoms, attempts are made to treat them to no avail, the patient is invited to confess his secret indulgences, whereupon the true causes of his plight are known. Either death or recovery could follow. Here, the medical practitioner indeed took on a priestly role, arrogating to himself the right to pry, to know and to pass judgement on a secret existence. The compulsion to discourse about 'unmentionable' acts and the demand to know about the sexuality of others by requiring them to give an account of themselves, which Foucault has written about, are thus well established in Tissot.[16]

A further issue is raised by the problem of finding an appropriate, non-erotic language for sexuality. Perhaps the analogy with witchcraft is useful here. There is considerable historical evidence that in some parts of Europe witch-hunts developed as a result of elite obsessions with the power of the devil, and that they accelerated with the use of torture, which encouraged people to talk about illicit activities and to denounce each other.[17] As a result, it becomes virtually impossible for historians to give any account of witchcraft itself, even assuming this is a feasible notion. Rather they must perforce study discourses about witchcraft, brought into existence by the interaction of different groups. It was the speaking and writing about magic that was significant, not the acts they purported to describe. Perhaps the same should be said about sexuality. In writing about Tissot, several historians have likened him to a witch-hunter in order to blame him retrospectively for persecuting people we now see as innocent victims. I can see how the analogy could be useful, not because we should pass judgement on him, but because it highlights the fact that it was reading, writing and speaking about the forbidden that was at issue in both cases. The similarities go further; Tissot gave a voice to that which was 'unmentionable', just as the witch-hunters had.[18] Both 'persecutor' and 'persecuted' had to speak the same language, enter into the same universe of meaning, agreeing about the potency of the phenomena at issue, even if one was righteous, the other a transgressor. Following early editions of the *Essay*, Tissot received many letters couched in the very terms he had set out. Tissot and others were engaged in constructing elaborate discourses which, while they condemned a whole range of activities as irresponsible, gave them acknow-ledgement, celebrated them in words, precisely by giving them a voice, a frame-work, an audience, and considerable power.

Just as the persecution of witchcraft allowed, indeed demanded, the re-counting of sexually transgressive activities, so Tissot relentlessly catalogued 'crimes' and positively enjoyed, so it seems, rehearsing gruesome details. There was no inherent limit to these recitations, and endless elaborations could be introduced: 'in a performance of this nature, where the writer must have less grounds to expect he shall convince by reasoning, than he has to hope he shall

---

16. Foucault, 1979; cf. McLaren 1973–74.

17. Watts, 1984, ch. 5; Merchant, 1982, ch. 5; *History Today*, November 1980 and February 1981; Barry *et al.*, 1996.

18. Belsey, 1985, pp. 185–91.

terrify by examples, too many cannot be recited'.[19] Thus, just as subordinate clauses can be added to sentences, so extra examples and further details could be added to Tissot's accounts. Discourses of sexuality proliferated promiscuously. An example of Tissot's approach will perhaps illustrate these points:

I was called upon, Feb. 10, 1760, to pay a visit in the country to a man, about forty years of age, who had been of a very strong and robust constitution; but who had been guilty of great excesses with women and wine, and who had greatly exerted himself in what may be stiled [sic] remarkable feats of that kind. [There follows a vivid description of the man's symptoms.]

It appeared to me that the original cause of the disorder was too free an use of women and wine; and I thought that the feats which he had often performed might be the cause of the muscles being more particularly affected.[20]

Tissot then recounted his contact with the patient over some four years. The case ends finally with death and a confession of having been abandoned to masturbation. Tissot's writing contains two distinct positions here: at an explicit level a cautionary tale is initiated in which a sinner will get his just deserts, but the repetition of his exploits together with the use of the word 'feats', which titillates readers and invites them to speculate about just what these 'feats' could be, indicates a rather different stance. On the one hand Tissot argued that too much sexual activity makes people ill, offering a persuasive case for this through his vivid language, while on the other the pleasures to be derived from thinking, writing, and reading about sexuality at length are also apparent.

Such ambivalence, of which I do not suppose the author to have been aware, goes deep into the structure of the book; it can be seen quite clearly in the issue of childhood sexuality:

A child of this city [Montpellier], at the age of between six and seven, instructed, as I imagine, by a servant maid, polluted himself so often, that a slow fever, which succeeded, finished him. His rage for this act was so great, that he could not be restrained from it to the very last days of his life. When he was informed that he thereby hastened his death, he consoled himself, in saying, that he should the sooner meet with his father, who died some months before.[21]

Here is a child apparently consumed with sexual passion, yet capable of fine sentiments. Moreover, his habit came not from within himself, but from an external agent of a different, lower social class. It is evident that Tissot had at his disposal a number of different explanations of masturbation, which carried distinct implications. The ambivalences and ambiguities of the book derive not only from the unstable coupling of illness and death with desire and pleasure, but from the existence of a number of models of how masturbation takes hold

19. Tissot, 1772, p. vi.
20. Ibid., p. 35.
21. Ibid., p. 23.

of people. In order to offer a general explanation for the devastating effects of masturbation, Tissot turned to the nature of seminal fluid itself, attributing to it formidable vital powers: 'the seminal liquor . . . has so great an influence upon the corporeal powers, and upon perfect digestion, which repairs them, that . . . the loss of an ounce of this humour would weaken more than that of forty ounces of blood. . . . can anyone doubt of the various ills that must necessarily flow from a profuse evacuation of a humour that is so precious?'[22] We can also apprehend the potency of 'seminal liquor' by the far-reaching physical changes that take place during male puberty and, conversely, as a result of castration. It is thus possible for Tissot to explain his pathological observations in physiological terms, although these hardly accounted for how such 'filthy practices' started and took hold of their victims.

When it came to particular cases of children, like the little boy from Montpellier, where Tissot had studied, he stressed the role of external agents to give a *social* account of the problem's origin. This is the advice he offered to parents on the subject of servants and preceptors. I give the passage in full in order to convey the range of metaphors Tissot employs:

I could produce but too great a number of young plants, who have been lost by the very gardener who was instructed with their rearing. There are in this kind of culture, gardeners of both sexes. But I shall be asked where is the remedy to this evil? The answer is within my sphere, and I shall give it in a concise manner. Be particularly careful in the choice of a preceptor, watch over him and his pupil with that vigilance, which an attentive and enlightened father of a family exerts to know what is done in the darkest recesses of his house; use that vigilance which discovers the coppice where the deer has taken shelter, when it has escaped all other eyes: this is always possible when it is earnestly pursued. . . . Never leave young people alone with their masters, if these are suspected; and prevent their having any correspondence with the servants.[23]

There is an undertow of violence here which is all the more striking for the contrast between the idea of children as plants, which was common at this time, and the idea of the father as a hunter. Likening children to plants could serve a variety of purposes, such as evoking a sense of latency, but generally it presented them as passive, adaptive and malleable, easily trained, and in the domain of nature.[24] The hunting image is not only strikingly violent, but it refers to deliberate, organised human behaviour, it contains movement, terror and persecution. But who or what is the father hunting? Is it the masturbating child, the corrupting tutor or sexuality itself that the deer stands for? Yet the father is more than a hunter: he is also to become an all-seeing eye or a beam of light which dispels darkness, and with it the privacy of the child. Tissot's solution to the 'problem' of childhood sexuality lay not in medicine but in the social arrangements of the household.

22. Ibid., p. 10.
23. Ibid., p. 43; I discuss this same passage in a different context in Chapter 10.
24. Book I of Rousseau's *Émile*, 1762, is full of such references. A less well-known example is Cadogan, 1748.

That Tissot's concerns were more social-cum-moral than narrowly medical is amply borne out by his treatment of other themes. Furthermore, he conceived the issue of the control of sexuality in terms of individual responsibility. We can see this in the fact that, concerned though he is with masturbation in adolescent boys, Tissot condemned *all* excessive sex, even within marriage. His examples moved between masturbation and heterosexual sex, and some of these stress that coition can be dangerous to some people even when not excessive. Individuals who do indulge themselves sexually are taking the first step on the road to suicide.[25] In addition, Tissot repeatedly stressed the melancholy of afflicted individuals, and melancholy is pre-eminently the disease of the self-absorbed; it was a recurrent theme in the literature on masturbation. In his edition of Tissot, the early nineteenth-century French hygienist Hallé nicely turned this association around by claiming that it is *reading* Tissot that induces melancholy![26]

When Tissot came to list the reprehensible habits likely to get the young into trouble, they were all associated with a self-indulgent, luxurious lifestyle: 'idleness and inactivity, lying too long a-bed, over soft beds, succulent aromatics, salt and vinous diet, suspicious friends, licentious productions . . . should sedulously be avoided'.[27] Narcissism seems to be the trouble here. Isolation and self-indulgence were to be deplored precisely because they were anti-social. Their likely outcome had to be recorded. To get this point across, Tissot launched into a list of symptoms which constituted a verbal attack of some force, where he seems to revel in the power of his own words:

A description of the danger to a person who is addicted to the evil, is perhaps the most powerful motive of correction. It is a dreadful portrait sufficient to make him retreat with horror . . . The whole mass fallen to decay; all the bodily senses and all the faculties of the soul weakened; the loss of imagination and memory; and imbecility, contempt, shame, ignominy, its constant attendants; all the functions disturbed, suspended, and painful; continued disorders, disagreeable, capricious, and disgusting; violent pains ever renewing; all the disorders of old age in the prime of youth; an incapacity for all the functions for which man was created; the humiliating character of being an useless load upon earth; the mortification to which it is daily exposed, a distaste for all decent pleasures; lassitude, an aversion for others, and at length for self; life appears horrible; the dread which every moment starts at suicide; anguish worse than pain; remorse, which daily increases; and which doubtless gains fresh strength; when the soul is no longer weakened by its union with the body; and serves perhaps for eternal punishment – a fire that is never extinguished.[28]

There is a relentlessness about Tissot's description that suggests an element of pleasure to be derived from the recounting of pain and misery in others. This prose displays one of the characteristics of discourses on sexuality identified

25. Tissot, 1771, see e.g. p. 5.
26. Lejeune, 1974, p. 1016.
27. Tissot, 1772, p. 124.
28. Ibid., p. 126.

earlier: it is potentially infinite, since more and more stories, examples and symptoms can be piled on top of one another. Even the sentence structure and punctuation confirm this. Equally interesting, however, is the content of Tissot's description-cum-denunciation.

By turning his attention inwards, the masturbator disintegrates as an individual self and as a social being. 'Useless load' is a term for social non-existence or, perhaps worse, for dependence upon others. Tissot's elaborate descriptions, case studies, anecdotes, quotations and stories can be read as pointing to a definition of health and its preservation in terms of the correct form of selfhood. In childhood, total control will be exercised over offspring so that their relationships with social inferiors in particular are mediated through the father. At a symbolic level, Tissot developed the idea of a precious gift being husbanded; parents patrol children to prevent the profligacy of precious resources. Such surveillance sets in place the habits which, for the rest of an individual's life, act as a guarantee against excessive introspection and self-indulgence. To do otherwise is to lose one's self, and hence to lose social legitimation – the consequences of the self-regarding dispersal of the most vital of vital fluids. It is ironic that Rousseau, according to Lejeune, also associated masturbation with introspection, but not in Tissot's sense.[29] Rather, for Rousseau, it was related to the creative imagination and reverie. Yet in *Émile* he condemned it, in terms very like those of Tissot, whom he admired.

We cannot, of course, know precisely how widespread this vision of ill-health and loss of selfhood as two facets of the same coin was, although the association between health and competence seems to have been common. Many medical advice books rehearsed similar arguments, even if relatively few of them developed such powerful images. Similarly, philanthropic and reformist literature of the period manifested precisely these concerns. Two examples spring to mind: writings about the reform of prostitutes, which concentrated on re-establishing self-control and self-esteem; and attacks on male homosexuality, which often registered fears about the loss of individual and class identity.[30] The notion of 'unnatural acts' links these areas. Such acts threatened to rob people of their fully human status, by making them closer to animals, or by degrading them into helplessness or dependence. Yet this notion of the 'unnatural' is deeply problematic in an era noted by many scholars as one in which all things natural were celebrated, the diversity of human existence explored and the commitment to sex as part of the natural order was particularly strong. Thus the boundary between 'natural' and 'unnatural' had to be negotiated with care at that time. I would suggest that this was achieved partly through a distinction between productive and unproductive sex. By this I do not simply mean procreative or non-procreative sex, although that is involved. Rather, 'productive' refers to those sexual activities which have positive outcomes for individuals and for society as a whole, not to a populationism that advocates babies at any price. Those who render themselves mentally,

29. Lejeune, 1974, pp. 1020–2.
30. Jones, 1978; Speck, 1980; Bray, 1982; Trumbach, 1977.

physically and socially incompetent through masturbation are clearly indulging in unproductive sex. By contrast, a married couple enjoying moderate sex, even if conception rarely results, would be an example of those who use their sexuality productively and responsibly.

Tissot was particularly concerned that young people who masturbated would be disinclined to marry – a concern which also featured in the contemporary literature on prostitution. Celibacy and sterility were feared consequences of onanism – according to Tissot, women in particular became averse to the marriage bed. Not surprisingly, Tissot worked with a profound commitment to gender difference. We may take gender here as a shorthand for the study of an aspect of nature and for a language-cum-framework through which wider issues could be explored. For example, denunciations of male homosexuality in this period often spoke of 'effeminacy' and 'degeneracy'. Tissot, by contrast, associated female homosexuality with the usurpation of a masculine role. It is notable that when discussing the effects of masturbation on women he moved so seamlessly to the question of homosexuality, without of course using that term. He attacked homosexual women on two grounds. First, he associated lesbianism (not his word) with deformed, over-large genitalia – that is, with monstrosity. Second, he accused them of being over-masculine: 'some women who were thus imperfect, glorying, perhaps, in this kind of resemblance, seized upon the functions of virility'.[31] In effect, it was being stated that two complementary beings were a necessary precondition for 'natural' sexual relations to take place. While these manoeuvres around unnaturalness might work quite well in relation to the sexuality of adults, the cases of children put them under considerable strain, because children were so frequently taken as a paradigm of 'the natural'.[32] If a sexual impulse was natural and children equally so, then an activity so often associated with children would seem to qualify for that epithet too. To resist this implication involved some elaborate reconceptualisations. For Tissot, the sexuality of children should be latent, not actualised.

We have already noted one of the ways in which Tissot accounted for precocious sexual activity in children – by identifying an external agent, often from a lower social class than the child, as the cause of corruption.[33] He also believed in the importance of education in the regulation of 'natural' propensities. Human nature, if it is not to be too disruptive, needs moulding in the correct forms. Here Tissot was in line with so many of his contemporaries, as he was too in the way in which he thought about this moulding, educative process as one that internalises moral norms. In children the process is still under way and hence necessarily incomplete, rendering them peculiarly vulnerable. Yet it must be completed if they are to become adults who are not socially dependent or too self-absorbed, both conditions which lead to inadequate development, signalled by poor health. Autonomy without narcissism, productive social relations without dependence were his goals. Tissot thus defined health in terms of a

31. Tissot, 1772, pp. 44–5.
32. Charlton, 1984, pp. 139–53.
33. Fairchilds, 1984, ch. 7.

particular kind of self, one that is not self-indulgent and hence has that degree of self-control and competence which allows it to function in society. There is a further implication: the location where such healthy selves are constructed is 'the family', an abstraction that can simultaneously hold a belief in sexuality as part of nature and a commitment to its moral regulation for social ends. While clearly not all health problems raised the particularly tricky problems that masturbation did, most of them could be related to questions of lifestyle, habit, constitution and temperament, suggesting precisely the same issues about the healthy self and its conditions of existence, as well as about its intimate relations with other selves, particularly within the family.[34]

Like other medical authors of advice books, Tissot presented means by which control could be successfully internalised, and, like them, he deluged the reader with a turbulent, conflict-ridden barrage of prose that created powerful images of adequacy and inadequacy, a dichotomy understood through gender, nature and the family, and which, above all, differentiated 'natural' from 'unnatural' development. At the same time, his text, which is acutely aware of its own practices and their potential transgressiveness, suggests, even draws attention to, the special pleasures to be derived from talking about forbidden topics. It is misleading to attribute to Tissot a reorientation of attitudes about masturbation and sexuality away from religion and towards medicine since he blended religious and medical idioms. Although he took health as a major criterion of judgement, the medical focus was far from exclusive. In fact his inclusiveness is striking. Notions of sin, evil, crime and punishment were all incorporated into a larger vision, which sets improper sexual activity in the context of class relations, family dynamics, responsibility and dependency, allowing him to move effortlessly between individual and social identity. Tissot shifted equally easily between patients' observable symptoms and their attitudes, feelings and unseen behaviour.

If it seems worthwhile to examine popular medical books as examples of particular kinds of discourses, a number of implications follow. First, we should be more attentive to the textual riches of such publications and make common cause with literary critics. Second, if specific examples of popular writing achieved prominence in the past, an explanation of this in terms of their literary properties may be more helpful than supposing, for example, that they cater to contemporary 'neuroses'.[35] Third, if the metaphors of medicine are constitutive of the ideas and theories of practitioners, then textual analysis necessarily becomes an indispensable historical tool. Fourth, since the writing itself has embedded within it a whole host of social preoccupations and tensions, understanding its language reveals how world-views are both confirmed and called into question. Finally, focusing on textuality helps us avoid the unfortunate dualism present in most treatments of 'popularisation', since language constitutes the common cultural core, which is no less fundamental to the science and medicine of the Enlightenment than it is to 'literature' as conventionally defined.

34. Donzelot, 1980; Foucault, 1979, vol. 1.
35. MacDonald, 1967, p. 431.

AFTERWORD

Since the first version of this chapter was written considerably more attention has been paid to medical popularisation and especially to the two outstanding eighteenth-century figures, Buchan and Tissot.[36] This shift reflects an increasing interest in the culture of medicine and in the ways in which medical values are formed and propagated. Furthermore, the new attention being given to popularisation fits in with current interpretations of the Enlightenment, and with an emphasis on the reformism generally present in eighteenth- and early nineteenth-century societies. We now give much greater prominence to the growth of consumerism over the eighteenth century, and purchasing popular medical works can be seen in just this way. At the same time historians argue that profound changes in economic and above all commercial relationships were inseparable from social and political shifts, for example, the development of a public sphere in which opinions were formed and debated. Hence it seems plausible to interpret the growth of medical publishing that openly sought extended audiences – I would include medical periodicals here along with popular works – as being indicative of broader social changes, such as rises in the production and consumption of printed materials, and growing interest in philanthropy and reform in the service of building a strong, stable nation, dedicated to the promotion of moderation in all things.

There can be no doubt that the popular medical literature of the later eighteenth century was reformist, although it arose out of a wide range of political positions. It was reformist in a highly specific sense. Much of it was directed at the prevention not only of misery, ill-health and death but also of quackery. It is true that several books contained remedies and cures, but the emphasis was on advice, self-management and precautions. Implicitly there was also a message to fellow medical practitioners about the need for regulation and control to prevent the people becoming the dupes of charlatans. The new actions these works hoped to provoke in their readers occurred at individual and familial levels, and involved thinking afresh about the conduct of daily life. Thus they were holistic in orientation, and bore directly on people's sense of themselves and of their intimate relationships. In this respect they laid little emphasis on medical ideas that were being developed at the same time and that have been seen as leading directly to the scientific medicine of the nineteenth century. Largely absent here was talk of localised pathologies, for example. Popular medicine concerned itself with daily experience, with lives as they were lived – this was not the static world of the autopsy, but the fluid world of regimen.[37] Although lifestyle medicine has never ceased to exist, and is now

---

36. Porter, 1992 is largely an analysis of Tissot and Buchan and of their influence and dissemination in a number of countries. Recent work on sexuality in the eighteenth century includes: Rousseau and Porter, 1987; Porter and Hall, 1995, chs 3 and 4; Porter and Teich, 1994, esp. ch. 6 (by Porter); Porter and Roberts, 1996, esp. ch. 6 (by Jones); Stanton, 1993; Bennett and Rosario, 1995.

37. I make this point because it might be thought that Tissot was constructing, in Laqueur's phrase, a set of 'humanitarian narratives'. One example he uses is reports of autopsies. Although the phrase is useful, it is not quite apt for Tissot, as I explain below – Hunt, 1989, ch. 7 (by Laqueur). Tissot does, however, do

healthier than ever before, its eighteenth-century form must be understood as the specific conjunction of a number of different conditions – the state of print culture, models of health, class formation, political priorities and so on.

Cultural historians of the eighteenth century have insisted on the larger importance of forms of writing which, while not invented in that century, came to prominence during it: the novel, case histories, periodicals and newspapers and so on.[38] Popular medical works are indeed interesting as forms of writing and they used narratives shaped by fiction, case histories and reportage. I suggested that a stress on their textual complexities is more fruitful than a concern about their epistemological status. Inquiries about the origins and quality of the knowledge they purported to impart are unproductive, because underlying them are assumptions about distinctions between high quality or pure knowledge on the one hand and diluted or applied knowledge on the other. The distinctions between popular and polite and high and low culture are equally problematic, and historians rarely use them now without glossing or seeking models that emphasise the interpenetration of forms of culture rather than two opposed types.[39]

It is not a coincidence that the eighteenth century has often been construed as a low point in medical advancement. Since historians cannot find valued innovations, they have turned to medical cultures. Of course a number of more positive trends in the field have encouraged the study of medicine as a form of culture. Nonetheless, work on popular medicine seems to me to have had difficulty ridding itself of older assumptions about progress, science and authoritative knowledge.[40] Publications classified as popular are sometimes treated as if they were lightweight, intellectually speaking. It is not that we should rate them otherwise on this particular scale, but that the scale itself is inappropriate. Rather than measure their weightiness, I propose that we unravel the emotional and social positions popular medical writings occupied.

Furthermore, an emphasis on the textual practices of popular medical writings helps us to, as it were, get inside the populariser's head. Naturally texts never give direct or unproblematic access to their authors, but they do establish moods, anxieties, furies, hopes, in this case providing evidence for the formation of medical identities. Texts reveal raw spots. For instance, in the case of Tissot's volume on onanism, we have identified a number of special anxieties – loss of coherent selfhood, the dangers of falling to the level of brutes, blurred gender roles, ambiguities between illness, sin and crime – that have wide historical resonances. When Tissot wrote about marital relations and domestic arrangements he was not alone, but adding his voice to existing ones – he fully participated in trends of the period, for example, in his concern

everything possible to assure readers of the truth of his accounts, for example, using exact dates, which is a point Laqueur draws attention to.

38. Armstrong, 1987 is an influential example. See also Shevelow, 1989.

39. Paulson, 1979 is an early and interesting attempt to make the distinction between popular and polite do rather different work. Brewer, 1997 draws on elite and popular culture without creating a simple dualism between them.

40. This is evident even in some of the chapters of Porter, 1992.

about the size and quality of the population. Furthermore, his ideas are inseparable from the forms in which he expressed them. His prose seeks to give a
level of truthful detail that will be both convincing and moving to readers. He
quotes from letters he has received, and their immediate intimacy fits with their
subject matter – sexual activity. In moving his readers, Tissot has not constructed a 'humanitarian narrative', since the remedies lie not in the sympathetic responses of readers to those whose woes are related, but in the possibility
that individuals and families will change their behaviour, indeed will change
their attitudes to themselves, and in this sense Tissot was more an exponent of
the cautionary tale than of stories that prompt first sympathetic identification
and then reformist action.[41] Insofar as Tissot provokes change, it is to be
largely inside the heads of his readers and their families.

Literary and cultural historians have recently found fresh ways of exploring
fiction and other genres in the eighteenth century so as to point up their
ideological centrality, particularly for gender relations and for the family.[42] In
their turn gender and family acted as mediators for just about every other
domain. Sexual disorder, like bodily conditions and the idea of health, was
commonly a figure for social and political chaos, and since the direct stakes
in individual and familial health were high, popular medical writings, which
addressed such issues and acted as a bridge between them, are of considerable
significance – a significance that attending to their textuality helps to bring out.

It may seem naive still to be asking questions about the nature of popularisation. Yet the innocent eye can be helpful, and there are further insights to
be derived from careful attention to writing strategies and to the manner in
which readers are constructed. Medicine was profoundly literary in the eighteenth century, and despite significant amounts of scholarship in this area over
the last ten years, the nature and implications of this literariness invite further
exploration.[43]

41. Hunt, 1989, ch. 7 where Laqueur stresses the philanthropic action that ought to follow the reading
of humanitarian narratives.

42. In addition to Armstrong, 1987, see Porter and Roberts, 1996, esp. ch. 6 (by Jones); Rousseau and
Porter, 1987; and Boucé, 1980, which contain many literary and cultural essays; see also Armstrong and
Tennenhouse, 1987; Zomchick, 1993.

43. Cf. Bynum and Porter, 1993a, ch. 65, Medicine and Literature (by Neve) and the journal *Literature
and Medicine*. Rosner, 1991 gives an interesting account of how what could be called literary issues were part
of a medical education.

CHAPTER SEVEN

Medical Mediations:
Mind, Body and the Guillotine

In myth and in history, the medicine of the French Revolution has long been celebrated. Philippe Pinel's loosing of the chains of the insane, and the 'birth of the clinic', that is, the rise of Paris hospital medicine, are the two most obvious examples.[1] There was, it has been asserted, a medical revolution that took place in France at this time, which enjoyed an intimate relationship with '1789':

the medical revolution that took place in these years constitutes a microcosm of the macrocosm that we call the French Revolution, and each revolution influenced the other. The transformation of institutions under a revolutionary public social philosophy affected the new course of health care for people. New medical approaches and techniques, as well as the new hospital system which emerged from this era, helped to lay the foundation for modern medicine in France. Revolution and war were not only the anvil and hammer that shaped a new France; they helped to forge a new medicine as well.[2]

Such a claim rests primarily on the institutional and professional innovations of the period. It is also common to identify the revolutionary period as a significant one for medical knowledge. In addition to Pinel, the anatomist Xavier Bichat is probably the best-known medical thinker of the period, although historians can point to a whole galaxy of medical theorists and practitioners who were major contributors to their fields.

Furthermore, a number of these men were totally caught up in the general stream of revolutionary events, and, in some instances, the nature of their revolutionary activity was closely linked to their medical formation.[3] An emphasis on 'great names', major institutions and professional organisation misses, however, the most striking quality of medicine – its cultural centrality. By its very nature such a presence is hard to describe. It involves, for instance, the use

---

An earlier version of this chapter appeared in Italian in 1984. Translations from the French are my own.

1. Foucault, 1973; Chabbert, 1974, vol. 10, pp. 611–14. Recent discussions of the revolution/medical revolution conjunction include Weiner, 1993, who mentions many of Guillotin's reformist activities; Outram, 1989; Williams, 1994.

2. Vess, 1975, p. 8.

3. Ackerknecht, 1967; Haigh, 1984; Staum, 1980, Weiner, 1993; Williams, 1994.

of metaphors of disease, ideas of public health, images of body parts, and play on the notion of therapy for both the body and the body politic. In addition, it involves the central issue explored here – the mediating properties of medicine. Medical discourses explored, often without the fact being openly stated, political and social concerns. Medical language is rich, wide-ranging and capable of touching such a broad spectrum of human experience that its potential as a mediator is unusually vast. Mind–body interaction – a pressing question raised by the guillotine – is an exceptionally good example of the mediation phenomenon, because it was, in its ideal form, an exemplification of ordered, coherent and harmonious relationships. The guillotine – that powerfully disruptive machine – was indeed an apt symbol of revolution.

Charlotte Corday d'Armont was guillotined for the murder of Marat on 17th July 1793. A story was immediately spread around that when the executioner held up her head to the crowd, and slapped one of her cheeks in retribution for her deed, she visibly showed her indignation. As one contemporary medical commentator put it: 'Who did not see Charlotte Corday's face blush with indignation when the detestable executioner, who held in his hand that calm and beautiful head, gave it a slap.'[4] The implication of this account of her last minutes was clear; death was not immediate upon decapitation, for the head was capable of movements: grinding of teeth, convulsions, movements of lips and eyes. These suggested the continued presence in the head of something that could be described, according to preference, as a soul, will, mind or self. It seemed to many observers that such signs were unambiguous expressions of conscious exertions on the part of the guillotine's victims, prompting the idea that pre-arranged signals between those sentenced to death and their friends would prove the issue one way or the other. Those who maintained that consciousness persisted after decapitation further argued that death was not painless, but, on the contrary, that the sensations produced by decapitation were exceedingly vivid. Consciousness could therefore continue, they believed, despite such drastic bodily mutilation.

The story about Charlotte Corday was only one, although certainly the most dramatic, of many anecdotes told about the persistence of life in severed heads and bodies during the French Revolution. Such mythology expressed a fundamental anxiety about the process of death which gripped the entire nation, and which provided a set of powerful images for European literature. Particularly significant was the way in which the guillotine became virtually synonymous with the entire revolutionary period. This was pre-eminently true in Charles Dickens's *A Tale of Two Cities* (1859), which, drawing heavily on Carlyle's conservative account of the French Revolution, never actually described an execution until the final dramatic scene, yet evoked vividly an image of the popular culture surrounding the guillotine.[5]

4. Oelsner, 1795, vol. 3, pp. 463–7, quotation from 464–5. General works on the death penalty and the guillotine include Goulet, 1981 and 1983; Kershaw, 1958; Laurence, n.d [1932]; Pertue, 1983; Arasse, 1989; Janes, 1991. For a narrative of Corday's encounter with Marat, see Schama, 1989, pp. 729–41.
5. Dickens, 1970. 'The guillotine's technical and visual character allowed it to acquire what we might term an *iconic resemblance* to the Jacobin Revolution' – Arasse, 1989, p. 5.

Medical practitioners occupied a central place in debates about the guillotine, for it was they, after all, who had given the machine their imprimatur. As early as October 1789, Dr Joseph-Ignace Guillotin, physician and freemason, raised the question of capital punishment in the Constituent Assembly. It was agreed that no distinction should be made between those of different social ranks where the form of execution was concerned – all should be decapitated, thereby extending a noble 'privilege' to the people. In his speeches in favour of the proposed new laws, Guillotin referred to a mechanical device to do the job quickly and efficiently. The basic idea was by no means new. It was received with enthusiasm because the guillotine appeared to be an instrument of humanity and equality. In addition, there were technical reasons why using swords on a routine basis for decapitation was unsatisfactory. A successful, that is quick and painless, execution could not be guaranteed.[6]

A guillotine was finally built after Antoine Louis, Permanent Secretary of the Academy of Surgeons, had given his opinion that a decapitating machine could easily be built 'the effect of which would be infallible. This apparatus . . . would cause no sensation and would hardly be noticed.'[7] In April 1792 trials were carried out at Bicêtre on three corpses, which were then examined by Guillotin and Louis among others. From the initial suggestion that such a machine be built through to its actual construction, medical practitioners were among the prime movers. It is not surprising therefore to find that, when a heated disagreement about the guillotine took place in 1795, very shortly after censorship of the press was relaxed, medical practitioners and medical arguments defined the terms of debate. Contributions to newspapers and magazines on the question of the guillotine in 1795 provide a valuable grid through which ideas then current about the relationship between mind and body can be examined.

The medical debate was sparked off in Brumaire, year 4 (October 1795), by a letter from the anatomist Samuel Thomas Soemmerring, published in the *Moniteur Universel*.[8] Soemmerring condemned the barbarity of the French for their use of the guillotine, setting out a number of physiological arguments in favour of hanging as an alternative that was considerably less painful. Interestingly, all commentators agreed that victims should, on humanitarian grounds, be spared as much pain as possible. It was the pronouncement of the death sentence, rather than its actual execution, that constituted the punishment. To support his views Soemmerring drew on accounts by those revived after hanging. In common with people who had nearly drowned, they described the sensations they had experienced as being like those of falling asleep. Furthermore, patients with damaged crania could be induced to sleep, Soemmerring claimed, by pushing on the exposed part of the brain. In hanging, blood accumulated in the brain and resulted in a build up of pressure which produced the

---

6. Soubiran, 1964, chs 9–12; Weiner, 1972, pp. 85–9; 'H.P.B', 1966, p. 230, Outram, 1989, ch. 7; Janes, 1991, esp. pp. 32–46.

7. Quoted in Soubiran, 1964, p. 131; the text of Louis's statement may also be found in Stewart, 1951, pp. 343–6.

8. Soemmerring, an IV, pp. 378–9; Soemmerring's letter was dated 20 May 1793.

sensation of sleepiness. Of course, there was no comparable first-hand evidence from those who had been decapitated!

The discussions on the guillotine therefore centred on how the persistent movements of heads and bodies should be interpreted, for they were the only empirical evidence afforded by decapitation. While those who entered the fray against Soemmerring, like the medical *idéologue* P.J.G. Cabanis, discounted the story about Charlotte Corday as pure fabrication, the general facts were never in dispute. Heads and bodies did move and convulsions could be induced by stimulating the exposed spinal cord. Furthermore, it was generally agreed that the brain could still receive sensations from amputated parts, while the Italian pioneer of work on electricity, Luigi Galvani, and others, had shown the persistence of reactivity in amputated limbs.

The disagreement concerned not what had been observed, be it in a clinical or an experimental context, or on the scaffold, but the significance that could legitimately be attached to these events. In the writings of those who discussed the guillotine's effects, several different levels of meaning can be discerned. The debates became a focus for the expression of a number of philosophical, scientific, moral and political concerns. There were two kinds of 'medical mediations' here. First, there was the question of the mediations between mind and body.[9] Descartes's legacy was in this respect a mixed blessing. He had framed a clear philosophical distinction between mind and body while leaving unresolved precisely how the interaction between the two took place. The Cartesian formulation was particularly troublesome because it separated into two what common sense suggested was inevitably tangled. It is important to recognise both the attraction of clear conceptual boundaries, and the equally strong revulsion felt for the simplification of daily experience that they represented. By the 1790s, there had emerged a complex set of languages, many of them drawing on 'the metaphor of organisation', through which the mediations between mind and body were explored, expressed, evaded and repressed.[10] Everyone agreed on the centrality of the mind–body question for natural philosophy and medicine, thereby making the issue of precisely how they interacted unavoidable. The vocabularies employed in such discussions were, however, conceptually rather loose. Many terms were used that had both common-sense and technical meanings, opening up the possibility of sometimes unpredictable and often hilarious imaginative associations arising. Literature again offers an instructive illustration: in the complex play on concepts of mind–body interaction as in Laurence Sterne's *Tristram Shandy* (1759–67). In fact, ambiguity was built in to key notions such as sensibility and irritability.[11]

There was a growing desire among those working in the life sciences in the late eighteenth century to avoid simply describing stable, physical characters and to capture instead physiological processes, which were constantly changing.

9. Rousseau, 1990; Smith, 1997.
10. Figlio, 1976. 'Organisation' meant, at its most basic, structural complexity, and its use in the life sciences usually indicated a pledge against dualism.
11. Sterne, 1967; Rogers, 1986. In France, Diderot's writings exhibited similar play with the ambiguity of key terms in the life sciences and with the complexity of mind–body relationships.

A vocabulary which stressed motion, dynamism, process and change was sought. For example, when the natural philosopher Lamarck wrote about the nervous systems of complex vertebrates and human beings, he evidently found it difficult to develop a language that avoided both materialism and vitalism. He resolved the difficulty primarily by the use of the nervous fluid as a physical intermediate between mind, that is, the operations of the brain, and the body.[12] There were a number of key terms in the bio-medical sciences of the late eighteenth century – irritability, sensibility, constitution, temperament, habit and consciousness – and they were used in a bewildering variety of ways.

The second kind of medical mediation in the guillotine debates stems from the broad social issues canvassed through them. The importance of general cultural themes and of symbolism in medical reactions to the guillotine is inescapable. We have already noted that relations between mind and body were at issue. More specifically, the implications of separating the head from the trunk by means of the guillotine were involved. The very ideas of 'head' and 'headship' were rich with meaning, moving as they do from a specific physical place to a form of social and political authority. First in Britain and then in France, kings had lost their heads in revolutionary episodes during which previous beliefs about monarchy and sovereignty had been challenged. Louis XVI had, less than three years earlier, been guillotined by a regime seeking to divest, not only him as an individual, but monarchy as a system, of power. The intention was to substitute the sovereignty of the people – a body that could survive without the old head. A new image of the body politic was being developed that involved extreme decentralisation, and, it has been argued, new physiological models of the body were simultaneously emerging with a corresponding emphasis. The sources of coherent action, be they political or physiological, and the conditions under which natural and social laws operated smoothly were called into question by the effects of the guillotine on its victims.[13]

The connection between the human body and the body politic is plain enough. Not only was the head and all it stood for highly significant, so also was the face of the victim. It was, of course, a commonplace that facial expressions, like body gestures, revealed the passions and also the moral content of human relationships.[14] According to physiognomists, what was publicly visible offered privileged insights into internal states, and these insights revealed, above all, the state of the soul, thereby giving rise to a devout knowledge of the inner life. In the case of guillotine victims it was the facial movements, perceived as expressions of consciousness, which elicited such passionate responses from commentators. Jean Joseph Sue, whose interests included physiognomy and artistic anatomy, entered the debate in support of Soemmerring's position that consciousness, and hence pain, persisted after decapitation; he saw the face as

12. Jordanova, 1981a; Corsi, 1988, esp. pp. 152–4 and 191–6. Lamarck is relevant here because of the close relationships, social and conceptual, between medicine and natural history, as several chapters in Jardine *et al.*, 1996 indicate.
13. Pickstone, 1981.
14. Bryson, 1981, esp. ch. 2. Bynum and Porter, 1993b. Chapter 3 also discusses physiognomy. Cf. Tytler, 1982; Jordanova, 1986a and 1993a; Shookman, 1993.

'a summary' of the three levels of sensations which characterised the three components of human life: the animal, the moral and the intellectual. Each one was expressed in a particular zone of the face. Sue thought that a form of death that separated these three tiers and their associated anatomical centres was the worst of all. The 'best' forms affected all three simultaneously, such as asphyxia. Although he was not explicit on this point, we may infer from Sue's physiognomical remarks that the contorted movements on the faces of the guillotined revealed precisely the gruesome disruption of the three vital levels which so deeply disturbed him.[15] Medical mediations in this second sense should emphatically not be viewed as involving elements that were extraneous to more central or more 'scientific' concerns. The links between the physiological, moral and political arguments were by no means tenuous or arcane, but intertwining strands in the cultural fabric, visible and clear.

The two kinds of medical mediations emerge on a closer examination of the debate on the guillotine. At its centre were six participants. Three of them, Soemmerring, Sue and Oelsner (who had met Soemmerring in Switzerland), argued that conscious life persisted after the separation of head from body, making victims suffer in a manner which was medically, morally and politically unacceptable.[16] Their three opponents were Cabanis, Wedekind from Göttingen, a convert to the French republican cause who served for several years in French military hospitals, and Le Pelletier, a Parisian practitioner.[17] They claimed that death by guillotine was instantaneous and painless. Both sides were united, however, in calling for the abolition of the death penalty and in expressing revulsion against its excessive use – feelings that could be more safely put into print since the law controlling the press had been repealed. We can discern in the writings of these people three distinct, though related, levels of argument: political, moral and physiological.

While no one wished to defend the unrestrained use of the guillotine, there was clearly a difference in the political attitudes of the two sides. Those who claimed that its victims suffered could easily use this as a basis for accusations of barbarity against the republic. Those who saw no evidence of suffering were, in fact, more sympathetic to a moderate revolutionary position. Among those who were convinced that pain was felt, Oelsner was the most explicit on the point, when he railed against 'abominable brutality':

Are you not ashamed of a stupid law that entrusts the rights of citizens to executioners! There is no need for an executioner in a well-ordered state; if they exist, such beings are marks of shame. I would never be a citizen of a country where the executioner would be my representative and judge.[18]

---

15. Sue, 1795. This was written by Jean Joseph Sue, a member of a medical family, several members of which were active in this period. Similar theories may be found in his other publications, 1788, 1797a (an V), 1797b (an VI). Corsi notes Sue's preoccupation with the nervous system (Corsi, 1988, p. 74).

16. Soemmerring, 1795; see also notes 4, 8, 18. The fact that Oelsner was a 'political writer' (Outram, 1989, pp. 111, 181) does not detract from the 'medical' nature of the debates as I have interpreted them here.

17. Cabanis, 1795, p. 155ff., also 1798, 1803, and in Lehec and Cazeneuve, 1956; Wedekind, an IV, pp. 395–6; Le Pelletier, an IV, p. 426. On Cabanis see Staum, 1980.

18. Oelsner, 1795, see note 1, p. 467.

Furthermore, he identified the use of the guillotine with political fanaticism, offensive because its public humiliation of the victim constituted a violation of human modesty on a par with female nakedness. The harm was done not just by the guillotine itself, but by those who were present when it was used – the mob, 'a rabble of cannibals' to use Oelsner's words. The guillotine stood for the breakdown of well-organised government – it was a symptom of decay in a young political being from which so much had been expected. Severed heads and writhing bodies bathed in blood represented the prevailing chaos in the body politic.[19]

Soemmerring, Oelsner and Sue, who were all more sympathetic to the idea of a vital principle than their opponents, saw in the convulsions of severed heads what Cabanis, somewhat sarcastically, called 'moral movements' – the human will striving to assert itself to the last. Volition was at the heart of these and related debates. Those like Lamarck and Cabanis who were committed to producing a naturalistic account of the human nervous system, sought to dispense with the will by redefining it as the product of a complex physiological faculty. They found that Napoleonic France provided a far less sympathetic environment for such ideas than the early 1790s had been. In fact a central feature of the conservative philosophy of the early nineteenth century was its reassertion of the concept of will in a reaction against the naturalism of earlier decades.[20]

The 'cannibalistic mob' was the embodiment of human passion run riot; it permitted the expression of the baser aspects of human nature. Although they were untroubled by the effect of the guillotine on the will, Cabanis and those who agreed with him were far from indifferent to the role of the mob in public executions. They too were concerned about the audience and their role in the public spectacle of death.[21] Capital punishment did not merely affect the unfortunate victim, it was closely related to general social attitudes. Cabanis, Wedekind and Le Pelletier actually condemned the guillotine for working too quickly, morally speaking; those present saw only blood, to the sight of which they quickly became habituated. Rather than executions serving as positive lessons in morality, the guillotine's effects were negative and principally served to harden attitudes. It was at this point that the political and the moral arguments intersected.

The most important moral question was the suffering of the victim. There was general agreement that once the death penalty had been pronounced, the

19. This perspective on the guillotine was expressed by those who were committed to a dualistic model of human beings, probably subscribed to some notion of an autonomous will, and were likely to espouse a conservative social, theological and political philosophy, emphasising external souces of authority and power. The similarities with Chateaubriand are remarkable; in describing his experiences of the Revolution, the totally unsettling image of severed heads, the lack of control – akin to sexual anarchy – and the charge of cannibalism are vividly evoked (Baldick, 1965, pp. 121, 127, 128–9), cf. Chapter 5. See also Paulson, 1983, e.g. p. 23 and, for an extremely stimulating discussion of how to think about violence in the Revolution, Fehér, 1990, ch. 8 (by Singer).

20. Boas, 1925; Chapter 5 of this volume.

21. Outram, 1989, ch. 7 is particularly concerned with the audience, both actual and as imagined by victims. In her analysis of responses to the guillotine, Outram stresses the class dynamics between largely middle-class victims and lower-class spectators. Janes, 1991 also considers the question of audiences.

condemned person was entitled to every consideration. Cabanis and Wedekind extended their concern to the relatives of those who lost their lives. They found Soemmerring and his supporters to be callous and irresponsible in making public their disquiet about the suffering the guillotine caused without the support of stronger evidence. Their writings might torment those who had lost loved ones and who would now have cause to believe that the guillotine tortured its victims by a slow and agonising death. If either side in the debate recognised specifically religious implications stemming from the guillotine, they did not say so. Only Sue voiced any thought of an explicitly spiritual kind, when he defined the vital principle as separate from matter, and suggested that after death it was reunited with 'this universal cause'.[22]

Thus, the guillotine was widely condemned on a variety of moral and political grounds, irrespective of whether death was thought to be painful or not. Cabanis, for example, concluded that, physiologically speaking, the guillotine represented a humane and efficient means of carrying out the death penalty, while on moral and political grounds he was resolutely opposed to it.

Turning to the physiological arguments, those on Soemmerring's side believed convulsions or movements of any kind to be signs of continued feelings, and they stressed that sensibility could continue even after movements ceased. Furthermore, it was claimed, the brain went on functioning even when no blood was flowing to it. Supporting evidence was drawn from experiments on animal electricity, from clinical observation of pathological conditions, and, in Sue's case, from teratology (the study of monstrosities). The use of zoological evidence that decapitated animals continued to move was, as Cabanis pointed out, problematic, for it implied that life persisted in the body as well as in the head. Only Sue was prepared to embrace this conclusion, which carried with it the implication that the soul or will was neither uniquely connected to the brain nor unitary in character. Soemmerring went so far as to rule out of court his own experiments on animals on the grounds that the relationship between brain and head was different in animals and human beings.

Sue argued that both trunk and head suffer upon separation. He based this conviction on the idea of 'co-relation'. For him, there were two types of sensation; the first was that immediately felt in the affected part, and the second was the consciousness of the sensation, experienced ultimately in the *sensorium commune*.[23] It was this relationship between peripheral and central nervous systems that Sue meant by the term co-relation. Together with his idea of a hierarchy of lives and of levels of sensation, co-relation played an important role in Sue's thought. These concepts expressed the harmony, integrity and equilibrium he attributed to living things, as indeed did all the participants in the debate. Notions like organisation commanded equally general consent as expressions of organic unity. However, whereas Cabanis and Lamarck used

22. Sue, 1795, p. 189.
23. The *sensorium commune* has been defined as 'an area of unified function which both presented all sensations to the mind and through which the will impressed itself upon the body. It was the place of the mind, yet a wholly material part of the nervous system and thereby closely tied to the body' (Figlio, 1975, p. 180).

organisation to convey the impossibility of separating the moral and the physical, Sue employed co-relation to suggest that organisms comprised three distinct levels of vitality, which could, and on occasions such as decapitation did, exist separately, at least on a temporary basis. These arguments were forcefully dismissed by Cabanis as antiquated Stahlianism – a mystifying vitalism – because they suggested a commitment to a separate vital principle that was no longer justified. Sue claimed that the guillotine isolated the animal, moral and intellectual lives, and hence was the worst of all possible deaths. Like Soemmerring and Oelsner, he preferred hanging, asphyxia or poison, all reputedly gentler, and, in the case of poison, the executioner need not even be present when death took place, a desirable further lessening of brutality, since death would then be private, not spectacularly public.

Whereas Sue condemned decapitation for being too quick and so more painful, Cabanis praised its speed. He used the experience of soldiers wounded in battle, who felt no immediate pain, to argue that guillotine victims did not suffer. There was simply not enough time for them to do so. The very act of cutting the neck happened too fast for the sensations to register. Cabanis believed that the blade did cut evenly, even through bone, while Soemmerring and his supporters asserted that it worked by crushing the vertebrae by virtue of its weight. Cabanis separated movement from sensation and convulsion from pain. He did not deny that painful sensations could exist in the central nervous system, merely that decapitation led to *conscious* feelings of pain. He paid particular attention to the nerves in the nape of the neck. This was the place, he pointed out, where, it had been recognised since time immemorial, animals and human beings could be killed at a stroke. He found it significant that electric shocks made their greatest impact in that part of the body. He did not claim that life in all its manifestations was extinguished with the fall of the blade, only that it was insofar as the conscious suffering of the victim was concerned.

The dispute between Soemmerring, Oelsner and Sue on the one hand, and Cabanis, Wedekind and Le Pelletier on the other, was a medical one in two senses. First, medical practitioners held a privileged position in that it was their advice and expertise that was sought, and they contributed the vast majority of the publications on the topic, which continued to be produced into the early twentieth century.[24] Second, the terms of reference established for the debate were medical ones, in that most of the evidence was drawn from clinical cases. Reference was also made to animal experiments, like those on frogs' legs, and to research on animal electricity in general, but anatomical and physiological approaches to the human body were paramount.

The issues embedded within the guillotine debates stretched far beyond the confines of medical ideas and practice, however. What the practitioners had was a fund of examples, drawn from clinical experience, experiments and autopsy findings. Other constituencies, such as natural historians, had their own

24. See the bibliographies in: Soubiran, 1964: see note 4, pp. 221–4; Tourneux, 1900, vol. 3, pp. 244–6; Devance, 1977, esp. p. 376.

sources; furthermore, they shared many of the conceptual preoccupations – the nature of life, organic change over time, models of the nervous system – that taxed medical practitioners. Three issues underlying the guillotine debates were of particular importance. These analytical challenges were present in the emerging life sciences of the period as guiding themes, they captured general intellectual, cultural and social concerns, and they were central to the systematic study of human nature.

The first issue was the definition of life and death. When the blade of the guillotine fell, according to Cabanis and his supporters, life in the sense of a whole functioning organism was annihilated immediately, whilst vital actions persisted. Both these phenomena were named 'life'. The definition of the concept of life itself was therefore crucial, and there was no consensus as to how to approach the problem. Many savants agreed that life could best be defined in terms of death. In addition to the obvious connection with Bichat's work in which life and death were mutually defining and death could be analysed into many smaller deaths, there was an important eighteenth-century tradition that used evidence provided by resuscitation following a variety of injuries; such near-deaths were natural experiments.[25] Similar injuries were also experimentally introduced in animals, as a means of revealing basic mechanisms of physiological functioning. The writings of Winslow, Bruhier d'Ablaincourt, Antoine Louis and Goodwyn exemplify the point.[26] Their experimental work examined the stages of death in their actual temporal sequences in order to throw light on physiological processes that were normally simultaneous and hence difficult to analyse.

The second issue was the manner in which organisms changed over time and the way in which time could be used as an analytical tool for uncovering the nature of life. Organic transformation took place at different paces, from the constant and relatively rapid processes of nutrition, respiration and excretion, through the alterations wrought by habits over a lifetime, to the exceedingly slow shifts that some naturalists believed took aeons to occur. Analysing these types of change was a shared preoccupation of medical practitioners and natural historians. For example, this was Lamarck's way in natural history, and his ideas were influenced by medical concerns resulting in an approach that was not only in line with that of the *idéologues*, but was also strikingly similar to that of Cabanis. Lamarck argued that the history of nature, understood from a transformist perspective, revealed the nature of life and the different forms it took. His theory of how animals had changed over time further explained how what are usually named 'mind' and 'body' interact. Lamarck showed that the nervous system became increasingly elaborate structurally and functionally with 'higher' animals. In other words, there were layers in the brain and nervous system, which, in their hierarchy of function, revealed a history. Time, taken in the exceedingly generous amounts Lamarck invoked, made each step of increasing complexity in the animal kingdom so small as to be plausible and easy

25. Entralgo, 1948; Haigh, 1981, esp. ch. 11; Chapter 9.
26. These writers will be mentioned in Chapter 9.

to imagine. Even the life history of individual animals illustrated the meta-
morphoses of which nature was capable. Lamarck was struck by the tadpole
becoming a frog, since it embodied a clear increment in complexity achieved
quite easily in a single lifetime.[27] Using the history of living things was one way
of exploring the different forms which this thing called life could take on. Such
an approach presupposed that organic nature was composed of phenomena
of different levels of complexity: anatomical, physiological, taxonomic and
historical. The guillotine debates also examined levels of organic complexity in
relation to time.

The 'problem of levels' was the third and the most general issue, and it
subsumes the first two since they both presupposed the use of hierarchical
models of organic functions. It may not be immediately apparent, however,
why ideas of natural levels or hierarchies posed problems. By the 1790s, anatomy
and physiology, like other sciences of life, certainly employed ideas of hierarchical levels both as analytical tools and as heuristic devices of self-evident
value for dealing with mind and body in a naturalistic manner. A further attraction of such models was the facility with which they could be extended to
include the social realm. Those committed to a naturalistic approach, like
Lamarck and Cabanis, could not satisfy all the criticisms of their contemporaries, who found such an approach levelling and hence threatening. For example,
Lamarck dealt with category distinctions, such as that between mind and body,
which many people took to be ones of kind, by turning them into differences
merely of degree. He dissolved large leaps into smaller ones, so that Descartes's
crisp distinction between mind and body was completely recast as the complex functioning of a nervous system, which gave rise to phenomena that had
sometimes been labelled as those of mind, at others those of body. The
human nervous system was only the most complex form of an organ found in
advanced vertebrates; it was not, therefore, unique. Similarly, Lamarck removed
the idea of will from its privileged position as a uniquely human faculty that
gave mankind a moral superiority sanctioned by God. He saw 'will' as a minor
faculty of the understanding, and the notion of free will as no more than a con.
Belief in the idea of free will derived from a false understanding of God's
creation, as opposed to a true appreciation of nature's productive powers. This
strategy led Lamarck to invoke a massive time scale for the history of the earth
and the history of life. If all natural changes had taken place incredibly slowly,
great things could be accomplished in the long term without the constituent
steps being difficult to imagine and explain. It was as if time itself worked
on an already laid-down substrate to produce each new level of organisation.
Here was one way in which the ideas of levels and layers did important work
in the life sciences of the period, and more specifically in models of the
nervous system.

27. Burkhardt, 1977, esp. chs 5 and 6; Corsi, 1988; Jordanova, 1984a. (Corsi's marvellous book shows
the intertwinings between medicine and natural history in the period.) For a cultural approach to natural
history, which also includes discussions of its medical dimensions, see Jardine, Secord *et al.*, 1996, esp.
chs 6 (by Cook) and 11 (by Spary).

Let us now return to the guillotine. It offered a conceptual challenge – how could its effects be explained when the actual act of decapitation took no time at all?[28] More specifically, what levels of life remained after the blade fell, and how did the guillotine separate out the different organic levels? What appeared on the surface as a dramatic instantaneous event forced people to think about its hidden complexity, not least because of the historical context in which the guillotine was used. In the distorted, uncoordinated movements of severed bodies and heads, biological and social dissolution, and chaotic, disordered life – both physiological and social – were put before the imagination of the people. Savants and medical practitioners, no less than other social groups, came to recognise that such disorder had, if possible, to be accommodated within their cognitive frameworks, which were rooted in their commitments to natural law and cosmic order.

Lamarck's peaceful transformism, in which highly complex organisms emerged gradually out of the mass of invertebrate life, and in which rational meritocracies were the desirable form of government, was based on a vision of the early 1790s. Its political counterpart may be seen in such writings as Volney's catechism *The Law of Nature* of 1793.[29] The Terror and the guillotine in their own ways offered a decisive challenge to that view, the latter by virtue of its biological, social and political ramifications. Lamarck appeared a trifle simplistic and naive when read through the eyes of the early nineteenth century because, like many others, he was unwilling to recognise the specialness of the human condition. Soemmerring and his supporters demanded precisely that. They wanted more than an acknowledgement of the existence of a soul, they strove for the recognition that the sudden death of a human being was a complex event that could only be fully understood if pain, suffering, consciousness and will were considered as particular expressions of a unique form of life. Even Cabanis had to admit that death was not truly instantaneous if all the available signs of life were taken into account.

Reactions to the guillotine, as to the Terror, focused a number of contemporary preoccupations with an unusual dramatic urgency. They raised the issue of natural, human and social order, and the relationship between these levels – to these debates the mind–body question was central. Medicine and the bio-medical sciences contributed to discussions of the guillotine a range of concepts, models and images through which debate could be conducted. In all the writings of medical practitioners on death in general and on decapitation in particular, concern about moral and political questions was present, largely in a mediated form. The physiological problems, challenging as they were in their own right, were vehicles for the expression of disagreements about ethics, about what it meant to be human, and, above all, about what forms of punishment

28. In a brilliant article Daniel Arasse argues that it was precisely this aspect of the guillotine that constituted its greatest threat. Death happened so fast that it could not be represented either verbally or visually. This is certainly true. Here I am concerned with how medical commentators used a range of analogous processes of longer duration to explore an apparently unobservable phenomenon: Arasse, 1982a, also 1982b and 1989.

29. Chapter 8 of this volume.

were morally permissible and with what social consequences. In this sense I have referred to medical commentaries on the guillotine as mediations of wider concerns. Within medical discourse itself there was the fundamental difficulty of explaining the relationship between mind and body, a difficulty suddenly rendered more acute by the guillotine.

I have suggested that those who wrote about the guillotine drew on a number of intellectual traditions, united by their common recourse to models of living nature as composed of levels or hierarchies. Yet a fully satisfying account of death, particularly of sudden death from a medical perspective, failed to emerge. This was because, however much shared clinical or experimental knowledge participants in the debate possessed, they invested such knowledge with different significance. Their distinct cognitive frameworks manifested themselves as political, social, moral and medical differences, and vice versa, making the only common ground their shared assumption that the guillotine dramatically demanded their attention.

CHAPTER EIGHT

Guarding the Body Politic: Volney's *Law of Nature*

Towards the end of a secular catechism, which first appeared in 1793, it was claimed that 'all the social virtues . . . may . . . be traced to the physical object of the preservation of man'.[1] It followed that individuals had to actively manage their bodily well-being, for their own sake, that of their family and of the nation to which they belonged. The message was familiar enough from the many advice books which, especially in the second half of the eighteenth century, preached moderation and a healthy lifestyle, expressed concern about population, and fulminated against luxury and self-indulgence. Volney's *Law of Nature* holds special interest, however. The catechism format, with its tightly controlled 'conversation', produced special effects which I explore in this chapter. This particular text spoke with no particular scientific or medical authority, although its creator was a well-known author and public figure by the time of its publication. Born in the 1750s when the Enlightenment was well under way, Volney held moderate political views, was particularly interested in the Middle East, and had been a member of the Estates General. He was influenced by and socialised with prominent thinkers who were liberal, interested in natural philosophy, and secularist in outlook.[2] For such a figure to recast the catechism, the cornerstone of French Catholic instruction, is particularly significant. Yet the result was complex; not a simple repudiation of Church authority and traditional Christian belief, but a strategic blend of sacred and secular, of faith and logic. As an *idéologue* with wide intellectual interests, Volney developed a naturalistic framework in this text into which all aspects of social, domestic and individual life could be slotted. The catechism contained admittedly only the bare bones of such a framework, and was designed to be a widely accessible and overtly didactic work. Volney's writing was certainly lucid – it displayed careful precision in its insistence on the scientific basis of morality. It should therefore be seen in the context of a whole range of moralising items that sought to alter the behaviour of their readers and viewers.

---

1. Volney, 1807, p. 391 (NB: all quotations from the text use this edition).
2. Gaulmier, 1951; Kennedy, 1978; Head, 1985.

Like his fellow authors on morality and health, Volney used a variety of strategies to promote the gathering together of individuals into communities through organic bonds of responsibility – individual and collective well-being were fused together. He developed a strict and rather mechanistic approach to nature and the moral precepts to be deduced from it, while negotiating a path between traditional Christianity on the one hand and a radical secularism on the other. God was by no means absent, although he was represented as working through nature. Volney chose the religious term, catechism, yet his little work was implicitly anti-clerical, carefully explaining, for example, why alms-giving could be harmful and celibacy bad for one's health!

Thus Volney's work, initially subtitled *Catechism for the French Citizen*, was not a scientific or medical text in any conventional sense; it was completely non-technical, dealt directly with nature's precepts rather than with explanations of natural phenomena, and it made no claims to specialised expertise. Here, the variety of physical nature was of no concern, although it was in some of Volney's other works.[3] Nonetheless it has much in common with popular medical and scientific works, and an analysis which brings out these shared themes can be particularly fruitful. The intricate relationships between ideas of life, health and pathology in late eighteenth- and early nineteenth-century France, which are explored in a number of chapters, constitute one context for Volney's text. I am particularly interested in the use of assumptions about health to bind people together as a step towards more organic social bonds – such discussions were frequently conducted under the rubric of medical police. The importance of medical police was the way it subsumed theories of health and disease, government policy, and local reforms and practices. As such, it was a significant aspect of the setting in which this text was written: medical police embraced a theory of nature, a political philosophy and simple moral precepts.[4]

La Loi Naturelle, ou Catéchisme du Citoyen Français, as it was called originally, later became *La Loi Naturelle ou Principes Physiques de la Morale Déduits de l'Organisation de l'Homme et de l'Univers*, thereby making explicit its deductive approach and consideration of the relationship between the physical and the moral, which lay at the heart of the science of man and of *idéologue* thought.[5] The early nineteenth-century English edition was published in a single volume with Volney's most celebrated work, *The Ruins*, and entitled *The Law of Nature, or Principles of Morality Deduced from the Physical Constitution of Mankind and the Universe*. Indeed, these works have been seen as complementary elements within a single intellectual project.[6] It was a grand title for what was after all a short piece, some 50 pages long, and written in the openly didactic form of questions and answers. The carefully wrought structure moved from general definitions of nature, laws of nature and morality, through the individual or private virtues

---

3. Especially his *Tableau du Climat et du Sol des États-Unis*, 1803.

4. See Chapter 9, and especially notes 1, 3, and 4, where the literature on medical police is cited.

5. On Volney as an *idéologue*, see Kennedy, 1978; Head, 1985. The person in his circle most associated with the physical/moral relationship was Cabanis: see Staum, 1980 and Williams, 1994, although it was widely debated in the period – see e.g. Fox *et al.*, 1995.

6. Gaulmier, 1951, p. 271.

to the social virtues and how these are best developed. It covered a wide range of moral issues from a somewhat rationalistic perspective, giving a privileged position to nature as a moral category, and to the physical well-being of the human race as the primary social and political goal.

Before discussing the text in more detail, something should be said about the catechism as a literary form. There was certainly nothing new in Volney's use of the catechism for primarily secular purposes, and even in its more conventional form, the catechism was a familiar part of religious and philosophical debates by the 1790s. *Catéchisme de l'Homme*, published anonymously in London in 1789, is an instructive example of a secular and deliberately subversive catechism. It sent up the genre itself by having the 'student' interrogate, challenge and contradict the master, rather than posing questions that are, in effect, foils for the demonstration of a superior's wisdom. The author conveyed a cogent argument for an alternative to despotism, according to principles which suggest the influence of Rousseau's *Du contrat social* (1761). By exploiting the dialogue form, the main objections to challenging the prevailing social order could be raised, as were doubts as to whether a viable alternative truly existed. The conclusion of the catechism was that it is morally permissible to challenge oppression, even that it is our responsibility to 're-establish the empire of reason on earth'.[7] An earlier example of a religiously inspired catechism shows another way in which the form could be extended. In 1758, a French priest, Gauchat, published a catechism based on Helvétius's book *De l'Esprit*, where conventional Christian questions were followed by passages from Helvétius in order to demonstrate the ungodly, materialistic character of contemporary French philosophy, particularly as manifested in the *Encyclopédie*. A similar range of catechisms can be found in eighteenth-century Britain.[8]

Despite their roots in Christian pedagogic practices, catechisms have a certain affinity with the dialogue of philosophical and scientific writings, especially in their shared assumption that knowledge comes with conversation. Yet there are also striking differences between these two types of written conversations. A comparison can be made between Volney's piece and Fontenelle's *Entretiens sur la Pluralité des Mondes* (1686), which brings these out. Most striking is the way in which, like Galileo, Fontenelle gave the participants characters and, furthermore, specified their class identity. Volney, on the other hand, simply provided a disembodied questioner and respondent. Conventional catechisms for use with children would obviously assume the roles of priest-instructor as respondent and religious novice as questioner, even if this was not explicitly stated. A degree of impersonality seems to be an integral part of catechisms since the human roles denote an abstract position. It is significant that Volney wrote so as to emphasise the abstract, impersonal nature of his tenets. Nonetheless the relationship between the two personae is fundamental, for it is their *inequality* which is crucial, especially in a catechism. Of course, there were many different forms of inequality: in Fontenelle, those between man and woman, savant and

7. M.W., 1789, pp. 14, 8. Gaulmier, 1951 discusses radical, secular catechisms before Volney, and charts the influence of the Encyclopédistes and other 'advanced' thinkers on Volney's ideas.

8. Gauchat, 1758; Darling, 1854.

aristocrat, expert and educated layperson were evoked. The traditional priest imagined by readers of catechisms was the experienced man of belief who can establish orthodox dogma for young novices, help them to learn it and establish its validity, using proofs from the Bible.

Catechisms conveyed, summarised, validated and controlled knowledge at the same time. Sometimes these distinct functions were demarcated physically in the text, for example by having a separate section devoted to confirming doctrine by 'Texts of Scripture' for the more able reader.[9] Volney brought these elements together by unfolding, step by step, the order of nature as the basis of morality, enunciating simple precepts while proving their correctness at the same time. Humour and play were entirely lacking, and the questions, far from seeming innocent and natural, appear as carefully set up for maximum didactic impact. This approach is best understood in the context of the *idéologue* philosophy espoused by Volney, which founded a theory of education, and of literary style, on a naturalistic analysis, sensualism, of how the mind works.[10]

Since catechisms are pedagogic devices, derived from systems of oral instruction and designed to assist the assimilation of a body of dogma, they express assumptions about the nature of 'knowledge' and the authority from which it derives, by virtue of their form and content. The knowledge catechisms contain is to be unquestioningly absorbed, simply as belief, and breaking it down into questions and answers merely expedites the task, renders it manageable. The question–answer form places a particular kind of authority in the hands of the respondent/author and their sources, while the pupil, and, by extension, readers, are controlled by the structure of the catechism, which withholds information and frames the questions that may be asked. Hence, the catechism not only structures what is known, but it excludes what may not. Its authoritarian mode of construction is expressed as much in the formulation of the questions as in the content of the answers. Despite closing off exploration and doubt, catechisms compel the reader/pupil to participate, to take up the role of questioner.

The fact that catechisms are composed of small units carefully organised into larger structures suggests that they contain classificatory systems, which are always tools for organising the world. A novel moral situation could, ideally, be slotted into this framework, just as a new animal or plant species could be in taxonomy. We can appreciate the structural similarities between catechisms and taxonomies, despite their different histories. Catechisms endow human moral experience with specific meaning and order, having already predetermined what forms that experience may permissibly take. They present worldviews in general, universalist terms, and, while their didactic mission is overt, their authority is conveyed as much in their organisation and language as in their content. Indeed, the very fact of presenting a universal framework is an authority-claim, and Volney's text does just this for a naturalistic world-view.

9. Paley, 1790; see also Some, 1792.
10. Picavet, 1971; Van Duzer, 1935; Williams, 1953. See also Lalande's 1928 definition of ideology, vol. 1, p. 336, which cites Destutt de Tracy's emphasis on the study of ideas as the constituents of consciousness, their nature and origin and their relationship to signs.

It is now evident that Volney exploited many of the features of the cat-echism discussed above, and at the same time rationalised it. It is hardly coin-cidental that he endowed the law of nature with ten major characteristics in a secular and abstract reworking of the ten commandments – a point that neatly illustrates his debt to and departure from religious forms. *La Loi Naturelle* represents his attempt to marry the order imposed by reason on human morality with the order present in nature itself. The text is organised according to naturalistic principles, not just in the sense that his starting point and base-line are in nature rather than God, but in the movement from the simple to the complex, from the particular to the general, in starting with the morality of individuals, passing through domestic, family relationships to society as a whole. Indeed, this is strongly reminiscent of the biological classification of Lamarck, which started with the simplest animals, and followed a scale of increasing complexity, culminating in the human race, thereby following nature's own order.[11] Acts of classification locate individuals in categories of different levels of generality – species, families, orders, classes and so on, which, in Volney's case, served to reinforce his point that individuals and collectives are part of the same (social-cum-natural) system.

Another way of conveying the hierarchical structure that Volney employed is to say that he rooted the social in the natural, and the moral in the physical, and that this too was typical of the *idéologue* approach, which is particularly clear in the ideas of his friends Cabanis and de Tracy. Volney's naturalistic ethics departed from the premise that the punishment and reward for human actions is built into nature itself. Thus, his notion of lawfulness stressed nature's im-manent power to command, rather than regularity or measurability; it is law as prescription rather than description that interested him. Although Volney granted that the law of nature came directly from God, the way it is built into the universe and cannot be evaded, together with the possibility of demonstrating it by human reason from observable facts, are the central themes of the work. It strikes the modern reader that Volney presented the law of nature as a secular belief system, yet it was not merely a matter of belief for him; it enjoyed the status of knowledge which could be indubitably proved:

Q. Since the law of nature is not written, may it not be considered as arbitrary and ideal? A. No, because it consists altogether in facts, whose demonstration may be at any time recalled before the senses, and form a science as precise and exact as those of geometry and mathematics: and this very circumstance, that the law of nature forms an exact science, is the reason why men, who are born in ignorance, and live in carelessness, have, till this day, known it only superficially.[12]

Thus human intellectual progress supports moral understanding.

Volney further stated that the principles of the law of nature as they relate to mankind are reducible to the single precept of self-preservation by seeking

11. Lamarck, 1809; see also Chapter 3.
12. Volney, 1807, p. 339.

pleasure and avoiding pain.[13] The goal of human existence is life, and the avoidance of death. Any behaviour which jeopardises the quality of life in a human body is anti-social sin. Volney's preoccupation with the quality of life echoed the vast eighteenth-century literatures on matters such as life insurance, pregnancy, childbirth and infant mortality, the use of life histories in medical writings, as well as philosophical questions on the definition of 'life' and the relationship between life and activity in the physical world. The well-being of citizens' bodies occupied the central space in his political theory, with the important corollary that health is not innate but learned, and that therefore ignorance is 'the true original sin'.[14] Civic responsibility is health-seeking behaviour. In stating this, Volney brought together the political-cum-moral abstractions of individual responsibility and social good, and mundane human existence in the form of bodily functions, such as eating and drinking, sleeping and sex. He could do this because of the multiple ways in which the body contained elaborate social meanings.[15] It was logical then for Volney to deny that virtue and vice are directed towards abstract, spiritual ends: 'they are always ultimately referable to . . . the destruction or preservation of the body'.[16] In other words, Volney sought to demonstrate as concretely as possible the palpable aggregate consequences of everyday acts as a means of changing people's practices. 'Habit' and 'education' were the relevant keywords.

As a structure, *La Loi Naturelle* was composed of three levels, with three corresponding classes of virtues: private (i.e. individual), domestic (i.e. familial) and social. Volney applied his basic principles to each level in turn by attacking excess, pleading for enlightened moderation and always maintaining his belief both in the capacity of individuals to change and in the efficacy of education as a major vehicle of self-improvement. There was nothing original in these themes, but Volney's text illustrates rather clearly a number of important issues: the use of nature as the ultimate authority, definitions of 'property', and the equation of human activity with labour.

Volney's text claimed authority by virtue of its organisation as well as its content. Structurally it gradually unfolded knowledge derived from nature and sanctioned by God, which it could do because nature boasts its own logic. The author has the privilege of conveying nature's order, and he also claimed that his words can be independently verified by anyone who chooses to do so. The author is authoritative because he can see, and then show to his reader, largely through deductive argument, the certain future consequences of particular acts. He thereby displayed not only his rational, fully enlightened knowledge of the world, but also his ability to calculate, to anticipate, to judge in advance – the 'prudential' insurance mentality. The role of the questioner is one of apparently innocent collusion, which always serves the telos of the text. The questions anticipate the correct answers, acting as foil for the display of simple, comprehensible truths.

13. Ibid., p. 340.
14. Ibid., p. 343.
15. This point is made by Outram, 1989, esp. Ch. 4, and is widely explored by scholars of the French revolutionary period.
16. Volney, 1807, p. 349.

The deeper force of Volney's arguments lay in their simplicity and perfect palpability. Nature is the ultimate arbiter and sanction, and nature lies not only all around, but inside each citizen. The origin of social order is not distant and separate from humanity, but contained within it: 'we have within us the germ of all virtue and of all perfection'.[17] An ideal 'community of citizens' emerges, so to speak, from the fabric of the body, 'our natural organisation', and from the realities of daily life.[18] Social-cum-moral orderliness is not imposed upon individuals, but is latent within them. This emergent, naturalistic style of authority must be understood in terms of citizenship, that is, the capacity of individuals to find within themselves the source of a well-regulated civil society, without recourse to a will imposed from the outside by a monarch, despot or God. The collectivity (body politic, *patrie*) arises out of natural sociability (sympathy) and groupings based in nature (the family). Volney, like many of his contemporaries, used the family as a bridge between the social and the biological.[19] For him, the '*patrie*' is a family, 'a community of citizens ... united by fraternal sentiments', and sheltered by a form of protective '*paternité*'.[20] This picture of responsible citizens constructing a well-organised civil society draws on a historically specific understanding of nature which stressed its immanence and the way in which the social and moral emerge from the physical, just as Volney, in constructing his text, allowed social virtues to emerge from their base in natural law.

Notions of immanence and emergence are of particular importance in the life sciences of the period, where there were a number of attempts to demonstrate that living things, including human beings, could not be satisfactorily explained by souls, spirits, or separate vital principles. Instead, it was the material organisation of an organic being which explained all its characteristics. In this way, the moral and spiritual aspects of a human being were not located in a separate entity, the soul, but dispersed so that they were evident in all parts of the body, since it was vital as an ensemble. It no longer made sense to many people to speak of some parts of the body as more 'human' than others, for it was the integrity and unity of life which was noteworthy. Life, then, was an ensemble of vital actions or processes. Physical organisation was the basis of morality, which gave this rendering of nature a particular political and social significance in challenging forms of authority and power which were separate from nature. Nature, in fact, had its own autonomous order, which, if followed, provided all that was needed for moral order to ensue. Volney was in the same circle as the medical thinker and political moderate Cabanis, and admired by him, thus it is not surprising to find affinities between his ideas and those current in medicine at the time. Certainly notions of 'organisation' and lifestyle have much in common with contemporary bio-medical thinking, yet Volney's

17. Ibid., p. 391.

18. Ibid., p. 390.

19. The theme of the family as a bridge between the natural and the social is also taken up in Chapter 10. The family was a central, if highly complex and contentious, concept for revolutionary politics in France: see, for example, Hunt, 1992.

20. Volney, 1807, pp. 390–1.

language stressed precision and exactitude, the affinities between social arguments and those of the 'hard' sciences. He did not refer explicitly to the life sciences, although traces of them are everywhere in the text, presumably because
he wanted to point up the rigour and certainty of the knowledge he deployed.[21]

The historical specificity of the vision of the social order emerging from the
natural is vividly illustrated by the conservative reaction with which it was met
in the first decades of the nineteenth century. The reaction challenged the view
of the immanence of nature on philosophical, political, religious and scientific
grounds. Paley's *Natural Theology* (1802) was typical of both British and French
conservative responses in reasserting a sense of psychic distance between man
and God, of nature as utterly distinct from its Creator, of man as vulnerable
in the hands of God, and needing nature principally as a vehicle of religious
revelation:

If one train of thinking be more desirable than another, it is that which regards the
phaenomena of nature with a constant reference to a supreme intelligent Author . . .
The world from thenceforth becomes a temple, and life itself one continued act of
adoration.

. . .

The works of nature want only to be contemplated.

. . .

Our happiness, our existence is in [the] hands [of this stupendous Being].[22]

Evidently for Paley, as for French conservatives such as de Maistre and de
Bonald, certain political consequences followed directly from the clear-cut
separation of God, man and nature. As George Boas argued a long time ago,
this was peculiarly compatible with conservative reaction to the excesses of the
French Revolution and with the triumph of Napoleon's imperial vision and
his *entente cordiale* with the Catholic Church.[23] But Volney was a man of 1789,
the representative of the third estate of Anjou at the meeting of the Estates
General, and his sights were appropriately rooted in improving human society
via knowledge of the physical world and not in the worship of a distant,
all-powerful God as Paley's were. For Volney, human happiness was in human
hands. Here were two contrasting assumptions not just about the role of
God, but about how the connections between knowledge (what we might call
'science') and politics should work.

For the devout, be they Protestant or Catholic, it was crucial that the
human body, moved as it was by the soul, was the instrument of divine will and
hence served a larger purpose in the worship and glorification of God. Some
eighteenth-century French writers on hygiene could thus castigate those who
carelessly misused their bodies for failing in their responsibility to God, who

21. On Cabanis see Staum, 1980 and Williams, 1994. Figlio, 1976 remains the best study of 'organisation'.
Lifestyle medicine is discussed in Chapter 6 and in Jordanova 1979/1997.
22. Paley, 1802, pp. 376, 577, 578 – Paley is also discussed in Chapter 3, while Chapter 5 explores this
conservative reaction in terms of 'the authoritarian response'.
23. Boas, 1925 and 1929.

had entrusted them with the care of their own bodies.[24] For Volney, on the other hand, the body was the most basic form of property, over which individuals had total control, which it was imperative they exercise in the most responsible manner. In both the secular and the Christian approaches, it is important to note, the same advice was given in favour of moderation and the avoidance of excess, but the inspiration for and purpose of such behaviour was entirely different for the two groups.

In Volney's political theory, the human body was the ultimate constituent element of any society, and since its misuse had social consequences, it must be tended, preserved and conserved. Not to do so threatened the whole fabric of society. Attaching high political stakes to the quality of life was a familiar part of the medical literature on hygiene, which invariably used the language of preservation and conservation. Macquart's *Dictionnaire de la Conservation de l'Homme* (1799) is an interesting example, where advice was given under headings, which were simply arranged alphabetically; presumably it was intended to be used as a handbook in times of need.

There was a twofold relationship between individuals and society with respect to health and disease. Individuals who, through their own neglect and carelessness, fell ill became agents of social deterioration. Venereal disease was a commonly cited example of this, for an affected man or woman leaves a pathological legacy to society through their children. Individuals are also affected by the environment, social, moral and physical, in which they live; their bodies bear traces of their lives, even of changes in social conditions. Although there were attempts to construe this as, somehow, the 'fault' of the individuals concerned, many of the causative factors, such as climate and working conditions, were not generally within an individual's control. The important point is that whatever the precise path of causation, there was a sense of dynamic interaction between individuals and the 'community of citizens' of which they were a part. In the broad political significance he attributed to health, Volney not only followed those traditions which attacked luxury and excess, but also medical writings which endowed the body with a special, sacred status and urged, in the public interest, that it not be desecrated.

Tissot's famous treatise on masturbation was perfectly clear on this point.[25] Excessive masturbation, like excessive heterosexual activity within marriage, leads to weakening of the body, and this, in turn, makes individuals no longer able to take care of themselves; they become dependent, with the result that society is burdened with the weak and dissipated bodies of the over-indulgent. Tissot's aim was not simply to regale us with grim stories about the physical symptoms resulting from masturbation, but to illustrate its consequences for social relations – his work might appropriately be described as a political economy of masturbation. In those who masturbate, their physical symptoms bear witness to their social pathology. In bodies, whether healthy or diseased, the traces, the sediment of social relations is deposited. And this account was

24. e.g. Le Bègue de Presle, 1763.
25. Tissot, 1760, who is the subject of Chapter 6.

based on a clear physiological conception of the maintenance of a healthy equilibrium of body fluids (nervous fluid, spermatic fluid and so on); it was through their dissipation that the body was weakened.

Since, as Volney remarked, 'every [man] is the absolute master, the entire proprietor of his body', people can use their energy productively or they can dissipate it through luxury and masturbation.[26] How people use that energy, their personal property, is, thus, of immense political importance, with the corollary that it is within the power of each individual to control their own actions. To this extent, each individual is construed as an autonomous unit, who can freely use their property, the body, responsibly or not, who is free to use activity (labour) as they please, providing, of course, that they pay the price nature exacts for any transgressions, and recognise the ripple effects of their behaviour. On the whole Volney put this point through logic, but there are moments when he employed the relentless cataloguing of symptoms that characterised Tissot's prose.[27]

In addition to owning their own bodies, citizens own the products of their labour.[28] Volney treats these terms – body and labour – as if they were roughly equivalent. He first introduced the question of labour when enumerating the principal private, i.e. individual virtues. Among these is 'activity, that is, the love of labour, and a proper employment of our time'.[29] Volney thereby extended a common equation of life with activity to construe the latter as the capacity to work. When he spoke of labour as a virtue and idleness and sloth as vices, he was partly restating familiar arguments against luxury, for inactivity engenders other vices, particularly sensual self-indulgence, which was at the heart of luxurious behaviour. Only legitimate labour entitles an individual to anything in return, that is, to consume. Those who consume in excess of what they have produced are luxurious, and have disrupted the correct balance between production and consumption. Luxury was merely a shorthand for an area where the rules of consumption were contested and required negotiation.[30]

Because of his condemnation of inactivity, Volney did not condone unlimited alms-giving for it might encourage 'indolence, which is hurtful both to the beggar and to the society'. He continued, 'no one has a right to enjoy the good or labour of another without rendering an equivalent by his own labour'.[31] Volney's moral precepts resemble a calculus, laying great emphasis on exact reciprocity as the basis of social relations.

Q. How can a man, according to the law of nature, repair any injury which he has committed?
A. By conferring a proportionable benefit upon those whom he has injured.
Q. Does this law allow him to repair it by prayers, vows, offerings to God, fastings, or mortifications?

26. Volney, 1807, p. 379.
27. Ibid., pp. 355–6.
28. Ibid., p. 379.
29. Ibid., p. 351.
30. On luxury see Berry, 1994.
31. Volney, 1807, p. 383.

A. No; for none of these things has any relation to the action which is meant to be atoned for . . .[32]

Calculation, measurement, proportion and prediction are repeatedly mentioned in the text. Achieving a precise matching between atonement and transgression is hardly easy, and Volney made little attempt to deal with the difficulties in a detailed way. Ultimately, we must assume, units of labour are the currency in which expiation is calculated. Since the activity of work is so important for Volney, the body has both political and economic significance. A naturalistic analysis of the conditions under which optimal functioning is obtained was therefore crucial. It was the duty of those who labour, as free agents, to maintain their bodies in good condition, and with it their domestic and social lives.

This assertion of human agency and responsibility allowed Volney to use a revitalised conception of sin, sanctioned by the contemporary medical literature on hygiene, which implied not the avenging hand of a distant creator, but nature's ultimately benevolent warning of the physical consequences of losing control over one's life. The language of sin in relation to health was remarkably widespread in this period and it fused quite easily with a naturalistic analysis. The marriage between aspects of traditional religious practice and a radical secular discourse on citizenship is displayed in the actual structure of *La Loi Naturelle*, combining as it does the impersonal authority of the catechism with demands for people to seize control of their own lives for the good of the community. But Volney was not simply concerned with morality and responsibility, he was concerned with labour, with calculation and with reciprocity in human, social relations. Volney's economism sits comfortably with the other themes of his text. His social relations are economistic transactions; a fair and just exchange being the object of the exercise. What was exchanged might be abstract – respect, honour, fidelity of spouses – but these, like the products of labour or labour itself, which are also exchanged, appear to find their ultimate roots in the quality of the human body.

Volney's text, of course, played on several overlapping levels here. His argument depended on using individual human bodies as the ultimate social constituents, and in that sense he treated persons as abstract moral units. The abstraction of human qualities is essential to the moral precepts of exact and fair exchange between citizens. The 'something' which is exchanged would seem to reduce to each person's labour. It is in the nature of human life to labour, for which physiological competence is crucial, just as it is for the 'work' of biological reproduction. This physiological competence is also treated as a thing to be consciously controlled by the individual. Volney's strategy was one which treated persons as commodities, as units of exchange, as abstract constituents of a 'community of citizens'. This was possible precisely because nature is self-sufficient, because the social order is immanent within the natural order, because each unit or person can deliberately act in such a way that an organic, moral society does emerge. All this was predicated on a particular

32. Ibid., p. 385.

vision of nature and of human nature as active, as containing the dynamic potential to generate a harmonious balance between production and consumption, a natural economy of forces. Imbalance can be perceived in the pathological signs present in individuals and society. Such traces of misused social relations can be corrected if the knowledge of nature and the understanding of its moral implications are used correctly. Bodies are products and agents in the social order, which is not the result of a passive nature moved by the hand of God, but is actively constructed by virtue of the powers immanent in each citizen. Volney's text sought, in both its form and its content, to elicit such participation, while also defining its terms.

La Loi Naturelle is highly suggestive of the social practices of the early 1790s in its repudiation of order imposed by distant authority in favour of an emerging natural order produced by citizens who were active in the marketplace, where just exchange created a moral world, where violations provoked severe punishments from nature itself, and where precise calculations were to underpin morality. Volney was indeed a man of 1789.

In 1789 women were active participants in many aspects of the revolutionary process, and over the next few years they formed clubs, wrote, argued and struggled.[33] Where were women in Volney's text? Like his contemporaries, he placed considerable emphasis on clear gender roles and on the family as a microcosm of society. The rare disruptions to the calm, utilitarian mood of the text occur when gender is at issue. One commentator has gone so far as to call Volney 'anti-feminist', and it is true that in the chapters on continence and on domestic virtues he revealed double standards characteristic of the time, and especially of Rousseau and his followers. This is especially notable since Volney has generally been seen as sceptical about cults of sensibility, which were so often associated with a Rousseauist world-view. A central part of this cult was an idealisation of feminine virtue, which readily switched to condemnation if women transgressed established moral norms. According to Volney, chastity was considerably more important for women than for men: women who bore children out of wedlock were rejected and impoverished, hence *their* need for greater self-control, and for the virtue of modesty, which, he made clear, is distinctively feminine. Certainly adultery is a crime, but 'the adulterous *woman* commits the most heinous of all robberies, giving heirs to her husband of foreign blood, who deprive of their lawful portion his true offspring'.[34] In the vehemence of this language, which is by no means unusual, it is apparent that the place of gender in the order of nature generated a quality of emotion that is quite distinct from the impersonal, abstract, calculated morality Volney's text advocated. In this respect too Volney was a man of 1789.

33. On women in revolution see Hufton, 1971; Levy *et al.*, 1979; and Abray, 1975 and Levy *et al.*, 1979, pp. 213–18, on the suppression of women's political clubs in 1793.
34. Volney, 1807, p. 374, my emphasis; see also pp. 361–2. Thomas, 1959; Rousseau, 1911.

CHAPTER NINE

Policing Public Health in France 1780–1815

Before embarking on an analysis of medical police and public health, we must acknowledge the difficulty of defining our object of study. The term 'medical police' was used in a variety of ways in the later eighteenth and early nineteenth centuries. Four main meanings were given to it: first, the administration of the health and well-being of the populace as a whole; second, the control of medical practice and practitioners; third, legal medicine; and fourth, the science of hygiene. Far from indicating confusion and ignorance, this diversity and richness of meaning reveals complex debates about the proper role of medical practitioners, their capacity to heal effectively, and their relationship to the people, government and legal structures. Underlying most discussions of medical police I found a crisis of confidence in the efficacy of conventional medical practice, expressed in strident demands for the control of 'charlatans' and the sale of specific remedies, and in the rejection of 'curing' as the primary and paradigmatic medical task, in favour of prevention. The search for alternative forms of practice was based on the conviction that many diseases had external, that is removable and controllable causes. In other words, environmental medicine was at the heart of medical police, however interpreted.[1]

Medical police was one of a cluster of closely related ideas. Sometimes it was taken as a synonym for legal medicine, at others for public medicine, public health or hygiene. It was frequently interpreted as that aspect of the science of government concerned with the health of the people. But in the latter half of the eighteenth century, particularly in France and Britain, it was most frequently used to denote the control of medical practice. This included means for excluding unlicensed medical practitioners, the rules governing professional societies, the etiquette and ethics of doctor–patient relationships, and the conduct between different groups of medical practitioners. Medical police encompassed apparently diverse aspects of medical theory and practice, which were held together by a number of shared assumptions and concerns. For the most part, what underlay this rich notion related to the general political and social

1. On the control of medical practice in France, see Ramsey, 1988 and Brockliss and Jones, 1997, chs 8, 9 and 10; on environmental medicine, Riley, 1987; Jordanova, 1979/1997; on medical police see White, 1983; La Berge, 1992, esp. ch. 1, Brockliss and Jones, 1997, esp. ch. 12.

preoccupations of that elusive entity the Enlightenment. Amongst the most important of these was the attempt to cater for the needs of a whole population, the people. A number of challenges resulted: finding ways of understanding the health of a collectivity, determining what forms of intervention were appropriate, and assessing the effectiveness of mass measures. As a result, hygiene, legal medicine, the control of medical practice, and public health became closely related aspects of a set of debates on health and the reform of society.

Environmentalism and the crisis over medical efficacy are themes of special importance here. Both of these led, though by different routes, to another facet of medical police, which was less explicit. This consisted of an emphasis on the moral-cum-political role of practitioners as those people who brought once poorly individuals into healthy communities, thereby eliminating the large proportion of sickness which was amenable to human control. This conviction that medical practice had a central part to play in forging a sense of collective identity was, during the period I am concerned with, increasingly expressed in the language of political economy instead of that of mercantilism and political arithmetic. Speaking about increasing national strength through the size of the population gave way to discussions of the management of a national economy through productivity. The shift was from concern for the *quantity* of the population to the *quality* of the health of the labouring, or potentially labouring, sector. Increasingly the emphasis was on 'managing the resources of a nation so as to increase its material prosperity'.[2]

Thus the idea of medical police is complex both conceptually and in its implications for administration and practice. In the nexus of beliefs and actions around medical police we can discern three distinct aspects which it may be helpful to bear in mind. First, there were the heated debates on the internal dynamics of the medical profession, nicely expressed in the title of a book I discuss later – *Medical Anarchy*. Second, there was an explicit relationship between practitioners and the official social policy of which they were agents. Here medicine and society were related in ways that it was commonplace to acknowledge. Third, medical theory and practice were enactments of social structure and social theory in an *implicit* way. What was said and done under the rubric of medical police had social and political meanings which were not fully articulated. The most important of these was the development of a collective consciousness via the responsibility of the individual to the group. To see these three dimensions in action, it is necessary to examine the theory and practice of medical police more closely.

The study of medical police presents some interesting comparative problems. Although it is usually associated with the German-speaking parts of eighteenth-century Europe, writings on the subject also came from Scotland, England, France and Italy. Historians became acquainted with medical police through two pioneering essays by George Rosen published in the 1950s.[3] He traced various

2. *Oxford English Dictionary*, vol. III, 1933, p. 35, definition of Political Economy (under Economy). See also Glass, 1978; Buck, 1982; Riley, 1985 and 1987. Coleman, 1982 explores the links between political economy and medicine in early nineteenth-century France.
3. Rosen, 1953 and 1957, reprinted in Rosen, 1974.

usages of the term and its approximate synonyms, political medicine and state medicine, from the seventeenth to the nineteenth centuries, and argued that the concept of medical police was by no means new in the writings of the German practitioner J.P. Frank with whom it is usually associated. Rosen placed medical police in the context of cameralist economic theories. He saw Frank's medical policies as expressions of forms of political power and of the economic ideals of the German-speaking states. The first volume of Frank's monumental work, *A System of Complete Medical Police*, appeared in 1779 and was quickly taken up in Italy, France and Britain, and reference was frequently made to Frank and other German writers. It is less common to find their arguments seriously questioned and discussed. For Rosen, medical police was essentially the doctrines promulgated in an absolutist state, which justified paternalistic control over the health of the people in order to increase the population, and so, by cameralist logic, the prosperity of the nation.

Medical police certainly needs to be seen in the context of eighteenth-century notions of police more generally and the concrete programmes of social action subsumed under the new science of police.[4] It is clear that police referred to the exercise of authority and to the agencies of management and control over the populace. Police was organised government and civil administration rather than a system specifically for the prevention and punishment of crime. However, prevention of unspecified harm to the populace, together with the establishment of regularity and order to ensure general safety and comfort, were important. Although policing was clearly a function performed by certain social strata, it would be misleading to associate the eighteenth-century form of police with either uniformed officials, a homogeneous state apparatus, or a unified professional structure for those jobs that involved policing. In France, under both the *ancien régime* and the Napoleonic state, the proliferation of institutions, committees and officials was far too great for them to represent a single class and set of interests. The three groups of medical practitioners, physicians, surgeons and apothecaries, definitely were involved in what might broadly be designated as policing activities, but they were merely some among many. Nor, of course, were medical practitioners themselves a homogeneous group, for the differences in education, income and status among them were immense. The rich variety of officialdom is illustrated in the statistical surveys of the departments of France compiled in the early years of the nineteenth century. For example, in year XII, the *préfet* of the *département du Nord*, Dieudonné, listed the public institutions for which Lille was the headquarters and their personnel – in addition to military and religious establishments, there were five justices of the peace, six police commissioners, directors, inspectors and controllers for taxes, mortgages, gold and silver, cloths, weights and measures, forests, roads and bridges, local commerce and the postal system among others. Lille also possessed a military hospital, an 'école primaire de

---

4. On concepts of police in the eighteenth century see Raeff, 1983. His examples come from Germany and Russia, and the discussion of medicine is somewhat Whiggish, but the conceptual framework of 'police' is usefully laid out. For brief definitions of 'police', 'cameralism' and 'mercantilism' see Black and Porter, 1996.

médecine', a botanical garden, a public assistance committee, a general hospital, five hospices for the old, orphaned and ill, a workhouse, two jails, and a departmental asylum for insane women. The population of the city at this time was 60,000.[5]

Perhaps one of the most important features of the system was that new committees and changing managerial tasks could easily be incorporated. Medical practitioners, so far as I can judge from evidence in the archives at Lille, worked closely with the municipal authorities on whom their licence to practise and form professional associations depended.[6] There certainly were disputes, although more often than not amongst practitioners themselves rather than between them and the magistracy. Practitioners visited cases of sudden death and accidents with a justice of the peace and made a full, written report. Perhaps the most extensive evidence of 'policing' activities comes from the hundreds of handwritten certificates which survive and which were signed by *chirurgiens* and *médecins jurés*. They relate to such matters as causes of death, state of mind, self-injury, capacity to work, seditious behaviour and stage of pregnancy. Many relate to the administration of poor relief, with which medical practitioners were closely involved, while others appear to touch on purely personal, family matters, such as whether a pregnant woman was fit to travel, where it is hard to imagine the reasons for medical involvement. In terms of the practical possibilities for medical intervention, the cases of sudden death and accidents are of particular interest because they illustrate the close relationship between medical police, public health and legal medicine. Many of the cases related to incidents of drowning – a topic to which I shall return later as it was in the forefront of attempts to promote preventative medical action in the name of social improvement and thus epitomises the eighteenth-century French manner of policing public health. There were other places where the ideas implicit in medical police and public health could be put into practice and from which we can gain more insight into what was envisaged in a programme of medical police. One such place was the legal system. Legal medicine, or medical jurisprudence, associated medicine with the execution of existing laws principally through the use of practitioners as expert witnesses at trials. Writings on legal medicine essentially followed, and sometimes sought to improve, existing judicial processes – by that token, they inevitably touched on some delicate moral and social issues, rape, virginity and illegitimacy among them. Legal medicine was not a specialism that arose *de novo* in the eighteenth century, and even a cursory look at writings on medico-legal topics reveals the long list of earlier authorities appealed to, together with a deep indebtedness to Roman law. As a subject it had certainly gained institutional backing – for example, by the foundation of chairs in the new medical faculties in 1795 – as well as intellectual respectability by the end of the eighteenth century. There were also a couple of standard texts in the field, by François Fodéré and Paul

5. Dieudonné, an XII, vol. 3, pp. 311, 313. The context for such regional statistics is elaborated in Perrot and Woolf, 1984, part 1. Coleman, 1982 also has much to say about Lille as an early industrial area.
6. The archival evidence comes from holdings in the Archives Municipales de Lille, and the Archives du Département du Nord, located in Lille.

Mahon.[7] These suggest the topics that, by consensus, formed the core of medical jurisprudence and the interweaving of legal themes with public hygiene and medical police.

An excellent example of these themes is the work of François Fodéré, the author of what appears to be the first systematic French publication on legal medicine, public hygiene and medical police. *Les Lois Éclairées par les Sciences Physiques ou traité de médecine légale et hygiène publique* first appeared in the year VII; it was revised, enlarged and given a new title in the Napoleonic period when, in 1813, it became *Traité de Médecine légale et hygiène publique ou de police de santé adapté aux codes de l'empire français et aux connaissances actuelles.*[8] Fodéré's clinical experience was immense and he had had ample opportunity to observe the administration of medical practice during his time as a surgeon in the army, being *médecin-juré* in Aosta and Bard, working in a hospital in Marseille, and running the École Centrale in Nice. Equally influential was his contact while a young man with the Parisian surgeon Antoine Louis, a noted author on medico-legal issues.[9] Fodéré's *Les Lois* was truly an encyclopedic work and there is ample evidence for its representative character. The three-volume first edition began with a general section setting out those circumstances which might place a patient outside the normal functioning of the law and which were determined through the examination of physiological variations with age, environment and sex, and mental condition. Military exemption and feigned illness were also discussed. The second section of the book dealt with civil cases, the majority of which related to sexual conduct – virginity, chastity, separation of spouses, conception, pregnancy, childbirth and the difficulties of determining paternity. Criminal cases, such as rape, abortion, infanticide, violent and accidental death, were dealt with in the third section. Finally, in the last section, Fodéré discussed public hygiene and medical police; in fact for him these two fields were inseparable, since neither made sense without the other. Hygiene was the science upon which medical police was based, and it was *public* hygiene because of the need to affect 'the totality of citizens'. 'Medical police is nothing other than the deployment of precepts demonstrated by hygiene.'[10] The fourth part began with an analysis of contagious diseases and the institutions established to deal with them. A whole range of epidemic and epizootic conditions were covered, together with inoculation. The other topics appear somewhat miscellaneous: foundlings, military health, health in towns, specific occupational hazards, maintaining health in prisons, hospitals and ships, and, finally,

7. Francois Fodéré was, in 1813, appointed to the second chair of legal medicine, in Strasbourg, the first being in Paris. Among his other important publications are *Leçons sur les Epidémies et l'Hygiène Publique*, 4 vols., Paris, 1822–24, and *Essai Historique et Morale sur la Pauvreté des Nations*, Paris, 1825. Paul Mahon's principal publication was *Médecine Légale*, 3 vols., Paris, 1801. La Berge, 1992 mentions Fodéré as an influential writer on public health issues. In 1795 Mahon was appointed assistant in legal medicine in Paris, and he was a contributor to the medical section of the *Encyclopédie Méthodique*. On legal medicine more generally, see Bynum and Porter, 1993a, ch. 69 (by Crawford), and Clark and Crawford, 1994, esp. introduction and part 2.

8. We may note the publication of a short-lived journal edited by Antoine Fourcroy called *La Médecine éclairée par les sciences physiques*, 1791–92, to which it is likely Fodéré was indebted for his title.

9. Antoine Louis published on such medico-legal issues as signs of death, and the normal length of human pregnancy in the 1750s and 1760s.

10. Fodéré, an VII, vol. 2, p. 359.

the difficulty of making a certain diagnosis of death. They were linked, however, by their importance to the population as a whole, by the potential threat to public safety and order if these matters were not attended to. Fodéré's treatise contained a wide range of the medico-legal and medical police topics current in the period. Although it was very much addressed to contemporary issues, it drew its legal precedents and classic cases largely from ancient Rome.

Medical police was closely bound up with programmes for positive health, individual and social, physical and moral. This goal was to be achieved through the control of external, environmental forces via administrative reforms and hygienist measures. Insofar as the latter were directed at individuals, therapy that involved altering human behaviour and lifestyle was stressed. But the main thrust of medical police and public health was to affect people en masse. These fields thereby became aspects of the science of management and the object they managed was the population, the people.

The idea of the health of the people was at the heart of medical police and public health, yet, as an idea, it is remarkably elusive. This is not just because of the challenges of imagining a collectivity such as 'the people', but also because 'health' is hard to define, being a desirable, ideal state rather than a phenomenon that can be measured. It may be helpful to distinguish three interpretations of the phrase which led to different forms of response: first, attempts to conceptualise and explain the level of health of a collectivity; second, the use of quantitative techniques; and third, the concern for the health of the 'popular classes' as opposed to the elite and the bourgeoisie. In considering approaches to collective health, we should note that there were a number of ways in which eighteenth-century political and social theorists, as well as medical practitioners, thought about the health of large groups. One of the best-known attempts was Rousseau's *Discours sur l'origine de l'inégalité* (1754), which argued that illness, a prominent feature of so-called civilised society, was entirely due to the harmful effects of that unequal way of life, coupled with the ignorance and incompetence of doctors.[11] These themes, that both increasing 'civilisation' and the intervention of medical practitioners were detrimental to general health, were taken up by many subsequent writers. In fact, thinking about society as pathogenic became quite commonplace, although the inferences drawn from that statement varied dramatically. The population was frequently seen as being composed of 'natural' subgroups defined by their shared lifestyle. The use of a physiology of lifestyle, based on the analysis of constitution, temperament and environment, and indebted to Neo-Hippocratism, was a major means to considering the health of groups.[12] Sub-groups within the population were sometimes determined by gender or age, at others by occupation, social or marital status. Hence, men and women, infants, aristocrats, peasants, the bourgeoisie and '*gens de lettres*', for example, were treated as significant medical constituencies.

11. Rousseau, 1974, pp. 149–50; Bynum and Porter, 1993a, ch. 27 (by Porter).
12. On Hippocratism see Sargent, 1982 and Bynum and Porter, 1993a, ch. 15 (by Hannaway); on constitution, see Bynum and Porter, 1993a, pp. 413–16; Brockliss and Jones, 1997 discuss the role of Hippocratic ideas in French medicine.

It was increasingly common during the eighteenth century to refer to the effects of epidemics or to mortality, especially that of children, as an indicator of general health standards. It is important not to underestimate the sophistication which demographic work relating to mortality had reached by the last quarter of the eighteenth century. This made possible the treatment of 'the population' and its constitutent groups as abstract entities. The mortality of those living in towns and the country, of the married and the single, of men and women, of the sane and the insane, of old and young, were all measured, analysed and considered, and data from different countries compared. As a result, a set of specific debates was generated which encompassed both public health and medical police – sex-ratios, longevity and life tables, causes of fertility and infant mortality, and the effects of inoculation and vaccination, lying-in hospitals, and so on. Practitioners, including relatively humble ones, became accustomed to collecting, using and criticising local statistics and to treating the population as a quantity for mathematical and manipulative administration – this was particularly true of Napoleonic France.[13]

Both the content and the language of writings on the health of the people suggest that another sense of the terms 'people' and 'population' was being invoked, that of the people as a *class*. In both the French and English languages of the period, 'the people' was defined as that part of the population that was *not* the nobility or the ruling class, but the 'commonality', 'the masses'. They were also those owned by a sovereign or a state.[14] Thus, to speak of the health of the people was to imply *both* the problems of those too ignorant, irresponsible and poor to deal with their own diseases, *and* the human resources of the labouring section of the community. William Cobbett was not far wrong when he said in 1817: 'we now frequently hear the working classes called "the population", just as we hear the animals upon a farm called "the stock" '.[15] The whole issue of the condition of the population was fraught with political tension, so it is no surprise to find indications of class conflict in writings on the subject. These were especially explicit when the 'traditional', 'superstitious' ways of the populace were castigated, and the option of reform via education was being advocated. Heated responses to quackery expressed anxieties about the gullibility of ordinary people, especially women, in relation to health matters.[16] But medical writers who wished to improve the health of the masses did not uniformly turn their attention towards the irresponsible multitudes, they frequently accepted that the spotlight should be on the medical fraternity itself.

13. Perrot and Woolf, 1984; Coleman, 1982; Frangsmyr *et al.*, 1990.

14. *Oxford English Dictionary*, vol. VII, 1933, p. 1126, under Population. See also vol. VII, pp. 661–2, under People; also Littré, 1878, vol. 3, pp. 1091–2 (Peuple), 1212 (Populace), 1213 (Population). The notion 'the people' continues to be problematic: see e.g. Smith, 1990, whose book, *The People's Health*, which first appeared in 1979, generated some puzzlement. Dealing with the period 1830–1910 in Britain it covers many of the issues practitioners in the late eighteenth and early nineteenth centuries were concerned with. Tissot's influential and widely read *Avis au Peuple sur sa Santé*, first published in 1761, is a significant marker, although its original aims were rather modest. For medicine specifically in relation to *citizens*, see Weiner, 1993.

15. *Oxford English Dictionary*, vol. VII, p. 1126.

16. Ramsey, 1988; Ackerman, 1990; Brockliss and Jones, 1997 consider the anxieties about quackery in France.

When examining their own and their colleagues' activities, medical practitioners were painfully aware of their own limited therapeutic capacities. This was so to such an extent that the crisis in medical efficacy became an integral part of approaches to policing the health of the people.

Attempts to deal with the health of the people posed practical as well as conceptual problems. Demands that medicine improve public health contrasted sharply with the limited therapeutic capacity of individual practitioners. The efficacy of medical practice was constantly being challenged by practitioners themselves: an excellent example is Jean-Emmanuel Gilibert's three-volume invective published in 1772 and provocatively entitled *L'Anarchie Médicinale, ou la médecine considerée comme nuisible à la société*. I would suggest that the dissatisfaction with contemporary medical practices and with existing provision for professional regulation expressed by Gilibert and others was reasonably widespread, especially among practitioners with hygienist sympathies. As a result, alternative forms of medical practice had to be considered, some of which entailed controlling practitioners while others led to different styles of therapy. There were four obvious, and to some extent overlapping, options which were readily available: environmental medicine, professional control, experimental medicine and preventative medicine.

The term 'environmental medicine' subsumes a variety of approaches, including the design of buildings, quarantine arrangements, drainage, canal construction and air purification. One of the most attractive features of a medicine which resorted to environmental control was that it could potentially affect large numbers of people and, since it used nature's own laws in the service of human beings, it was considered both more efficacious and less dangerous than therapies which relied on drugs, or, worse still, secret specific remedies.[17]

Diatribes against specific remedies abounded, as did demands for licences to sell them. Many people believed that remedies themselves were only part of the problem, and that it was the practitioners selling them who constituted a threat to the nation's health. Those who marketed specifics were frequently, but by no means universally, those who had no formal permit to practise, and it was such 'quacks', along with midwives and wisewomen, who were castigated as medical anarchists. One solution, therefore, was to rigidly exclude from practice all those who were inadequately educated and trained, and who sold such specifics. Accordingly, many practitioners advocated medical police, that is, policing medical practice, a task which was taken quite seriously during Napoleon's reign, and which was executed in part by regional 'medical juries'. The reports submitted by the juries give some indication of the difficulties posed by the overseeing of practitioners.[18] The policing of medical practice was not, in the sources I have consulted, seen as an unwarranted intrusion: rather the development of explicit medical ethics was welcomed. Acceptance of regulations

17. Riley, 1987 discusses environmental medicine. See also Weiner, 1993, ch. 10. It worth noting how other fields, such as medical topography, explored the possibilities of environmental medicine by trying to correlate disease patterns with social and environmental factors for well-defined geographical areas in the hope of improving human conditions there – a form of medical police.

18. Material relating to Medical Juries is in Archives Départementales du Nord, Serie M. 231.

may have been made easier by the sense that it was medical practitioners themselves rather than 'outsiders' who were initiating and executing means of control. There is, of course, a temptation to see desire for control and 'ethics' as a decisive step in the inevitable formation of a modern professional consciousness. Historians are increasingly uncomfortable with such teleological models. Indeed, it is becoming clear that the late eighteenth and early nineteenth centuries were crucial for the processes of professionalisation – it is equally clear how complex these processes actually were. That the situation was far from simple is revealed by the extent of interpersonal rivalry and dispute so evident in the case of Lille. Medical police, in the sense of controlling practice, entailed not just the hounding of so-called charlatans and empirics, but the elaboration of precise rules of conduct between various groups of licensed practitioners and between those of different ranks. Midwives, however, generally bore the heaviest criticism of 'unprofessional' behaviour.[19]

Along with these forays into stricter control of practice went attempts to define and redefine correct medical roles. The arguments were not primarily conducted in terms of expertise, but in terms of public utility – the medical calling was very often presented as akin to that of the philanthropist and politician. Furthermore, in the name of public service, practitioners of all classes advocated and employed experimental surgical techniques and vivisectional experiments. Two justifications were offered – first, that new surgical methods would only save lives if the surgeon had plenty of practice, and second, that certain medical judgements, particularly in legal medicine, were based on physiological fantasy instead of fact. It was not enough, for instance, to ascertain that a subject was dead, it was vital to establish the exact cause and *mechanism* of death because this might lead to the prevention of other deaths. It was commonly admitted that determining the cause of death was a difficult operation, and it could hardly be investigated experimentally by drowning, suffocating or hanging living subjects – puppies could be used instead. Exponents of such experiments explicitly stated that knowledge of anatomy alone was insufficient in such matters.[20] In addition to experimental work on mechanisms of death, a great deal of attention was devoted to Caesarean section, no doubt because it seemed doubly capable of becoming a widely-used, lifesaving operation. The Lille medical and surgical organisations debated the issue several times in the last two decades of the eighteenth century. One was actually performed in the city in May 1780; the woman survived and was even accorded a pension by the magistrates.[21] In his treatise on legal medicine and medical police of 1801, Paul Mahon advocated the use of sections on *all* women dying

---

19. On the development of medical ethics see Baker, 1993; Baker *et al.*, 1993; on French midwives see Gelis, 1984 and 1988.

20. There is a direct connection here with the debates on the guillotine discussed in Chapter 7. On ideas of death (and life) see Bynum and Porter, 1993a, ch. 13 (by Albury), esp. pp. 252–6. McManners, 1981 explores the social history of attitudes towards death in eighteenth-century France.

21. Warocquier, 1782 on methods of Caesarean section refers to the section performed by his father in 1780. This thesis together with others on related topics and pamphlets sent from Paris on the medical problems of childbirth are in the Archives Municipales de Lille.

in childbirth shortly *before* delivery, partly in the hope of saving the babies, but also to give surgeons experience in refining their techniques.[22]

Such radical medical intervention could become unnecessary once preventative techniques were fully developed. So said the formidable array of hygienists who wrote manuals and pamphlets urging people to live better, less passionately, more moderately, avoiding tea and coffee and so on, through the endless rules and regulations, which, we must assume, were absorbed by the middle classes if they were by anyone. This medical advice literature was couched in a peculiar combination of religious and political language. The first step was to castigate the irresponsibility of those who betrayed the sacred trust of their health. Le Bègue de Presle moralised on the subject in 1763:

One can only be astounded and frightened when one perceives the large number of dangers to which people expose themselves everyday by imprudence, recklessness, ignorance; and how often they risk their health, their very lives needlessly . . . for pleasure neither the intensity, the extent nor the duration of which are worth the smallest of the ills which are the price one pays for such pleasures.[23]

From this follows the moral duty to preserve one's health, in this case expressed more in religious than in social terms: 'Life and health, since they are vested in us by the Deity, their preservation should be reckoned among the most sacred and necessary of duties.'[24] Illness was sin; it could be avoided through the salvation that comes from sound understanding. In matters of health, as in those of religion, knowledge and education were the keys to self-improvement. The duty to seek health was also in the interests of the state, so that, according to Gilibert, for example, the individual and the common good were equally served by those who strove to cherish their bodies. It was by prolonging the lives of heads of families and by preserving more children who would become artisans, agriculturalists and soldiers, that hygienic practices would save and regenerate society.[25] This fusion of religious and enlightened medical discourses may seem odd at first sight since we tend to think of them as starting from radically opposed premises. But both discourses appealed to individuals to transcend their immediate needs and interests for the good of the group and the sanctions invoked were moral and not overtly repressive in character. The extent to which formal laws and punishments were seen as necessary and desirable is obviously a continuum. Many writers had no need to appeal to artificial man-made laws: nature punished sin herself and the human body was the terrain on which the forces of good and evil did battle. One such person was Constantin Volney, whose *La Loi Naturelle* (1793) epitomised the marriage of religion and secular naturalism. For Volney, incorrect health behaviour was a sin against nature and against society.

22. Mahon, 1801, vol. 3, pp. 197–216.
23. Le Bègue de Presle, 1763, p. ix.
24. Ibid., pp. xx–xxi. Le Bègue de Presle's sentiments have much in common with those of Tissot (see Chapter 6) and Volney (see Chapter 8). They were also expressed in many popular medical writings – Porter, 1992, ch. 4 is on France.
25. Gilibert, 1772, esp. vol. 3, pp. 133, 333.

Q. What is understood by Physical good or evil?
A. By the word physical is meant whatever acts immediately upon the Body; health is a physical good; sickness is a physical evil. . . .
Q. What is vice according to the law of nature?
A. It is the practice of actions prejudicial to the individual and to society.
Q. Have not virtue and vice an object purely spiritual . . . ?
A. No; they are always ultimately referable to a physical end; and this end is invariably the destruction or preservation of the human body.[26]

The issue, then, was citizenship. What happened to an individual human body had repercussions, so good citizens were knowledgeable about health and actually put their knowledge into practice because of their sense of civic responsibility. The politics of the body and illness as naturalised punishment for sin are themes found in many writers of the period from Voltaire to the Marquis de Sade.

I now wish to consider another aspect of citizenship and health, which brings us squarely back to the policing of public health – the attempts to generate organised concern for the well-being of others. Medical police was not just an issue for debate among elite medical circles. The ensemble of beliefs already outlined found expression in concrete practice of a number of different kinds. One well-known example was the control of epidemic disease; the response in Marseilles to the 1720 outbreak of plague and the organisation of their Bureau de Santé were frequently cited as admirable models. Doubtless, administrative precedents, which already existed under the *ancien régime*, had considerable influence. In a number of European countries during the eighteenth century elaborate provision was made for the treatment and attempted resuscitation of the drowned. The organisation involved, the political interventions and written sources illustrate types of practical action as well as attitudes towards the people's health: they provide us with insight into concrete situations in terms of both widespread beliefs and local arrangements. Fortunately, a wide range of materials bearing on the question is available, from the handwritten certificates of practitioners to treatises on theories of asphyxiation.

The themes of this diverse literature include the use of experiments on living animals, the castigation of traditional practices, the functioning of laws relating to death and the allegedly widespread fear of premature burial.[27] Although it is unclear how such a fear is to be explained, it was evidently taken seriously and the Lille authorities invested considerable time, energy and money in attempts to save drowned people. Drowning and asphyxiation appear to have been quite common, not just in places like Amsterdam with its canals, London with its river, and Liverpool with its docks, but in inland towns, such as Lille, as well.[28] Fairly representative were cases like that of Pierre Courbe,

26. Volney, 1807, pp. 347, 349.

27. On attitudes to death in eighteenth-century France, see McManners, 1981.

28. See, on Amsterdam, Kool, 1855; the society was founded in 1767, and on England, Thomson, 1963. The certificates dealing with drowning and asphyxiation are in the Archives Municipales de Lille. On such matters in Paris, see Brockliss and Jones, 1997, p. 744.

153

aged 51, who fell into a trough of water on 2 August 1784 while drunk and was revived by Decroix, a local apothecary. Even more common was the asphyxiation of poor people who lived in small cellars with no ventilation, like the elderly couple overcome by fumes on 12 June 1785. They lived in a cellar measuring 12×22 feet and containing open latrines.

As a well-defined area of debate, the problem of drowning gained prominence in France in the 1740s, both at local government level and in the printed medical literature. Under the latter head, the most important contributions were a dissertation on the signs of death (1742) by the anatomist Jacques Bénigne Winslow and a *mémoire* by Jacques Jean Bruhier d'Ablaincourt on avoiding premature burial (1745).[29] In 1752, the prominent surgeon and practitioner of legal medicine Antoine Louis published his *Lettres sur la certitude des signes de la mort où l'on assure les citoyens de la crainte d'être enterrés vivans, avec des observations et des expériences sur les noyés*. There followed a stream of publications contradicting, agreeing with or elaborating upon the work of Winslow, Bruhier and Louis as well as that of ancient writers. Among the best-known of such works was Edmund Goodwyn's *The Connexion of Life with Respiration*, published in 1786, 1788 and 1798 in Latin, English and French respectively.[30] Care of the drowned was also a preoccupation of the French government from the 1740s onwards and the printed debate was joined by departmental administrations. In the year VII, for example, we find the health council of Calvados publishing a pamphlet containing a taxonomy of forms of asphyxia, suggesting cures and means of accurately determining death.[31] The available material on drowning demonstrates a number of points: its importance as an issue in legal medicine; the existence of a widespread conviction that many of those submerged were still alive and should be treated for what Goodwyn speaks of as a disease – asphyxia; the use of experimental techniques to elucidate physiological mechanisms as a means to a practical effective cure; and the enthusiasm for devising 'machines' and instruments for use in resuscitation.

Chronologically, local government concern for the drowned and printed debate went hand in hand. In Lille in 1755 there was an 'Ordonnance pour les précautions à prendre au sujet des gens qui tombent dans l'eau et que l'on croit noyées' issued by magistrates. This lengthy and detailed regulation began by regretting the reluctance of the public to help the drowned and postulated as an explanation a general fear of acting illegally. 'Charitable' intervention, even where the victim appears dead, is permissible on condition that a surgeon is summoned immediately. Public-spirited people, who helped victims and called surgeons, were to be rewarded. Detailed instructions on what to do followed: keep trying to revive the patient for at least two hours, get them to vomit using a feather, undress them and wrap them in covers in a warm bed and use warm compresses. In order to stimulate the body, it must be moved frequently, and victims should be forced to gargle spirits, warm urine or a mixture of pepper and vinegar. Additional key procedures were bleeding from the jugular vein,

29. Winslow, 1742; Bruhier, 1745–46.
30. Goodwyn, 1798.
31. Conseil de Santé du Département du Calvados, an VII.

blowing air into the lungs (Goodwyn invented a special pump to do this), and injecting tobacco smoke or other irritants into the intestines using a syringe. By 1757 the use of warm coals was being advocated through a detailed case history, and arrangements were made for some to be available in case of emergencies. In 1772 the magistrates pronounced themselves dissatisfied with the provisions, presumably because people were not coming forward to help as they should. A syringe for fumigation was provided, and punishments in the form of fines introduced for bar- and inn-keepers who failed to provide heated rooms for victims of drowning. Those helping, on the other hand, including the surgeons, were to be recompensed and have their expenses refunded, all within one week. By 1780, the organisation was even better, with one surgeon and one apothecary having special kits of instruments for the treatment of the drowned. And, people are exhorted once again to act:

Those who are genuinely beneficent and worthy of praise, who consent to help the drowned, deserve moreover the wholehearted gratitude of their fellow citizens, and what greater satisfaction can a sentient being experience than that of having saved the life of a citizen.[32]

The regulation ended with an attack on traditional responses to the drowned, such as hanging them up by their feet.

Three types of provision were made by the magistrates to help the drowned. First, there were administrative and practical arrangements, such as the supply of special kits, coal and syringes. Second, they employed an educational mode, disseminating information on large posters as a means of countering customary practices and instilling new ones. The posters distributed by Humane Societies in Britain were remarkably similar. Third, magistrates invoked juridical procedures by threatening punishment and fines and offering rewards. But all of these strategies had a common aim – to enlist the help of both practitioners and the populace through creating a sense of collective responsibility. Such an approach was viable because submersion and suffocation were presented as having effects which could quite easily be mitigated in many cases. It was the possibility of saving lives for the nation that made elaborate preventative measures worthwhile. To achieve this saving of life, the magistrates, the medical practitioners and the populace worked together for the common good.

I have suggested that medical police and public health involved a delicate balance between the interests of the individual as a private citizen, and those of the collective, the 'public'. Many commentators recognised that the interrelationships between the health of individuals and that of society were exceedingly complex and they sought ways to elucidate the connections in the hope of finding points for medical intervention. But they also attempted to separate the medical problems of individuals from those of groups, using the distinction between public and private. In the medical section of the *Encyclopédie Méthodique*, the prominent hygienist Jean-Noël Hallé differentiated public from

32. *Ordonnances du Magistrat*, 410, pp. 209–210v (Archives Municipales de Lille).

private hygiene and complained that hitherto this separation had been mostly ignored.[33] For him, it was not just the treatment of individuals or collectivities that marked the difference, but the fact that, as a public hygienist, 'the philosophically-aware medical practitioner becomes the counsellor and the soul of the legislator'. Broadly speaking, private hygiene involved regimen while public hygiene included the analysis of general environmental factors and of those features of social structure deemed to determine health. It is interesting to note the repeated assertion that those who undertake to heal society through practising public hygiene are responding to a higher calling both spiritually and politically than the humbler practitioner who deals directly with individual patients.

It may be useful to put such uses of 'private' and 'public' in the context of the distinction between domestic and political economy, the former dealing with the management of a household, the latter with that of a political and economic entity. There were two forms of medicine to match. Domestic medicine, with its reliance on regimen and good advice, paid particular attention to women and children, to the regulation of sexuality, and to proper conduct within the family. In its attention to personal responsibility, the vast literature on domestic medicine echoed a theme of great importance to the politics of the late Enlightenment – the family as the point of mediation and transition between individuals and the nation.[34] The medicine of political economy, on the other hand, addressed itself to the collectivity, and most particularly to its labouring fraction, with others, such as children, being seen as valuable only insofar as they were potential labourers. Such an analysis linked health, defined as productive capacity, to abstract features of the social structure, and it, too, subjected to severe scrutiny the efficacy of conventional medical practice.

Looking at health as the result of historical, supposedly 'civilising' processes aided the project of developing a 'political medicine'. Partly, as I indicated earlier, this was conducted in the terms laid down by political theorists such as Rousseau, and his heirs in the 1790s and 1800s continued to discuss 'the state of nature', the effects of nomadic patterns of life, and the association between the concentration of population and disease in cities. This could lead to an interest in specific environmental pathogens, so that technical literatures grew up on the effects of soil, deforestation, housing, diet, air, occupation and so on. Such an approach tended to emphasise a single causal factor and to offer the possibility of elucidating the exact impact of each parameter on physiological processes. Other writers went directly to social structures in attempting to

33. Hallé, 1798, vol. 7, pp. 373–437. Coleman, 1982, La Berge, 1992 and Weiner, 1993 emphasise Hallé's importance as a major influence on nineteenth-century French hygiene. Hallé was the first holder of the chair of hygiene in the reformed Paris medical faculty – Fourcroy defined the qualities expected in the incumbent, and in doing so distinguished between public and private hygiene, Coleman, 1982, p. 17.

34. Chapter 6 discusses and cites literature on domestic/popular medicine. The distinction between public and private, which Hallé for example used, is extraordinarily complex and has been the subject of a good deal of recent scholarship more in relation to gender and to the nature of the Enlightenment than to medicine. Recent trends are evident in Castiglione and Sharpe, 1995, which also reveals the extensive influence of Habermas in shaping current approaches to the 'public sphere' of the eighteenth century. The family is the subject of part 3. Cf. Hunt, 1992.

understand disease patterns in terms of economic trends and requirements. Population as a concept remained at the core of such work, but it carried new meaning following the work of Thomas Malthus. Malthus was indeed the fundamental reference point for such practitioners as C.F.V.G. Prunelle and Étienne Sainte-Marie, both associated with medicine at Montpellier at various stages of their careers.[35]

There is a clear statement of the political economy approach, as well as a good deal of ambivalence about the real effects of medical intervention, in Clement Prunelle's *De l'action de la médecine sur la population des états* (1818), the opening lecture of his course on medical police at Montpellier. Prunelle was convinced that medical care had little social impact in combating the ill effects of civilisation and overpopulation compared with the positive role of industry in increasing wealth and improving the general conditions of life. It was only through prolonging the lives of industrial workers and combating disease which prevented work, that medicine had any impact. Prunelle shifted the debate away from mortality to morbidity; he was concerned not with the quantity of life, but with its quality. And quality ultimately reduced to production – we find him approvingly quoting the economist J.B. Say, 'nothing can make population increase which does not also favour production, and nothing can diminish it . . . which does not also undermine the sources of production'.[36]

When he spoke of population, Prunelle meant its wealth-creating sections, and he employed arguments which were economistic in the extreme. Prunelle did not attach great importance to the deaths of babies and new-borns, for, as he says, even counting the real costs of the lost work of the mothers and the medical fees connected with childbearing, the loss was small compared to that of an adult:

the death of a person who has reached the age of sixteen destroys simultaneously the capital that has accumulated upon them and the revenues which this capital was about to produce. Medicine is employed to enable people to live longer, not to increase their numbers.[37]

Using such arguments, Prunelle arrived at clear conclusions about the role of practitioners in policing public health. Under his interpretation of medical police three types of activity were envisaged. First, it had to produce an adequate and healthy population through intervention in marriage, housing, nutrition – including discovering new forms of subsistence, clothing, work, leisure and so on. This was essentially the preventative aspect of medical police. But along with this went the second type of activity: extensive policing of medical practitioners and their education. Prunelle did not totally neglect the value of curative medicine – the third type – in combating the ills due to excessive population growth: the control of contagious diseases, improving the lot of the

35. Prunelle, 1818; Sainte-Marie, 1824 and 1829; La Berge, 1992 is revealing about the role of both men in French public health movements, esp. pp. 23, 33, 132, 133.
36. Prunelle, 1818, pp. 13–14.
37. Ibid., pp. 22–3, 26 note 1.

homeless, poor, sick and destitute, indeed of all those whose health was already suffering.

There is little doubt that historians have been considerably hampered in their study of medical police and public health by the difficulty of defining their terms – a difficulty which is highly suggestive of recurrent conflicts and tensions within medicine itself. These surround the problem of the efficacy of medical intervention, especially with respect to large groups, and the differential weightings given to preventative and to curative medicine. These medical preoccupations must be seen in the broader setting of what forms of health control are possible and permitted within a historically specific social, political and economic arena. For the purposes of defining a research task, a contextual approach to the history of public health could take two forms. The first, and the more conventional, would be a study of organisations and institutions in the context of local and central government, the pressures from various sections of the community, financial resources and legislative backing. The second would address such questions as the class dynamics implicit in public health, the forms of power and control both advocated and enacted, and the political, social, cultural and economic value assigned to health. I am not, of course, advocating that these two approaches be pursued separately; quite the contrary, the two need, ideally, to be fused. However, the first has been far more enthusiastically undertaken than the second. There are a number of reasons for this, but one of them is very simple, although extraordinarily hard to combat. The history of public health remains one of the bastions of truly Whiggish history and for a rather specific reason. A linear progression of increasing enlightenment and knowledge leading to specific reforms and innovative techniques – sewage control, purification of water and air and so on – can be discerned. What is more, these developments appear logical, inevitable, self-evidently good and in line with common sense – once we know that dirt causes disease, how could we not try to eliminate dirt for the safety of all citizens? This caricatured sentiment shows how intimately a belief in *philanthropic* reform is bound up with our presuppositions about public health. By what appears a natural extension of this position, most attention has been devoted to pioneering individuals and the institutions with which they were associated.[38]

In stark contrast to the Whig history of public health is the fact that matters of health, and most especially of public health, are deeply political in that they partake of prevailing power structures and social relations. So that, without forcing a schism between ideology and material conditions, we must, nonetheless, give a prominent place in our studies to the real power of ideas and ideologies, which permit some things, but not others, to be said and done in relation to health. And this situation is explained, not by varying degrees of philanthropic benevolence, but by the day-to-day workings of a social system, including the enactment of its beliefs. I am far from denying the historical

38. Rosenberg's edited collection in honour of George Rosen, 1979, contains some recent work which illustrates the hagiographic and Whiggish modes, as well as one piece, by Rosenberg himself, which suggests the importance of ideologies in campaigns for practical reform. On medicine and philanthropy see Bynum and Porter, 1993a, ch. 62 (by Jones). Recent work on French public health has been cited in earlier notes.

importance of philanthropy; on the contrary, it seems to be one of the most powerful impulses of the period I have been discussing. 'Philanthropy' was a capacious term which, in addition to describing charitable activities and organisations, conveyed a sense of the social relationships, the responsibilities and the rights attached to them. Inevitably, philanthropy conveyed ideas of proper behaviour in relation to health, no less than to work, sexuality and religion. From this it follows that we might usefully try to pin down the specific place of public health in the complex ensemble which philanthropy represents. One way of doing this would be through detailed comparative studies: for example, the provisions for that ultimate preventative measure, the saving of lives, could be compared for, say, Britain, France, and the Netherlands, with respect to the drowned, asphyxiated and the prematurely buried. Naturally, this was only one small aspect of public health activities in the eighteenth century, but it serves as an example of the relationship between administrative procedures, forms of 'persuasion' through education, and ideas of lifesaving as a civic responsibility. Even here, control and coercion were just below the surface.

In looking at the multiplicity of themes subsumed under medical police, I found a number of preoccupations which shed light on public health. There was a crisis over the efficacy of medicine, which was used as a springboard, both to develop new forms of practice and to reform practitioners themselves. All this was done on the somewhat hubristic assumption that a large proportion of ill health was removable, controllable and preventable by conscious human action. In this sense public health and medical police were deeply indebted to environmental medicine.[39] There was a specific economic-cum-political imperative behind the drive for positive health for the collectivity. In mercantilist logic, people were wealth; more people, especially healthy ones, generate more wealth. It was an easy step to make the healthy body into an icon; freedom from debilitating ills was as important as social responsibility and political rights, even a precondition for them. But the treatment of the people, the population, as a homogeneous entity was not entirely satisfactory, and the process of breaking it down into fractions with specific health characteristics was evidently taking place during the late eighteenth and early nineteenth centuries, and was indeed a significant part of what I have referred to as 'lifestyle' medicine. I noted a concomitant shift from quantity of population to the durability of the working population as the index of the people's health and guide to the forms of policing required. Policing public health was, I would argue, integral to the broader transition from political arithmetic to political economy.

39. Jordanova, 1979/1997 and Riley, 1987.

PART III

FAMILY VALUES

It is hard to think of any aspect of eighteenth-century culture where an interest in the family did not manifest itself. While it is immediately evident that philanthropists, demographers, lawyers and poor-relief administrators had to deal with familial issues, and that the eighteenth-century novel took its central themes from domestic life, it is less clear precisely how medical and natural knowledge were concerned with the family. It is the purpose of the essays in Part 3 to show how this could work. 'Family' is an ambiguous term, not just because what counts as 'family' at any given historical moment is underdetermined, but also because it functions in a number of distinct ways. It was simultaneously a metaphor, a legal category, and a means of classifying people. Family and household, while closely related in the period, were not identical. My interest is not in co-residence, but in intertwined ideas of kinship and gender. More particularly, I examine how kin relations were rooted in nature. Indeed, the family was freshly and urgently naturalised in the eighteenth century. Its constituent relationships were not construed in terms of genetic endowment, but in much looser terms of affinity and invested with intense emotionality. In practice, there were many such relationships, and, given high levels of mortality, the legal and emotional complexities of serial marriages and stepchildren could be formidable. In the sources I have examined, however, such issues were marginal; instead they focused on two types of relationship – between man/ father/husband and woman/mother/wife, and between parents, especially mothers, and their children. Such relationships were paradigmatic – they seemed the most 'natural', the most important in terms of health and survival, and the most piercingly intimate. It was possible to oscillate, when writing about the family, between the particular and the abstract, between specific relationships and nature's norms. I use the term 'kinship' to stress abstract thinking about the family, but I intend it to evoke, not so much the social practices through which relationships were managed, as the system, the implicit framework, through which intimate affinities were understood. It is immediately apparent that these are matters of classification – kinship is a taxonomic system. Reciprocally, the terms in which animals, plants and minerals were classified in the eighteenth century owed much to thinking about the family and human reproduction.

Once again the chapters that make up Part 3 have much in common, although originally conceived within distinct problematics. 'Naturalising the Family' was written with the relationships between science and literature in mind. It explores the ways in which reproduction and sexuality were linked, often in a euphoric literary style, in both scientific and fictional writings. It hints at the existence of a dynamic between a naturalistic view of the family and one that gives more weight to what I would call its sacred aspects – a theme taken up in the final chapter. 'Gender, Generation and Science' explores in more detail one particular naturalistic vision of reproduction, that of William Hunter. I offer an interpretation of his images of pregnancy in terms of contemporary ideas of mother–child relationships. The immediate inspiration for this chapter was the growth of interest in eighteenth-century medicine as a social and cultural phenomenon. I return to William Hunter and his brother John in the final essay of the book, 'Cultures of Kinship'. This was written specifically in order to reveal the possibilities of a cultural history that cast its net wide in terms of sources and ideas. I wanted to show something of how people thought and felt about kinship, to evoke its capacity to mobilise the most complex and raw responses, without neglecting its intellectual dimensions.

It is easy to be dismissive of the sentimentalism connected with the family, just as it is to despise the mobilisation of 'family values' for political ends. To succumb to either temptation is an abdication of the historian's responsibility to her materials. I have tried to offer a sympathetic, but not uncritical account of representations of the family, whether these were presented as authoritative knowledge, as entertainment or as aids to meditation and reflection.

CHAPTER TEN

Naturalising the Family: Literature and the Bio-medical Sciences of the Late Eighteenth Century

Family, gender and sexuality are themes common to eighteenth-century science and literature. The bio-medical sciences were concerned with reproduction and gender as natural phenomena to be explored along with other facts of nature. At the same time, bio-medical writings on these themes may be understood as a literary tradition in that they drew on a specific fund of writing styles, images and metaphors. Elements of this discourse were used in novels, as well as in philosophical and political writings. In this sense we may speak in general of shared cultural resources, and more specifically of a language of nature, which achieved its force partly because it raised important social questions about the family as a natural moral unit. Eighteenth-century literary traditions in general were marked by a special interest in the world of nature, often as the mirror of human feeling, a source of moral norms or as an escape from society, and in the world of kinship, where love and intimacy could be expressed within the legitimate bounds of the family. Equally, they explored what was unstable and disturbing in both nature and the family. This chapter examines issues around family, gender and sexuality that were present in both 'science' and 'literature', paying particular attention to their implications for the relations between the domain of nature and that of culture and society.[1]

Referring to a set of particular literary, medical and scientific interests in late eighteenth-century France, I am concerned with a range of historically specific factors: the definition of human sexuality in scientific-cum-medical terms, and the preoccupation with the family as a biological and social unit – a privileged zone of life. When eighteenth-century commentators discussed such matters as pregnancy, childbirth and adolescence, they did so with a lively realisation of their dual physiological and social character. Furthermore, physiological processes were tools with which social events could be explored, and may therefore be said to stand in a mediating relationship to them. The preoccupation – one might almost say obsession – with reproduction makes little sense in isolation

---

1. The field of science and literature has grown exponentially in the last fifteen years. My own approach has been greatly influenced by the work of Gillian Beer. For recent surveys see Olby *et al.*, 1990, ch. 9 (by Golinski), ch. 51 (by Beer), and Bynum and Porter, 1993a, ch. 65 (by Neve). A valuable collection of Beer's essays appeared in 1996.

from the institution which gave it meaning (and a legal framework) – the family. There can be no doubt about the widespread interest among late eighteenth-century writers in the family, both as idea and as lived experience.[2] In relation to languages of nature, the crucial point is that in the family we have an idea which is at once natural and social. It was such an integral element of human existence that its value as a subject of study could scarcely be disputed. Furthermore, it could be treated in a variety of ways: by painters, writers, lawyers, political theorists, economists, administrators, churchmen, medical practitioners and politicians. In the literature and art of the period, both idealised and problematic relationships between family members featured so prominently that their significance cannot be denied.[3] Historians of science and medicine have been less willing than cultural historians to admit that here, where the social and biological met, a language of nature, ripe for analysis, existed. To decipher such a language in the context of eighteenth-century images of the family is to do more than illuminate an aspect of culture shared by the humanities and the sciences, as we now think of them: it is to perceive the mediation of social relations.

This language of nature was strongly dichotomous in character in that it drew on related pairs of opposite terms as its structuring concepts.[4] These potent, metaphorically-rich binaries were, in the end, ideas, used for doing cultural business, not descriptions of the social complexities of the eighteenth century. Nowhere was this feature more marked than in writings on the family and sexuality – male/female is such a powerfully evocative opposition.[5] I refer to a number of such pairs:

female	male
nature	culture/society
private	public
family	society
inside (interior)	outside
body	mind
passion (feeling)	reason

The dichotomous approach can be illustrated by the treatise on *Physiognomy*, first published in 1775–78, by the Swiss pastor Lavater, in which he drew up a series of paired characteristics designed to evoke the differences between the sexes.

Man is more solid; woman is softer.

Man is straighter; woman is more supple.

Man walks with a firm step; woman with a soft and light one.

Man contemplates and observes; woman looks and feels.[6]

2. Flandrin, 1979; Forster and Ranum, 1976; Traer, 1980; Jacobs *et al.*, 1979; Foucault, 1979; McLaren, 1973–74; Edmiston, 1985; Charlton, 1984; Hunt, 1992. O'Day, 1994 offers a comparative perspective.

3. Bryson, 1981; Duncan, 1973, 1981; Hautecœur, 1945; Edmiston, 1985; Goodden, 1989; Charlton, 1984.

4. Williams, 1975, 1983; Jordanova, 1989a; Elshtain, 1981; Castiglione and Sharpe, 1995; MacCormack and Strathern, 1980.

5. In addition to the works cited above, Maclean, 1980 provides useful background.

6. Lavater, 1841, p. 172; for some recent approaches to physiognomy see Shookman, 1993.

These images of masculinity and femininity pervaded medical and scientific writings, and enabled a holistic view of the human body to be built up. Furthermore, the overlap between these pairs produced a language which incessantly evoked associations, so that to speak of women, for example, was to suggest the realm of private domesticity; one pair stood for and represented the others. It would be a mistake to construe these pairs as static, with stable meanings: on the contrary, sometimes, as in Lavater, there was a continuum, not a mutually exclusive relationship, between the terms. Similarly, whereas female was often related to unmediated nature, as in the power to reproduce, male could also be so related as in its association with brute sexual desire. In these ways a set of complex changing images was built up which both constrained and expressed tension and contradiction.

Scientific and medical writings are composed of clusters of images and packages of ideas. The importance of textual analysis is increasingly being recognised as a way of unpacking these clusters. It is equally important to consider items of culture as entities, where all their elements – style, language, medium and so on – are working together. The approach, which involves treating cultural products as integrated wholes, may be applied to any kind of writing or art. The example of visual culture is a particularly appropriate one, for it alerts us to the importance of 'ways of seeing', to their capacity to *re*structure, that is, to *re*-present ideas, experiences and social conditions. In doing so worldviews and ideologies are given expression.[7] The language of late eighteenth-century writings in the bio-medical sciences was significant in three respects: first, it employed terms with both common-sense and technical meanings and thereby exploited the imaginative associations they gave rise to; second, there was a deliberate attempt to formulate a common language for mind and body so that different levels of organic complexity could be dealt with in the same explanatory framework; and, finally, there was a growing desire to give notions previously construed as descriptions of stable, physical characters a physiological meaning, reflecting constantly changing internal biological processes. A vocabulary of vital action became necessary which stressed motion, dynamism, process and change; all these fundamental features of nature demanded expression.[8]

Take the common eighteenth-century notion of 'habit', for example. This concept was of growing importance in the biology and medicine of the period. Standing at the borderline of mind and body, habit expressed common experience, and conveyed the idea of organisms as products of their own life histories. It represented the possibility of behavioural responses to stimuli being incorporated into the physical make-up of living things. For the biologist

7. Berger, 1972, 1980; Bryson, 1981; Williams, 1975, 1983. Michael Baxandall's approach to visual culture is exceptionally generative: 1985; 1988 (first published 1972); 1995.

8. Charlton, 1984 covers many of the themes of this chapter from a different historiographical perspective. Useful background on eighteenth-century scientific developments may be found in Roger, 1963/1993; Olby *et al.*, 1990, ch. 19 (by Sloan); Hankins, 1985; Reill and Wilson, 1996, especially the entries for Generation and Vitalism. I find the use of the term 'vitalism' problematic, and Reill and Wilson define it rather strictly, nonetheless, many historians have noted a shift in the second half of the eighteenth century towards an interest in life as active and in the distinctiveness of organic phenomena. Cf. Williams, 1994.

Lamarck, habit expressed the active relationship between plants and animals and their environment. It explained the characteristics both of individuals and of species as they developed during the long history of the natural world.[9] A similar argument can be applied to terms like 'temperament', 'constitution' and 'sensibility', which were linked in having habit as one of their major sources. The distinctive skeletons and musculature of the sexes, the physician Cabanis explained, arise from use and habit and not from rigid, determining structures. Feminine sensibility derived, therefore, from the general habits of women, while it in turn influenced the broad parameters of women's lives.[10] The focus was increasingly on the analysis of internal physiological processes. This search for deeper knowledge may be understood both literally and metaphorically, since the most inaccessible areas of the body and those organic processes that were hardest to observe claimed greater attention. There was a special allure exercised by the idea of comprehending the previously unseen.

The concern with the recesses of the living body carried levels of meaning beyond the explicit claim of physiology to be a new and more sophisticated bio-medical perspective. Those studying the interiors of organisms paid particular attention to the female form and its generative powers, thereby raising cultural, social, political and economic questions. But these resonances can only be reconstructed if we accept the full symbolic load carried by the human, and particularly by the female body. The connections between different realms of social life were imaginative, as much as anything. Analysing mediations therefore entails revealing the metaphors on which they were built and their employment in a particular cultural setting. In investigating the reasons for the prominence of reproduction and sexuality in many different forms of eighteenth-century writings, literary and visual materials are particularly valuable. They may, for example, contain elements 'censored' from scientific and medical writings, either consciously or unconsciously, and for a variety of reasons. While we acknowledge the fundamental structural affinities between science and literature, it is nonetheless also the case that the rationalistic conventions of Enlightenment thought adhered to by many natural philosophers allowed fewer open spaces for tensions and unresolved problems than did fiction and poetry of the same period. This does not mean that late eighteenth-century science and medicine evaded the ambiguous and intractable aspects of the world, but rather that, in expressing their ideas in written form, natural philosophers strove extremely hard to manage and dominate their materials – a project in which they were, inevitably, only partially successful.

I shall explore the use of natural imagery in eighteenth-century writings on the family and reproduction by discussing works of fiction such as *Paul et Virginie* (1788) by Bernardin de Saint-Pierre, and *Les liaisons dangereuses* (1782) by Choderlos de Laclos, and medical writings such as *Rapports du Physique et du*

---

9. Lamarck, 1809, vol. 1, ch. vii; Jordanova, 1984a, pp. 54–6. For a more literary approach to sensibility see Brookner, 1972, chs 1–3; Rogers, 1986; Goodden, 1989; cf. Benjamin, 1991. Webster, 1970 has a helpful definition of sensibility from the perspective of someone who was not only around at the time but intensely interested in science and medicine – see note 38 below.

10. Cabanis, 1956, vol. 1, pp. 272–315; Tissot, 1772.

Moral de l'Homme (1802) by the medical practitioner Cabanis, with its lengthy analysis of female physiology.

A major impulse towards a naturalistic study of sexuality and the family came from that characteristic eighteenth-century project, the application of scientific techniques to all aspects of human existence to create a 'science of man'.[11] The science of man took many forms, but two questions with which this chapter is concerned were invariably present. First, there was the issue of the male and female forms of 'man' – a curiously abstract notion which belies the insistent exploration of sex differences. Second, there was the question of the relationship between individuals and groups, at a given moment in time and over human history. The passage from the state of nature to society, whether historical or metaphorical, was undoubtedly problematic. Making the simple assumption that people were, by definition, social beings was hardly totally satisfying, given the huge variety of cultures that were known to and actively being examined by Enlightenment writers. There was too much wrong with some societies for them to be identified simply with 'nature', while the 'natural' virtues of individuals were rarely rewarded in so-called civilised environments. In discussions about the history of human development, about social organisation, and about the relationships between individuals and groups, the family occupied a pivotal position – it was there that individuals became social. The idea that the family could be taken as a prototype and microcosm of society as a whole was widely held and extremely attractive. By virtue of gender differences and reproduction, the family was rooted in nature, and so was constructed as a legitimate foundation for the sexual division of labour and the separation between public and private life.[12] Commentators used the family as a natural-cum-social object to explore a wide range of issues.[13] The very inseparability of its natural and social aspects is fundamental. Furthermore, in speaking about the family, the gendered nature of parental authority, and the obligations and duties between spouses, were widely debated. Hence, an examination of late eighteenth-century writings on family and sexuality, be they political, fictional, medical or scientific, reveals in the language of nature a discourse about power.

The naturalness of the family revolved around two sets of relationships: those between man and woman, and those between parent and child. While some writers discussed relations between siblings, this was usually to make a specific point, to which I shall return shortly. Of all possible combinations, the bond between mother and child held a special place as both the most basic biological and the most significant social relationship. This took the form of a vast literature on pregnancy, childbirth, infanticide, breast-feeding, wet-nursing, swaddling and illegitimacy.[14] Such writings did not necessarily take the precise nature of maternity for granted, however. The medical practitioner William

11. Bryson, 1968; Phillipson, 1981; Staum, 1974 and 1980; Fox *et al.*, 1995.
12. Okin, 1980; Elshtain, 1981 and 1982; Castiglione and Sharpe, 1995, esp. chs 4, 5 and 6.
13. Diderot is a wonderful example of the point: e.g. Edmiston, 1985 and *Greuze & Diderot*, 1984.
14. Indications of these literatures may be found in Knibiehler, 1976; Forster and Ranum, 1980; Jackson, 1996; Laqueur, 1990, esp. ch. 5; Wilson, 1995, as well as in the Wellcome Library in London, which can be searched by keywords. Much of the popular medical literature of the eighteenth century related to these issues, e.g. Porter, 1992.

Cadogan was not alone in aiming in his *Essay on Nursing* (1748) to delineate a more active and significant role for the father in the process of childrearing. The respective contributions and responsibilities of mothers and fathers to their children were not rigid and fixed, but subject to continual re-evaluation.

The fact remains that it was the mother's relationship to her child, a symbol of the synthesis of nature and society, which dominated much writing in late eighteenth-century France. The intensity of the relationship began during pregnancy, and was expressed in terms of 'sympathy', an idea of exceptional richness, which in this period was employed in a number of new ways, adding significant levels of meaning to its originally medical connotation of two parts of the body affecting each other.[15]

The Mother gives the first Impression or Impulse to the Child, from Whence it is returned with greater Force, by the natural mutual Sympathy and Communication between two equal Sufferers.[16]

The special sympathy between mother and child could not be explained in mechanical terms. It was, on the contrary, a physiological and hence an organic relationship.[17] The physiological language, which alone was appropriate for its discussion, contained psychological and social dimensions, precisely because it was a language of life, a vocabulary which conveyed the qualities only the living possessed. Extending the argument about maternal sympathy, Cabanis, doctor and *idéologue*, argued that only women possess the refined and delicate responses necessary for the care of vulnerable infants. For him, maternal love was based in the sensibility which is specific to the female sex. There were degrees of sympathy – that between mother and foetus was even more intense than that between mother and baby. There were several levels and types of sympathy – between different parts of the same physiological system, between different areas of the body – and it was manifested in different degrees according to age, sex and the part in question.[18]

Sympathy and sensibility were closely linked. For Cabanis, sensibility lay at the heart of life itself. It was the closest it was possible to get to a vital principle, but it could only be studied through its effects since its ultimate cause was unknowable.[19] Sensibility explained all aspects of life including human intelligence. Its seat was the brain and nervous system through which all the organs and muscles were connected, providing a physical basis for sympathy. But sensibility was not a passive organic property, it was an active faculty which acted through the brain on sensations and impressions received by the senses. Sensibility was thus central to the late eighteenth-century project of developing a science of life.[20]

15. French, 1969, chs 4 and 7; Lawrence, 1979; Marshall, 1988.
16. Morgan, 1735, pp. 220–1, is typical of the period.
17. For this reason, the placenta, the organ where mother and child met, was of special interest, as discussed in Chapter 12.
18. Cabanis, 1956, vol. 1, pp. 275, 280, 295, 305.
19. Ibid., pp. 195–6, 198, 539–40; vol. 2, pp. 266–7, 291–2, 496–7, 498–9.
20. Figlio, 1975 and 1976; Corsi, 1988; Roger 1963/1993; Williams, 1994.

Sensibility varied with age, sex and behaviour. Woman's distinctive sensibility was lively but unstable. Together with female weakness by comparison with men, the sensibility of women served to captivate the male sex. Man had a different but complementary sensibility which, moreover, served a larger goal: the maintenance of morality. Furthermore, Cabanis explained: 'All civil societies invariably have as their foundation, and equally necessary for their regulation, the primitive society which is the family.'[21] Society, morality and civilisation all rested upon the union of two opposite elements, male and female, both part of nature, yet finely adapted to their moral functions and social goals, which were expressed through the family.

In sexual reproduction, eighteenth-century writers found a convenient combination of biological, moral and social elements. Cabanis summarised the distinctive features of human gestation to which the key was the special nature of the uterus with its highly developed sensibility. The peak of sensibility reached by the womb during pregnancy served to stimulate the growth of the embryo, and constituted the ability to pass on life. Unlike other species, human babies were not capable of surviving unaided, hence the need for parental care, which women alone could provide by virtue of their physiological delicacy and associated psychological traits.[22] These characteristics determined the sorts of work to which the female sex was generally best suited: sedentary, requiring no muscular force, but demanding fine skills and preferably working on small objects.[23] In Cabanis's view they were emphatically not to do brain work.[24]

In his *Rapports du Physique et du Moral de l'Homme*, Cabanis moved easily from anatomical through physiological and psychological considerations and on to moral and social ones, aided by concepts like sensibility on the one hand, and by his broad conception of sexuality on the other. From the science of man, he was led on to the dual study of sex differences and social institutions, employing in the process powerful images of femininity and masculinity. But in the fifth section, which dealt with 'the influence of sex on the nature of ideas and on moral feelings', the two sexes were not treated with equal attention or in similar detail.[25] This part was, in fact, almost exclusively devoted to women, as if sex were more fundamental to female physiology than to male, and the feminine a deviation from a male norm. The use of dichotomies and metaphor was central to the arguments he developed about the importance of sexuality. He associated women with the inside of the home, the care of children and distance from danger, with modesty, and with weakness, timidity and secretiveness. Masculinity, by contrast, was associated with public debate, politics, reason, forceful energetic personalities, and with strength, daring, enterprise, hard work and the desire to dominate nature.

21. Cabanis, 1956, vol. 1, p. 293.
22. Ibid., pp. 272, 291–2, 295, 305.
23. Ibid., vol. 1, pp. 278–9.
24. Ibid., p. 298; L. Wilson, 1993 concerns the 'maladies des femmes' debates: esp. ch. 4 is interesting on the degree to which women could exercise intellectual authority.
25. Cabanis, 1956, vol. 1, pp. 272–315.

The specialness of the mother as the embodiment of femininity is vividly illustrated in Bernardin de Saint-Pierre's *Paul et Virginie*, an extraordinarily popular sentimental novel, written by a man with a strong interest in natural history, which idealises the moral goodness of nature. Paul and Virginie are brought up on lush Martinique by their mothers, neither of whom has a husband, to become admirable human beings. Their mothers, from very different social backgrounds, are both presented as founts of natural, innate wisdom. It is their destiny to convey simple virtues to their children. Fathers, by implication, are entirely dispensable: the principal role men play in the book is that of mediator between the new moral micro-society in which Paul and Virginie live with their mothers and servants, and the old world, the *ancien régime* of deceit, luxury, artificiality and sorrow. The arbitrary use of power in corrupt Europe had destroyed the simple happiness of human beings, and particularly of these women. The rewards they have in their new lives are linked, not only with their virtue, but with their exotic environment. Bernardin was tapping into a particular curiosity about the family and sexuality in such settings.[26]

Bernardin de Saint-Pierre places the mother/child dyad at centre stage. Both children enjoy exceptionally intense closeness with their mothers. Great importance is also attached to the relationship between the two children, described as that between brother and sister – they shared the breast milk of both women – although they are not, of course, biologically related. This natural bonding between children was given a political inflection by Mary Wollstonecraft in her *Vindication of the Rights of Woman* (1792), when she suggested that true equality had its origins and its prototype in the mutual respect and love of siblings.[27] Comradeship began with real brothers and sisters; the family was the school for equality and political responsibility.

Bernardin de Saint-Pierre's micro-society has an interesting family structure:

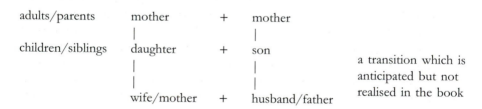

There is sufficient ambiguity in the relationship between Paul and Virginie to raise, in the modern reader's mind at least, the question of incest. In Bernardin's ideal society, mother/child relationships are characterised by maternal sacrifice and transmission of the gift of natural virtue. Those between 'siblings' display sharing, identification and sympathy. We never see a full sexual relationship

---

26. Charlton, 1984, ch. 6, Outram, 1995, ch. 5; inevitably Diderot was a prime example of the trend; the best short introduction remains France, 1983.

27. Wollstonecraft, 1975, pp. 86, 113, 129, 279. It should be noted that Wollstonecraft, who was a novelist as well as being steeped in natural philosophy, discusses many of the key concepts of this chapter – habit, sympathy, sensibility, motherhood, the distinction between public and private, for instance, deftly manipulating a number of gendered dualisms to make her points. Cf. Hunt, 1992, ch. 3.

between a man and a woman, for the story does not permit the love between Paul and Virginie to be consummated, and their mothers lead virtuous, celibate lives. However, despite the tragedy of thwarted love, Virginie's death is in its own way an erotic climax.

Bernardin presents the story as a true one, and so, by implication, an account of a way of life which is in principle attainable. His treatment of the physical environment is integral to the plan. The goodness of the micro-society derives partly from its environment: a natural world which is exceptionally fecund, beautiful, and relatively free from human intrusion. Although guided by natural theology, and containing an unconcealed idealisation of a 'natural' society, *Paul et Virginie* contains a dramatic disruption. That the perfect equilibrium should be shattered is unavoidable, even *natural*, not just for the sake of an exciting plot, but for the simple reason that children grow up. And growing up means awakening sexuality. Or, to put the same point differently, within traditional narratives one cannot stay in the garden of Eden forever. Woman not man precipitated that particular expulsion. Bernardin implies, however, that in an ideal world, Virginie's expulsion would never have happened; she was, after all, completely innocent (see plate 18, p. 172).

In *Paul et Virginie*, Virginie's sexuality is the decisive disruption, both because she reaches sexual maturity first, and because the potential consequences of her desires – pregnancy – make her more vulnerable than Paul. Prompted by such fears, her mother sends her back to France. Her visit proving a failure, Virginie returns to her tropical paradise only to be drowned in a storm on the way back because she refuses to remove her clothes and swim to safety with a naked sailor. Her death is caused by her *modesty*, the quintessentially 'natural' female virtue.[28] The changes of puberty were taking place before she left the island, but she was unable to understand what was happening. Her transformation from child to woman is expressed through images of variation, crisis, instability and unpredictability, manifest in mind, body and the physical environment. The picture of awakening sexuality is identical to that found in any number of contemporary scientific and medical treatises. For example, Cabanis characterised puberty as a 'general commotion', 'a general change of all human existence', which demonstrated the effect of the reproductive organs, whose highly developed sensibility set up sympathetic responses in other parts of the body through the fluids they secreted and through the nervous system.[29] The important point is that the 'natural' passage from childhood to adulthood, which physiological changes inevitably produced, is a cause of disruption and conflict as well as a crucial part of human and social continuity.

Bernardin's treatment of adolescence, and his refusal to allow the story to narrate Virginie's successful attainment of full womanhood, raises the question of how growing up was conceptualised and socially marked. Was it by autonomy from parental control, by entry into the market-place if socially appropriate, by marriage, by becoming sexually active, or by the birth of children?

28. Robinson, 1982. On *Paul et Virginie*, see also Goodden, 1989, Charlton, 1984; and Hunt, 1992, esp. pp. 29–32.
29. Cabanis, 1956, vol. 1, p. 285.

PLATE 18. *Jean-Baptiste Greuze,* Innocence, *1790s, oil on panel. Reproduced by Permission of the Trustees of the Wallace Collection, London. The girl's large eyes, skimpy clothing and intermediate state between childhood and adulthood indicate how a female figure could be simultaneously pure and erotically suggestive.*

Something of all of these was involved, linked as they were by prevailing ideas about sexuality and family. Indeed, by stressing the sexual dimension of adolescence, Bernardin implied the related changes in marital status and fertility, with their economic implications. Adolescence, the in-between state, was deeply threatening. For example, concern about illegitimacy frequently focused on young girls living away from home, working as servants and craving the comfort of a stable relationship, yet lacking the guiding discipline of parents to steer them into a correct marriage.[30] Similarly, the premature apprenticeship of young children was offensive to many people who feared that seduction and exploitation were the inevitable consequences; sexual and economic vulnerability went hand in hand, the twin sequelae of lack of parental control.[31] No matter how attaining adulthood was envisaged, a link was made between sexuality and growth – sex develops, and thus was not seen as a fixed essence but as a dynamic biological process whose natural history could be described.[32]

Sexuality had two meanings which were in tension. It had a positive sense if construed as the impulse to procreate responsibly, portrayed in the almost erotic intimacy of mothers and children in paintings from the second half of the eighteenth century.[33] It was seen more negatively if sexual expression was premature, illicit, excessive, or simply for carnal gratification. Although in theory this applied equally to men and women, surfeit of passion or voluptuousness was stereotypically associated with feminine weakness. The sense that sexuality disrupts, exploits, is open to both sexes and highly dangerous unless disciplined, is explored by Laclos in *Les liaisons dangereuses*.[34] He portrays an exceedingly clever woman, the Marquise de Merteuil, who, being a widow unhampered by husband, children or fear of pregnancy, is capable of playing the power games of the bedroom – a monstrous creature.

Laclos constructs the book as a series of letters, and, like Bernardin de Saint-Pierre, he strives to create the illusion of veracity. The epistolary form gives the impression that convention and custom are exceedingly artificial, for the letters show how, beneath the surface, people seek power over others. Life is depicted as a manipulative game akin to the military strategies with which Laclos was familiar; people are rarely what they appear to be, since, in order to play the game, appearance must mask reality. Human beings are not motivated by passion or true feeling, but by the idea of victory; hence, they do not experience loving and living directly, but instead they take pleasure from the power they hold over others. Individuals are caught in webs of intrigue. Women are just as good at the games as men, maybe even better. Laclos certainly does not depict all human beings as equally corrupt, only *potentially* so. This is because of the sheer strength of human sexuality. Laclos claimed his book was a moral tale, designed to instruct mothers in particular of the consequences of excessively liberal attitudes towards children. But by virtue of its capacity to explore the nature of human sexuality, as game and intrigue, as duty, and as natural passion, it is profoundly unsettling – now as then.

The power of *Les liaisons dangereuses* derives from the perfect matching of the two main protagonists, a man, the Vicomte de Valmont, and a woman, the

---

30. Spacks, 1978; Shorter, 1976; Fairchilds, 1978.

31. Ariès, 1973; Gillis, 1974; Sommerville, 1982.

32. Laqueur, 1990 deals with similar issues from a different perspective.

33. Duncan, 1973; Chapter 11 explores a particular visual rendering of the intimacy between mother and child. Some of Greuze's paintings, especially the *Much-Loved Mother*, 1769, suggest the fusion of reproduction and sexuality.

34. Laclos, 1979; Thody, 1975; Goodden, 1989; Hunt, 1991, ch. 2.

Marquise de Merteuil, who plot the downfall of others by sexual means and who are equally capable of playing the game of life – a game which ends with disaster for them both.[35] They also both stand outside the normal family structures, which should serve as a moral framework. Laclos shows what happens when the two interacting elements of authority and obedience are lacking. The young girl, Cécile Volanges, whose virtue is at stake, has no father, only a naive mother. Nor, recasting the argument at another level, does reason prevail over the passions, for people, even exemplary ones like the Présidente de Tourvel, do succumb to their sexual desires – the forces which, although natural, sow the seeds of disorder. However 'bad' the seducer Valmont is, his female equivalent, the Marquise, is presented as worse and is seen as such by other characters in the novel. Laclos implies that (male) authority is required to check (feminine/sexual) disorder. Yet he does not seem to be arguing for absolute (male) rule and passive (female) obedience, but for a coherently organised society rooted in a particular kind of family.

Laclos portrays a society somehow adrift, but he could hardly be said to approve of such a situation, despite what early critics of the work claimed. In fact, he shows an intuitive reluctance to believe in the possibility of a truly moral society emerging from human nature. Sexuality appears to him so potentially dangerous and subversive that there have to be rules to constrain its (ab)use, which will restore the proper social distinctions between husbands and wives, parents and children, men and women. Families, like society, require a framework of discipline, something which *Les liaisons dangereuses* shows mothers alone to be unable to provide. The very absence of male authority figures in the novel is the most powerful argument for their social importance. The lack of strong men indicates not Laclos's idealisation of motherhood, but his conviction that fathers (and husbands) are vital. Sexuality, then, might be a powerful natural force – Laclos's descriptions of the Présidente's emotional reactions to Valmont suggest as much – yet it needs to be tempered by a framework, the family, which bridges the natural and the social.

Like the remarkable works of the Marquis de Sade, we must understand Laclos's book as an inversion of dominant ideology. When he shows men and women equally playing the power games of sex, he is in fact supporting a radical demarcation between the sexes of the kind found in Cabanis. Exaggerating the luxury of the rich and idle which Laclos, like many of his contemporaries, associated with the Parisian court aristocracy, he portrays a society which is the precise opposite of the one he himself wished to see. While de Sade uses some of the same techniques, this is clearly to argue a different case. What these writers have in common, however, must not be lost sight of: namely that sexuality, however 'natural', is a powerfully disruptive force at the heart of social relations.

While sexuality and adolescence, despite being natural phenomena, seemed threatening forces in late eighteenth-century culture, the responses to their

35. This point is precisely the one addressed in the split images discussed in Chapter 2. By putting a male half and a female half together and showing that there is an inherent mismatch, these images imply the fundamental differences between men and women.

174

presence in men and women were radically different. In placing Virginie, her rise to sexual maturity, and her virginal death at the centre of his book, Bernardin de Saint-Pierre evoked a special association between the female body and the living organism capable of reproducing itself. At one level this was simply the recognition of the distinctively female contribution to procreation: pregnancy and suckling. The theme of generation was at the core of the life sciences during the eighteenth century.[36] Just as the 'sexuality' and reproductive organs of plants elicited enormous interest, so did hermaphrodites and monsters, as well as healthy human reproductive systems, all of which were to be catalogued, described, classified and depicted. Women were the carriers and givers of life, and, as a result, a pregnant woman was both the quintessence of life and an erotic object.[37] This is, of course, quite consistent with an emphasis on the heightened sensibility of women and their wombs, for sensibility was a fundamental organic property.

A better understanding of the identification of femininity with life can be achieved if the significance of the concept of life itself is considered.[38] In the late eighteenth century, life was commonly associated with activity and plasticity, with the adaptive powers of organisms to respond to the environment, and with organisation, that is, the structural complexity of a living being, a concept used to explain the special properties of animals and plants. Life was a notion of synthesis, system and fusion. Appropriately enough, it sustained an approach to sexuality which stressed, not the reproductive organs or genitals, but the whole organism. Every fibre of a female body carried femininity within it – a femininity which was acquired by custom and habit. Furthermore, this total femaleness was adapted to specific biological and social purposes; it fulfilled a social role. This perspective can be termed 'organicist' in that it stressed the whole co-ordinated organism, which then became a model for other entities, such as human societies.[39] A rigid demarcation between mind and body thus made no sense, since the organism was one integrated whole. Hence, clearly, the moral and the social emerged out of the natural organisation of living matter. Life, then, was a fertile concept. If we think for a moment of some of its associations, its cultural significance can be brought into sharper focus: life blood, life science, life style, life history, life and death. Living phenomena were systematically explored, for example, by correlating behaviour with health, by tracing life events as they affected the body, by comparing similar organisms in different environments. All manner of social relationships were integral to

36. Roger, 1963/1993; Delaporte, 1982; Hankins, 1985, ch. 5.

37. Jordanova, 1980a; images of pregnancy are discussed in Chapter 11.

38. Figlio, 1975 and 1976; Canguilhem, 1971; Jordanova, 1984a, pp. 44–57. Webster, 1970 (first published 1828), gives 25 distinct meanings! Although of a later generation (Webster was the same generation as Cabanis and Volney), Littré's definition of 'vie' is also instructive (and considerably more detailed), containing many eighteenth-century examples – 1878, vol. 4, pp. 2482–4. Littré had a strong interest in medicine and its classical heritage. The first meaning he gives stresses organisation, and includes sensibility as a defining characteristic of animals (2482).

39. Like vitalism, organicism is a problematic term. Charlton, 1984 uses it extensively, e.g. pp. 15, 72, 77, 78, 160. Cf. Williams, 1983, pp. 227–9 on 'organic'. I use it to mean the intense interest in organic wholes and the use of 'life' as a holistic concept.

an understanding of living phenomena because of the dialectical relationship between the living being and its conditions of existence.[40]

Since it was not reproductive organs alone which made men and women different, natural philosophers looked elsewhere for the distinction. Organisms interacted with their surroundings, giving sexuality a behavioural dimension, in that females became full women by doing womanly things, like breast-feeding their children; to refuse the task was to denature or unsex oneself, as also happened when women took on 'male' occupations such as scholarship. Cabanis asserted that male and female children were strikingly *similar* and concluded that sex differences emerge only in the course of development.[41] As a result, the social and psychological environment, including the family, in which an individual was nurtured became of paramount importance. Each life history, seen from this point of view, was a complex story, and the body bore the signs of accumulated experience. One could read a body like a book: it told the story which the medical practitioner interpreted and recorded in case notes. Both the inside of the body and its general appearance or physiognomy were scrutinised for evidence of how the female and the male diverge. This was accomplished by, for example, analysing the nervous system, fibres and tissues. The language of fibres and tissues is of great interest because it spoke about the unobservable. In descriptions of the smallest constituents of women's bodies, images of softness, rotundity, delicacy, feebleness and childishness were used. Their muscles were weak and the female nervous system was possessed of great sensibility, and was softer than a man's. But women were also presented as supple, strong, durable and flexible, and their greater life expectancy was adduced as evidence of this.[42]

Thus the inside of an organism was seen in terms of its sensibility, a term which bridged the physical and the moral or mental, and united them in a single organic base. Significantly, the febrile feminine sensibility was seen as particularly akin to that of children. Although sensibility was rooted in the nervous system, the glands were equally important in the physiology of sex. Glands, including the testicles and ovaries, powerfully affected all other parts of the body through substances they released, changes they prompted in the circulatory system beginning in puberty, and their swelling at this time. Glands formed a physiological system with sympathetic links between member organs. An emphasis on the fine structure of the body went hand in hand with an interest in body fluids. The prominent Montpellier physician Barthez claimed that women lived longer than men partly because of the rejuvenating effects of menstruation.[43] Spermatic fluid was also deemed to have healthful properties for the women who received it, while losing it illegitimately, through sexual excess or masturbation, had dire consequences for men.[44] Blood was clearly of

40. Environmentalism, the sense that organisms were responsive and adaptive, and the belief that the family was an environment that shaped its members, went together: on environmentalism see Glacken, 1967; Jordanova and Porter, 1979/1997; Riley, 1987.

41. Cabanis, 1956, vol. 1, p. 276.

42. Barthez, 1858, pp. 181, 184.

43. Ibid., p. 184.

44. Tissot, 1772, pp. 9–11; Chapter 6, this volume.

great biological and metaphorical significance. Sex organs affected the rest of the body through the circulatory system, inaugurating new directions in blood flow during puberty which were accompanied by increased tone of blood vessels, more heat, and greater frequency of haemorrhages. Most important was the onset of menstruation at the correct time. The blood of women as their life force was bizarrely depicted by de Sade in *Justine* (1791), where an aristocrat bled to death a succession of young wives for his erotic satisfaction.[45]

Most late eighteenth-century anatomical and physiological accounts assumed that reproduction and sexuality were inseparable. The pregnant woman was thus an object of desire, for she had attained the peak of femininity. The fusion of procreation and sexuality was a consequence of taking the whole, integrated organism as the object of study. The particular interest of de Sade's writings is their *separation* of sexuality and reproduction, one of the most immediately shocking of his ideas. Furthermore, he argued that the separation stemmed from nature herself.[46] Thus he took totally seriously, and sought to theorise, what Laclos evoked in a spirit of social criticism. For Sade, women and men could indeed be treated equally as vehicles for sexual pleasure. He gave no special status to women because of their capacity to bear children – a striking contrast to the idealisation and mystification of female biology found in scientific and medical writings. De Sade raised quite openly the question of infanticide, one of the most highly charged subjects of the period. Infanticide could, he implied, be seen as a rational rather than a criminal act. The world, he allowed one of his protagonists to assert, is overpopulated anyway, and why, he went on to ask, should we bring forth more children to be neglected and rejected by parents who lack the economic resources to care for them?[47] The argument brutally called into question common assumptions about the value of human life.

As a perceptive critic of his own society, de Sade must be listened to attentively. Whatever he did or did not advocate in terms of personal conduct, he threw into sharp focus a number of important zones of tension. The most noteworthy of these were the questions of power and money as they impacted upon individual bodies. De Sade showed, in relentless detail, how vulnerability to sexual exploitation was connected with poverty and lack of social status. By separating sexuality and reproduction, he allowed the possibility that the human body, male or female, could be an instrument of pleasure; any part of the body could be an erotic zone. It was not the purpose of anatomical parts that interested him, but their capacity for sensuality. In abolishing the sanctity with which human reproduction had been invested, especially in relation to motherhood, he refused to accord any special value to female life-giving powers. Women, like men, take and give pleasure. Women, like men, buy, sell, trade and steal for the sake of sexual gratification and power. If sex is the

45. Sade, 1966, pp. 633ff.; Webster, 1970 offers 'blood' as one meaning of life in the eighteenth century: '7. Blood, the supposed vehicle of animation. "And the warm *life* came issuing through the wound." Pope' (vol. 2, pages not numbered).

46. Sade, 1966, p. 489; on Sade see Carter, 1979; Goodden, 1989; Hunt, 1992, ch. 5.

47. Sade, 1966, pp. 470–1, 650.

ultimate form of power, it is important to recognise that wealth is the principal means by which it is achieved. Those who are economically and sexually weak will be robbed; the rich can buy or just take whatever pleasures they want. Sex, in other words, is a commodity. In fact, de Sade argued, it was already treated that way if only the surface veneer were skimmed off. The body, for him, was already in the market-place. It was an object bought and sold daily, frequently under the guise of institutions like marriage, which supposedly protected and cherished human beings while in fact treating them as cattle.[48]

Thus, de Sade's view was the reverse of the medical organicism discussed earlier. Where the medical writers saw life, resisting the reduction to the status of an object, he saw the reduction already accomplished. Where they revered the feminine, he demystified it. Where they treated the human race as a natural unit, a biological entity, he perceived its fragmentation into the rich and powerful, the poor and weak. The insight that sex was treated as a commodity was hardly new with de Sade. Writers on prostitution had noted that sexual and economic exploitation went hand in hand.[49] They generally assumed that treating women merely as instruments of sexual pleasure was wrong because it prevented them from fulfilling their proper destiny as wives and mothers. Furthermore, they implied that whereas there was little inherently wrong with men treating sex as a commodity, there was when women did so. This asymmetry in the argument prompts us to ask why it was so important for women to be placed in the mystified, sacred role of life-giver.

Concern with the value of life and of individual lives as impersonal abstractions dominated many areas of scientific, medical and philosophical enquiry. Some examples were the attempts to produce adequate morbidity and mortality statistics, reliable life tables for insurance purposes, and analyses of infant mortality.[50] Here the bare facts of life and death were quantified, and ways suggested for improving the quality as well as the quantity of life. Early demographic work was an attempt to bridge the public and private domains because aggregate population, and its profile, was the concern of the state, even if produced by the actions of individuals in their most intimate relationships. An individual's capacity to give life depended on many physiological and anatomical variables as well as on psychological and social ones. Private, individual acts of sex and reproduction had public consequences in the size and health of the population and its labouring potential. Quantification was one way of dealing with the problem of how to manage human resources. Improving the quality of mothering was seen as an important step towards the goal of bettering the population. The private behaviour of women as reproductive beings and their physiological competence were of great interest to those attempting to develop a scientific, quantitative analysis of human life. Each life was assigned a value

---

48. Critiques of marriage in the period from the woman's perspective made similar points, likening wives to, for example, slaves. Particularly poignant examples may be found in the two anthologies edited by Roger Lonsdale, 1984 and 1989.

49. Jones, 1978; Merians, 1996, chs 1, 2, 7, 14, 15.

50. Rosen, 1976; Glass, 1978; Cullen, 1975, pp. 1–16; Gonnard, 1923; Coleman, 1977a, b, 1982; Buck, 1982; McManners, 1981, ch. 4.

based on what it could produce: work in the case of men, healthy children in the case of women. This value was expressed in numerical terms if life insurance or membership of friendly societies was involved. In this sense human life was already treated as a commodity; the mentality of mercantilism was well established.[51]

In seeming contrast, the mentality of the organicist approach was based on the assumption that living things were integrated wholes, ensembles of functions. Such views tended to lead to assertions about the inviolability of life. Since the distinctive features of living things did not adhere in any one part of them, as they would according to mechanist or dualist presuppositions, but were diffused through every fibre of the body, vivisection or ruthless experimentation raised anxieties, although for many practitioners exhaustive anatomical dissections were major means of improving natural knowledge. The sacred value of *life* had to be respected. Furthermore, there were degrees of living complexity or organisation, with those beings which were most structurally elaborate, closest to the peak of life, being given special status.

This special status was also assigned to women and young children: women because they gave life, children because they had recently received it. In them the full mystery of life was manifest. One can state this another way by saying that women and children became those people it was least acceptable to treat as objects or commodities. Life was placed in opposition to commodity. To the sets of pairs mentioned at the beginning of the chapter, some more may now be added:

nature	society
women and children	men
life	commodity
sacred	material
privacy of the home/protection	public market-place

We can now go a stage further and ask about the implicit meanings of such dichotomies. The central issue here is the treatment of human life as if it were a thing. If we want to understand the special significance of the feminine and the infantile as natural categories, we should look at what their mystification concealed. A form of social relations which treated persons as objects was veiled by a language of nature in which reproduction and sexuality were made both natural and sacred via the anatomy and physiology of women. Since the language was a predominantly masculine one, it may be understood as a projection onto the feminine of something men felt they were actually, or in danger of, losing. This 'something' was captured and retained by being associated with the other – woman and child. The family then became the principal occasion for the mingling of these elements, hence the need to stabilise the family through the physical presence of women and children within the home as symbols of life and personhood. For this reason the apparent violation of

51. Rosen, 1974; Wilson, 1958; Reill and Wilson, 1996, entries for cameralism and mercantilism. For further references see Chapter 9.

children through labour carried a very strong symbolic load. None of this, it must be emphasised, was a simple description of lived experience, but a complex conceptual grid through which that experience was passed, and, in the process, transformed.

One of the most potent expressions of these ideas in the eighteenth century may be found in the writings of Rousseau, especially in *Émile* (1762). He was in fact virtually the only author Cabanis referred to when writing about sexuality. Other medical writers concerned with femininity and sexuality, such as the French physician Pierre Roussel, as well as authors of more conventionally literary works like Bernardin de Saint-Pierre, were similarly indebted to Rousseau.[52] Rousseau spawned a literary and ideological tradition, seductive for its capacity to draw together political, personal and scientific elements, and with a strong aesthetic dimension. This tradition was highly compatible with the approaches to natural history at the Muséum National d'Histoire Naturelle (formerly the Jardin du Roi) in Paris, with which Bernardin was briefly associated and which nourished the imagination of several generations of Frenchmen in the eighteenth and nineteenth centuries.[53]

The metaphorically-rich idea of privacy was evoked in a number of ways as a result of giving women and children the status of not-commodity, carriers of life. Privacy was identified with domesticity, with surveillance of intimate acts, with voyeurism and the erotic, and with the interior of the body, what was not normally seen, the 'private parts'. Hence the force of calling prostitutes 'filles publiques'. In the very process of separating off the female and private from the male and public in the domain of the imagination and of ideology, the impulse to examine, probe, violate and penetrate the former was generated. Curiosity and reverence are perfectly compatible. At the same time as Cabanis waxed lyrical about the suppleness of the fibres of the female body, sex organs were increasingly explicitly depicted in medical treatises, and erotic elements were present in conventional anatomical drawings and models. Medical practitioners probed, and then wrote about, the most private aspects of people's lives. They made moral tales out of case histories; but the drive to know about the private aspects of people's lives went far deeper than that. In his famous treatise on masturbation, the Swiss physician Tissot took the notion that it is important to penetrate into the most private aspects of people's lives a stage further.[54] He did not advocate *medical* instrusion, but rather that parents should oversee children at every possible moment in order to guard against their masturbating tendencies.[55] Such advice presupposes an intimacy between parents and children that gives the former the right to see and know all in relation to their offspring.

Children were placed in an ambiguous situation when associated with the female aura of domestic privacy. Women could be conceptualised in this way

52. Roussel, 1775; Schwartz, 1984; MacCormack and Strathern, 1980, chs 2 and 3; Le Doeuff, 1981–82; Knibiehler, 1976.
53. Huss, 1986; Kaplan, 1977; Jordanova, 1980b; Corsi, 1988; Jardine *et al.*, 1996, ch. 15.
54. Tissot, 1772; Donzelot, 1980.
55. e.g. Tissot, 1772, p. 43.

by presenting their sexuality and their reproductive capacities as one and the same thing. For children the situation was more equivocal when they reached adolescence, as we saw in the case of Virginie. In *Paul et Virginie* children were shown as non-sexual beings, and Bernardin de Saint-Pierre did not describe the whole transformation from childhood to full sexual maturity. It was too explosive, too threatening, for him to be able to do so. Yet in practice children had to make the transition from childhood to adulthood, from being subject to their parents to being parents themselves.

Tissot's concern about masturbation implied that, in some sense, children already *were* sexual beings; why else would their secret activities need to be controlled? The awkwardness of growing up, both in reality and in imagination, could not be solved easily. One approach was to select an age at which the passage from one status to another could be deemed to have taken place. The tensions and difficulties of so doing are nicely portrayed in debates on the age at which children should work or be considered legally competent. At a deeper level, these debates were about when children might pass from the private to the public, when they might enter the world of commodities, and when they might become sexually active. Once working, they lost their special status close to the source of life; they entered the public domain, became economic actors, and could no longer represent innocence. Hence the concern about child prostitution, which violated the economic, the sexual and the social dimensions of childhood simultaneously.[56]

Forms of cultural shorthand were developed to designate the special way in which women and children were carriers of life. The pictorial treatment of children in the period as innocent, as simple, as close to nature, playful and, most significantly, as implicitly erotic, is one example (see plate 18, p. 172; see also plates 10, 11, pp. 41, 42).[57] Another is the treatment of the breast, which took on symbolic significance in the ways it was extolled for its beauty and its valuable biological function. It also stood for the attraction between men and women, since it was a visible sign of femininity which suggested the importance of reproduction.[58] It did so all the more powerfully in an environment where wet-nursing was commonplace and a known killer of babies.[59] The mother's refusal or willingness to give her breast to the child meant, symbolically, and sometimes literally, death or life. The arrival and departure of the wet-nurse were common themes in painting of the period, which also on occasion depicted the mother giving suck or about to do so.[60] This shorthand

---

56. I have tried to explore some of these questions, using English materials, in Jordanova 1987a. Charlton, 1984, esp. pp. 140ff., discusses childhood. A classic, if much criticised, account is Ariès, 1973; see also Scarre, 1989.

57. Pointon, 1993, ch. 7. Images of Emma Hamilton – the girl pin-up – are pertinent here: see Jenkins and Sloan, 1996, e.g. pp. 269–70; Greuze is the painter most associated with suggestive little girls, that much is clear from Diderot's comments: see Brookner, 1972 and *Greuze & Diderot*, 1984. The crucial point is that young girls could suggest both innocence and latent sexuality.

58. Roussel, 1803, p. 16; on the history of the breast see Yalom, 1997; and, more specifically on the eighteenth century, Schiebinger, 1993, ch. 2; Perry, 1991.

59. Sussman, 1982.

60. Gelis *et al.*, 1978 reproduces some of these images. Hunt, 1991 contains an exceptionally stimulating chapter by Mary Sherriff, which discusses wet-nursing pictures, pp. 14–40.

was predicated on the ability of putatively natural objects and processes to contain and express a wide range of social and cultural meaning.

This chapter has explored some of the issues involved in late eighteenth-century treatments of sexuality, reproduction and the family as phenomena which were at once natural and social. There were important political, economic, social and ideological questions raised by such treatments. The language in which these questions were couched, shared by scientific, medical and literary accounts, is among the most important keys to their historical significance. It was indeed a language of nature, full of tensions, ambiguities, and fruitful associations, and serving to conceal as well as reveal. It drew upon anatomy and physiology, and was sustained by the growing scientific and medical interest in a science of life. To chart the development of the new science of biology without considering the larger cultural context that gave meaning to the concept of life, or to read novels depicting sexual experience and kin relations in isolation from the scientific and medical treatments of those subjects, results in a partial and distorted historical perspective. Science and literature, united in eighteenth-century culture, must be reunited by the historian.

Gender, Generation and Science: William Hunter's Obstetrical Atlas

An early nineteenth-century description of the Hunterian Museum in Glasgow lavished special praise on the exhibits illustrating the gravid uterus:

There are above five hundred Preparations under this division. They are prepared with the greatest taste and care, are exceedingly beautiful, making this department the most valuable perhaps of any in the world. Many splendid and valuable engravings were taken from these, and a volume of them published under Dr Hunter's superintendence.[1]

This chapter discusses the volume in question: William Hunter's *The Anatomy of the Human Gravid Uterus*, published in a large format in 1774. Both the foregoing description, with its excess of superlatives, and the huge, often dramatic plates of Hunter's obstetrical atlas suggest that the social and cultural meanings of images of pregnancy were complex, and that far from lying on the surface, they were embedded in visual and verbal texts. What follows is an attempt to analyse Hunter's book, to place it in its cultural context, and to examine the deeper meanings it contained.

Hunter made revealing claims for the knowledge of nature his book afforded. The assertion that seeing was knowing, which was integral to his project, raised the issue of how the mind acquires knowledge of nature. It also prompted the question, what sort of a phenomenon is nature? The explicit epistemology and the implicit notions of man and nature the atlas contained indicate that the illustrations to medical books such as Hunter's were not ornamental additions, nor were they convenient diagrams; they were their very *raison d'être*. The primacy of the visual was clear in Hunter's philosophy of education:

In explaining the structure of the parts, if a teacher would be of real service, he must take care, not barely to describe but to shew or demonstrate every part. What the student acquires in this way, is solid knowledge, arising from the information of his own senses. Hence his ideas are clear and make a lasting impression upon his memory.[2]

1. Laskey, 1813, p. 51.
2. Hunter, 1784, p. 87.

Furthermore, Hunter was far from naive where art was concerned. Professor of Anatomy at the newly-founded Royal Academy between 1768 and 1783, he had decided views on art. For him 'the superiority of Nature over Art' seems to shine forth in almost every thing – an opinion many Academicians did not share. Hunter was also a collector and connoisseur who enthused over the rediscovered Leonardo drawings at Windsor Castle and bought the work of such artists as Rembrandt and Chardin.[3]

The Anatomy of the Human Gravid Uterus has frequently been praised in the highest terms as one of the great artistic achievements of medicine. It is indeed a remarkable book, not the least important aspect of which is the enormous size of the plates, which Hunter took care to defend in the preface. For him, the technical quality of the plates was of particular importance; they combined descriptive clarity with beauty. The work contains thirty-four plates of different kinds; some depict several objects, others a life-size section of the human body – the female trunk between the abdomen and the middle of the thighs. Some plates are packed with detail, others are more schematic, showing large parts in outline only. Facing each plate are a short description and a key to the letters placed on the engraving to mark specific anatomical parts. The text, in both Latin and English, is arranged in parallel columns. Hunter used words sparingly in the atlas, a feature that serves to focus attention more completely on the images. The plates show various stages of dissection from the open skin on the pregnant abdomen to the empty womb and the placenta. The last two engravings show 'abortions' and 'conceptions' from the early stages of foetal development.

There is no doubt that some of the plates have a peculiar force; they arrest and may even shock the modern eye for reasons that require careful probing. Their power derives in part from the way the foetus is shown, with great attention to details like hair and fingers, and very tightly wedged into its mother's body. This differs strikingly from earlier representations of the foetus *in utero*, which often showed it as a miniature adult floating in space.[4] The impact of Hunter's images is further heightened by a technique that was common in eighteenth-century anatomical pictures and models. Parts of the body are shown beautifully intact, often with great attention given to facial features, hair and so on, while other parts are cut off, such as the tops of thighs, giving a dislocated impression – the body is realistically whole, but also amputated to show human flesh resembling chunks of meat. We can take the analogy with meat further, in that the human flesh of these anatomical images is, like meat, somewhere between the full vitality of life and the total decay of death. The body was captured in visual form as if at the moment of death: it was made to look fresh, just like flesh for eating, which should be safely dead without being decomposed. The startling effect of combining realism with butchery was commonly

3. Kemp, 1975, p. 38; *idem*, 1976, pp. 144–8; Laskey, 1813. On Hunter's collecting activities see Bynum and Porter, 1985, esp. ch. 10 (by Rolfe); Brock, 1990, 1994 and 1996. It should also be stressed that Hunter was a busy and thoughtful *practitioner* of midwifery: Wilson, 1995, esp. ch. 13.
4. Examples of early images of the foetus may be found in Eccles, 1982; Thornton and Reeves, 1983 and in Newman, 1996.

given by medical representations of the period. Anatomical illustrations frequently provided scrupulously lifelike detail in parts other than those that were the explicit subject of the picture. For example, in Jacques Gautier d'Agoty's *Anatomie de la Tête* (1748) the interior of the brain and the facial sinuses were illustrated in a plate of three male heads close together in a conspiratorial pose. The faces of two are clearly visible and naturalistically shown; one has the top of his head cut off to show the brain, the other is missing the front of his face on one side. On the one hand we see a group of people, and on the other we see anatomical objects displayed.[5]

In Hunter's atlas, this juxtaposition of dissected and whole parts is made all the more arresting by the part of the body chosen for depiction. For example, in perhaps the most striking plate of all, Plate VI, which 'represents the child in the womb, in its natural situation', we see a full frontal view of a female trunk with legs apart; the viewer's eye is drawn towards the vagina, which is made all the more prominent by the external genitals having been cut away (see plate 19, p. 186). The net result is an image that is intimate yet impersonal, suggestive of humanity yet butchered, celebrating the act of generation, yet also conveying violated female sexuality. The sense of violation is reinforced by Plate IV, where the clitoris has been cut in two, although this organ has no relevance to the plate or, indeed, to the book as a whole (see plate 20, p. 187). Indeed, there is a notable contrast in the depictions of mother and child – the latter is treated tenderly while the former appears mutilated.

Hunter's plates can be compared with those in Jenty's *Demonstratio Uteri Praegnantis Mulieris* of 1761, a work of particular relevance since the drawings on which the plates of both books were based were done by the same artist, Jan van Rymsdyk, as were those for Smellie's obstetrical atlas, published in 1754 (see plates 21, 22, pp. 188, 189). In Jenty's work, however, a different printing technique was used, mezzotint, which emphasised soft contours, and the thighs were not sectioned. Furthermore, the torso was surrounded by soft folding drapery. Some plates in Smellie's volume included drapery, yet the treatment of female genitalia is more explicit here than in either Hunter's or Jenty's atlas. The effect of this is mitigated somewhat by the explanation Smellie offered the reader that he 'intended to shew in what manner the Perinaeum and external parts are stretched by the Head of the Foetus'. Smellie's intended audience, young male practitioners, may have had an impact on his choice of plates. Hunter and Jenty offered no comparable accounts. That a variety of ways were available for producing anatomical images heightens the significance of those specifically chosen by Hunter, his artists and engravers.[6]

The preface to *The Anatomy of the Human Gravid Uterus* shows that Hunter was quite deliberately putting across a particular view of the body, its representation and the role of careful looking in medicine.

---

5. The d'Agoty plate is reproduced in *La Découverte du Corps Humain*, 1978, p. 18; see also Ciardi, 1981; Lanza *et al.*, 1979; Roberts and Tomlinson, 1992, esp. pp. 523–9.

6. Jenty, 1758, 1759 and 1761–65; Smellie, 1754, the quotation is from the commentary facing plate XV; Thornton, 1982; Roberts and Tomlinson, 1992, ch. 12.

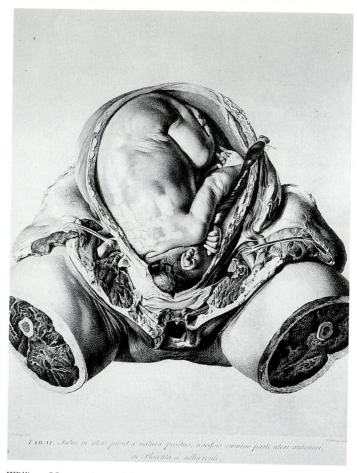

TAB VI. Fœtus in utero prout a natura positus, resectis omnino parte uteri anteriori, ac Placenta ei adhærente.

PLATE 19. *William Hunter,* Anatomia Uteri Humani Gravidi, *1774, engraving, plate VI,* 'This represents the child in the womb in its natural situation.' *Wellcome Institute Library, London.*

The art of engraving supplies us, upon many occasions, with what has been the great desideratum of the lovers of science, an universal language. Nay, it conveys clearer ideas of most natural objects, than words can express; makes stronger impressions upon the mind; and to every person conversant with the subject, gives an immediate comprehension of what it represents.[7]

Hunter, of course, begs the most important question: what *is* being represented? He wished to suggest that this was self-evident; we must refuse his suggestion. Images, he was asserting, are vital means for the communication of natural knowledge. Seeing is itself an act of understanding and knowing. Hunter held up the immediate perception of supposedly unacted-upon nature as an epistemological ideal. As he said of Plate VI, 'Every part is represented just as

7. Hunter, 1774, Preface.

186

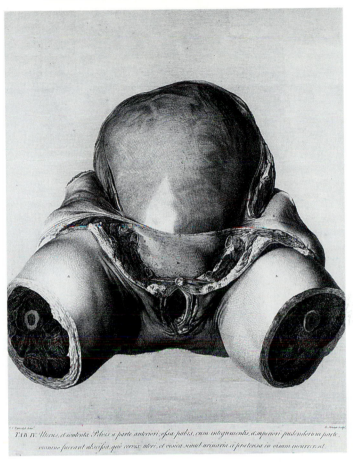

TAB. IV. Uterus, et contenta Pelvis a parte anteriori, ossa pubis, cum integumentis, et superiori pudendorum parte, omnino fuerant abscissa, quo cervix uteri, et vesica simul urinaria è pretensa in visum incurrerent.

PLATE 20. *William Hunter,* Anatomia Uteri Humani Gravidi, *1774, engraving, plate IV,* *'A fore-view of the womb, and of the contents of the pelvis; the ossa pubis, with the muscles and* *integuments which cover them being removed.' Wellcome Institute Library, London.*

it was found, not so much as one joint of a finger having been moved.' Hunter appealed to an apparently unambiguous nature through simple naturalistic images of physical reality. We can see this as an attempt to create the illusion that there need be no mediations between nature and the human mind – for him truth was all on the surface. There were no limits to the imitation of nature, so that 'a painter or sculptor in executing a single figure in the ordinary situation of quiet life cannot copy Nature too exactly, or make deception too strong'. Thus scrupulously exact bodily details, including surface blood vessels, were essential for giving a 'natural appearance'.[8]

There were, according to Hunter, two traditions of anatomical illustration. The first made simple portraits of nature showing the object just as it was seen, in the manner of the Dutch anatomist Bidloo. Hunter contrasted this first

8. Kemp, 1975, pp. 39, 35.

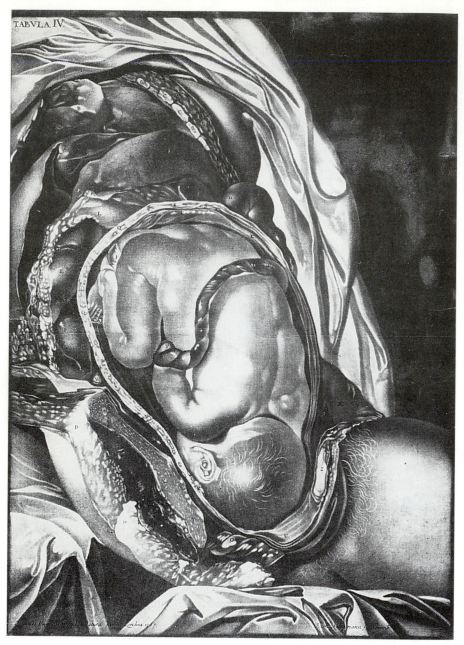

PLATE 21. *Charles Nicholas Jenty*, Demonstratio Uteri Praegnantis Mulieris, *1761, mezzotint, plate IV, 'This figure shows a foetus positioned in the passage by which it is naturally expelled.' Wellcome Institute Library, London.*

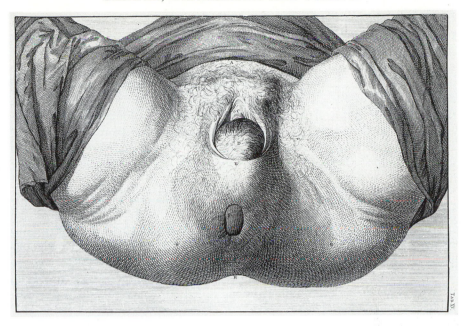

PLATE 22. *William Smellie,* A Sett of Anatomical Tables, *1754, engraving, plate XV, Wellcome Institute Library, London. 'The Fifteenth Table is intended principally to shew in what manner the* Perinaeum, *and external parts are stretched by the Head of the* Foetus, *in a first* pregnancy, *towards the end of Labour'.*

tradition, his own, with one in which nature is imaginatively reconstructed in the minds of anatomists and artists. Although he could see disadvantages with the first tradition and advantages with the second, in the last analysis pictures 'which represent what was actually seen' are the ones carrying 'the mark of truth', and are 'almost as infallible as the object itself'.[9] For Hunter, the former tradition produced images with 'the elegance and harmony of the natural object', the latter possess 'the hardness of a geometrical diagram'. Despite his assertions about the close representation of nature, Hunter's work did not reflect nature but fabricated it. For example, the bodies from which the pictures were drawn were dead, and had often been so for a long time. The plates are designed to give the impression of vitality, as in the way the umbilical cord seems to gleam as if it were still wet.

A lifelike effect was partly achieved by injecting blood vessels with wax to keep their shape.

Filling the vascular system with a bright coloured wax, enables us to trace the large vessels with great ease, renders the smaller much more conspicuous, and makes thousands of the very minute ones visible, which from their delicacy, and the transparency of their natural contents, are otherwise imperceptible.[10]

9. Hunter, 1774, Preface. See also Bynum and Porter, 1993b, ch. 6 (by Kemp).
10. Hunter, 1784, p. 56.

In general, Hunter found anatomical preparations to be of great value for revealing both structures requiring 'considerable labour to anatomize' and those not commonly seen. Although he preferred wet preparations to dry ones, he was enthusiastic about making wax models from dead bodies. Wax enjoyed a considerable vogue in this period for modelling and sculpting purposes as well as for anatomical ones. The Italians specialised in producing wax figures designed to be beautiful, alluring ornaments as well as anatomically informative, although Hunter was sceptical about waxworks not cast from real subjects.[11] But however they were made, these models, like Hunter's plates, suggest an urgent search for verisimilitude, and wax, with its potential for resembling human flesh, was a particularly attractive medium.

For Hunter anatomical pictures ought to reveal 'true nature, that is, the peculiar habit and composition of parts, as well as the outward form, situation and connection of them'.[12] The plates in the *Gravid Uterus* show the extent to which he was concerned with the topography of the body, the spatial relationships between parts, their surface features and particularly their texture. Anatomy, for Hunter, was a study of three dimensions, like sculpture or wax modelling, portraiture or landscape painting. He had little of the architect's concern with inner structure – the skeleton – as the German anatomist Soemmerring had. Rather, Hunter's enterprise was closely akin to that of a cartographer, lovingly recording all the details of the terrain – flesh, vessels and tissues. There was no smoothing out here but, rather, corrugations depicted in loving detail. When the mapping had been completed, the human body would, in some significant sense, be known and understood.[13]

Hunter himself employed a topographical analogy, and considerably developed it by likening the medical practitioner to a general, and the human body to a country under civil war or invasion:

To do his duty with full advantage, a general, besides other acquirements, useful in his profession, must make himself master of the Anatomy and Physiology, as we may call it, of the country. He may be said to be master of the *Anatomy* of the country, when he knows the figure, dimension, situation, and connection, of all the principal constituent parts; such as, the lakes, rivers, marshes, mountains, precipices, plains, woods, roads, passes, fords, towns, fortifications, etc. By the *Physiology* of the country, which he ought likewise to understand, is meant, all the variety of active influence, which is produced by the inhabitants.[14]

The notion of topographical exactitude was of considerable importance in British art during the eighteenth century, especially among landscape painters and portraitists.[15]

11. Ibid., pp. 89–91, 56; see also Lanza *et al.*, 1979; Lemire, 1990.
12. Hunter, 1774, Preface.
13. On topography see note 15. Smoothing out flesh was associated with classicism: see note 20.
14. Hunter, 1784, p. 70.
15. *Polite Society*, 1983, p. 12; Paulson, 1982, pp. 40–1; on portraiture in the period see Pointon, 1993; on topography see Michael Charlesworth's stimulating piece on panoramic drawing in the eighteenth century, 1996.

Hunter's epistemology was fundamentally a visual one. There is no space here for refined, abstract analysis. Instead, all was known by means of sight. It may be worth considering the significance of the sense of sight and of ideas of light for conceptions of human knowledge in this period. Not only were these three elements (vision, light, knowledge) commonly associated, but light was the dominant metaphor of the progress of the human intellect. The connection between light and science was, of course, commonly made, for example in references to Sir Isaac Newton.[16] The themes of sight, light and knowledge, and the intricate relationships between them, were taken up in the visual arts by Joseph Wright of Derby, who consistently called into question diverse kinds of human knowledge by depicting the 'scientist', philosopher, alchemist, ana-tomist, connoisseur and artist contemplating their objects of study. Light itself and its various sources were clearly of considerable interest to Wright. But the complexities of looking, and more generally of vision, are also explored in his paintings. Seekers after knowledge, and those who expound knowledge, are frequently depicted in the company of others whose view of their activities is rather different. Many of his pictures further allude to the problem of compre-hending death, a problem most sharply brought into focus by the horror that awaits those who plunder graves in *Miravan Opening the Tomb of his Ancestors* (1772). It shows a young nobleman who has broken into an ancestral tomb in the belief that he will find treasure there. What he finds is a skeleton – a re-velation about death – and, with new awareness, turns away, covering his eyes.[17]

Wright's distinctive manner of treating light pictorially was closely connected with his exploration of the ways in which human beings understand nature, their attitudes to knowledge and the gender differences involved. In *An Experi-ment on a Bird in the Air Pump* (*c.*1767–69), he hinted at a tension between the search for scientific knowledge and femininity. While the natural philosopher demonstrates the air pump, one girl turns away from the apparatus, fearing that the bird will die in the experiment, and a smaller girl looks on in puzzlement. Wright would seem to be drawing on the idea, frequently articulated by thinkers of the Enlightenment, that there was a potential incompatibility between women and scientific knowledge. Often this was done by associating the feminine with nature and the masculine with reason; the former became thereby objectified and passive, the latter active and enquiring.[18] The example of Joseph Wright of Derby is instructive not because he gave visual expression to scientific values, as is often claimed. In fact his pictures are considerably more complex than that. They are instructive because they show how looking and knowledge were problematised in the visual culture of Hunter's day and because, as scholars

16. For a very different view of the status of the visual in the eighteenth century see Stafford, 1991. On Newton see Nicolson, 1946 and Fauvel, 1988, esp. chs 1, 4 and 11.

17. Nicolson, 1968 is the standard source on Wright: on Miravan see vol. 1, pp. 53–4 and 243 and vol. 2, plate 107; Paulson, 1982, pp. 49, 58, ch. 8, p. 113; M.H. Nicolson, 1946. There has been a dramatic growth of interest in Wright in recent years: of particular interest are Barrell, 1992, esp. chs 3 (by Solkin), 5 (by Bermingham) and 7 (by Daniels); Daniels, 1994, ch. 2; Egerton, 1990, on Miravan, pp. 93–4 and 241; Solkin, 1993, ch. 6.

18. A particularly interesting discussion of the air pump picture is Schupbach, 1987, pp. 340–7. Jordanova, 1980a, 1989; Lloyd, 1984.

have recently shown, they engage with a wide range of contemporary debates. Furthermore their style, which gives viewers a strong sense of their verisimilitude, is authoritative in a manner similar to the engravings in *The Anatomy of the Human Gravid Uterus*. Such authority had to be carefully fashioned; and since in doing so a value system was given visual expression, its premises could be called into question by those with a different world-view.

Hunter's epistemology was soon challenged, even by those who saw themselves as extending his work. Samuel Thomas von Soemmerring, for example, prepared his *Icones Embryonum Humanorum* (1799) as a supplement to Hunter's *Gravid Uterus*. It showed mainly embryos in the early stages of pregnancy. Soemmerring was allied with the tradition of anatomical illustration that Hunter associated particularly with Bartholommeo Eustachi. According to Soemmerring, the anatomist should select from his material the most beautiful, perfect and undamaged specimens in order to 'find the true norm of the organs'. Furthermore, 'we have to let our intelligence detect and remedy such deviations as occur in specimens taken from cadavers, in consequence of death, preparation, or preservation'.[19]

The espousal of the ideal as a goal in science and art was widespread. It took the form of the 'classicisation of anatomical study' to which Kemp refers. In *The Nude Male*, Walters suggests that the neoclassical nude was accepted only at its farthest remove from the naked human body – signs of organic life such as veins and sinews were smoothed away. Her statement 'the nude is idealised almost to death' is particularly applicable to the Italian wax anatomical models mentioned earlier.[20] By contrast, Hunter wished all such details to be faithfully depicted. Another form of the 'ideal' was the assertion of the priority of imagination over reason, which was such a fundamental aspect of critiques of the Enlightenment in the 1790s. Such critiques were a vital part of debates within the British artistic community of the period, and they found powerful expression in the works of William Blake and his friend John Flaxman, whose admiration for Hippocrates and Galen was part and parcel of his classicism.[21]

Hunter saw nature's truths as being on the surface, ready to be received by the trained, observant mind/eye, whereas Soemmerring saw them as being below the surface, requiring an active intellect to bring them out in their pure form, a form in which they might never actually exist. There can be no doubt of the general cultural significance of the positions held by Hunter and Soemmerring respectively, going back as they do to Aristotelian and Platonic

19. Soemmerring is quoted by Choulant, 1945, pp. 302–3; Hunter, 1774, Preface. Schiebinger, 1989 and 1993, discusses Soemmerring's interest in the skeleton from the point of view of race and gender.

20. Kemp, 1975, pp. 26–7; Walters, 1979, p. 206; on neoclassicism, see Honour, 1968 and Irwin, 1997. Crow, 1995 is particularly attentive to the ways in which David and his associates portrayed the human, especially the male, body. Kemp points out (21) that Hunter was sceptical about Winckelmann's classicism; on Winckelmann, see Irwin, 1997 and Potts, 1994.

21. Flaxman, 1829; Hagstrum, 1966. Reynolds, who was President of the Royal Academy when Hunter was professor of Anatomy there, also valued the ideal and the general above the particular, as his *Discourses* make plain.

traditions. Soemmerring's view, indicative of the growing anti-rationalism of the time, was informed by an intense dislike of what he took to be the materialism of much contemporary physiology – a point that came out clearly in the hostile stance he took towards the guillotine during the French Revolution.[22] Soemmerring's attack on materialism and the French Revolution was linked to his anatomical and aesthetic views, which led him to an epistemology in marked contrast to that of Hunter, which stressed the visible, material world. This does not mean that Hunter was a radical materialist. On the contrary, he was an ardent defender of the King and held orthodox religious views, extolling the works of the Supreme Being who was the creator and director of the universe.[23] Yet it was the real world of nature in all its infinite variety that captured Hunter's interest, and especially the 'machinery' of the human body. Real detail, not ideal form, was his object of study.

The relationships between words and images are varied and intricate. In the case of Hunter's volume, it is by no means obvious how the book was to be used, which groups it was intended for, or, indeed, what kind of work, beyond a sumptuous one, Hunter intended to produce. At one level, the images are clearly 'medical' in that they show anatomical preparations carefully and knowledgeably designed to display internal organs, and we have seen the emphasis Hunter placed on such demonstrations when teaching. However, unlike Smellie, Hunter did not structure the book around the needs of a young *accoucheur*. The anatomical tables in Smellie's volume were designed to accompany his midwifery textbook. Both were aimed at the young male practitioner, as is clear from the plates explaining the use of forceps.[24] To the extent that Hunter's atlas can be labelled 'medical', commentators tend to disregard the other elements it contains.

Medicine is like other forms of culture in containing meanings that are best interpreted in relation to myths, symbols and beliefs. Furthermore, medicine in general, and *The Human Gravid Uterus* in particular, raise directly such issues as death, birth, production and creativity – all these combine elements of human experience with the mythical and symbolic, working at many levels of consciousness. The historical relationship between art and anatomy bears out this point. It is misleading to construe this as a continuous, progressive joint quest for accuracy and technical perfection. Male and female figures were commonly depicted as Adam and Eve, female figures with children as Madonnas, while reminders of death abound in anatomical images. These were part of iconographical traditions, and are best understood in the same terms as those art historians or historians of culture have developed. It follows that 'realism' can no longer be seen as the unproblematic commitment of art and anatomy, nor must it be allowed to develop into a spurious criterion of value. Realism is, in

22. Chapter 7, this volume; Outram, 1989, ch. 7.

23. Hunter's volume was dedicated to the King and he enjoyed a Royal appointment. My assumption has been that we can take at face value Hunter's comments about his respect for the King and about religion. In Bynum and Porter, 1985, however, Porter offers a compelling reading of Hunter as a skilled and highly self-aware opportunist – pp. 7–34, see esp. 29–30.

24. Smellie, 1752–64.

fact, itself a historical contruct, not an unproblematic and self-evidently valuable analytical term.[25]

To acknowledge the presence of mythic and symbolic elements in anatomical images is also to say that they are mediations, in that they re-present social and cultural relations in an experiential form. Anatomical depictions may assist in papering over, accommodating and exploring tensions and contradictions not fully explicit in the image itself. Such latent levels may be about sexual modesty or desire, fear of death, disease and mutilation, the bonds between parents and children, or the sexual act itself. Anatomical images of pregnancy mediate gender and family relations in particular. Family and gender are ideological constructs as well as powerful human experiences, and medicine has played a central role in constructing familial relationships, especially that between mother and child – this role was particularly prominent in the eighteenth century (see plate 23, p. 197). Hunter produced *The Gravid Uterus* at a time of intense medical concern with domestic medicine – the health practices of families, of which the wife and mother was the main architect.[26]

The clusters of ideas around male and female, nature and science, also underlay anatomical treatments of women's bodies. Early anatomical images were rather discreet generally when it came to sexuality. The genitals, particularly of women, were mostly veiled or covered in some way. Female sexual characters were often removed, as in the omission of pubic hair, which was shown in a sketchy way and without relentless naturalism if present at all. Similarly breasts were not emphasised, and on occasion the whole body was masculinised, leaving only the head hair as unambiguously feminine. But Hunter and some of his contemporaries showed female genitals in unrelenting detail. This revealed to open view what was normally concealed, and revealed it furthermore in a context of dissection, mutilation and death – a situation commonly construed at the time as one of violation, as Hogarth made clear in *The Reward of Cruelty*, the last print of his *Four Stages of Cruelty* (1751). There a dissection is performed on a man who has killed his pregnant lover. Anatomical illustrations linked medical knowledge to sight, and, in the case of eighteenth-century depictions of women, to seeing parts of nature previously deemed private, thereby forging additional links with sexual-cum-intellectual penetration and with the violence of the dissecting-room.[27]

Hunter made aesthetic claims for his atlas just as Laskey did when he described the Hunterian Museum in Glasgow. Yet the content of the images and the manner in which they had been composed diverged most markedly

25. Bryson, 1981, 1983. Realism remains a tricky concept, normally discussed by art historians in relation to nineteenth-century images. Fried's 1987 discussion remains compelling. Cf. Levine, 1993. For a range of anatomical figures see *The Quick and the Dead*, 1997, as well as general works on art and anatomy cited elsewhere in the notes.

26. Buchan, 1769; Lawrence, 1975; Rosenberg, 1983; W. Hunter's other work in the area of reproduction is outlined in Brock, 1983, pp. 12, 17, 20–2, 23, 47, 59, 63; on popularisation see Porter, 1992.

27. Examples of women in anatomical illustrations can be found in Thornton and Reeves, 1983 and in Hahn *et al.*, 1962; on the broader significance of such images see Jordanova, 1980a and 1984b; the Hogarth prints are in Shesgreen, 1973, plates 77–80, see also *The Quick and the Dead*, 1997, pp. 34, 38, 104–5. Roberts and Tomlinson, 1992 and Cazort, Kornell *et al.*, 1996 contain a range of high-quality reproductions.

from the normal canons of taste in the period, unlike many other anatomical illustrations. Those by Albinus, for example, were set against elaborate backgrounds of plants, trees, hills, animals, lakes and buildings. Joseph Wright made an exact copy of one figure for his *The Old Man and Death* (1774).[28] The content of Hunter's plates is not directly comparable to contemporaneous 'polite art', nor do they seek to be decorous. By making a public proclamation about the legitimacy of all natural objects being known and seen, Hunter was countering the mystification and concealment of certain anatomical parts, which had been justified by reference to religious convention and modesty, and he was also basing his aesthetic firmly in nature. Whatever the eye could see was true, and it was beautiful because it was natural: 'what imitates Nature most is most striking; and . . . it will be likewise *more pleasing* if the subject be properly adapted to our passions'.[29] Artificial convention should give way to the reality of nature. There was a precedent for this approach in the anatomical drawings of Leonardo, and Hunter saw his project in this tradition. Furthermore, such affinities with a Renaissance artist of genius served as a powerful legitimation for later practices.[30]

However unusual the content of some anatomical illustrations may have been, our understanding of their implications, and those of anatomical models so far as gender is concerned, can nonetheless be furthered by comparing them with more conventional works of art. For example, the Italian wax models that functioned as collectors' items, with their glass, coffin-like cases, pearl necklaces, luxuriant hair and ecstatic facial expressions, are reminiscent of Bernini's statue of Saint Teresa (1646–52), whose face suggests both religious ecstasy and sexual transports. The use of such recognisable patterns and of accoutrements in anatomical models and illustrations shows that gender differences and the perception of sexuality were important elements in the medical realm also. Thus, in the case of women we can demonstrate the close relationships between medical images and those in the culture more generally, and note the mixture of eroticism, violence and idealisation in the drive to know and see more of feminine nature.[31]

The case of the foetus is altogether more complex and elusive than is that of women.[32] Few depictions of children prior to the eighteenth century satisfy our canons of naturalism, and perceptions and theories of childhood underwent some dramatic changes between the seventeenth and nineteenth centuries. Many early pictures of foetuses treat their bodily shape as being essentially that of an adult. An alternative way of expressing these ideas would be to say that earlier it had not seemed so pressing to present an accurate, naturalistic depiction of a foetus as it did to Hunter, for example. Placing changes in medical illustrations of embryos, babies and children in the context of changes

28. Nicolson, 1968, vol. 1, p. 56.

29. Kemp, 1975, p. 39 (emphasis in original).

30. Iversen, 1983, esp. pp. 213, 215–16; Kemp, 1976; Hunter, 1784, pp. 37–9.

31. Jordanova, 1980a; Cooke and Wollen, 1995, pp. 178–201 (ch. by Warner); Lemire, 1990; on Bernini, see Wittkower, 1979, chs 8 and 9, a photograph of Saint Teresa is on p. 175.

32. Newman, 1996.

in portraiture might be revealing. Hunter saw his atlas as containing portraits, after all. It depicted specific anatomical subjects; which particular one is always noted, and individual peculiarities included. Over the eighteenth century, British portraiture moved towards giving its subjects, and children especially, a more embodied, fleshly look, and showed them in less formal, more 'natural' poses. The *Gravid Uterus* portrayed flesh – sometimes, as in the case of the mother's body, it is meaty, but at others, as in the child's, it is chubby, fresh, substantial. Hunter's full-term foetus strives to be realistic – it has long elegant fingers and magnificent hair. It is almost too perfect, and it was the perfection, completeness and beauty of the new-born child that contemporary medical opinion stressed. The plates in the *Gravid Uterus* showing the full-term child nearly bursting out of the womb were totally different from the tiny adult body floating in an enormous cavity in a variety of postures, found in early illustrations, and persisting in some popular eighteenth-century prints (plate 26, p. 214).

Children were a central element in images of the family in the eighteenth century. Whereas for Blake, for example, there was no natural identity of interest between parents and children, for the vast majority of writers and artists there was a growing sense of natural fusion, of an organic link between the different family members, particularly between mother and child. This fusion was represented visually by showing an intertwining intimacy between women and their offspring. Sometimes this was achieved by actually blending figures together, as Gainsborough did in *The Baillie Family* (c.1784), where the clothes of the mother and those of the baby she is holding on her knee appear continuous. This is just what Reynolds did in *Mrs Richard Hoare and Her Son* (1763; see plate 23, p. 197), where the whole composition as well as the palette suggests intense emotional engagement between mother and child and places it in the context of nature. He produced a similar emotional effect in *Lady Cockburn and Her Three Eldest Sons* (1774) by encircling the mother with her children and showing them scantily dressed, which serves to emphasise their 'naturalness' – a pictorial formula suggestive of the theme of charity (cf. plate 30, p. 223). The associative chain – mother, child, nature . . . – was all the more effective when women's sexuality and their reproductive powers were treated as inseparable, and this was particularly marked in the work of the French painter Greuze, as in his *La Mère Bien-Aimée* (*The Much-Loved Mother*, c.1769), where the wife is rapturously greeted her husband while numerous children throng around embracing her.[33]

To return to the foetus, it is worth recognising both the difficulties of imagining life before birth and how highly charged such ideas are. Two issues are present here: the nature of the birth process and the way in which the foetus develops before its passage to the outside world. Birth is an event that marks, in an apparently natural manner, a fundamental transition. All societies see birth as a dramatic moment infused with significance, as the heroic myths associated with those 'born' through Caesarean section bear witness. Images of

33. Damon, 1965; Blake, 1970; Bryson, 1981, ch. 5, esp. pp. 136–7; Duncan, 1973; Hautecœur, 1945; Brookner, 1972, esp. pp. 64–5; *Greuze & Diderot*, 1984, esp. pp. 76–8.

PLATE 23. *Sir Joshua Reynolds*, Mrs Richard Hoare and Son, *1767–68, oil on canvas. Reproduced by Permission of the Trustees of the Wallace Collection, London. The blending of mother, child and nature is suggested in a number of ways, including the 'rhyme' of the flowers on her dress with those growing close by.*

the foetus, especially when it is made to look like a person, evoke beliefs about the act of birth. Because of the advent of man-midwifery, the management of childbirth was one of the most controversial topics in Britain in the second half of the century. These fierce debates hinged on gender roles, on the interpretation of nature, and on the proper management of a major ritual. Ideas

197

about growth and development were also given expression in depictions of life before birth. Hunter's atlas must therefore be placed in the context of ideas about embryology. In order to understand changes in the ways foetuses were shown, a brief discussion of theories of preformation and *emboîtement*, which enjoyed a wide following during the eighteenth century, may be helpful. These theories presumed 'that the gradual appearance and apparent creation of the parts observed, as the ovum turned into the embryo and then into the adult, were simply due to an increase, in size and in hardness, of parts that were already present'.[34] All living things were created at the beginning, later generations being enclosed within earlier ones. The formation of an individual was simply the expansion of an already existing being. Although not new in the seventeenth century, these theories came to prominence with the work of Swammerdam in the 1660s, and remained influential throughout the eighteenth century. Preformationism, where the baby is essentially like an adult, removes the need to think about foetal growth and the human status of the child. Within this framework, the infant always was human and complete; it merely had to grow bigger. For those committed to the alternative hypothesis, epigenesis, the full-term foetus had emerged gradually from a beginning that was radically distinct from its final form. It is worth remembering how preposterous this latter view seemed to many, so that Claude Perrault could say in 1680, 'If the egg consists of homogeneous matter as is presumed on this hypothesis [epigenesis], it can only develop into a foetus by a miracle, which would surpass every other phenomenon in the world.'[35]

The uterine space around the 'preformationist' embryo, as we may call the little people of early images, possibly suggests the further growth yet to come. But it might also represent a separation between the would-be adult and its immediate environment – its mother. Hunter's plates, in contrast, convey an almost oppressive intimacy between mother and child, an intimacy ceaselessly expressed in medical writings of the period. Although birth scenes – that is, the room and its occupants during or soon after a birth – were common, particularly in the sixteenth and seventeenth centuries, the actual process of birth was rarely depicted. Smellie, however, did show the head just appearing in his *Sett of Anatomical Tables* (1754). This absence of depictions of the moment of separation gives Blake's portrayal of birth as an act of releasing untameable human energy a peculiar power. In *The Marriage of Heaven and Hell* (1790), he showed a child half out of its mother, already actively embracing life with its outstretched arms. Blake's picture is notable because it expresses so forcefully a particular conception of childhood. In its moment of birth, the new being affirms its vitality and energy, those elements of the human spirit that Blake's

---

34. Gasking, 1966, p. 41.

35. Quoted ibid., p. 37; I am most grateful to Dr Helen Brock for her advice on what Hunter's own views about the preformation *versus* epigenesis debate may have been, for he never stated them unequivocally. Dr Brock suggests that Hunter inclined towards epigenesis, and this has been my assumption in this essay. She says, 'All Hunter's drawings of early stages of human embryology give no suggestion of a complete individual nor did John Hunter's drawings' (personal communication). On preformationism see also Charlton, 1984, pp. 73–5.

works celebrate in so many different forms. In this sense the child was an emblem or symbol for Blake, playing an important role in his metaphysical and mythological systems.[36] Children and foetuses in medical illustrations represent equally complex, if very different ideas.

The vitality of generation appears in Hunter's *Gravid Uterus* not as force or energy but in the fullness and texture of the internal organs. He used the bodies of a number of women who had died at different stages of pregnancy. The outer layers of tissues were carefully peeled off to reveal the foetus beneath, just as the wax modellers made removable flaps and organs for their female figures, which often contained a pregnant uterus at their deepest layer. Clearly, Hunter was fascinated by different tissues and their textures. The importance he attached to stripping off layers can be seen in Plate XXI, taken from a drawing by Alexander Cozens. Hunter described it as 'from a seventh subject at seven months. The womb opened by a crucial incision, and the four corners carefully separated . . . so as to shew the child, and waters, through the enclosing membranes.' The result is an indistinct and blurred effect whose very lack of clarity conveys the sense of looking *through* tissues, of the foetus being contained by them, even pressing against them. Simultaneously, the viewer sees the anatomical closeness of foetus and womb, and acquires a sense of the deep recesses of the body marked by layers of tissues. Smellie's atlas contained a similar plate.[37]

In the anatomical plates, the mother's body framed and moulded the foetus, the two lives being portrayed as a single interconnected system.[38] Both Hunter's and Jenty's plates displayed these features, which were absent, however, in those made by Stubbs at the very beginning of his career for John Burton's *An Essay Towards a Complete New System of Midwifery* (1751). Stubbs made the uterus into an abstract capsule connected with other physical objects only through a disembodied hand reaching up into the womb in one of the etchings. However, Stubbs's later work on human and animal anatomy, some of it for William Hunter himself, eschews such abstractions, and displays the same relentless search for a form of embodied literalism as we find in the *Gravid Uterus*.[39]

The sense of the woman and child being as one was particularly strongly asserted when it appeared in danger of violation, as, for example, in the case of illegitimate children, who elicited increasing amounts of anxiety over the eighteenth century. These children were more likely to be killed, abandoned or otherwise deprived than those born to legally married parents, although marriage itself was far from being unambiguous, either in theory or in practice. The ambiguities about kinship, property and inheritance, which were among the most threatening aspects of illegitimacy, reveal how relationships between parents, especially mothers, and children were imagined through the idioms of

36. Blake, 1975, plate 3; Damon, 1965, esp. pp. 81–2; Coveney, 1967.

37. Marks, 1967; Smellie, 1752–64, plate XI.

38. Hunter's interest in the relationship between the circulatory systems of mother and child and in the nature of the placenta is discussed in Brock, 1983, pp. 47–8; Chapter 12, this volume.

39. Burton, 1751, plate 10, see also plate 13; two of Stubbs's plates are reproduced in Taylor, 1971, plates 1 and 2; see also Gilbey, 1898, pp. 6–8; Paulson, 1975, ch. 10, esp. p. 173; Egerton, 1984.

blood, responsibility, legality, ownership. To be more precise, ideally the special maternal relationship was to be expressed only within the confines of civil law so that the different aspects of parenting were in harmony with one another. For example, for Rousseau, children conceived in a wife's adulterous relationship violated natural rights, making them robbers of the husband's name and estate. Legitimate children, by logical extension, were lawful possessors of their parental heritage; the common family interest consisted of shared and natural rights to property, and also to the love and devotion of their mothers and fathers.[40] Natural languages, such as those around breast-feeding and gestation, existed for thinking about such matters, and these were important precisely because of the increasing authority of nature in the period.

Hunter's foetuses possessed and confidently inhabited their mothers' bodies. In contrast, earlier, proto-adult 'preformationist' foetuses lived in a different world, where they seemed lost in the waters of the womb. They appeared as temporary tenants, with no 'natural' rights of possession. From the point of view of imagery, they were born into a looser family structure, one that easily permitted children to leave home for work or training without shattering a sacred bond with the mother, which, by the end of the century, was construed as at once natural, legal and social. Also connected are the general acceptance of child labour, which was beginning to be seriously questioned for the first time at the end of the eighteenth century on the grounds that the children required parental protection by virtue of their very nature, and the common practice of informal adoption in earlier periods. Both child labour and informal adoption made sense in a culture where the death of parents before children reached adulthood was common, making parents temporary custodians of their progeny, where there was less emphasis on 'correct' blood relationships, and where children were considered to be socially and economically competent at a young age. The medical literature of the second half of the eighteenth century, in contrast, emphasised that maternal and child welfare were necessarily connected, and the need to protect and carefully nurture infants as natural resources; furthermore, it sought to woo fathers into greater responsibility for the upbringing of children.[41]

The 'preformationist' image of the foetus appears to us to be manifestly 'artificial', whereas the Hunterian portrayal seems more 'natural'. This difference prompts us to see the latter as an unmediated, indeed a better, representation of nature. Yet this would be a mistake, since both are cultural products, and as such carry within them levels of meaning deriving from the ideas, assumptions, tensions and contradictions of their times. There is no unmediated nature, only different mediations, some of which conform more closely to our current conceptions than others. Different mediations can arise at the same historical moment. If we compare Hunter's obstetrical atlas with that of Jenty, both differences and similarities emerge, and both are equally important. They

40. Rousseau, 1911, esp. Book 1; Brinton, 1936; Okin, 1980; Jackson, 1996.
41. Ariès, 1973; Flandrin, 1979; the role of fathers is emphasised in Cadogan, 1748; and in Tissot, 1772; Hanway, 1785 outlines some of the arguments against child labour.

share a precise naturalism and an emphasis on the identity of mother and child. They differ in that Hunter's is more impersonal and reifying where Jenty's, partly by virtue of its different printing technique, is both softer and more holistic. This contrast is clear in the comparison between the cross-sectioned thighs shown in Hunter's book and the more complete ones depicted in Jenty's. These works share many features that clearly separate them from anatomical pictures in different and earlier traditions. The search for satisfying portrayals of the human body, a quest that unites art and anatomy, lay behind the work of men like Hunter and Jenty. As Hunter put it: 'in Painting and Sculpture the power of representing the human body in all the variety of its circumstances as near as possible to the original reality must be an aquisition of the greatest consequence, because it is so essential to the effect of the work'.[42] The history of representations of the human figure can be fully understood only by reaching for a more fundamental level of human experience – that of myth and symbol. The religious reasons for attempts to capture human form are of special importance. John Flaxman made this clear when he lectured on sculpture at the Royal Academy in the early nineteenth century. His fourth lecture, 'On Science', stressed 'the circle of knowledge', an expression he used to imply the need for a synthesis of art and science if the human figure were to be properly represented. He approvingly quoted Socrates as saying, 'The human form is the most perfect of all forms, and contains in it the principles and powers of all inferior forms.' He reinforced the point by referring to the view of the ancients that man was a microcosm, to 'Revelation', and to the general assent given, even in pagan countries, to the idea that the most beautiful human form was divine.[43]

Once it can be agreed that naturalism and realism must be analysed and not taken for granted, as too many works dealing with medical images still do, then attention can be turned to cultural motifs and historically-specific themes. Some possibilities relating to Hunter's atlas have been suggested in this chapter. In addition to the theory and practice of kinship and theories of human development, they include areas ranging from epistemology and theories of representation, on the one hand, to law and political theory, on the other, and include such art-historical topics as style, tradition and patronage. In other words, anatomical images raise extremely broad issues. Furthermore, they impinge on those boundaries in which societies have profound, if concealed, stakes. Depictions of medical subjects may be counted among those cultural artefacts that sustain fundamental distinctions and give them meaning. The *Gravid Uterus* touched on a number of such boundaries, most easily expressed through their related dichotomies: male/female, life/death, foetus/child, child/adult, science/nature. The divide between life and death was called into question quite sharply during Hunter's lifetime, especially by the medical community, both in their investigations into the possibilities for reviving the drowned or hanged, and in their efforts at preventing maternal and, above all, infant death. It is surely

42. Kemp, 1975, pp. 40–1.
43. Flaxman, 1829, pp. 102–3; cf. Clark, 1985.

important that so many anatomical pictures served as *memento mori*, as is most obvious in those that contain skulls and skeletons, particularly where the latter are sitting up in response to the trumpet blast that heralds the Last Judgement. Lessons about death were often contained in the gesture and position of the figure, and the background and accompanying objects. These are far from extraneous to the image: on the contrary, they render it meaningful. They frame the image morally speaking, give it a mood, and guide viewers as to what they should attend to.[44] The life–death dichotomy was raised in two forms by Hunter's work and by similar productions. First, they dissected the dead in order to reveal, lay bare and ultimately comprehend the living, and second, in so doing, they opened for inspection the process of gestation, the giving of life and the coming into life, the implied opposite of which was non-existence, death. In producing his magnificent book, William Hunter did not capture an image of nature with an 'innocent eye'; instead he unveiled historically specific cultural constructs and social relationships.

44. The skeleton sitting up in response to a trumpet call is in Gamelin's *Nouveau Recueil d'Ostéologie* (1779) and is reproduced in Bynum and Porter, 1985, p. 411; on death and related matters see McManners, 1981; *La Découverte du Corps Humain*, 1978, esp. p. 20; Hall, 1969, *memento mori* are discussed under 'Skull', p. 284 and 'Still Life', pp. 291–2; on attempts to revive the drowned see Chapter 9.

CHAPTER TWELVE

Cultures of Kinship

The title of this final chapter includes two ideas that are notoriously difficult to handle. This does not mean that I am beginning with an apology. I am starting rather with an acknowledgement. The elusive qualities of 'culture' also constitute one of its main attractions. The allure of cultural history will not be revealed by any neat definition of its concepts, methods or sources. I therefore propose not to set out an agenda for this field, but to discuss an area – cultural constructions of the family in the eighteenth century – that has intrigued me for the last fifteen years or so.[1] 'An area' is perhaps too bland a way of putting it; these are matters that have absorbed me because they are at once intellectually and methodologically challenging, emotionally complex, and important to me in my life as a whole. They can be examined through a range of sources that I find delightful and endlessly absorbing – and I make no apology for that. Here I want to do some cultural history, even as I am implicitly reflecting on what the field is about.

My use of the notion of kinship also demands a brief introductory comment. I chose it not just for its capacity to alliterate with culture, but because its use in anthropology has served to establish it as a general abstract term in a way that 'family', with its undertow of the particular, resists. It is perhaps unfortunate that when historians have used the term 'kinship' it has generally been of rules governing marriage, inheritance and household organisation. This is not my concern here. For me, kinship evokes the sense both that in a given society people are constantly and actively using ideas of affinity and that cultural historians can piece these uses together to produce general accounts of that society.[2]

---

1. In addition to other chapters in this volume, see, for example, Jordanova, 1987a; Scarre, 1989, pp. 3–24; Jordanova, 1991. My interest in the history of the family started in the mid-1970s; I am tremendously indebted to Leonore Davidoff for many conversations on the subject since 1980. Since most of the larger issues dealt with here have been discussed earlier, the reader is referred to earlier chapters for the relevant literatures.

2. Davidoff and Hall, 1987; Elshtain, 1982; Flandrin, 1979; Forster and Ranum, 1976; Gillis, 1974; Ginsburg and Rapp, 1995; Hunt, 1992; MacCormack and Strathern, 1980; O'Day, 1994; Traer, 1980; Strathern, 1992. Cf. Williams, 1983 for his definition of 'family'. I am particularly grateful to Marilyn Strathern for her inspirational and challenging writings on gender and kinship as well as numerous conversations on these topics.

'Cultures of kinship' could encompass a great deal; here I am narrowing my focus in three ways – by taking a specific period, a particular problem, and a thematic case study. My material, which is largely British, comes from the second half of the eighteenth century – an era of decisive transformation in relation to what I am summing up in the word 'kinship'. However, the particular problem that intrigues me is not, I suspect, confined to the eighteenth century. It is this: scientific and medical modes of thought, of central importance for kinship in Western societies, understand their object of study, nature, in terms of the properties of things. In this period, it was the demonstrable, visible properties of matter that formed the most secure basis for authoritative knowledge. There is a great deal that this emphasis on what was visible in objects leaves out and cannot adequately conceptualise. It becomes difficult to give due attention to what is magical, holy, ideal, mysterious. It is possible, in fact, that as medicine in particular claimed to know more and more about reproduction, sexuality and ageing, all of which are central to kinship, more was left out, even extruded. Modes of imagining human relationships, especially the most intimate ones, were peripheral to scientific and medical discourses, which certainly could approach them in a mediated way and often recognised their significance, but nonetheless had to adopt special stances towards them. How then, and this is the problem that interests me, do cultures cope with this – what do they do with the bits that their most authoritative discourses, in this case science and medicine, find problematic, bits that are central to lived experience? My thematic case study, designed to explore these questions, is the relationship between mother and child, a prominent motif of the time. It was a subject of particular interest to medical practitioners, and it was invested with a reverence, an idealised quality, that indicates it was carrying elaborate investments. This relationship was on the one hand studied scientifically, on the other made mysterious.

What I have said so far may appear to be lacking in the very characteristic that supposedly makes history what it is – concreteness. Let me therefore turn immediately to a specific example, which vividly shows how lived kinship and represented kinship were intertwined in eighteenth-century England.

Ann Ford, born in 1737, was a young, beautiful and talented woman, who sang and played at informal gatherings in her father's house. But her life started to go badly wrong. She was courted by an old (married) aristocrat, she fell out with her father and uncle because she had repelled his advances, she tried to earn money by performing in public, she felt her reputation to have been impugned by the aristocrat's public and dishonest treatment of her and by her father and uncle's repudiation of her. To defend her reputation she published a pamphlet with a satirical ballad appended to it. She was not, however, 'ruined'; Ann Ford married and had children, published other works, and was immortalised in a splendid portrait by Gainsborough (see plate 24, p. 205).[3]

---

3. Hayes, 1975, pp. 37, 210, plate 54; Armstrong, 1904, pp. 102, 176–81; Leppert, 1988, pp. 40–2; Williamson, 1972, pp. 110–13; Lindsay, 1981, pp. 53–4; Todd, 1984, 302–3.

PLATE 24. *Thomas Gainsborough,* Portrait of Mrs Philip Thicknesse, *1760, oil on canvas, Bequest of Mrs Mary M. Emery, Cincinnati Art Museum. Ann Ford married Philip Thicknesse in 1762.*

Ann Ford was the daughter of a lawyer, Thomas Ford, and the niece of John Ford, a surgeon and midwife. Her pamphlet, *A Letter from Miss F——d, addressed to a person of distinction*, was first published in 1761, and, while technically anonymous, it was easily attributable to her. It is a masterly piece of writing, carefully designed to elicit the sympathy of readers for her plight. The pamphlet consists of a blow by blow account of her relationship with a member of the aristocracy, whose intentions towards her are presented in an unpleasant light. The general scenario, a respectable young woman without fortune being pursued by an older man of higher status, was hardly unique. What sets Ann Ford's pamphlet apart is, first, her absolute insistence that her perspective be publicly recorded and judged; second, her indictment of her father and uncle for colluding with his 'L——d——p' rather than supporting and protecting her; third, her status as a young unmarried women, who desired to make a musical career for herself, who asserted, in other words, her independence; and fourth, her active manipulation of words and music for her own ends.

It is surely no coincidence that, as a musician, she adapted that most robust of musical forms, the ballad, for her own, very different purposes. In her musical version of the story, 'A New Song to the Tune of Chevy-Chase', the ballad has become a dirge, a relentless re-telling of her misfortunes:

'Tis of a noble L——d I sing;
An E——l of high renown;
Of whose achievements fame doth ring,
Throughout this mighty town.

Youthful and handsome once was he,
And am'rous all his life;
And all historians do agree
That once he lov'd his wife.

By Cupid arm'd with all his art
T'assist the wanton trade;
Among the gentle virgins hearts
He grievous havock made.

He laughing play'd with Cupid's snares;
It but his Hours amused;
And often has been heard to swear,
He never was refused.

Time who destroy'd the walls of Troy,
This Champion did defy;
He kept the post of youth and joy,
Nor from love's field wou'd fly.

In that vile place, the city call'd,
A lovely maiden dwell'd;
Whose charms his mighty heart subdued,
And all his valour quell'd.

One day as am'rous Phaebus deign'd
This pupil to inspire;
While she to learn her lesson feign'd,
She stole his fav'rite lyre.

His stolen prize, in spight of shame,
To all the world is known;
Its praises too she boldly claims,
And wears them as her own.

He saw her smile; he heard her sing;
He felt the raging smart;
The pain so often felt before,
Again possess'd his heart.

Upon his knees the hero fell,
He sigh'd, he wept, he swore;
Offer'd his heart, his life, his soul,
And eke his wealthy store.

He try'd all ways that those who love
Use to express their pain;
From her white hand he took——her glove,
And drew it on again.

Then to the charmer of his heart,
He made his ardent pray'r,
And vow'd to settle on his part,
Eight hundred pounds a year!

The Maid with scorn his fruit repell'd;
Her virtue stood the field;
Her heart refused to be compell'd
On such base terms to yield.

This island L——d was sorely griev'd
To find she stood her ground;
His pride was picqu'd, his hope deceiv'd,
Its first repulse had found.

Dishonest love can never bear
True virtue's pride and scorn;
Repulsed, its refuge is despair,
Or to revenge will turn.

I scorn my fate, the maiden said;
The world's applause I'll try;
While vice her votaries has paid,
Shall virtue silent die?

The p——r inform'd of her design,
Most meanly condescends
To soil her fame, her project spoil's
In whispers to her friends.

With idle tales of this and that,
He female ears amused;
To shew his zeal, and his revenge,
Five guineas he refused.

Now God reform all noble L——ds,
That lead unrighteous lives;
May shame be still their just reward,
That do defraud their wives.[4]

In relating her experiences in this way, Ann Ford mobilised a story, perhaps
we should say a myth, that enjoyed a certain currency by the 1760s, the fall
of a young innocent woman, through the loss of her sexual virtue to a man of
the world. The end point of that fall was, successively, prostitution, venereal
disease and death – a fall that always stands in implied contrast to an ideal
female life of chaste courtship, a well-chosen marriage, and responsible, happy
motherhood.[5] This scenario lurks in Ford's text, which makes clear her heroism
in not actually succumbing. Her real anxiety becomes explicit when she speaks
of whether Lord Jersey could imagine it possible to 'purchase my person'.[6]
The alternative to prostitution, even in its most genteel of forms, was a musical
career, which she claims should be 'looked upon in as favourable a light, as a
surgeon or midwife' – a biting reference to her uncle, and his profession, which
was far from being morally stable.[7] Ann Ford had to tread a delicate path, since
her decision to go public could, in fact did, elicit hostile comments about
washing dirty linen in public – a charge that was more barbed because she was
a woman, a woman furthermore who had placed herself outside the protection
of her male kinsfolk. Ann Ford's mother, we should note, is absent, presumably
dead. While she may have detached herself from her family, she was firmly
allied with other networks. Ann Ford moved in fashionable circles, and this is
how she met both Gainsborough and the man who in 1762 was to become her
husband, the pugnacious Philip Thicknesse. He had been married twice before,
was the author of at least 24 works, but enjoyed no stable career. His whole life
suggests an inability to settle, either literally, in terms of occupation and home,
or metaphorically, in terms of people or ideas. He engaged in lengthy legal
battles over family property and was on spectacularly bad terms with his son
by his second wife, whom he attacked in his memoirs. Gillray's splendid cartoon of 1790 portrayed him as Dr Gallstone; its surfeit of detail, both visual
and textual, conveys his multifarious interests and activities as well as his bile
(see cover illustration).[8]

4. Ford, 1761, pp. 41–7.
5. Lonsdale, 1984, no. 438 is Thomas Holcroft's remarkable 1785 poem, *The Dying Prostitute, an Elegy*. On
morals and prostitution see Roberts, 1992, ch. 10; Andrew, 1989; Compston, 1917; Speck, 1980.
6. Ford, 1761, p. 38.
7. Ibid., p. 17.
8. On Thicknesse see Gosse, 1952; Chapter 2 of this volume; the works on Gainsborough cited in
note 3 above, *Dictionary of National Biography*, vol. XIX, pp. 612–13.

Of particular interest for our explorations of kinship, however, is one of Thicknesse's publications on medical/health issues – he had briefly worked for an apothecary – entitled *Man-Midwifery Analysed*, first published in 1764. His diatribe, for that is what it was, went through three editions, in 1764, 1765 and 1790 respectively, and the last one is dedicated to none other than John Ford, Ann Ford's uncle, the surgeon and midwife. The dedication, which was sarcastic rather than laudatory – he called Ford his 'sinister uncle' – became an occasion for yet more unbridled hostility towards what Thicknesse dubbed the 'obstetric gentry'.[9]

The basic arguments that Thicknesse put forward had become common-place by the 1790s. He advanced simultaneously on a number of fronts – the indecency of having men attend women in childbirth, the superiority of 'Goody Nature' in this regard, the foolishness of women in agreeing to be delivered by men, and the association of man-midwifery with what was foreign and fashion-able.[10] Thicknesse's language was intense, heightened, venomous. For instance, he suggested that man-midwifery was a step on the road to prostitution: 'But, husbands, I ask you, whether Doctors are not men? and whether you are not fools to submit to such insults? If the women will have the male gender about their persons, let them send to Italy for castrato operators.' And in the pages that followed, Thicknesse made it plain that 'the preservation of the Empire' depended on eradicating such male practitioners.[11] The work is full of spite, double entendres and horror stories – some probably autobiographical.

The lives and writings of Ann Ford and Philip Thicknesse neatly exemplify a number of important themes in eighteenth-century cultural life. Both of them were exceptionally explicit about the tensions that existed around not just the conduct of family life and of sexual relationships but how these were to be represented and debated. The materials relating to this admittedly unusual couple enable us to apprehend particularly vividly the energies that animated their concerns, to see these concerns at work in a number of domains including art, medicine, music and literature, to watch the varied forms they took.

Their concerns were in no way idiosyncratic. I take both Ann Ford and Philip Thicknesse to be preoccupied with matters of kinship, with the organ-isation of family life and with the cultural patterns that determine, express, and alter patterns of intimacy. They reveal something of the cultural stakes, the psychic-cum-political investment, the symbolic charge that contemporaries found in the autonomy of women and the conduct of childbirth. I am summing up such issues by the word 'kinship'. I am interested in something that has been a dimension of this word since its earliest uses in English around the middle of the nineteenth century.[12] This 'something' has two aspects: the idea that in specific societies 'family' is a structured element, which has a systematic quality that can be reconstructed by scholars, and that when this has been done gen-eral features of that society can be understood. In using 'systematic' here, I do

9. Thicknesse, 1790, p. 71.
10. Thicknesse, 1764, p. 3.
11. Thicknesse, 1790, pp. 80, 82.
12. *Oxford English Dictionary*: see the entries for 'kin' and its cognates.

not mean to suggest there was only one way of experiencing and representing kinship at any one time. I hope that my explorations show, among other things, that very different notions of familial relationships co-existed at a given time and place. I use 'systematic' to suggest that models of kinship had entailments, implicit logics, that even if fully coherent paradigms did not exist, people, more or less consciously, worked through the implications of their beliefs about the nature of the family. As a cultural historian, I want to watch them doing this.

Inevitably, the cultural history of the family is a vast topic. Every cultural artefact is touched in some way or other by so fundamental a zone. I am concentrating here on relations between mothers and children and I should like to explain briefly why. Eighteenth-century thinkers found the family profoundly interesting. Many did so because they took it to be a natural unit, the first society, the most fundamental and universal unit of human organisation. Of all its parts, motherhood was the most natural. My contention is that the equation between the family and nature in the eighteenth century only makes sense in the context of the rise to dominance of a taxonomic mode of thought, that is, an obsession with classifying all nature's products, together with an infatuation with the charisma of 'nature', which impelled people to search for naturalistic accounts of familial relationships. The relations between mother and child were especially interesting, since they seemed of all kin relations the most deeply embedded in nature. There were many further shifts, preoccupations and social processes that led eighteenth-century culture-makers to the mother/child bond – it was overdetermined that philanthropists, lawyers, medical practitioners and so on should become interested in this relationship. But explaining, under-standing and representing it presented huge challenges to all these groups. Finding an adequate imagery for the relationship that went beyond the banal strained the imaginative capacities of writers and artists alike.

My argument has two complementary facets; first I shall trace one way in which naturalistic explanations of the mother/child relationship were pursued by those professionally committed to the scientific study of medicine. I shall do so by examining the interest in exactly how the placenta functioned, which first became a topic of intense medical concern in the second half of the eighteenth century. Second, I will explore what this relentless naturalisation leaves out, denies, renders fugitive – I shall call this remnant 'the sacred'. I will consider how the sacredness of motherhood is imagined in the eighteenth century, using among other examples the popularity of *Stabat Mater*, the medieval poem of uncertain authorship that officially entered the Roman Missal and Breviary in 1727, and that continued to attract composers, writers and audiences alike throughout the nineteenth century.[13]

I have set up this argument through the examples of Ann Ford and Philip Thicknesse in order to indicate how what might appear to be abstract concerns could be grounded in the lives of real people, and also to convey something of the affect with which they were invested. It was not just that man-midwifery was controversial, that feelings about it ran high, but that these were precisely

13. Sadie, 1980, vol. 18, pp. 36–7; Julian, 1957, vol. 2, pp. 1081–4.

focused on the physical and moral intrusion that a man touching a parturient woman constituted, and on the contagious quality of this intrusion, which could spread, like an infectious disease, to a whole nation.[14] Man-midwifery was unsettling. This perceived threat to an entire social order was bound up with the sense that Nature had been displaced. Nature, personified as 'the old Lady', 'Goody Nature', was presented by Thicknesse as the suffocated victim of French male midwives. When he fulminated about this threat, the name he most often invoked was that of William Smellie, whose writings on midwifery were indeed directed to young male practitioners wishing to make careers that included midwifery.[15] He might just as easily have directed his venom at William Hunter, who enjoyed a certain notoriety as well as fame when it came to obstetrics. I am interested in Hunter in this context not so much because of his activities in actually delivering children, but because of his relentless curiosity about reproductive processes. If, as in the typical denunciation of men-midwives, it was considered that they touched and saw inappropriately, Hunter did so on a grand scale, because he felt driven, not only to procure the bodies of women who had died at different stages of pregnancy for the purposes of dissection, but also to represent these dissections in words and images, and to pursue an experimental approach towards the tissues he studied. So far as I know he was not a vivisectionist, but he was interested in fiddling around with human parts, so to speak, an interest he shared with his younger brother John, one of the great heroes of nineteenth-century British medicine.[16]

Interest in the placenta was by no means new: it goes back to the earliest systematic work on medicine and was given new energy with Harvey's work on the circulation of the blood.[17] My interest in late eighteenth- and early nineteenth-century controversies about the placenta lies, at least in part, in the fact that they were technical, requiring detailed anatomical and physiological knowledge and a proven record of observation and experiment if participants were to be taken seriously. While the writings of Ford and Thicknesse are revealing, they do not possess this more technical dimension, thus, while they are useful in revealing the quality of affect that surrounded disputed kinship, and something of the circumstances in which such disputes were rooted, like all sources they are limited. Two assumptions are being made here: first, putting diverse sources together is helpful not just because they are diverse but because we can trace particular resonances between them; second, any engagement with sources that appealed to nature as a norm, a set of laws, must take seriously the complexities of the most authoritative natural knowledge. William and John Hunter's views of the placenta claim our attention precisely because of the authority with which they were invested, both by themselves and by their

14. Porter, 1987a; Fores, 1793.

15. Thicknesse, 1764, pp. 5–6, 21, and 1765, pp. 34, 41–4; Smellie, 1752–64 and 1754. Wilson, 1995, esp. ch. 9.

16. It should be stressed that, as Adrian Wilson has pointed out, as a practitioner of midwifery William Hunter was notably non-interventionist, 1995, ch. 13. On John Hunter and his reputation see Jacyna, 1983. Cf. Lawrence and Shapin, 1998, ch. 5 (by Lawrence), and Jordanova, 1997.

17. Adams, 1858; De Witt, 1959.

followers, because of the powerful technologies through with they broadcast their claims – I am thinking particularly of their visual representations – and because of the coherent overall vision of gestation that they elaborated in the process.

The famous atlas that William Hunter published in 1774 with its parallel Latin and English texts and lavish illustrations includes pictures of a number of placentas, but very little commentary on what was already a vexing physiological and anatomical issue – what was the placenta, how did it work, was it of the mother, the child or both? We know more about William Hunter's ideas on this subject by virtue of the nineteenth-century editions of a manuscript left unpublished at his death in 1783. Medical interest in the placenta continued to grow over the nineteenth century, even if the issues that animated it shifted somewhat. For the Hunters the challenge was twofold – to give an accurate account of placental structure and to explain its mode of operation, both of which involved sorting out the contributions of the mother and of the foetus to this puzzling organ. Here is William Hunter on the subject:

[The placenta's] internal surface . . . is glossy, hard and compact in its texture, and beautifully marked with ramifications of the umbilical vessels.

The human placenta, as well as that of quadrupeds, is a composition of two parts intimately blended, an umbilical or infantile, and an uterine portion. One is a continuation of the umbilical vessels of the foetus, the other is an efflorescence of the internal part of the uterus.

He concluded:

in the umbilical portion the arteries terminate in the veins by a continuity of canal, whereas in the uterine portion, there are intermediate cells, into which the arteries terminate, and from which the veins begin.[18]

Hunter's account is revealing in a number of respects. He located his findings within the implied framework of comparative anatomy – a field in which his brother was especially prominent. His evidence was derived from dissection, from injecting blood vessels with different coloured waxes and from preparing tissue so as to reveal its true composition. He understood the placenta to be both maternal and foetal; an intimate blending. He responded aesthetically to its physical qualities, even as he recognised that the different membranes surrounding the child resist separation and cannot be visually represented. The images of placentas in William Hunter's atlas are striking, by virtue of their abstract, almost surreal quality (see plate 25, p. 213).

I have discussed William Hunter's studies of the placenta for three reasons – to show the complexity and range of responses this organ elicited in him, to draw attention to his focus on a physical structure that, as it were, carried

18. Hunter, 1843, pp. 32, 33, 39.

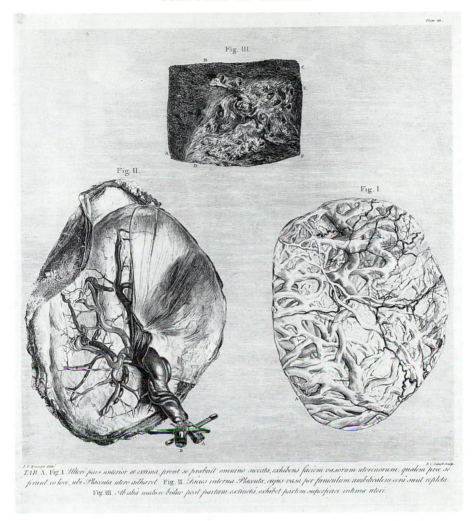

PLATE 25. *William Hunter*, Anatomia Uteri Humani Gravidi, *1774, engraving, plate X,* '*Fig. 1 A view of the outside of the forepart of the womb, as it appeared when quite dry; exhibiting a specimen of the uterine vessels, at the part where the placenta adhered. Fig. 2 The inside of the placenta, which was injected by umbilical vessels after it was taken out of the womb. Fig. 3 A portion of the internal surface of the womb, from a woman who had died two days after delivery*' *Wellcome Institute Library, London.*

within it a familial relationship, and to point out that his model of mother/ child interaction is one of intense intimacy. Earlier generations certainly believed in a direct, unmediated connection with mother and embryo, and the capacity of the maternal imagination to affect the child *in utero* remained a topic of discussion in the eighteenth century. The surgeon Samuel Sharp also assumed a direct connection when, returning from his European travels, he noted in his *Letters from Italy* of 1767 a propensity to goitre in Savoy:

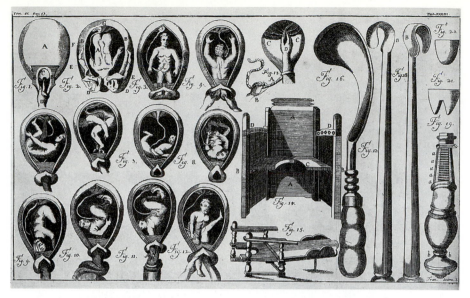

PLATE 26. *F. Sesone,* Thirteen diagrams of fetuses in the womb in varying positions, two obstetrical chairs and several instruments, *not dated, etching, Wellcome Institute Library, London.*

I was curious in my examination, whether any children were born with this malady upon them: I did not know but that the blood of the mother, imbued with snow-water, might operate this effect upon the foetus before the birth . . .[19]

If there were a number of ways in which the mother/foetus link was imagined, so too a variety of visual idioms co-existed. Despite the prominence of the Hunterian vision of tight physical embrace and intimate blending, which is found to varying degrees in many medical illustrations of the second half of the eighteenth century, images suggesting a looser fit between the two beings, if I can put it that way, were also in circulation. For some the foetus remained a mannikin – an idea that persisted in eighteenth-century encyclopedia illustrations. We may note the adult bodily proportions given to the child, the spaces surrounding it and the undifferentiated placenta (see plate 26, above).

Let me now turn briefly to John Hunter, a man, by all accounts, somewhat lacking in charm but possessed of abundant self-importance. In his paper, 'On the Structure of the Placenta', Hunter set out his claims to have discovered the precise nature of 'the connexion between the mother and foetus in the human subject' in 1754: 'The facts now being ascertained and universally acknowledged, I consider myself as having a just claim to the discovery of the structure of the placenta, and its communication with the uterus.'[20] He made it perfectly clear that he had led William to the idea, that other opinions on the subject

19. Sharp, 1767, p. 298. On maternal imagination see Huet, 1993, ch. 3.
20. John Hunter, 1837, vol. 4, pp. 60, 62.

PLATE 27. *James Palmer, ed.,* The Works of John Hunter, *1837, plates volume, plate XXXIV, 'Fig. 1 A part of a uterus at the ninth month of utero-gestation, with a portion of the placenta, to show the mode in which the blood-vessels of the mother communicate with it ... Fig. 2 Is a section of the monkey figured in [earlier] plates...' (p. 19). Wellcome Institute Library, London.*

were worthless, and that his, John's, authority on this matter should prevail. The text implies that he drew this authority from three specific sources: comparative anatomy, embryology, and pathology, i.e. extra-uterine pregnancies.

Hunter provided a picture to back up his argument (see plate 27, above). This was important since, in the last analysis, his position rested on visual inspection, on others seeing what he saw. Many did not. The best example of this refusal, which I interpret as a refusal not just of the Hunter brothers' detailed claims about the placenta, but of their claims to authority in general and of their vision of the maternal/foetal relationship in particular, came from

Jesse Foot, whose scandalous biography of John Hunter was published in 1794, a mere year after his death – scandalous because its principal aim was to make Hunter appear ridiculous. Foot died in 1826, but four years previously he had cut up a copy of his biography and mounted it in three albums with many additional pictures, some prints, and some original water-colours of scenes from Hunter's life. One of his jibes against John Hunter is particularly striking – the claim, backed up by an appropriate print, that Hunter's picture of the placenta looks like a map of the moon; both images are equally unhelpful and speculative.[21] What purported to be a literal representation of nature has been recast as science fiction. Foot homed in on his target with uncanny accuracy. The images of the placenta produced by both William and John Hunter were indeed abstract, they strained to represent the topography of placental flesh, to give that flesh a structure, to make real, concrete and comprehensible a part of the organic world to which a bit of mystery clung then as it continues to cling now.[22] As such their images could elicit disbelief, revulsion and ridicule.

It is possible for the cultural historian to recognise the existence of mystery without perpetuating it. The mystery emanates, I suggest, in this case from three sources: from long-held 'popular' assumptions about the special qualities of the afterbirth, which were allied with anxieties about birth itself; from the genuine difficulty in making out the constituent parts of the placenta by visual inspection; and from the very invisibility of conception and gestation, which necessarily made them fertile ground for the imagination. Precisely because of the emotional energies that gathered around pregnancy, birth and infant death in the eighteenth century, the attempts of men such as William and John Hunter to bring a self-consciously scientific point of view to bear upon these topics were controversial. On the one hand they could be placed within the main stream of Enlightenment thought and practice – careful, observational work, adding to the sum of human knowledge, and increasing human well-being. Understanding the placenta and how to manage it had obvious payoff – one of the women William Hunter dissected for his atlas had 'died of a flooding in the last month of pregnancy', her placenta was 'inside the mouth of the womb, under the child's head, and detached from the womb; the occasion of the fatal hemorrhage'.[23] On the other hand the Hunters' activities could equally well be construed as meddling and hubristic – a position taken up even by some medical practitioners, such as Francis Adams, who commented on their work.

Claims to secular knowledge have long been vulnerable to this type of criticism, but it finds it mark considerably more easily where matters of kinship are concerned. More specifically, knowledge of processes of reproduction can readily be construed as profoundly threatening. This is because reproductive processes

21. Foot, 1794, p. 222; the Grangerized version is in the Wellcome Institute Library, London and I am particularly grateful to John Symons for drawing my attention to this rich source. Hunter, 1835–37; Adams, 1858; on Jesse Foot's attack on John Hunter see also Jordanova, 1997.

22. I am grateful to Robin Dixon for drawing my attention to this point and for many stimulating conversations on kinship arising from his doctoral work at the University of Essex on the couvade and fatherhood in modern Britain, which is based on extensive oral history interviews.

23. Hunter, 1774, commentaries on plates XI and XII; Adams, 1858.

constitute a moral, social, political and psychic scaffolding, so that tinkering with one part, or rearranging the parts, causes a ripple effect. This is a general proposition that may apply to many times and places, but it has a perfectly specific relevance to the second half of the eighteenth century. At that time reproductive matters had the capacity to profoundly unsettle people, and this accounts for the almost insanely violent responses, as they seem to our eyes, to many aspects of midwifery in the period.[24]

Why? Let me put it quite bluntly. The work of men such as the Hunters made visible for the first time foetuses at different stages of development, the uterus at different stages of pregnancy. They brought together images that purported to tell it as it really was. They did so by cutting up women who had died at various stages of pregnancy and by investigating pregnant animals. The cultural context in which they did all this was permeated by an enthusiasm for knowing and naming the parts of nature. In the circumstances it was inevitable that, not always consciously, there was a powerful dynamic set up between reproduction as it was felt and as it had previously been represented, and scientific and medical approaches to it – we would do well to remember that 'reproduction' was itself a new word at the time, which for some commentators carried with it precisely the threat of a scientific demystification of the sacred in a way that the earlier term 'generation' had not.[25] I am noting not only the novelty of the Hunters' project, but the historical specificity of this era with respect to an uneasy relationship between naturalistic views of procreation and a sense of the sacredness of the mother/child bond. I am emphatically not suggesting, however, that the eighteenth century was the first time when people grieved over the premature death of children or worried about their capacity to procreate successfully; I am indicating that the quality of their griefs and anxieties, the forms of their expression, are historically specific.

We may be struck, for example, by the number of poems written by women on abortion, infant death, pregnancy and birth in the two wonderful anthologies of eighteenth-century verse compiled by Roger Lonsdale. These poems mostly deploy what might be called an everyday religious language combined with languages of nature. They convey an emotional intensity not in any way metaphysical or high-flown as well as a passionate identification of the mother with her child – the theme of the *Stabat Mater* poem. What makes these eighteenth-century poems all the more striking is that one of the most eloquent of them, entitled *To a Little Invisible Being who is Expected Soon to Become Visible*, composed in 1795, was by a woman, Anna Laetitia Barbauld, who never herself bore a child. It is a poem of anticipation and longing, which, while it extols the 'germ of new life', also acknowledges the simultaneous separateness and dependency of the foetus:

---

24. The association of man-midwifery with Frenchness is a case in point. On the (gendered) use of Frenchness in English moralising of the period see Cohen, 1996 and Donald, 1996. It has been very hard for historians to explain why the management of childbirth elicited such powerful emotional responses, partly because they have tended to see it in terms of professionalism. A new historiography is beginning to emerge, however, e.g. Bynum and Porter, 1985; Marland, 1993; Wilson, 1995.

25. Jordanova, 1995a pursues these issues in more detail.

... the stranger guest,
fed with her life through many a tedious moon.[26]

A poetic example, or indeed a visual one, makes the point particularly force-fully that a relationship is in question. It is, if I can so express myself, what happens in the metaphorical space between mother and child that interests Barbauld. Once the child is conceived, this space opens up, filled at first by the mother's fantasies and those of others around her and then by the newly visible being and its reactions, and eventually by dynamic interactions between the key players. Through such interactions something new comes into being, which goes beyond the individuals involved. It was difficult, perhaps impossible, to build a fully naturalistic language through which such a complex relation-ship was satisfactorily conceptualised, and yet these multi-faceted affinities were nonetheless vividly apprehended. This difficulty lent attraction to the scientific-cum-medical approach, which examined natural objects for their per-manent characteristics, and found ways of explaining them in their material composition. The naturalistic mode of thought, which *recast* relationships as the physical properties of natural objects, was readily available, and was attractive in being already the centrepiece of natural history and natural philosophy. The idea of taxonomy, with its emphasis on visible traits, was its kernel; the concern was to develop systems of classification certainly for all of nature, and, for many savants of the eighteenth century, for social and cultural phenomena as well. The passion for classification that swept the educated classes of this period, and the broad appeal of natural history, especially botany, are too well known to require elaboration here.[27]

The infatuation with nature-with-a-capital-N took many forms, among them collecting, preserving, representing and identifying specimens, especially of plants, shells, fossils and animals of manageable size. This was the era of nosologies – tables of diseases and their symptoms, listed as if they were flowers or stones.[28] It was also the era of fierce controversies over precisely how objects were to be classified, whether by some convenient, but artificial system – one that is, thought up by human beings – or by some natural system, that is, by using characteristics in the objects themselves that genuinely expressed their relation-ships to one another. Common to both sides in the controversies was a widely shared belief in the importance of classification as an analytical tool and a com-mon taxonomic vocabulary – a language of kinship. Affinity, likeness, relation-ship, family were key terms, and clusters of animals and plants were increasingly represented in branching diagrams that resembled family trees. Classification stood for a particular way of knowing the natural world, primarily through carefully observing the characteristics of objects. It was in this period a largely static form of knowledge – hence to note an affinity was to register formal resemblances,

26. Lonsdale, 1989, no. 201, lines 1, 23–4.
27. Delaporte, 1982; Jardine *et al.*, 1996, part 2; Benjamin, 1991, ch. 4; Pointon, 1997, ch. 4; Hankins, 1985, ch. 5.
28. The works of Linnaeus and Cullen exemplify the point. See Bynum and Porter, 1993a, ch. 17 (by Bynum), esp. pp. 343–8.

not to assert that one was the progenitor of the other or that they had common ancestry. Indeed it could be argued that evolutionary ideas, which were beginning to be explored in the last two decades or so of the eighteenth century, became explosive exactly because they offered a scientific way of understanding relationships of kinship over aeons of time, and by that token explicitly challenged one of the pockets where a sense of the sacred had been placed.[29]

I now want to consider the sacred in slightly more detail, and to examine ways of understanding the relationships between mothers and children that sought to acknowledge and celebrate them as bonds that were not to be violated because they were in some sense holy. Such a statement does not imply a romanticised view of the past – often the sacred was used quite manipulatively, especially in attempts to mobilise philanthropic and reformist sentiment around the family in the eighteenth century. Rather, it involved what appears to us as a conservatism about motherhood in stressing the transcendent joys of maternity and in mystifying, often for nakedly political ends, the unique status of the mother. I am not criticising naturalisations of kinship and applauding its sacralisation. On the contrary, I want to reveal the dynamics between them at a specific historical moment, in order to appreciate the energy this generated. To do so involves, I believe, turning to the funds of Christian imagery that were not only available but also attractive to Catholics and Protestants alike in the eighteenth century (see plate 28, p. 220). I suspect that Mary, mother of Christ, appealed to both groups not least because there were so many variations that could be elaborated on the original theme. Other Christian imagery also maintained its appeal – the figure of the penitent Magdalen, visions of charity as a woman suckling a baby, often surrounded by children, Mary and Elizabeth with their respective sons, the judgement of Solomon, the massacre of the innocents and so on (see plate 29, p. 221).[30]

Take the example of Solomon, who, according to the first book of Kings, chapter 3, married the daughter of Pharaoh (or, as the King James version put it, 'made affinity' with her), asked God for wisdom – 'an understanding heart to judge thy people, that I may discern good and bad' – and put his wisdom to the test when two harlots came before him each claiming to be the mother of a baby boy. They had given birth within a few days of each other, but one of the infants died, and his mother swapped the babies round, claiming the live one as her own.

24 And the king said, Bring me a sword. And they brought a sword before the king.
25 And the king said, Divide the living child in two, and give half to the one, and half to the other.

The unknown librettist of Handel's *Solomon*, written in 1748, continued with the first harlot, the real mother, imploring Solomon, with a maternal pathos reminiscent of Mary's suffering by the cross, not to kill her child:

29. In relation to early 'evolutionary' ideas, on Eramus Darwin's theories, see McNeil, 1987; on Lamarck's see Corsi, 1988.
30. Warner, 1976; Warner, 1985 is also relevant.

THE AMIABLE MOTHER.

PLATE 28. *Anon.*, The Amiable Mother, *1790, mezzotint, Wellcome Institute Library, London. This image of simple motherhood, which is indicative of the general enthusiasm for good mothering in the period, is also displaced in time and place, by implication to a better world, possibly that of Renaissance Italy.*

PLATE 29. *John Michael Rysbrack,* Charity, *1745, terracotta,* © *Indianapolis Museum of Art, gift of Mrs Albert J. Beveridge. This statuette is related to the white marble relief frieze of* Charity, *which Rysbrack produced for and donated to the Foundling Hospital. It was set in a mantelpiece that was installed in 1746.*

221

Can I see my infant gor'd?
With the fierce relentless sword?
Can I see him yield his breath,
Smiling at the hand of death?
And behold the purple tides
Gushing down his tender sides?
Rather be my hopes beguil'd,
Take him all – but spare my child.

The king's summing up both asserted his special insight:

The stern decision was to trace with art,
The secret dictates of the human heart.

and defined the qualifications for genuine motherhood:

She who would bear the fierce decree to hear,
Nor send one sigh, nor shed one pious tear,
Must be a stranger to a mother's name –[31]

Commentators agree that this scene is the centrepiece of the opera, first performed at Covent Garden in 1749, when, significantly enough, the three main female parts, Solomon's Queen, the first harlot and the Queen of Sheba, were all sung by the same performer.[32] The opera is emotionally eloquent, and it also produces a sense of stability. Solomon dedicates his temple, enters a happy marriage, dispenses wisdom and justice, and brings off a diplomatic coup when the Queen of Sheba pays him extravagant homage. Handel's librettist created a vision that was especially apt for mid-eighteenth-century Britain in its celebration of conjugal bliss, devoted motherhood and paternal wisdom. Although these were presented as desirable, attainable goals, they are also invested with a certain mystique. Being a loving wife and a good mother was given a sacred quality, and these virtues were mobilised in organised attempts to reform and improve the family.

A combination of realistic reform and idealised domesticity was a common motif in eighteenth-century responses to collapsed kinship. It spurred the foundation of the Foundling Hospital, with which Handel, like Hogarth, was so closely associated, the Magdalen Hospital for Penitent Prostitutes, and many other organisations. Prominent among such institutions were those for which Jonas Hanway, the indefatigable merchant philanthropist, worked. In a sense I have derived my main theme from Hanway, and in particular from his *Sentimental History of Chimney Sweepers*, published in 1785, which is the most overt example I know of the deliberate cultivation of an aura of specialness around

31. Handel, 1965, pp. 4–5.

32. I have quoted from a modern translation, available with the CD of *Solomon*; for a more 'old-fashioned' version see Handel, 1965, pp. 4–5. On *Solomon*, see Deutsch, 1955, p. 660; Keates, 1986, pp. 285–6. Smith, 1995 offers a subtle analysis of the political resonances of *Solomon*, esp. pp. 309–17.

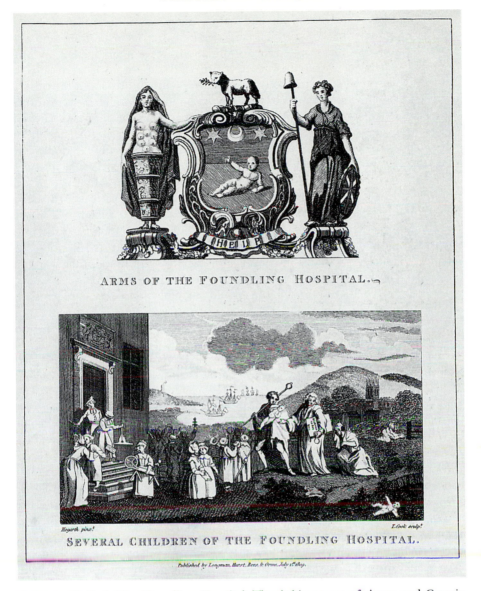

ARMS OF THE FOUNDLING HOSPITAL.

Hogarth pinx.ᵗ   T. Cook sculp.ᵗ

SEVERAL CHILDREN OF THE FOUNDLING HOSPITAL.

Published by Longman, Hurst, Rees, & Orme, July 1ˢᵗ 1809.

PLATE 30. *T. Cook*, The Foundling Hospital: The Achievement of Arms, and Captain Coram and several Children, Carrying Implements of Work, a Church and Ships in the Distance, *engraving, 1809, after William Hogarth, 1739, Wellcome Institute Library, London.*

the relations between parents and children, in the name of preserving, both physically and morally, the lives of infants – indeed, for him infancy was 'a sacred state of life' (see plate 30, above).[33]

33. Hanway, 1785, p. 44; Taylor, 1979 and 1985; Hutchins, 1940, chs 2 and 5; Compston, 1917; Andrew, 1989, esp. chs 2, 3, 4; McClure, 1981.

Thus the sacredness of kinship had many aspects, which became evident not only in representations of mothers and children, but in institutions and the animating concerns that inspired their foundation. Accordingly, while London's Foundling Hospital was controversial, those who supported it were able to draw on widespread concern about the wastage of infant life, about the misery of fallen women, about threats to marriage as an institution. Here were forms of collapsed kinship that demanded reform, that is, to be returned to their sacred state. These concerns had their hard edge, being born of anxieties about population, national vigour and mercantile strength. They also had another side, a desire for identification with idealised figures or states, which was a necessary corollary in fact to the condemnation of bad mothering, sexual immorality, infanticide, child neglect and so on. It is for this reason that the image of the happy mother, which often included either a naked breast or a child suckling and was reminiscent of representations of Charity, came into such prominence in the second half of the eighteenth century – it stood for what was simultaneously natural and sacred, healthy and moral, practical and symbolic. The breast-feeding woman was a somewhat magical figure, a talisman perhaps, so that commentators could imagine that, with enough such women, their society would all right. She embodied profound benevolence (see plates 28, 29, pp. 220–1).[34] But exuberant, lactating maternity could all too easily turn into maternity ruptured, through the grief of bereavement.

A specific inflection was given to maternal grief in this period, I contend, by the passionate belief, a new phenomenon, that death could indeed be held at bay. Indeed, many medical practitioners were explicit on this point – to a significant degree they built their professional identity around their imagined capacity to prevent disease and death. Certainly only some diseases, some deaths were thought to be preventable, but the crucial issue is practitioners' growing desire to achieve this and their growing belief that they actually could. Philanthropists similarly believed it was their duty to reduce unnecessary deaths, especially of small children. It seems to me that the public at large, if I may invoke so crude a notion, shared a sense of the injustice of much death and disease, and of the realistic possibility that they could be staved off. Nowhere was this clearer than in relation to infant mortality, which, *à la mode de* Hanway, became a highly, and increasingly emotive subject over the eighteenth century.[35] As a result, the grief of the mother at her loss could be framed in a new way, as a tragedy that should not have happened. If, in the freshly sentimental view of motherhood in the eighteenth century, families could be supremely happy in an uncomplicated way, so, if things went wrong, could they justly be distraught. In *Solomon*, even a harlot is portrayed as devastated at the loss of her child, which was not to condone her dishonesty in passing another's child off

---

34. Depictions of 'charity' that included a breast-feeding woman exemplify the point. Much has been made of Rousseau's enthusiasm for breast-feeding and of the fashionable status it acquired. Duncan, 1973 remains an excellent study of images of motherhood in the period. See also Schiebinger, 1993, ch. 2.

35. Rosen, 1976; Buchan, 1769 opened his *Domestic Medicine* with some trenchant comments on the importance and the real possibility of reducing infant mortality.

as her own. A baby's death came to be construed as unnecessary, as a trial almost beyond endurance, indeed as a collective loss – hence the need for reforming institutions and philanthropic activists.

Consider, for example, the poem written by the sister of John and Charles Wesley, Mehetabel Wright, and published in 1733, *To an Infant Expiring the Second Day of its Birth*:

> Tender softness, infant mild,
> Perfect, purest, brightest child;
> Transient lustre, beauteous clay,
> Smiling wonder of a day;
> Ere the last convulsive start
> Rends the unresisting heart;
> Ere the long-enduring swoon
> Weights thy precious eyelids down;
> Oh! regard a mother's moan,
> Anguish deeper than thy own!
> Fairest eyes, whose dawning light
> Late with rapture blessed my sight,
> Ere your orbs extinguished be,
> Bend their trembling beams on me,
> Drooping sweetness, verdant flower,
> Blooming, withering in an hour,
> Ere thy gentle breast sustains
> Latest, fiercest, vital pains,
> Hear a suppliant! Let me be
> Partner in thy destiny![36]

Wright's desire to die with her child was taken up, in reverse as it were, by Jane Cave, in her poem *Written a Few Hours before the Birth of a Child*, published in 1786, which ends:

> One wish to name I'd humbly dare,
> If death thy pleasure be;
> O may the harmless babe I bear
> Haply expire with me.[37]

Both poems express an intense identification of mother with child, and it is precisely this theme that is so striking an element of the *Stabat Mater* verses, with the significant addition of the identification of the poet with the grieving mother. There is a merging of griefs in the poem, as there was in Mehetabel Wright's:

---

36. Lonsdale, 1989, no. 81.
37. Ibid., no. 247, lines 13–16.

Is there one who would not weep
Whelm'd in miseries so deep
Christ's Dear Mother to behold?

Can the human heart refrain
From partaking in her pain
In that Mother's pain untold?

. . .

O thou Mother! fount of love!
Touch my spirit from above;
Make my heart with thine accord.[38]

These lines are from an eighteenth-century translation of the poem, which was set to music a number of times in the period. The one most people know is Pergolesi's setting of 1736, but especially relevant to my themes is Haydn's *Stabat Mater*. Its exact date of composition is unclear, but significantly enough it was written, so the composer once claimed, as a 'token of thankfulness' 'in honour of the blessed Virgin' after recovering from a life-threatening illness, possibly in the late 1760s. It gained considerable popularity across Europe towards the end of the eighteenth century. Here are two later verses:

Let me mingle tears with thee,
Mourning Him who mourned for me,
All the days that I may live.

By the cross with thee so stay,
There with thee to weep and pray,
Is all I ask of thee to give.[39]

I have wished to find some way of conveying the continued capacity of an idealised image of motherhood, whether joyful or sorrowful, to move people during the high point of the Enlightenment, to keep alive in them a spiritualised understanding of a relationship that was, at that very moment, being subjected to an unparalleled scrutiny, to a probing and literalist representation that sought to explain mother–child relations in terms of the fabric of the body. The sacredness of kinship was not made manifest only in maternal grief, for in the evocations of happy motherhood there was an erotic dimension that suggested its own kind of spirituality.

Two themes have been running through this account, and it is time in con-clusion to return to them. The first is my curiosity about what the consequences were of claiming, as so many high priests of Enlightenment science and medicine did, that their domain, Nature, knew no bounds, that their methods had no inherent limits but could be applied universally, thereby embracing phenomena such as the family. The second is my curiosity about how relationships between

---

38. Robertson, 1967, p. 134.
39. Ibid.; Robbins Landon, 1976, pp. 57–8; *idem*, 1978, pp. 144, 234–6, 268, 412–13.

people were imagined and represented at this time, given the vitality of medicine particularly in rethinking areas such as generation, marriage, sexuality, which presuppose intimate human interactions, not an abstracted human body. My assumption has been that although these questions are not restricted to the second half of the eighteenth century, they emerged at that time with a peculiar urgency and intensity.

Of course, relationships between people, including intimate ones, can be imagined in many other ways than through kinship – citizenship or comradeship, for example, friendship or fellowship, partnership or patronage. But the cultural richness of languages of kinship is inescapable, embracing as they do natural, legal, emotional, spiritual, political and religious affinities. This subject has become something of a minefield, given that we live in a situation where all the main political groupings wish to be seen as on the side of 'the family', to mobilise those riches for ends that are rightly to be regarded with suspicion. But having said this, we have not thereby purged languages of kinship of their emotive dimensions, which can in fact be difficult to avow fully. It may be that cultural history has something valuable to offer here in suggesting how ideas take root, how they are challenged, the means by which they gather affect. This is not a history of one dominant framework giving way to another, but of something altogether more dialectical, in the sense both that alternative, diverse views co-exist and that distinct modes of thought play off each other. Thus authoritative assertions about understanding motherhood in terms of objects, that is materially, were in dynamic interaction with equally vigorous claims and assumptions about its sacred qualities, indeed each served to sharpen the other.

In using the term 'kinship' I wanted to evoke an abstract idea that could be seen to have a cultural life detached from but never fully independent of the messiness of everyday life. Over the lifecourse of notions such as 'family', 'affinity', 'kinship' and their cognates, the makers of culture actively, if not always consciously, mould ideas or clusters of ideas in complex ways. It is properly the business of cultural history to examine and take apart for further inspection the cultural life of abstract ideas, especially when those ideas are at once part of the most authoritative and powerful systems of knowledge ever devised and integral to the very fabric of life, as it pulsates in individuals, in families and in nations.

Bibliography

Abir-Am, P. and Outram, D., eds (1987), *Uneasy Careers and Intimate Lives: Women in Science, 1789–1979*, New Brunswick and London, Rutgers University Press.

Abrams, M.H. (1993), *A Glossary of Literary Terms*, Fort Worth, Tex., Harcourt Brace Jovanovich.

Abray, J. (1975), 'Feminism in the French Revolution', *American Historical Review* 80: 43–62.

Ackerknecht, E. (1967), *Medicine at the Paris Hospital 1794–1848*, Baltimore, Johns Hopkins University Press.

Ackerman, E.B. (1990), *Health Care in the Parisian Countryside*, New Brunswick and London, Rutgers University Press.

Adams, F. (1858), *On the Construction of the Human Placenta. An Historical Sketch*, Aberdeen, A. Brown and Company.

Agulhon, M. (1981), *Marianne into Battle: Republican Imagery and Symbolism in France, 1789–1880*, Cambridge, Cambridge University Press.

Aikin, J. (1775), *A Specimen of the Medical Biography of Great Britain; with an Address to the Public*, London, J. Johnson.

Aikin, J. (1780), *Biographical Memoirs of Medicine in Great Britain*, London, J. Johnson.

Allen, D. (1981), 'The Women Members of the Botanical Society of London, 1836–1856', *British Journal for the History of Science* 13: 240–54.

Anderson, B. (1991), *Imagined Communities: Reflections on the Origin and Spread of Nationalism*, London, Verso (revised edition).

Andrew, D. (1989), *Philanthropy and Police: London Charity in the Eighteenth Century*, Princeton, Princeton University Press.

Anon. (1772), *The Danger and Immodesty of the Present too General Custom of Unnecessarily Employing Men-midwives*, London, J. Wilkie.

Appel, T.A. (1987), *The Cuvier–Geoffroy Debate: French Biology in the Decades before Darwin*, New York, Oxford University Press.

Arasse, D. (1982a), 'La Guillotine ou l'Inimaginable *Effet d'une Simple Mécanique*', *Revue des Sciences Humaines* 186–7: 123–44.

Arasse, D. (1982b), 'La Guillotine et la Terreur ou la Révolution Consacrée', *Corps Écrits* 2: 91–105.

Arasse, D. (1989), *The Guillotine and the Terror*, London, Allen Lane.

Ariès, P. (1973), *Centuries of Childhood*, Harmondsworth, Penguin.

Ariès, P. (1983), *The Hour of Our Death*, Harmondsworth, Penguin.

Armstrong, N. (1987), *Desire and Domestic Fiction: A Political History of the Novel*, New York, Oxford University Press.

Armstrong, N. and Tennenhouse, L. (1987), *The Ideology of Conduct: Essays on Literature and the History of Sexuality*, London, Methuen.

Armstrong, W. (1904), *Gainsborough and his Place in English Art*, London, Heinemann.

Baker, R. (1993), 'The History of Medical Ethics', *Companion Encyclopedia of the History of Medicine*, W. Bynum and R. Porter, eds, London and New York, Routledge: 852–87.

Baker, R., Porter, D. *et al.*, eds (1993), *The Codification of Medical Morality: Historical and Philosophical Studies in the Formalization of Western Medical Morality in the Eighteenth and Nineteenth Centuries*, Dordrecht, Boston and London, Kluwer Academic Publishers.

Baldick, R., ed. (1965), *The Memoirs of Chateaubriand*, Harmondsworth, Penguin.

Bann, Stephen, ed. (1994), *Frankenstein, Creation and Monstrosity*, London, Reaktion Books.

Barker, F., Bernstein, J. *et al.*, eds (1982), *1789: Reading Writing Revolution*, Colchester, University of Essex.

Barrell, J., ed. (1992), *Painting and the Politics of Culture: New Essays on British Art 1700–1850*, Oxford, Oxford University Press.

Barry, J., Hester, M. *et al.*, eds (1996), *Witchcraft in Early Modern Europe: Studies in Culture and Belief*, Cambridge, Cambridge University Press.

Barthes, R. (1993), *Camera Lucida*, London, Vintage.

Barthez, P.J. (1858), *Nouveaux Éléments de la Science de l'Homme*, Paris, Baillière (first published 1778).

Baxandall, M. (1985), *Patterns of Intention: On the Historical Explanation of Pictures*, London and New Haven, Yale University Press.

Baxandall, M. (1988), *Painting and Experience in Fifteenth-Century Italy: A Primer in the Social History of Pictorial Style*, Oxford, Oxford University Press (revised edition).

Baxandall, M. (1995), *Shadows and Enlightenment*, New Haven and London, Yale University Press.

Beer, G. (1983), *Darwin's Plots: Evolutionary Narrative in Darwin, George Eliot, and Nineteenth-Century Fiction*, London, Routledge and Kegan Paul.

Beer, G. (1986), 'The Face of Nature: Anthropomorphic Elements in the Language of "The Origin of Species"', *Languages of Nature: Critical Essays on Science and Literature*, L. Jordanova, ed., London and New Brunswick, Free Association Books and Rutgers University Press: 207–43.

Beer, G. (1996), *Open Fields: Science in Cultural Encounter*, Oxford, Clarendon Press.

Beier, L. (1985), 'In Sickness and in Health: A Seventeenth-Century Family's Experience', *Patients and Practitioners: Lay Perceptions of Medicine in Pre-Industrial Society*, R. Porter, ed., Cambridge, Cambridge University Press: 101–28.

Beik, P. (1970), *The French Revolution Seen from the Right: Social Theories in Motion, 1789–99*, New York, Howard Fertig.

Belsey, C. (1985), *The Subject of Tragedy: Identity and Difference in Renaissance Drama*, London, Methuen.

Benjamin, M., ed. (1991), *Science and Sensibility: Gender and Scientific Enquiry 1780–1945*, Oxford, Basil Blackwell.

Bennett, J. (1991), *Lilies of the Hearth: The Historical Relationship between Women and Plants*, Ontario, Camden House.

Bennett, P. and Rosario, R., eds (1995), *Solitary Pleasures: The Historical, Literary, and Artistic Discourses of Autoeroticism*, London and New York, Routledge.

Berger, J. (1972), *Ways of Seeing*, Harmondsworth, Penguin.

Berger, J. (1980), *About Looking*, London, Writers and Readers.

Bergeron, L. (1981), *France Under Napoleon*, Princeton, Princeton University Press.

Berman, M. (1978), *Social Change and Scientific Organisation: The Royal Institution 1799–1844*, London, Heinemann.

Bernardin de Saint-Pierre, J.H. (1966), *Paul et Virginie*, Paris, Garnier-Flammarion.

Bernardin de Saint-Pierre, J.H. (1982), *Paul and Virginia*, London, Peter Owen.

Berry, C.J. (1994), *The Idea of Luxury: A Conceptual and Historical Investigation*, Cambridge, Cambridge University Press.

Best, G. (1988), *The Permanent Revolution: The French Revolution and its Legacy 1789–1989*, London, Fontana.

Bindman, D. (1989), *The Shadow of the Guillotine: Britain and the French Revolution*, London, British Museum Publications.

Black, W. (1782), *An Historical Sketch of Medicine and Surgery, from their Origin to the Present Time*, London, J. Johnson.

Black, J. and Porter, R., eds (1996), *The Penguin Dictionary of Eighteenth-Century History*, London, Penguin.

Blake, J.B. (1979), *A Short Title Catalogue of Eighteenth Century Printed Books in the National Library of Medicine*, Bethesda, Md., US Department of Health, Education, and Welfare.

Blake, W. (1970), *Songs of Innocence and Experience*, London, Oxford University Press.

Blake, W. (1975), *The Marriage of Heaven and Hell*, London and New York, Oxford University Press.

Bloor, D. (1979), 'Polyhedra and the Abominations of Leviticus', *British Journal for the History of Science* 11: 245–71.

Boas, G. (1925), *French Philosophies of the Romantic Period*, Baltimore, Johns Hopkins University Press.

Boas, G. (1929), *The Adventures of Human Thought: The Major Traditions of European Philosophy*, New York and London, Harper and Brothers.

Boas, G. (1964), *French Philosophies of the Romantic Period*, New York, Russell and Russell.

Boas, G. (1966), *The Cult of Childhood*, London, Warburg Institute.

Bonney, R. (1987), 'Absolutism: What's in a Name?', *French History* 1: 93–117.

Boucé, P.-G. (1980), 'Aspects of Sexual Tolerance and Intolerance in Eighteenth-Century England', *British Journal for Eighteenth Century Studies* 3: 173–91.

Boucé, P.-G., ed. (1982), *Sexuality in Eighteenth-Century Britain*, Manchester, Manchester University Press.

Bowler, P.J. (1992), *The Fontana History of the Environmental Sciences*, London, Fontana.

Bray, A. (1982), *Homosexuality in Renaissance England*, London, Gay Men's Press.

Brewer, J. (1997), *The Pleasures of the Imagination: English Culture in the Eighteenth Century*, London, HarperCollins.

Brinton, C. (1936), *French Revolutionary Legislation on Illegitimacy, 1789–1804*, Cambridge, Mass., Harvard University Press.

Brock, C.H., ed. (1983), *William Hunter 1718–1783: A Memoir by Samuel Foart Simmons and John Hunter*, Glasgow, University of Glasgow Press.

Brock, C.H. (1990), *Dr William Hunter's Papers and Drawings in the Hunterian Collection of Glasgow University Library: A Handlist*, Cambridge, Wellcome Unit for the History of Medicine.

Brock, H. (1994), 'The Many Facets of Dr William Hunter (1718–83)', *History of Science* 32: 387–408. (*H. Brock also publishes as C.H. Brock.*)

Brock, C.H. (1996), *Calendar of the Correspondence of Dr William Hunter 1740–1783*, Cambridge, Wellcome Unit for the History of Medicine.

Brockliss, L.W.B. and Jones, C. (1997), *The Medical World of Early Modern France*, Oxford, Clarendon Press.

Brooke, J.H. (1974), 'Natural Theology in Britain from Boyle to Paley', *New Interactions between Theology and Natural Science*, Milton Keynes, Open University Press.

Brooke, J.H. (1985), 'The Relations between Darwin's Science and his Religion', *Darwinism and Divinity: Essays on Evolution and Religious Belief*, J. Durant, ed., Oxford, Basil Blackwell: 40–75.

Brooke, J.H. (1991), *Science and Religion: Some Historical Perspectives*, Cambridge, Cambridge University Press.

Brookner, A. (1972), *Greuze: The Rise and Fall of an Eighteenth-Century Phenomenon*, London, Elek.

Bruhier, J.-J. (1745–46), *Mémoire sur la Nécessité d'un Règlement Général au Sujet d'Enterrements et Embaumements*, Paris, Morel jnr.

Bryson, G. (1968), *Man and Society: The Scottish Inquiry of the Eighteenth Century*, New York, A.M. Kelley.

Bryson, N. (1981), *Word and Image: French Painting of the Ancien Régime*, Cambridge, Cambridge University Press.

Bryson, N. (1983), *Vision and Painting: The Logic of the Gaze*, London, Macmillan.

Buchan, W. (1769), *Domestic Medicine*, Edinburgh, Balfour, Auld and Smellie.

Buck, P. (1982), 'People who Counted: Political Arithmetic in the Eighteenth Century', *Isis* 73: 28–45.

Burgess, R. (1973), *Portraits of Doctors and Scientists in the Wellcome Institute of the History of Medicine*, London, Wellcome Institute for the History of Medicine.

Burke, P. (1990), *The French Historical Revolution: The Annales School 1929–1989*, Cambridge, Polity Press.

Burke, P., ed. (1991), *New Perspectives on Historical Writing*, Cambridge, Polity Press.

Burke, P. (1992), *The Fabrication of Louis XIV*, New Haven and London, Yale University Press.

Burkhardt, R.W. (1977), *The Spirit of System: Lamarck and Evolutionary Biology*, Cambridge, Mass., Harvard University Press.

Burlingame, L.J. (1973a), 'Lamarck', *Dictionary of Scientific Biography*, C.C. Gillispie, ed., New York, Charles Scribner's Sons, 7: 584–94.

Burlingame, L.J. (1973b), 'Lamarck's Theory of Transformism in the Context of His Views of Nature', Cornell University, Ph.D. thesis.

Burn, A.E. (1910) 'Creeds', *Encyclopaedia Britannica*, 11th edition, New York, Encyclopaedia Britannica Inc., 7: 392–400.

Burton, J. (1751), *An Essay Towards a Complete New System of Midwifery, Theoretical and Practical*, London, James Hodges.

Butler, M.A. (1978), 'Early Liberal Roots of Feminism: John Locke and the Attack on Patriarchy', *American Political Science Review* 72: 135–50.

Butterfield, H. (1931), *The Whig Interpretation of History*, London, Bell.

Bynum, W.F., Lock, S. *et al.*, eds (1992), *Medical Journals and Medical Knowledge: Historical Essays*, London and New York, Routledge.

Bynum, W.F. and Porter, R., eds (1985), *William Hunter and the Eighteenth-Century Medical World*, Cambridge, Cambridge University Press.

Bynum, W.F. and Porter, R., eds (1993a), *Companion Encyclopedia of the History of Medicine*, London and New York, Routledge, 2 vols.

Bynum, W.F. and Porter, R., eds (1993b), *Medicine and the Five Senses*, Cambridge, Cambridge University Press.

Cabanis, P.J.G. (1795), 'Note sur l'Opinion de MM. Oelsner et Soemmerring, et du Citoyen Sue, Touchant le Supplice de la Guillotine', *Magasin Encyclopédique* 5: 155ff.

Cabanis, P.J.G. (an VI, 1798), *Mémoires de la Société Médicale d'Émulation*, 1: 278–93.

Cabanis, P.J.G. (an XI, 1803), *Du Degré de Certitude de la Médecine*, Paris.

Cabanis, P.J.G. (1956), *Œuvres Philosophiques de Cabanis*, C. Lehec and J. Cazeneuve, eds, Paris, Presses Universitaires de France, 2 vols.

Cadogan, W. (1748), *An Essay upon Nursing and the Management of Children from their Birth to Three Years of Age*, London, J. Roberts.

[Calvados] Conseil de Santé du Département du Calvados (an VII), *Instruction sur le Traitement des Asphyxiés*, Caen.

Canguilhem, G. (1971), *La Connaissance de la Vie*, Paris, J. Vrin, 2nd edition.

Cantor, P.A. (1984), *Creature and Creator: Myth-Making and English Romanticism*, Cambridge, Cambridge University Press.

Carter, A. (1979), *The Sadeian Woman: An Exercise in Cultural History*, London, Virago.

Castiglione, D. and Sharpe, L., eds (1995), *Shifting the Boundaries: Transformation of the Languages of Public and Private in the Eighteenth Century*, Exeter, University of Exeter Press.

Catalogue des livres de la Bibliothèque de Feu M. Le Chevalier J.-B. de Lamarck (1830), Paris, Barrois et Benou.

Cazeneuve, J. and Lehec, C., eds (1956), *Œuvres Philosophiques de Cabanis*, Paris, Presses Universitaires de France.

Cazort, M., Kornell, M. *et al.* (1996), *The Ingenious Machine of Nature: Four Centuries of Art and Anatomy*, Ottawa, National Gallery of Canada.

Chabbert, P. (1974), 'Philippe Pinel', *Dictionary of Scientific Biography*, C.C. Gillispie, ed., New York, Charles Scribner's Sons, 10: 611–14.

Chapin, C.F. (1955), *Personification in Eighteenth-Century English Poetry*, London, King's Crown Press.

Charlesworth, M. (1996), 'Thomas Sandby Climbs the Hoober Stand: The Politics of Panoramic Drawing in Eighteenth-Century Britain', *Art History*, 19: 247–66.

Charlton, D.G. (1984), *New Images of the Natural in France: A Study in European Cultural History 1750–1800*, Cambridge, Cambridge University Press.

Chartier, R. (1988), *Cultural History: Between Practices and Representations*, Cambridge, Polity Press.

Chartier, R. (1994), *The Order of Books: Readers, Authors and Libraries in Europe between the Fourteenth and Eighteenth Centuries*, Cambridge, Polity Press.

Chateaubriand, F.R. de (1966), *Génie du Christianisme*, Paris, Garnier-Flammarion.

Choulant, J.L. (1945), *History and Bibliography of Anatomic Illustration*, New York and London, Schuman's.

Christie, J. (1990), 'The Development of the Historiography of Science', *Companion to the History of Modern Science*, R. Olby. *et al.*, eds, London and New York, Routledge: 5–22.

Church, W.R., ed. (1964), *The Influence of the Enlightenment on the French Revolution: Creative, Disastrous or Non-Existent?*, Lexington, Mass., Heath.

Ciardi, R., ed. (1981), *L'Anatomia e il Corpo Humano*, Milan, Gabriele Mazzotta.

Clark, K. (1985), *The Nude*, London, Penguin Books (first published 1956).

Clark, M. and Crawford, C., eds (1994), *Legal Medicine in History*, Cambridge, Cambridge University Press.

Clarke, M.L. (1974), *Paley: Evidences for the Man*, London, SPCK.

Cohen, M. (1996), *Fashioning Masculinity: National Identity and Language in the Eighteenth Century*, London and New York, Routledge.

Coleman, W. (1974), 'Health and Hygiene in the Encyclopédie: A Medical Doctrine for the Bourgeoisie', *Journal of the History of Medicine* 29: 399–421.

Coleman, W. (1977a), 'L'Hygiène et l'État selon Montyon', *Dix-Huitième Siècle* 9: 101–8.

Coleman, W. (1977b), 'The People's Health: Medical Themes in 18th Century French Popular Literature', *Bulletin of the History of Medicine* 51: 55–74.

Coleman, W. (1982), *Death is a Social Disease: Public Health and Political Economy in Early Industrial France*, Madison, University of Wisconsin Press.

Colley, L. (1992), *Britons: Forging the Nation, 1707–1837*, New Haven and London, Yale University Press.

Commager, H.S. (1978), *The Empire of Reason: How Europe Imagined and America Realized the Enlightenment*, London, Weidenfeld and Nicolson.

Compston, H.F.B. (1917), *The Magdalen Hospital: The Story of a Great Charity*, London, SPCK.

Cooke, L. and Wollen, P., eds (1995), *Visual Display: Culture Beyond Appearances*, Seattle, Bay Press.

Cooter, R. (1984), *The Cultural Meaning of Popular Science: Phrenology and the Organization of Consent in Nineteenth-Century Britain*, Cambridge, Cambridge University Press.

Copleston, F. (1975), *A History of Philosophy. Volume IX: Maine de Biran to Sartre*, London, Search Press.

Corsi, P. (1988), *The Age of Lamarck: Evolutionary Theories in France, 1790–1830*, Berkeley, University of California Press.

Coveney, P. (1967), *The Image of Childhood: The Individual and Society: A Study of the Theme in English Literature*, Harmondsworth, Penguin.

Crow, T. (1995), *Emulation: Making Artists for Revolutionary France*, New Haven and London, Yale University Press.

Cullen, M.J. (1975), *The Statistical Movement in Early Victorian Britain*, Hassocks, Harvester.

Cunningham, A. and Jardine, N., eds (1990), *Romanticism and the Sciences*, Cambridge, Cambridge University Press.

Cuno, J. (1989), *French Caricature and the French Revolution 1789–1799*, Berkeley and Los Angeles, Grunwald Centre for Graphic Arts, University of California.

Curtis, L.A. (1981), 'A Case Study of Defoe's Domestic Conduct Manuals Suggested by *The Family, Sex and Marriage in England 1500–1800*', *Studies in Eighteenth Century Culture* 10: 409–28.

Damon, S.F. (1965), *A Blake Dictionary: The Ideas and Symbols of William Blake*, Providence, RI, Brown University Press.

Daniels, S. (1994), *Fields of Vision: Landscape Imagery and National Identity in England and the United States*, Cambridge, Polity Press.

Darling, J. (1854), *Cyclopedia Bibliographica: A Library Manual of Theological and General Literature, and Guide to Books for Authors, Preachers, Students, and Literary Men. Analytical Bibliographical, and Biographical*, London, J. Darling.

Darnton, R. (1968), *Mesmerism and the End of the Enlightenment in France*, Cambridge, Cambridge University Press.

Darnton, R. (1984), *The Great Cat Massacre and Other Episodes in French Cultural History*, London, Allen Lane.

Daudin, H. (1926), *Les Classes Zoologiques et l'Idée de Série Animale en France à l'Époque de Lamarck et de Cuvier (1790–1830)*, Paris, Félix Alcan.

Davidoff, L. and Hall, C. (1987), *Family Fortunes: Men and Women of the English Middle Class, 1780–1850*, London, Heinemann.

Davis, N.Z. and Farge, A., eds (1993), *A History of Women: Renaissance and Enlightenment Paradoxes*, Cambridge, Mass. and London, The Belknap Press of Harvard University.

Davy, H. (1812), *Elements of Chemical Philosophy*, London, J. Johnson.

Day, A. (1996), *Romanticism*, London, Routledge.

Delaporte, F. (1982), *Nature's Second Kingdom*, Cambridge, Mass., Harvard University Press.

Desmond, A. (1987), 'Artisan Resistance and Evolution in Britain, 1819–1848', *Osiris* 2nd series 3: 77–110.

Desmond, A. (1989), *The Politics of Evolution: Morphology, Medicine and Reform in Radical London*, Chicago, Chicago University Press.

Deutsch, O.E. (1955), *Handel: A Documentary Biography*, London, Adam and Charles Black.

Devance, L. (1977), 'Le Féminisme pendant la Révolution Française', *Annales Historiques de la Révolution Française* 49: 341–76.

De Witt, F. (1959), 'An Historical Study on Theories of the Placenta to 1900', *Journal of the History of Medicine and Allied Sciences* 14: 360–74.

Dickens, C. (1970), *A Tale of Two Cities*, Harmondsworth, Penguin.

Dieudonné (an XII), *Statistique du Département du Nord*, Douai (reprinted, n.d., Brionne, Gerard Monfort), 3 vols.

Dixon, R. (1997), 'Re-interpretation of the Couvade', University of Essex, Ph.D. thesis.

Donald, D. (1996), *The Age of Caricature: Satirical Prints in the Reign of George III*, New Haven and London, Yale University Press.

Donnison, J. (1977), *Midwives and Medical Men: A History of Inter-Professional Rivalries and Women's Rights*, London, Heinemann Educational.

Donzelot, J. (1980), *The Policing of Families: Welfare Versus the State*, London, Hutchinson.

Douglas, M. (1966), *Purity and Danger: An Analysis of Concepts of Pollution and Taboo*, London, Routledge and Kegan Paul.

Douglas, M. (1973), *Natural Symbols: Explorations in Cosmology*, Harmondsworth, Penguin.

Douglas, M., ed. (1973), *Rules and Meanings: The Anthropology of Everyday Knowledge*, Harmondsworth, Penguin.

Duchet, M. (1971), *Anthropologie et Histoire au Siècle des Lumierès: Buffon, Voltaire, Rousseau, Helvétius, Diderot*, Paris, François Maspero.

Duncan, C. (1973), 'Happy Mothers and New Other Ideas in French Art', *Art Bulletin* 55: 570–83.

Duncan, C. (1981), 'Fallen Fathers: Images of Authority in Pre-Revolutionary French Art', *Art History* 4: 186–202.

Dunning, W.A. (1920), *A History of Political Theories from Rousseau to Spencer*, New York, Macmillan.

Durant, J., ed. (1985), *Darwinism and Divinity: Essays on Evolution and Religious Belief*, Oxford, Basil Blackwell.

Easlea, B. (1983), *Fathering the Unthinkable: Masculinity, Scientists and the Nuclear Arms Race*, London, Pluto.

Eccles, A. (1982), *Obstetrics and Gynaecology in Tudor and Stuart England*, London, Croom Helm.

Edmiston, W. (1985), *Diderot and the Family: A Conflict of Nature and Law*, Saratoga, Calif., ANMA.

Egerton, J., ed. (1984), *George Stubbs 1724–1806*, London, Tate Gallery.

Egerton, J., ed. (1990), *Joseph Wright of Derby*, London, Tate Gallery.

Ehrenreich, B. and English, D., eds (1979), *For Her Own Good: 150 Years of the Experts' Advice to Women*, London, Pluto.

Elshtain, J.B. (1981), *Public Man, Private Woman: Women in Social and Political Thought*, Oxford, Basil Blackwell.

Elshtain, J.B., ed. (1982), *The Family in Political Thought*, Brighton, Harvester.

Emch-Deriaz, A. (1992), *Tissot: Physician of the Enlightenment*, New York, P. Lang.

Emerson, R. (1990), 'The Organisation of Science and its Pursuit in Early Modern Europe', *Companion to the History of Modern Science*, R. Olby *et al.*, eds, London and New York, Routledge: 960–79.

Engelhardt, H.T. (1974), 'The Disease of Masturbation: Values and the Concept of Disease', *Bulletin of the History of Medicine* 48: 234–48.

Entralgo, P.L. (1948), 'Sensualism and Vitalism in Bichat's "Anatomie generale"', *Journal of the History of Medicine* 3: 47–64.

Eynard, C. (1839), *Essai sur la Vie de Tissot*, Lausanne, Marc Ducloux.

Fairchilds, C. (1978), 'Female Sexual Attitudes and the Rise of Illegitimacy: A Case Study', *Journal of Interdisciplinary History* 8: 627–67.

Fairchilds, C. (1984), *Domestic Enemies: Servants and their Masters in Old Regime France*, Baltimore, Johns Hopkins University Press.

Fauvel, J. *et al.*, eds (1988), *Let Newton Be! A New Perspective on his Life and Works*, Oxford, Oxford University Press.

Fehér, F., ed. (1990), *The French Revolution and the Birth of Modernity*, Berkeley and Los Angeles, University of California Press.

Feldman, P. and Scott-Kilvert, D., eds (1987), *The Journals of Mary Shelley*, Oxford, Clarendon Press, 2 vols.

Fiering, N.S. (1976), 'Irresistible Compassion: An Aspect of Eighteenth-Century Sympathy and Humanitarianism', *Journal of the History of Ideas* 37: 195–218.

Figlio, K. (1975), 'Theories of Perception and the Physiology of Mind in the Late Eighteenth Century', *History of Science* 13: 177–212.

Figlio, K. (1976), 'The Metaphor of Organisation: A Historiographical Perspective on the Bio-Medical Sciences of the Early Nineteenth Century', *History of Science* 14: 17–53.

Filmer, R. (1991), *Patriarcha and Other Writings*, Cambridge, Cambridge University Press.

Flandrin, J.-L. (1979), *Families in Former Times, Kinship, Household, and Sexuality*, Cambridge, Cambridge University Press.

Flaxman, J. (1829), *Lectures on Sculpture*, London, John Murray.

Fodéré, F. (an VII, 1798), *Les Lois éclairées par les sciences physiques, ou traité de médecine légale et hygiène publique*, Paris, Croullebois, 3 vols.

Fodéré, F. (1822–24), *Leçons sur les Epidémies et l'Hygiène Publique*, Paris, Levrault.

Fodéré, F. (1825), *Essai Historique et Morale sur la Pauvreté des Nations*, Paris, Huzard.

Fontenelle, B. d. (1955), *Entretiens sur la Pluralité des Mondes*, Oxford, Clarendon Press (ed. R. Shackleton).

Foot, J. (1794), *The Life of John Hunter*, London, T. Becket.

Ford, A. (1761), *A Letter from Miss F——d, Addressed to a Person of Distinction*, London, no publisher given.

Fores, S.W. (1793), *Man-Midwifery Dissected; or, The Obstetric Family Instructor*, London, S.W. Fores.

Forster, R. and Ranum, O., eds (1976), *Family and Society*, Baltimore and London, Johns Hopkins University Press.

Forster, R. and Ranum, O., eds (1980), *Medicine and Society in France*, Baltimore and London, Johns Hopkins University Press.

Foucault, M. (1970), *The Order of Things*, London, Tavistock.

Foucault, M. (1973), *The Birth of the Clinic: An Archaeology of Medical Perception*, London, Tavistock.

Foucault, M. (1979), *The History of Sexuality*, London, Allen Lane, vol. 1.

Fox, C., Porter, R. *et al.*, eds (1995), *Inventing Human Science: Eighteenth-Century Domains*, Berkeley, Los Angeles and London, University of California Press.

France, P. (1983), *Diderot*, Oxford, Oxford University Press.

Frangsmyr, T. *et al.*, eds (1990), *The Quantifying Spirit in the Eighteenth Century*, Berkeley and Los Angeles, University of California Press.

French, R.K. (1969), *Robert Whytt, the Soul, and Medicine*, London, Wellcome Institute for the History of Medicine.

French, R. and Wear, A., eds (1991), *British Medicine in an Age of Reform*, London, Routledge.

Fried, M. (1987), *Realism, Writing, Disfiguration: On Thomas Eakins and Stephen Crane*, Chicago and London, University of Chicago Press.

Garlick, K. (1954), *Sir Thomas Lawrence*, London, Routledge and Kegan Paul.

Garlick, K. (1989), *Sir Thomas Lawrence: A Complete Catalogue of Oil Paintings*, Oxford, Phaidon.

Gascoigne, R. (1985), *A Historical Catalogue of Scientific Periodicals, 1665–1900 with a Survey of their Development*, New York, Garland.

Gasking, E. (1966), *Investigations into Generation 1651–1828*, Baltimore, Johns Hopkins University Press.

Gauchat, L.G. (1758), *Catéchisme du livre de l'Esprit, ou élémens de la philosophie de l'Esprit, mis à la portée de tout le monde*, Paris, no publisher given.

Gaulmier, J. (1951), *L'idéologue Volney, 1757–1820: Contribution à l'histoire de l'orientalisme en France*, Beyrouth, Université de Paris.

Gay, P. (1985), *Freud for Historians*, New York and Oxford, Oxford University Press.

Gelfand, T. (1993), 'The History of the Medical Profession', *Companion Encyclopedia of the History of Medicine*, W.F. Bynum and R. Porter, eds, London and New York, Routledge, II: 1119–50.

Gélis, J. *et al.*, eds (1978), *Entrer dans la Vie*, Paris, Gallimard.

Gélis, J., ed. (1979), *Accoucheur de Campagne sous le Roi Soleil: Le Traité d'Accouchement de G. Mauquest de la Motte*, Toulouse, Privat.

Gélis, J. (1984), *L'Arbre et le Fruit: La Naissance dans l'Occident Moderne (XVIe–XIXe siècle)*, Paris, Fayard.

Gélis, J. (1988), *La Sage-femme ou le Médecin: Une Nouvelle Conception de la Vie*, Paris, Fayard.

George, M.D. (1942), *Catalogue of Political and Personal Satires*, London, British Museum.

George, M.D. (1967), *Hogarth to Cruikshank: Social Change in Graphic Satire*, London, Allen Lane.

Gilbey, W. (1898), *Life of George Stubbs*, London, Vinton and Co.

Gilibert, J.-E. (1772), *L'Anarchie Médicinale, ou la Médecine Considérée Comme Nuisible à la Société*, Neuchatel, no publisher given, 3 vols.

Gillis, J.R. (1974), *Youth and History: Tradition and Change in European Age Relations, 1770 – Present*, New York and London, Academic Press.

Gillispie, C.C. (1959), *Genesis and Geology: A Study in the Relations of Scientific Thought, Natural Theology, and Social Opinion in Great Britain 1790–1850*, New York, Harper and Row.

Gillispie, C.C., ed. (1970–80), *Dictionary of Scientific Biography*, New York, Charles Scribner's Sons.

Gillispie, C.C. (1980), *Science and Polity in France at the End of the Old Regime*, Princeton, Princeton University Press.

Gillray, J. (1968), *The Works of James Gillray*, New York, Blom.

Ginsburg, F.D. and Rapp, R., eds (1995), *Conceiving the New World Order: The Global Politics of Reproduction*, Berkeley, Los Angeles and London, University of California Press.

Glacken, C. (1967), *Traces on the Rhodian Shore: Nature and Culture in Western Thought from Ancient Times to the End of the Eighteenth Century*, Berkeley.

Glass, B., Temkin, O. *et al.*, eds (1968), *Forerunners of Darwin, 1745–1859*, Baltimore, Johns Hopkins University Press.

Glass, D. (1978), *Numbering the People: The Eighteenth-Century Population Controversy and the Development of Census and Vital Statistics in Britain*, London, Gordon and Cremonesi.

Gonnard, R. (1923), *Histoire des Doctrines de la Population*, Paris, Nouvelle Librairie Nationale.

Goodden, A. (1989), *The Complete Lover: Eros, Nature, and Artifice in the Eighteenth-Century Novel*, Oxford, Clarendon Press.

Goodman, D.C., ed. (1973), *Science and Religious Belief, 1600–1900: A Selection of Primary Sources*, Milton Keynes, Open University Press.

237

Goodwyn, E. (an VI, 1798), *La Connexion de la Vie avec la Respiration ou Recherches Expérimentales sur les Effets que Produisent sur les Animaux Vivans, la Submersion, la Strangulation, et les Diverses Espèces de Gas Nuisible*, trad. de l'anglais par Hallé, Paris, Mequignon snr.

Gosse, P. (1952), *Dr Viper: The Querulous Life of Philip Thicknesse*, London, Cassell.

Goulet, J. (1981), 'Robespierre: Le Peine de Mort et la Terreur', *Annales Historiques de la Révolution Française* 53: 219–38.

Goulet, J. (1983), 'Robespierre: Le Peine de Mort et la Terreur', *Annales Historiques de la Révolution Française* 55: 38–64.

Greene, J.C. (1981), *Science, Ideology, and World View*, Berkeley, University of California Press.

Greuze & Diderot: Vie Familiale et Éducation dans la Seconde Moitié du XVIIIème Siècle (1984), Clermont-Ferrand, Service Information de la ville de Clermont-Ferrand.

Gusdorf, G. (1978), *La Conscience Révolutionnaire: Les Idéologues*, Paris, Payot.

Hagstrum, J. (1966), 'William Blake Rejects the Enlightenment', *Blake: A Collection of Critical Essays*, N. Frye, ed., Englewood Cliffs, NJ, Prentice-Hall: 142–55.

Hahn, A. *et al.*, eds (1962), *Histoire de la Médecine et du Livre Médical*, Paris, O. Perrin.

Hahn, R. (1971), *The Anatomy of a Scientific Institution: The Paris Academy of Sciences, 1666–1803*, Berkeley and London, University of California Press.

Haigh, E. (1984), *Xavier Bichat and the Medical Theory of the Eighteenth Century*, London, Wellcome Institute for the History of Medicine.

Hall, J. (1969, 1974, 1979, revised edition), *Dictionary of Subjects and Symbols in Art*, London, John Murray.

Hallé, J.-N. (1798), 'Hygiène', *Encyclopédie Méthodique Médecine*, 7: 373–437.

Hallie, P.P. (1959), *Maine de Biran: Reformer of Empiricism 1766–1824*, Cambridge, Mass., Harvard University Press.

Hampson, N. (1968), *The Enlightenment*, Harmondsworth, Penguin.

Handel, G.F. (1965), *Solomon: An Oratorio*, Ridgewood, NJ, Gregg Press.

Handel, G.F. (1985) *Solomon*, Philips (CD).

Hankins, T. (1985), *Science and the Enlightenment*, Cambridge, Cambridge University Press.

Hanway, J. (1785), *A Sentimental History of Chimney Sweepers in London and Westminster*, London, Dodsley.

Hare, E.H. (1962), 'Masturbatory Insanity: The History of an Idea', *Journal of Mental Science* 108: 1–25.

Haslam, F. (1996), *From Hogarth to Rowlandson: Medicine in Art in Eighteenth-Century Britain*, Liverpool, Liverpool University Press.

Hautecœur, L. (1945), *Les Peintres de la Vie Familiale: Evolution d'un Thème*, Paris, Galerie Charpentier.

Haydn, J. (1977), *Stabat Mater*. Vocal Score, London, Faber Music.

Haydn, J. (1992), *Stabat Mater*, Decca (CD).

Hayes, J. (1975), *Gainsborough: Paintings and Drawings*, London, Phaidon.

Head, B. (1985), *Ideology and Social Science: Destutt de Tracy and French Liberalism*, Dordrecht, Nijhoff.

Helvétius, C.-A. (1758), *De l'Esprit*, Paris, Durand, 2 vols.

Hill, D. (1976), *The Satirical Engravings of James Gillray*, New York, Dover.

Hobsbawm, E.J. (1962), *The Age of Revolution: Europe, 1789–1848*, London, Weidenfeld and Nicolson.

Hogarth, W. (1955), *The Analysis of Beauty*, Oxford, Clarendon Press.

Honour, H. (1968), *Neo-Classicism*, Harmondsworth, Penguin.

Hornbeak, K. (1938), 'Richardson's *Familiar Letters* and the Domestic Conduct Books', *Smith College Studies in Modern Languages* 19: 1–29.

H.P.B. (17 August 1966), 'Joseph-Ignace Guillotin (1738–1814), Physician and Reformer', *British Medical Journal*: 230.

Huet, M.-H. (1993), *Monstrous Imagination*, Cambridge, Mass., Harvard University Press.

Hufton, O. (1971), 'Women in Revolution 1789–1796', *Past and Present* 53: 90–108.

Hulme, P. and Jordanova, L., eds (1990), *The Enlightenment and its Shadows*, London and New York, Routledge.

Hume, D. (1948), *Dialogues Concerning Natural Religion 1779*, New York, Hafner.

Hunt, L., ed. (1989), *The New Cultural History*, Berkeley and London, University of California Press.

Hunt, L., ed. (1991), *Eroticism and the Body Politic*, Baltimore and London, Johns Hopkins University Press.

Hunt, L. (1992), *The Family Romance of the French Revolution*, Berkeley and Los Angeles, University of California Press.

Hunter, J. (1835–37), *The Works of John Hunter*, London, Longman, Rees, Orme, Brown, Green and Longman, 4 vols + Atlas (edited by J.F. Palmer).

Hunter, W. (1774), *Anatomia Uteri Humani Gravidi Tabulis Illustrata*, Birmingham, J. Baskerville, S. Baker and G. Leigh.

Hunter, W. (1784), *Two Introductory Lectures Delivered by Dr William Hunter, his Last Course of Anatomical Lectures, at his Theatre in Windmill-Street*, London, J. Johnson.

Hunter, W. (1843), *An Anatomical Description of the Human Gravid Uterus and Its Contents*, London, H. Rendshaw (edited by E. Rigby).

Huss, R. (1986), 'Michelet and the Uses of Natural Reference', *Languages of Nature: Critical Essays on Science and Literature*, L. Jordanova, ed., London, Free Association Books: 289–321.

Hutchins, J.H. (1940), *Jonas Hanway, 1712–1786*, London, SPCK.

Hutt, M. (1995), 'Medical Biography and Autobiography in Britain, *c*.1780–1920', unpublished D. Phil. thesis, University of Oxford.

Huxley, A. (1950), *Themes and Variations*, London, Chatto and Windus.

Illich, I. (1983), *Gender*, London, Boyars.

Inkster, I. (1981), 'Seditious Science: A Reply to Paul Weindling', *British Journal for the History of Science* 14: 181–7.

Inkster, I. and Morrell, J., eds (1983), *Metropolis and Province: Science in British Culture, 1780–1850*, London.

Irwin, D. (1997), *Neoclassicism*, London, Phaidon.

Iversen, M. (1983), 'The New Art History', *The Politics of Theory*, F. Barker *et al.*, eds, Colchester, University of Essex: 212–19.

Jackson, M. (1996), *New-Born Child Murder: Women, Illegitimacy and the Courts in Eighteenth-Century England*, Manchester and New York, Manchester University Press.

Jacobs, E. *et al.*, eds (1979), *Woman and Society in Eighteenth-Century France*, London, Athlone Press.

Jacyna, L.S. (1983), 'Images of John Hunter in the Nineteenth Century', *History of Science* 11: 85–108.

Janes, R. (1991), 'Beheadings', *Representations* 35: 21–51.

Jardine, N., Secord, J. *et al.*, eds (1996), *Cultures of Natural History*, Cambridge, Cambridge University Press.

Jenkins, I. and Sloan, K. (1996), *Vases and Volcanoes: Sir William Hamilton and His Collection*, London, British Museum Press.

Jenty, C.N. (1758), *The Demonstrations of a Pregnant Uterus of a Woman at her Full Time*, London, the author.

Jenty, C.N. (1759), *Demonstration de la Matrice d'une Femme Grosse et de Son Enfant a Terme*, Paris, Charpentier.

Jenty, C.N. (1761–65), *Demonstratio Uteri Praegnantis Mulieris*, Nuernberg (*sic*), Felssecker.

Jones, C. (1978), 'Prostitution and the Ruling Class in Eighteenth-Century Montpellier', *History Workshop Journal* 6: 7–28.

Jordanova, L. (1976), 'The Natural Philosophy of Lamarck in its Historical Context', University of Cambridge, Ph.D. thesis.

Jordanova, L. (1979), 'Earth Science and Environmental Medicine: The Synthesis of the Late Enlightenment', *Images of the Earth*, L. Jordanova and R. Porter, eds, Chalfont St Giles, British Society for the History of Science: 119–46, 2nd edition, 1997.

Jordanova, L. (1980a), 'Natural Facts: A Historical Perspective on Science and Sexuality', *Nature, Culture and Gender*, C. MacCormack and M. Strathern, eds, Cambridge, Cambridge University Press: 42–69.

Jordanova, L. (1980b), 'Romantic Science? Michelet, Morals and Nature', *British Journal for the History of Science* 13: 44–50.

Jordanova, L. (1981a), 'La Psychologie Naturaliste et le "Probleme des Niveaux": La Notion de Sentiment Intérieur chez Lamarck', *Lamarck et son Temps, Lamarck et notre Temps*, Paris, J. Vrin: 69–80.

Jordanova, L. (1981b), 'Policing Public Health in France 1780–1815', *Public Health*, T. Ogawa, ed., Tokyo, Saikon: 12–32 [Chapter 9].

Jordanova, L. (1982), 'Guarding the Body Politic: Volney's Catechism of 1793', *Reading Writing Revolution*, F. Barker *et al.*, eds, Colchester, University of Essex: 12–21 [Chapter 8].

Jordanova, L. (1984a), *Lamarck*, Oxford, Oxford University Press.

Jordanova, L. (1984b), 'Body Image and Sex Roles in the Eighteenth Century: Anatomical Models and Pictures', *Kos* 2: 82–7.

Jordanova, L. (1984c), 'Medical Mediations: Mind and Body in the Guillotine Debates during the French Revolution', *Kos* 10: 68–80 [Chapter 7].

Jordanova, L. (1985), 'Gender, Generation and Science: William Hunter's Obstetrical Atlas', *William Hunter and the Eighteenth-Century Medical World*, R. Porter and W.F. Bynum, eds, Cambridge, Cambridge University Press: 385–412 [Chapter 11].

Jordanova, L. (1986a), 'Physiognomy in the Eighteenth Century: A Case Study in the Relationships Between Art and Medicine', University of Essex, MA thesis.

Jordanova, L., ed. (1986b), *Languages of Nature: Critical Essays on Science and Literature*, London and New Brunswick, NJ, Free Association Books and Rutgers University Press.

Jordanova, L. (1986c), 'Naturalising the Family: Literature and the Bio-Medical Sciences in the Late Eighteenth Century', *Languages of Nature: Critical Essays on Science and Literature*, L. Jordanova, ed., London, Free Association Books: 86–117 [Chapter 10].

Jordanova, L. (1987a), 'Conceptualising Childhood in the Eighteenth Century: Love, Labour and Investment', *British Journal for Eighteenth Century Studies* 10: 189–99.

Jordanova, L. (1987b), 'The Popularisation of Medicine: Tissot on Onanism', *Textual Practice* I: 68–79 [Chapter 6].

Jordanova, L. (1989a), *Sexual Visions: Images of Gender in Science and Medicine between the Eighteenth and Twentieth Centuries*, Hemel Hempstead, Harvester Wheatsheaf.

Jordanova, L. (1989b), 'Medical Mediations: Mind, Body and the Guillotine', *History Workshop* 28: 39–52 [Chapter 7].

Jordanova, L. (1989c), 'Nature Powers: A Reading of Lamarck's Distinction between Creation and Production', *History, Humanity and Evolution*, J.R. Moore, ed., Cambridge, Cambridge University Press: 71–98 [Chapter 3].

Jordanova, L. (1991), 'The Representation of the Family in the Eighteenth Century: A Challenge for Cultural History', *Interpretation and Cultural History*, A. Wear and J. Pittock, eds, London and New York, Macmillan and St Martin's Press, 109–34.

Jordanova, L. (1992), 'The Hand', *Visual Anthropology Review* 8: 2–7, and in *Visual Theory*, L. Taylor, ed., New York, Routledge, 1994: 252–9.

Jordanova, L. (1993a), 'The Art and Science of Seeing in Medicine: Physiognomy 1780–1830', *Medicine and the Five Senses*, W.F. Bynum and R. Porter, eds, Cambridge, Cambridge University Press: 122–33.

Jordanova, L. (1993b), 'Has the Social History of Medicine Come of Age?', *Historical Journal* 36: 437–49.

Jordanova, L. (1993c), 'Gender and the Historiography of Science', *British Journal for the History of Science* 26: 469–83.

Jordanova, L. (1993d), 'Museums: Representing the Real?', *Realism and Representation: Essays on the Problem of Realism in Relation to Science, Literature, and Culture*, G. Levine, ed., Madison and London, University of Wisconsin Press.

Jordanova, L. (1994), 'Melancholy Reflection: Constructing an Identity for Unveilers of Nature', *Frankenstein, Creation and Monstrosity*, S. Bann, ed., London, Reaktion Books: 60–76, 198–201 [Chapter 4].

Jordanova, L. (1995a), 'Interrogating the Concept of Reproduction in the Eighteenth Century', *Conceiving the New World Order: The Global Politics of Reproduction*, F. Ginsburg and R. Rapp, eds, Berkeley, Los Angeles and London, University of California Press, 369–86.

Jordanova, L. (1995b), 'The Social Construction of Medical Knowledge', *Social History of Medicine* 8: 361–81.

Jordanova, L. (1996), 'Science and National Identity', *Sciences et Langues en Europe*, R. Chartier and P. Corsi, eds, Paris, École des Hautes Études en Sciences Sociales.

Jordanova, L. (1997), 'Medical Men 1780–1820', *Portraiture: Facing the Subject*, J. Woodall, ed., Manchester, Manchester University Press: 101–15.

Jordanova, L. (1998), 'Science and Nationhood: Cultures of Imagined Communities', *Imagining Nations*, G. Cubitt, ed., Manchester, Manchester University Press: 192–211.

Jordanova, L. and Porter, R., eds (1979), *Images of the Earth: Essays in the History of the Environmental Sciences*, Chalfont St Giles, British Society for the History of Science, 2nd edition 1997.

Julian, J. (1907), *A Dictionary of Hymnology*, London, John Murray, revised edition.

Kaplan, E.K. (1977), *Michelet's Poetic Vision: A Romantic Philosophy of Nature, Man and Woman*, Amherst, University of Massachusetts Press.

Keates, J. (1986), *Handel: The Man and His Music*, London, Hamish Hamilton.

Kemp, M. (1975), *Dr William Hunter at the Royal Academy of Arts*, Glasgow, University of Glasgow Press.

Kemp, M. (1976), 'Dr William Hunter on the Windsor Leonardos and his Volume of Drawings attributed to Pietro da Cortona', *Burlington Magazine* 118: 144–8.

Kennedy, E. (1978), *A Philosophe in the Age of Revolution: Destutt de Tracy and the Origins of 'Ideology'*, Philadephia, The American Philosophical Society.

Kennedy, E. (1989), *A Cultural History of the French Revolution*, New Haven and London, Yale University Press.

Kershaw, A. (1958), *A History of the Guillotine*, London, John Calder.

Klukoff, P. (1970), 'Smollett's Defence of Dr Smellie in *The Critical Review*', *Medical History* 14: 31–41.

Knibiehler, Y. (1976), 'Les Médecins et la "Nature Feminine" au Temps du Code Civil', *Annales ESC* 31: 824–45.

Knight, D. (1967), 'The Scientist as Sage', *Studies in Romanticism* 6: 65–88.

Kool, J.A. (1855), *Aperçu Historique au Sujet de la Société pour Secourir les Noyées, Instituée à Amsterdam*, Amsterdam, J. de Ruijter.

Kristeller, P.O. (1983), '"Creativity" and "Tradition"', *Journal of the History of Ideas* 44: 105–13.

Kroeber, A.L. and Kluckhohn, C. (1952), *Culture: A Critical Review of Concepts and Definitions*, Cambridge, Mass., Peabody Museum of American Archaeology and Ethnology.

Kronick, D. (1991), *Scientific and Technical Periodicals of the Seventeenth and Eighteenth Centuries: A Guide*, Metuchen, NJ, Scarecrow.

La Berge, A.F. (1992), *Mission and Method: The Early Nineteenth-Century French Public Health Movement*, Cambridge, Cambridge University Press.

La Découverte du Corps Humain (1978), Paris, Musée de l'Homme.

Laclos, P.-A.-F.C. de (1979), *Les Liaisons Dangereuses*, Harmondsworth, Penguin.

Lalande, A. (1928), *Vocabulaire Technique et Critique de la Philosophie*, Paris, Librairie Félix Alcan, 2 vols.

Lamarck, J.-B. (1809), *Philosophie Zoologique, ou considerations relatives à l'histoire naturelle des Animaux; à la diversité de leur organisation et des facultés qu'ils en obtiennent; aux causes physiques qui maintiennent en eux la vie et donnent lieu aux mouvemens qu'ils executent; enfin, à celles qui produisent, les unes le sentiment, et les autres l'intelligence de ceux qui en sont doués*, Paris, Dentu, 2 vols.

Lamarck, J.-B. (1815–22), *Histoire naturelle des animaux sans vertèbres*, Paris, Déterville, 7 vols.

Lamarck, J.-B. (1820), *Système analytique des connaissances positives de l'homme, restreintes à celles qui proviennent directement ou indirectement de l'observation*, Paris, A. Berlin.

Lamarck, J.-B. (1830), *Catalogue des livres de la Bibliothèque de Feu, M., Le Chevalier, J.-B. de Lamarck*, Paris, Barrois et Benou.

Landrieu, M. (1909), *Lamarck, le fondateur du transformisme, sa vie, son œuvre*, Paris, Société zoologique de France.

Lane, J. (1985), 'The Doctor Scolds Me: The Diaries and Correspondence of Patients in Eighteenth-Century England', *Patients and Practitioners: Lay Perceptions of Medicine in Pre-Industrial Society*, R. Porter, ed., Cambridge, Cambridge University Press: 205–48.

Lanza, B. *et al.*, eds (1979), *Le Cere Anatomische della Specola*, Florence, Arnaud.

Laplanche, J. and Pontalis, J.-B. (1988), *The Language of Psychoanalysis*, London, Karnac and the Institute of Psychoanalysis.

Laqueur, T. (1990), *Making Sex: Body and Gender from the Greeks to Freud*, Cambridge Mass. and London, Harvard University Press.

Larson, J.L. (1971), *Reason and Experience: The Representation of Natural Order in the Work of Carl von Linné*, Berkeley, University of California Press.

Laskey, J. (1813), *A General Account of the Hunterian Museum, Glasgow*, Glasgow, J. Smith.

Laslett, P., ed. (1965), *John Locke: Two Treatises of Government*, New York, Mentor.

Laurence, J. (pseudonym of J.L. Pritchard) (n.d.[1932]), *A History of Capital Punishment*, London, Low Marston.

Lavater, J.-G. (1841), *La Physiognomonie ou L'Art de Connaître les Hommes d'après les Traits de Leur Physiognomie*, Paris, Librairie Française et Étrangère (first published 1775–78).

Lawrence, C. (1975), 'William Buchan: Medicine Laid Open', *Medical History* 19: 20–35.

Lawrence, C. (1979), 'The Nervous System and Society in the Scottish Enlightenment', *Natural Order: Historical Studies of Scientific Culture*, B. Barnes and S. Shapin, eds, Beverly Hills, Sage.

Lawrence, C. and Shapin, S., eds (1998), *Science Incarnate: Historical Embodiments of Natural Knowledge*, Chicago and London, University of Chicago Press.

Le Bègue de Presle, A.G. (1763), *Le Conservateur de la Santé, ou avis sur les dangers qu'il importe à chacun d'éviter, pour se conserver en bonne santé et prolonger sa vie. On y a joint des objets de règlements de police relatifs à la santé*, Paris, P.F. Didot, jnr.

Le Doeuff, M.L. (1981–82), 'Pierre Roussel's Chiasmas: From Imaginary Knowledge to the Learned Imagination', *Ideology and Consciousness* 9: 39–70.

Le Pelletier, L. (24 Brumaire an IV, 1795), *Moniteur Universel*: 426.

Leask, N. (1992), 'Shelley's "Magnetic Ladies": Romantic Mesmerism and the Politics of the Body', *Beyond Romanticism: New Approaches to Texts and Contexts, 1780–1832*, S. Copley and J. Whale, eds, London, Routledge: 53–78.

Lebrun, R. (1969), 'Joseph de Maistre, Cassandra of Science', *French Historical Studies* 6: 214–31.

Lefanu, W. (1984), *British Periodicals of Medicine, 1640–1899*, Oxford, Wellcome Unit for the History of Medicine (revised edition).

Lejeune, P. (1974), 'Le "Dangéreux Supplément": Lecture d'un Aveu de Rousseau', *Annales ESC* 29: 1009–22.

LeMahieu, D.L. (1976), *The Mind of William Paley: A Philosopher and His Age*, Lincoln, Nebr., University of Nebraska Press.

Lemire, M. (1990), *Artistes et Mortels*, Paris, Raymond Chafond.

Lepenies, W. (1992), *Melancholy and Society*, Cambridge, Cambridge University Press.

Leppert, R. (1988), *Music and Image: Domesticity, Ideology and Socio-Cultural Formation in Eighteenth-Century England*, Cambridge, Cambridge University Press.

Levere, T. (1990), 'Coleridge and the Sciences', *Romanticism and the Sciences*, A. Cunningham and N. Jardine, eds, Cambridge, Cambridge University Press: 295–306.

Levey, M. (1979), *Sir Thomas Lawrence, 1769–1830*, London, National Portrait Gallery.

Levine, G., ed. (1993), *Realism and Representation: Essays on the Problem of Realism in Relation to Science, Literature, and Culture*, Madison and London, University of Wisconsin Press.

Levine, G. and Knoepflmacher, U.C., eds (1983), *The Endurance of Frankenstein: Essays on Mary Shelley's Novel*, Berkeley, University of California Press.

Levy, D.G., Applewhite, H.B. *et al.*, eds (1979), *Women in Revolutionary Paris 1789–1795*, Urbana, University of Illinois Press.

Limoges, C. (1975), 'Pluche', *Dictionary of Scientific Biography*, C.C. Gillispie, ed., New York, Charles Scribner's Sons, 11: 42–4.

Lindsay, J. (1981), *Thomas Gainsborough: His Life and Art*, London, Granada.

Littré, E. (1878), *Dictionnaire de la Langue Française*, Paris, Hachette, 4 vols.

Lively, J., ed. (1965), *The Works of Joseph de Maistre*, New York, Macmillan.

Lloyd, G. (1984), *The Man of Reason: 'Male' and 'Female' in Western Philosophy*, London, Methuen.

Lonsdale, R., ed. (1984), *The New Oxford Book of Eighteenth-Century Verse*, Oxford, Oxford University Press.

Lonsdale, R., ed. (1989), *Eighteenth-Century Women Poets: An Oxford Anthology*, Oxford, Oxford University Press.

Loudon, I. (1992), 'Medical Practitioners 1750–1850, and the Period of Medical Reform in Britain', *Medicine in Society: Historical Essays*, A. Wear, ed., Cambridge, Cambridge University Press: 219–47.

Lovejoy, A.O. (1936), *The Great Chain of Being: A Study of the History of an Idea*, Cambridge, Mass., Harvard University Press.

Lovejoy, A.O. (1948), *Essays in the History of Ideas*, Baltimore, The Johns Hopkins University History of Ideas Club.

Lyons, M. (1994), *Napoleon Bonaparte and the Legacy of the French Revolution*, Basingstoke and London, Macmillan.

McClure, R. (1981), *Coram's Children: The London Foundling Hospital in the Eighteenth Century*, New Haven and London, Yale University Press.

MacCormack, C. and Strathern, M. eds, (1980), *Nature, Culture and Gender*, Cambridge, Cambridge University Press.

McCullough, L. (1993), 'John Gregory's Medical Ethics and Humean Sympathy', *The Codification of Medical Morality: Historical and Philosophical Studies of the Formalization of Western Medical Morality in the Eighteenth and Nineteenth Centuries*, R. Baker, *et al.*, eds, Dordrecht, Boston and London, Kluwer Academic Publishers: 145–60.

MacDonald, R.H. (1967), 'The Frightful Consequences of Onanism: Notes on the History of a Delusion', *Journal of the History of Ideas* 28: 423–31.

Maclagen, D. (1977), *Creation Myths: Man's Introduction to the World*, London, Thames and Hudson.

McLaren, A. (1973–74), 'Some Secular Attitudes toward Sexual Behaviour in France 1760–1860', *French Historical Studies* 8: 604–25.

Maclean, I. (1980), *The Renaissance Notion of Woman*, Cambridge, Cambridge University Press.

McManners, J. (1981), *Death and the Enlightenment: Changing Attitudes to Death among Christians and Unbelievers in Eighteenth-Century France*, Oxford, Oxford University Press.

McNeil, M. (1987), *Under the Banner of Science: Erasmus Darwin and His Age*, Manchester, Manchester University Press.

Macquart, L.-C.-.H. (an VII, 1798/99), *Dictionnaire de la Conservation de l'Homme ou d'hygiène, et d'éducation physique et morale. Ouvrage élémentaire et à la portée de tous les citoyens; dans lequel on s'applique à détruire les préjugés, à fournir des précautions utiles aux différens états de la société, et à donner des avis pour les accidens qui exigent les plus prompts secours*, Paris, Bidault, 2 vols.

MacQueen, J. (1970), *Allegory*, London, Methuen.

Mahon, P. (1801), *Médecine Légale*, Paris, F. Buisson, 3 vols.

Maistre, J. de (1994), *Considerations on France*, Cambridge, Cambridge University Press.

Marin, L. (1988), *Portrait of the King*, Basingstoke, Macmillan.

Marks, A.S. (1967), 'An Anatomical Drawing by Alexander Cozens', *Journal of the Warburg and Courtauld Institutes* 30: 434–8.

Marland, H., ed. (1993), *The Art of Midwifery: Early Modern Midwives in Europe*, London, Routledge.

Marshall, D. (1988), *The Surprising Effects of Sympathy*, Chicago, University of Chicago Press.

Maulitz, R. (1987), *Morbid Appearances: The Anatomy of Pathology in the Early Nineteenth Century*, Cambridge, Cambridge University Press.

Mellor, A. (1988), *Mary Shelley: Her Life, Her Fiction, Her Monsters*, London, Routledge.

Merchant, C. (1982), *The Death of Nature*, London, Wildwood.

Merians, L.E., ed. (1996), *The Secret Malady: Venereal Disease in Eighteenth-Century Britain and France*, Lexington, The University Press of Kentucky.

Michels, R. (1948), 'Authority', *Encyclopedia of the Social Sciences*, E.R.A. Seligman, ed., New York, 1: 319–21.

Minder-Chappuis, G. (n.d.[1973]), 'Auguste Tissot: Sa Correspondance avec A. de Haller et ses Œuvres durant la Période de 1754 à 1761', Berne Faculté de Médecine, thesis.

Moore, F.C.T. (1970), *The Psychology of Maine de Biran*, Oxford, Oxford University Press.

Moravia, S. (1974), *Il Pensiero degli Ideologues: Scienza e Filosofia in Francia*, Florence, La Nuova Italia.

Moravia, S. (1980), 'The Enlightenment and the Sciences of Man', *History of Science* 18: 247–68.

Morgan, T. (1735), *The Mechanical Practice of Physic*, London, T. Woodward.

Morrell, J. (1990), 'Professionalisation', *Companion to the History of Modern Science*, R. Olby *et al.*, eds, London and New York, Routledge: 980–9.

Morrell, J. and Thackray, A. (1981), *Gentlemen of Science: Early Years of the British Association for the Advancement of Science*, Oxford, Oxford University Press.

Morris, R., Kendrick, J. *et al.* (1807), *Edinburgh Medical and Physical Dictionary*, Edinburgh, Bell and Bradfute.

Morrison-Low, A. (1991), 'Women in the Nineteenth-Century Scientific Instrument Trade', *Science and Sensibility: Gender and Scientific Enquiry, 1780–1945*, M. Benjamin, ed., Oxford, Basil Blackwell: 89–117.

Musselwhite, D.E. (1987), *Partings Welded Together: Politics and Desire in the Nineteenth-Century English Novel*, London, Methuen.

M.W. (1789), *Catéchisme de l'Homme Publié par M.W.*, London, no separate publisher given.

The New English Hymnal (1986), Norwich, Canterbury Press.

Newman, K. (1996), *Fetal Positions: Individualism, Science, Visuality*, Stanford, Calif., Stanford University Press.

Nicolson, B. (1968), *Joseph Wright of Derby: Painter of Light*, London and New York, Pantheon, 2 vols.

Nicolson, M.H. (1946), *Newton Demands the Muse*, Princeton, Princeton University Press.

Nicolson, M.H. (1976), *Science and Imagination*, Hamden, Conn., Archon Books.

Nihell, E. (1760), *A Treatise on the Art of Midwifery*, London, A. Morley.

Nussbaum, F. (1984), *The Brink of All We Hate: English Satires on Women, 1660–1750*, Lexington, University Press of Kentucky.

O'Day, R. (1994), *The Family and Family Relationships, 1500–1900: England, France and the United States*, Basingstoke and London, Macmillan.

Oelsner, C.-E. (1795), 'Sur le Supplice de la Guillotine, par le Professeur Soemmerring', *Magasin Encyclopédique* 3: 463–7.

Okin, S.M. (1980), *Women in Western Political Thought*, London, Virago.

Olby, R., Cantor, G. *et al.*, eds (1990), *Companion to the History of Modern Science*, London and New York, Routledge.

Outram, D. (1978), 'The Language of Natural Power: The "Éloges" of Georges Cuvier and the Public Language of Nineteenth Century Science', *History of Science* 16: 153–78.

Outram, D. (1984), *Georges Cuvier: Vocation, Science, and Authority in Post-Revolutionary France*, Manchester, Manchester University Press.

Outram, D. (1989), *The Body and the French Revolution: Sex, Class and Political Culture*, New Haven, Yale University Press.

Outram, D. (1995), *The Enlightenment*, Cambridge, Cambridge University Press.

Packard, A.S. (1901), *Lamarck, the Founder of Evolution: His Life and Work*, New York, Longmans, Green and Co.

Paley, W. (1790), *The Young Christian Instructed*, Carlisle, F. Jollie.

Paley, W. (1802), *Natural Theology: Or Evidences of the Existence and Attributes of the Deity, Collected from the Appearances of Nature*, London, R. Faulder.

Paley, W. (1836–38), *The Works of William Paley*, London, Longman and Co.

Palmer, R.R. (1959, 1964), *The Age of the Democratic Revolution*, Princeton, Princeton University Press, 2 vols.

Partridge, E. (1961), *A Dictionary of Slang and Unconventional English*, London, Routledge and Kegan Paul.

Paul, C. (1980), *Science and Immortality: The Éloges of the Paris Academy of Sciences (1699–1791)*, Berkeley, University of California Press.

Paulson, R. (1972), *Rowlandson: A New Interpretation*, London, Studio Vista.

Paulson, R. (1975), *Emblem and Expression: Meaning in English Art of the Eighteenth Century*, London, Thames and Hudson.

Paulson, R. (1979), *Popular and Polite Art in the Age of Hogarth and Fielding*, South Bend, In., and London, Notre Dame University Press.

Paulson, R. (1982), *Literary Landscape: Turner and Constable*, New Haven and London, Yale University Press.

Paulson, R. (1983), *Representations of Revolution (1789–1820)*, New Haven and London, Yale University Press.

Peabody, R. (1968), 'Authority', *International Encyclopedia of the Social Sciences*, D.L. Sills, ed., New York, 1: 473–7.

Penny, N. (1986), *Reynolds*, London, Weidenfeld and Nicolson.

Perrot, J.-C. and Woolf, S.J. (1984), *State and Statistics in France 1789–1815*, London, Paris and New York, Harwood Academic Publishers.

Perry, R. (1991), 'Colonizing the Breast: Sexuality and Maternity in Eighteenth-Century England', *Journal of the History of Sexuality* 2: 204–34.

Perry, G. and Rossington, M., eds (1994), *Femininity and Masculinity in Eighteenth-Century Art and Culture*, Manchester, Manchester University Press.

Pertue, M. (1983), 'La Révolution Française et l'Abolition de la Peine de Mort', *Annales Historiques de la Révolution Française* 55: 14–37.

Phillipson, N. (1981), 'The Scottish Enlightenment', *The Enlightenment in National Context*, R. Porter and M. Teich, eds, Cambridge, Cambridge University Press: 19–40.

Picavet, F. (1971, first published 1891), *Les Idéologues: Essai sur l'Histoire des Idées et des Théories Scientifiques, Philosophiques, Religieuses*, New York, Burt Franklin.

Pickstone, J. (1981), 'Bureaucracy, Liberalism and the Body in Post-Revolutionary France: Bichat's Physiology and the Paris School of Medicine', *History of Science* 19: 115–42.

Plattner, M. (1979), *Rousseau's State of Nature: An Interpretation of the Discourse on Inequality*, DeKalb, Northern Illinois University Press.

Plumb, J.H. (1975), 'The New World of Children in Eighteenth-Century England', *Past and Present* 67: 64–95.

Pointon, M. (1993), *Hanging the Head: Portraiture and Social Formation in Eighteenth-Century England*, New Haven and London, Yale University Press.

Pointon, M. (1997), *Strategies for Showing: Women, Possession and Representation in English Visual Culture 1665–1800*, Oxford, Oxford University Press.

Polite Society by Arthur Devis 1712–1787: Portraits of the English Country Gentleman and his Family (1983), Preston, Harris Museum and Art Gallery.

Pollock, L. (1983), *Forgotten Children: Parent–Child Relations from 1500–1900*, Cambridge, Cambridge University Press.

Poovey, M. (1980), 'My Hideous Progeny: Mary Shelley and the Feminization of Romanticism', *Publications of the Modern Language Association of America* 95: 332–47.

Porter, R., ed. (1985), *Patients and Practitioners: Lay Perceptions of Medicine in Pre-Industrial Society*, Cambridge, Cambridge University Press.

Porter, R. (1987a), 'A Touch of Danger: The Man-Midwife as Sexual Predator', *Sexual Underworlds of the Enlightenment*, G. Rousseau and R. Porter, eds, Manchester, Manchester University Press: 206–32.

Porter, R. (1987b), *Disease, Medicine and Society in England 1550–1860*, Basingstoke and London, Macmillan.

Porter, R. (1989), *Health for Sale: Quackery in England, 1660–1850*, Manchester, Manchester University Press.

Porter, R., ed. (1992), *The Popularization of Medicine 1650–1850*, London and New York, Routledge.

Porter, R. (1993), 'Diseases of Civilization', *Companion Encyclopedia of the History of Medicine*, W.F. Bynum and R. Porter, eds, London and New York, Routledge, I: 584–600.

Porter, R., ed. (1995), *Medicine in the Enlightenment*, Amsterdam, Rodopi.

Porter, R., ed. (1997), *Rewriting the Self: Histories from the Renaissance to the Present*, London and New York, Routledge.

Porter, R. and Hall, L. (1995), *The Facts of Life: The Creation of Sexual Knowledge in Britain, 1650–1950*, New Haven and London, Yale University Press.

Porter, R. and Roberts, M.M., eds (1996), *Pleasure in the Eighteenth Century*, Basingstoke and London, Macmillan.

Porter, R. and Teich, M., eds (1981), *The Enlightenment in National Context*, Cambridge, Cambridge University Press.

Porter, R. and Teich, M., eds (1988), *Romanticism in National Context*, Cambridge, Cambridge University Press.

Porter, R. and Teich, M., eds (1994), *Sexual Knowledge, Sexual Science: The History of Attitudes to Sexuality*, Cambridge, Cambridge University Press.

Postle, M. (1995), *Sir Joshua Reynolds: The Subject Pictures*, Cambridge, Cambridge University Press.

Potts, A. (1994), *Flesh and the Ideal: Winckelmann and the Origins of Art History*, New Haven and London, Yale University Press.

Prunelle, C. (1818), *De l'Action de la Médecine sur la Population des États*, Paris, Fengueray.

Pugh, Simon (1988), *Garden–Nature–Language*, Manchester, Manchester University Press.

Puttfarken, T. (1985), *Roger de Piles' Theory of Art*, New Haven and London, Yale University Press.

The Quick and the Dead (1997), London, Hayward Gallery.

Raeff, M. (1983), *The Well-Ordered Police State: Social and Institutional Change through Law in the Germanies and Russia, 1600–1800*, New Haven and London, Yale University Press.

Ragan, B.T. and Williams, E.A. eds (1992), *Re-Creating Authority in Revolutionary France*, New Brunswick, NJ, Rutgers University Press.

Ramsay, D. (1801), *A Review of the Improvements, Progress and State of Medicine in the XVIIIth Century*, Charleston, W.P. Young.

Ramsey, M. (1988), *Professional and Popular Medicine in France, 1770–1830: The Social World of Medical Practice*, Cambridge, Cambridge University Press.

Raven, C.E. (1953), *Natural Religion and Christian Theology*, Cambridge, Cambridge University Press.

Reedy, W.J. (1981), 'Burke and Bonald: Paradigms of Late Eighteenth-Century Conservatism', *Historical Reflections* 8: 69–93.

Reedy, W.J. (1983), 'Language, Counter-Revolution and the "Two Cultures": Bonald's Traditionalist Scientism', *Journal of the History of Ideas* 44: 579–97.

Reill, P.H. and Wilson, E.J. (1996), *Encyclopedia of the Enlightenment*, New York, Facts on File.

Rendall, J. (1985), *The Origins of Modern Feminism: Women in Britain, France and the United States 1780–1860*, London, Macmillan.

Reynolds, J. (1992), *Discourses*, London, Penguin (edited by P. Rogers).

Ribiero, A. (1986), *Dress and Morality*, London, Batsford.

Richardson, G. (1979), *Iconology*, New York and London, Garland Publishing (1st edition London, G. Scott, 1779).

Richardson, R. (1988), *Death, Dissection and the Destitute*, London, Routledge and Kegan Paul.

Riley, J. (1985), *Population Thought in the Age of the Demographic Revolution*, Durham, NC, Carolina Academic Press.

Riley, J. (1987), *The Eighteenth-Century Campaign to Avoid Disease*, Basingstoke and London, Macmillan.

Ripa, C. (1971), *Baroque and Rococo Pictorial Imagery: The 1758–1760 Hertel Edition of Ripa's 'Iconologia'*, New York, Dover Publications.

Robbins Landon, H.C. (1976), *Haydn: Chronicle and Works. Haydn in England 1791–1975*, London, Thames and Hudson.

Robbins Landon, H.C. (1978) *Haydn: Chronicle and Works. Haydn at Eszterhaza 1766–1790*, London, Thames and Hudson.

Roberts, J. (1990), *The Counter-Revolution in France, 1787–1830*, Basingstoke, Macmillan.

Roberts, J. (1995), *The Penguin History of the World*, London, Penguin.

Roberts, K.B. and Tomlinson, J.D.W. (1992), *The Fabric of the Body: European Traditions of Anatomical Illustration*, Oxford, Clarendon Press.

Roberts, M. (1993), 'The Male Scientist, Man-Midwife and Female Monster: Appropriation and Transmutation in Frankenstein', *A Question of Identity: Women, Science and Literature*, M. Benjamin, ed., New Brunswick, NJ: 59–74.

Roberts, N. (1992), *Whores in History: Prostitution in Western Society*, London, HarperCollins.

Robertson, A. (1967), *Requiem: Music of Mourning and Consolation*, London, Cassell.

Robinson, N.K. (1996), *Edmund Burke: A Life in Caricature*, New Haven and London, Yale University Press.

Robinson, P. (1982), 'Virginie's Fatal Modesty: Some Thoughts on Bernardin de Saint-Pierre and Rousseau', *British Journal for Eighteenth-Century Studies* 5: 35–48.

Roche, D. (1980), 'Talent, Reason, and Sacrifice: The Physician during the Enlightenment', *Medicine and Society in France*, R. Forster and O. Ranum, eds, Baltimore and London, Johns Hopkins University Press.

Roger, J. (1963), *Les Sciences de la Vie dans la Pensée Française du XVIII Siècle*, Paris, Armand Colin.

Roger, J. (1993), *Les Sciences de la Vie dans la Pensée Française du XVIIIe siècle: La Génération des Animaux, de Descartes à l'Encyclopédie*, Paris, Albin Michel.

Rogers, J. (1986), 'Sensibility, Sympathy, Benevolence: Physiology and Moral Philosophy in *Tristram Shandy*', *Languages of Nature: Critical Essays on Science and Literature*, L. Jordanova, ed., London, Free Association Books: 117–58.

Rosen, G. (1953), 'Cameralism and the Concept of Medical Police', *Bulletin of the History of Medicine* 27: 21–42.

Rosen, G. (1957), 'The Fate of the Concept of Medical Police 1780–1890', *Centaurus* 5: 97–113.

Rosen, G. (1974), *From Medical Police to Social Medicine: Essays on the History of Health Care*, New York, Science History Publications.

Rosen, G. (1976), 'A Slaughter of Innocents: Aspects of Child Health in the Eighteenth-Century City', *Studies in Eighteenth-Century Culture* 5: 293–316.

Rosenberg, C., ed. (1979), *Healing and History: Essays for George Rosen*, New York and London, Science History Publications and Dawson.

Rosenberg, C. (1983), 'Medical Text and Social Context: Explaining William Buchan's *Domestic Medicine*', *Bulletin of the History of Medicine* 57: 22–42.

Rosner, L. (1991), *Medical Education in the Age of Improvement: Edinburgh Students and Apprentices*, Edinburgh, Edinburgh University Press.

Ross, I.S. (1995), *The Life of Adam Smith*, Oxford, Clarendon Press.

Rotberg, R. and Rabb, T., eds (1988), *Art and History: Images and their Meaning*, Cambridge, Cambridge University Press.

Rousseau, G.S., ed. (1990), *The Languages of Psyche, Mind and Body in Enlightenment Thought*, Berkeley and Los Angeles, University of California Press.

Rousseau, G. and Porter, R., eds (1980), *The Ferment of Knowledge: Studies in the Historiography of Eighteenth-Century Knowledge*, Cambridge, Cambridge University Press.

Rousseau, G. and Porter, R., eds (1987), *Sexual Underworlds of the Enlightenment*, Manchester, Manchester University Press.

Rousseau, J.-J. (1911), *Émile*, London, Dent.

Rousseau, J.-J. (1973), *The Social Contract and Discourses*, London, Dent.

Rousseau, J.-J. (1974), *The Essential Rousseau*, New York, Mentor.

Roussel, P. (1775), *Système Physique et Moral de la Femme*, Paris, Vincent.

Roussel, P. (1803), *Système Physique et Moral de la Femme*, Paris, Crapart, Caille et Ravier.

Rudwick, M.J.S. (1985), *The Great Devonian Controversy: The Shaping of Scientific Knowledge among Gentlemanly Specialists*, Chicago and London, University of Chicago Press.

Russell, C.A., ed. (1973), *Science and Religious Belief: A Selection of Recent Historical Studies*, London, University of London Press.

Sade, D.A.F. de (1966), *Justine, Philosophy in the Bedroom and Other Writings*, New York, Grove Press.

Sadie, S., ed. (1980), *The New Grove Dictionary of Music and Musicians*, London, Macmillan, 20 vols.

Sainte-Marie, E. (1824), *Précis Elémentaire de Police Médicale, Ouvrage destiné aux Administrateurs*, Paris, Cormon et Blanc.

Sainte-Marie, E. (1829), *Lectures Relatives à la Police Médicale faites aux Conseils de Salubrité de Lyon et du Département du Rhône*, Paris, J.-B. Baillière.

Sargent, F. (1982), *Hippocratic Heritage: A History of Ideas about Weather and Human Health*, New York and London, Pergamon.

Scarre, G., ed. (1989), *Children, Parents and Politics*, Cambridge, Cambridge University Press.

Schaffer, S. (1990a), 'Genius in Romantic Natural Philosophy', *Romanticism and the Sciences*, A. Cunningham and N. Jardine, eds, Cambridge, Cambridge University Press.

Schaffer, S. (1990b), 'States of Mind: Enlightenment and Natural Philosophy', *The Languages of Psyche: Mind and Body in Enlightenment Thought*, G.S. Rousseau, ed., Berkeley, University of California Press: 233–90.

Schama, S. (1989), *Citizens: A Chronicle of the French Revolution*, London, Viking.

Schiebinger, L. (1989), *The Mind Has No Sex? Women in the Origins of Modern Science*, Cambridge, Mass., Harvard University Press.

Schiebinger, L. (1993), *Nature's Body: Gender in the Making of Modern Science*, Boston, Beacon Press.

Schochet, G.J. (1975), *Patriarchalism in Political Thought*, Oxford, Basil Blackwell.

Schofield, R.E. (1963), *The Lunar Society of Birmingham: A Social History of Provincial Science and Industry in Eighteenth-Century Britain*, Oxford, Clarendon Press.

Schupbach, W. (1987), 'A Select Iconography of Animal Experiment', *Vivisection in Historical Perspective*, N.A. Rupke, ed., London, Croom Helm: 340–60.

Schwartz, J. (1984), *The Sexual Politics of Jean-Jacques Rousseau*, Chicago and London, University of Chicago Press.

Secord, J.A. (1985), 'Newton in the Nursery: Tom Telescope and the Philosophy of Tops and Balls, 1761–1838', *History of Science* 23: 127–51.

Shapin, S. and Schaffer, S. (1985), *Leviathan and the Air Pump, Hobbes, Boyle and the Experimental Life*, Princeton, Princeton University Press.

Sharp, S. (1767), *Letters from Italy*, London, R. Cave, 2nd edition.

Shelley, M. (1985), *Frankenstein*, Harmondsworth, Penguin (edited by M. Hindle).

Shesgreen, S. (1973), *Engravings by Hogarth: 101 Prints*, New York, Dover.

Shevelow, K. (1989), *Women and Print Culture: The Construction of Femininity in the Early Periodical*, London and New York, Routledge.

Shinn, T. and Whitley, R., eds (1985), *Expository Science: Forms and Functions of Popularisation*, Dordrecht, Reidel.

Shklar, J.N. (1972), 'Subversive Genealogies', *Daedalus* 101: 129–54.

Shookman, E., ed. (1993), *The Faces of Physiognomy: Interdisciplinary Approaches to Johann Caspar Lavater*, Columbia, SC, Camden House.

Shorter, E. (1976), *The Making of the Modern Family*, London, Collins.

Shortland, M. and Yeo, R., eds (1996), *Telling Lives in Science: Essays on Scientific Biography*, Cambridge, Cambridge University Press.

Silverman, D. (1989), *Art Nouveau in Fin-de-Siècle France: Politics, Psychology and Style*, Berkeley, University of California Press.

Smellie, W. (1752–64), *A Treatise on the Theory and Practice of Midwifery*, London, D. Wilson, 3 vols.

Smellie, W. (1754), *A Sett of Anatomical Tables, with Explanations, and an Abridgement of the Practice of Midwifery, With a View to Illustrate a Treatise on that Subject, and Collection of Cases*, London, no publisher given.

Smith, F.B. (1990), *The People's Health, 1830–1910*, London, Weidenfeld and Nicolson, 2nd edition.

Smith, G. (1985), 'Prescribing the Rules of Health: Self-Help and Advice in the Late Eighteenth Century', *Patients and Practitioners: Lay Perceptions of Medicine in Pre-Industrial Society*, R. Porter, ed., Cambridge, Cambridge University Press: 249–82.

Smith, R. (1995), *Handel's Oratorios and Eighteenth-Century Thought*, Cambridge, Cambridge University Press.

Smith, R. (1997), *The Fontana History of the Human Sciences*, London, Fontana.

Soemmerring, S.T. (1795), 'Lettre de M. Soemmerring à M. Oelsner', *Magasin Encyclopédique* 3: 468–77.

Soemmerring, S.T. (18 Brumaire, an IV, 1795), *Moniteur Universel*: 378–9.

Solkin, D. (1993), *Painting for Money: The Visual Arts and the Public Sphere in Eighteenth-Century England*, New Haven and London, Yale University Press.

Some, D. (1792), *The Assembly's Catechism Explained, and the Principles of Religion therein contained, confirmed by the Holy Scriptures*, Edinburgh, Society for Propagating Religious Knowledge among the Poor.

Sommerville, J. (1982), *The Rise and Fall of Childhood*, Beverly Hills, Sage.

Soubiran, A. (1964), *The Good Doctor Guillotin and his Strange Device*, London, Souvenir Press.

Spacks, P.M. (1978), 'The Dangerous Age', *Eighteenth-Century Studies* 11: 417–38.

Speck, W. (1980), 'The Harlot's Progress in Eighteenth-Century England', *British Journal for Eighteenth Century Studies* 3: 127–39.

Stafford, B.M. (1991), *Body Criticism: Imaging the Unseen in Enlightenment Art and Medicine*, Cambridge, Mass., MIT Press.

Stanton, D., ed. (1993), *Discourses of Sexuality: From Aristotle to AIDS*, Ann Arbor, University of Michigan Press.

Staum, M. (1974), 'Cabanis and the Science of Man', *Journal of the History of Behavioural Sciences* 10: 135–43.

Staum, M. (1980), *Cabanis: Enlightenment and Medical Philosophy in the French Revolution*, Princeton, Princeton University Press.

Steinberg, L. (1983), *The Sexuality of Christ in Renaissance Art and Modern Oblivion*, New York, Pantheon Books.

Sterne, L. (1967), *The Life and Opinions of Tristram Shandy*, Harmondsworth, Penguin.

Stewart, J.H. (1951), *A Documentary Survey of the French Revolution*, New York, Macmillan.

Stocking, G. (1982), *Race, Culture and Evolution*, Chicago, University of Chicago Press.

Strathern, M. (1992), *After Nature: English Kinship in the Late Twentieth Century*, Cambridge, Cambridge University Press.

Sue, J.J. (1788), *Élémens d'Anatomie*, Paris, l'Auteur, Mequignon, Royer, Barrois.

Sue, J.J. (1795), 'Opinion du Citoyen Sue, Professeur de Médecine et de Botanique, sur le Supplice de la Guillotine', *Magasin Encyclopédique* 4: 170–89.

Sue, J.J. (1797a, an V), *Essai sur la Physiognomonie des Corps Vivans Considerée depuis l'Homme jusqu'à la Plante*, Paris, Du Pont.

Sue, J.J. (1797b, an VI), *Recherches Physiologiques, et Expériences sur la Vitalité*, Paris, Fuchs.

Sussman, G. (1982), *Selling Mothers' Milk: The Wet-Nursing Business in France, 1715–1914*, Urbana, Ill., University of Illinois Press.

Tarczylo, T. (1980), '"Pretons la Main à la Nature . . .": L'Onanisme de Tissot', *Dix-Huitième Siècle* 12: 79–96.

Taylor, B. (1971), *Stubbs*, London, Phaidon.

Taylor, J.S. (1979), 'Philanthropy and Empire: Jonas Hanway and the Infant Poor of London', *Eighteenth-Century Studies* 12: 285–305.

Taylor, J.S. (1985), *Jonas Hanway: Founder of the Marine Society: Charity and Policy in Eighteenth-Century Britain*, London, Scolar.

Temkin, O. (1973), 'Health and Disease', *Dictionary of the History of Ideas*, P. Weiner, ed., New York, Scribner, 2: 395–407.

[Thicknesse, P]. (1764), *Man-Midwifery Analysed: and the Tendency of that Practice Detected and Exposed*, London, R. Davis.

[Thicknesse, P.] (1765), *Man-Midwifery Analysed: and the Tendency of that Practice Detected and Exposed*, London, R. Davis and T. Caslon.

[Thicknesse, P.] (1790), *Man-Midwifery Analysed; or the Tendency of that Indecent and Unnecessary Practice Detected and Exposed*, London, Fores.

Thody, P. (1975), *Laclos: Les Liaisons Dangereuses*, London, Edward Arnold, revised edition.

Thomas, K. (1959), 'The Double Standard', *Journal of the History of Ideas* 20: 195–216.

Thompson, J.M., ed. (1934), *Napoleon's Letters*, London, Dent.

Thomson, E.H. (1963), 'The Role of Physicians in the Humane Societies of the Eighteenth Century', *Bulletin of the History of Medicine* 37: 43–51.

Thornton, J.L. (1982), *Jan van Rymsdyk: Medical Artist of the Eighteenth Century*, Cambridge and New York, Oleander Press.

Thornton, J.L. and Reeves, C. (1983), *Medical Book Illustration: A Short History*, Cambridge and New York, Oleander Press.

Tissot, S.A.A.D. (1758), *De la Santé des Gens de Lettres*, Lausanne, Franç. Grasset et Cie.

Tissot, S.A.A.D. (1760), *L'Onanisme; ou, Dissertation Physique, sur les Maladies Produites par la Masturbation*, Lausanne, A. Chapuis.

BIBLIOGRAPHY

Tissot, S.A.A.D. (1761), *Avis au Peuple sur sa Santé*, Lausanne, Zimmerli.

Tissot, S.A.A.D. (1766), *Onanism*, London, the translator.

Tissot, S.A.A.D. (1767), *Avis aux gens de lettres et aux personnes sédentaires sur leur santé*, Paris, chez J. Th. Herissant fils.

Tissot, S.A.A.D. (1768), *An Essay on Diseases Incidental to Literary and Sedentary Persons*, London, E. and C. Dilly.

Tissot, S.A.A.D. (1768), *Advice to the People in General With Regard to their Health*, London, T. Becket & P.A. De Hondt.

Tissot, S.A.A.D. (1771), *An Essay on the Disorders of People of Fashion*, London, Richardson and Urquhart.

Tissot, S.A.A.D. (1772), *An Essay on Onanism*, Dublin, James Williams.

Todd, D. (1995), *Imagining Monsters: Miscreations of the Self in Eighteenth-Century England*, Chicago, University of Chicago Press.

Todd, J., ed. (1984), *A Dictionary of British and American Women Writers 1660–1800*, London, Methuen.

Topham, J. (1992), 'Science and Popular Education in the 1830s: The Role of the Bridgewater Treatises', *British Journal for the History of Science* 85: 397–430.

Tourneux, M. (1890–1913), *Bibliographie de l'Histoire de Paris pendant la Révolution Française*, Paris, Imprimerie Nouvelle, 5 vols.

Towers, J. (1766–80), *British Biography; or, an Accurate and Impartial Account of the Lives and Writings of Eminent Persons in Great Britain and Ireland*, London, R. Goadby.

Traer, J.F. (1980), *Marriage and the Family in Eighteenth-Century France*, Ithaca, NY, Cornell University Press.

Trumbach, R. (1977), 'London's Sodomites: Homosexual Behaviour and Western Culture in the Eighteenth Century', *Journal of Social History* 11: 1–33.

Tytler, G. (1982), *Physiognomy in the European Novel: Faces and Fortunes*, Princeton, Princeton University Press.

van Duzer, C.H. (1935), *The Contribution of the Idéologues to French Revolutionary Thought*, Baltimore, Johns Hopkins University Press.

Vess, D. (1975), *Medical Revolution in France, 1789–1796*, Gainesville, Fla, Florida State University Press.

Volney, C.-F. (1807), *The Ruins: or, A Survey of the Revolutions of Empires to which is added the Law of Nature, or Principles of Morality deduced from the Physical Constitution of Mankind and the Universe*, London, J. Johnson.

Volney, C.-F. (1934), *La Loi Naturelle ou Catéchisme du Citoyen Français*, Paris, Librairie Armand Colin.

Volney, C.-F. (1968), *A View of the Soil and Climate of the United States of America*, New York, Hafner (first published 1803).

Walker, R. (1985), *Regency Portraits*, London, National Portrait Gallery, 2 vols.

Walters, M. (1979), *The Nude Male: A New Perspective*, Harmondsworth, Penguin.

Warner, M. (1976), *Alone of All Her Sex: The Myth and Cult of the Virgin Mary*, London, Weidenfeld and Nicolson.

Warner, M. (1983), *Joan of Arc: The Image of Female Heroism*, Harmondsworth, Penguin.

Warner, M. (1985), *Monuments and Maidens: The Allegory of the Female Form*, London, Weidenfeld and Nicolson.

Warocquier, F.-J. (1782), *Thèse Anatomico-Chirurgicale . . .* , Lille.

Watts, S. (1984), *A Social History of Western Europe 1450–1720*, London, Hutchinson.

Wear, A., ed. (1992), *Medicine in Society: Historical Essays*, Cambridge, Cambridge University Press.

Webster, C. (1983), 'The Historiography of Medicine', *Information Sources in the History of Science and Medicine*, P. Corsi and P. Wendling, eds, London, Butterworth.

Webster, N. (1970), *An American Dictionary of the English Language*, New York and London, Johnson Reprint Corporation, first published 1828, 2 vols.

Wedekind, G. (20 Brumaire, an IV, 1795), *Moniteur Universel*: 395–6.

Weindling, P. (1980), 'Science and Sedition: How Effective were the Acts Licensing Lectures and Meetings', *British Journal for the History of Science* 13: 139–53.

Weiner, D. (1972), 'The Real Doctor Guillotin', *Journal of the American Medical Association* 220: 85–9.

Weiner, D. (1993), *The Citizen Patient in Revolutionary and Imperial Paris*, Baltimore and London, Johns Hopkins University Press.

Weinsheimer, J. (1987), 'Mrs Siddons, the Tragic Muse, and the Problem of *As*', *Journal of Aesthetics and Art Criticism* 36: 317–28.

White, B.M. (1983), 'Medical Police: Politics and Police: The Fate of John Roberton', *Medical History* 27: 407–22.

White, N. (1947), *Shelley*, London, Secker and Warburg, 2 vols.

Whitley, R. (1984), *The Intellectual and Social Organisation of the Sciences*, Oxford, Clarendon Press.

Wiley, B. (1962), *The Eighteenth-Century Background: Studies on the Idea of Nature in the Thought of the Period*, Harmondsworth, Penguin.

Williams, E.A. (1994), *The Physical and the Moral: Anthropology, Physiology, and Philosophical Medicine in France, 1750–1850*, Cambridge, Cambridge University Press.

Williams, L.P. (1953), 'Science, Education and the French Revolution', *Isis* 44: 311–30.

Williams, R. (1975), *The Country and the City*, St Albans, Paladin.

Williams, R. (1981), *Culture*, London, Fontana.

Williams, R. (1983), *Keywords: A Vocabulary of Culture and Society*, London, Fontana, revised edition.

Williamson, G. (1972), *The Ingenious Mr Gainsborough*, London, Robert Hale.

Wilson, A., ed. (1993), *Rethinking Social History: English Society 1570–1920 and its Interpretation*, Manchester, Manchester University Press.

Wilson, A. (1995), *The Making of Man-Midwifery: Childbirth in England, 1660–1770*, London, UCL Press.

Wilson, C. (1958), *Mercantilism*, London, Routledge and Kegan Paul for the Historical Association.

Wilson, D. (1993), *Signs and Portents: Monstrous Births from the Middle Ages to the Enlightenment*, London and New York, Routledge.

Wilson, L. (1993), *Women and Medicine in the French Enlightenment: The Debate over Maladies des Femmes*, Baltimore and London, Johns Hopkins University Press.

Wilton, A. (1992), *The Swagger Portrait: Grand Manner Portraiture in Britain from Van Dyck to Augustus John, 1630–1930*, London, Tate Gallery.

Winslow, J. (1742), *Dissertation sur l'Incertitude des Signes de la Mort. Traduite et Commentée par Jacques-Jean Bruhier*, Paris, Morel le jeune.

Wittkower, R. (1979), *Sculpture: Processes and Principles*, Harmondsworth, Penguin.

Wolf, J.B. (1968), *Louis XIV*, London, History Book Club.

Wollstonecraft, M. (1975), *A Vindication of the Rights of Woman*, Harmondsworth, Penguin.

Woodall, J., ed. (1997), *Portraiture: Facing the Subject*, Manchester, Manchester University Press.

Woolf, S.J. (1991), *Napoleon's Integration of Europe*, London, Routledge.

Yalom, M. (1997), *A History of the Breast*, London, HarperCollins.

Yeo, R. (1979), 'William Whewell, Natural Theology and the Philosophy of Science in Mid-Nineteenth-Century Britain', *Annals of Science* 36: 493–516.

Yeo, R. (1991), 'Reading Encyclopedias: Science and the Organisation of Knowledge in British Dictionaries of Arts and Sciences, 1730–1850', *Isis* 82: 24–49.

Zomchick, J.P. (1993), *Family and the Law in Eighteenth-Century Fiction*, Cambridge, Cambridge University Press.

Index

Dates of birth and death are given as appropriate, and n denotes a reference in a footnote.

256